A Computer Science Reader

A Computer Science Reader
Selections from ABACUS

Edited by
Eric A. Weiss

Springer-Verlag
New York Berlin Heidelberg
London Paris Tokyo

Eric A. Weiss
Associate Editor, ABACUS
Springer-Verlag New York
175 Fifth Avenue
New York, NY 10010, USA

QA 76.24
C 658
1988

Library of Congress Cataloging-in-Publication Data
A computer science reader.
   Includes index.
   1. Electronic data processing.   2. Computers
I. Weiss, Eric A.   II. Abacus (New York, N.Y.)
QA76.24.C658   1987   004   87-9804

Typeset by David Seham Associates, Metuchen, New Jersey.
Printed and bound by R.R. Donnelley & Sons, Harrisonburg, Virginia.
Printed in the United States of America.

9 8 7 6 5 4 3 2 1

ISBN 0-387-96544-0 Springer-Verlag New York Berlin Heidelberg
ISBN 3-540-96544-0 Springer-Verlag Berlin Heidelberg New York

Dedication

On 22 December 1986, while this book was being prepared, Walter Kaufmann-Bühler, Mathematics Editor at Springer-Verlag in New York, died suddenly at the age of 42. The founding and survival of ABACUS are due more to him and his enthusiasm than to any other person, and it was at his suggestion and with his support and encouragement that this collection was put together. His most untimely death was a great loss to everyone associated with ABACUS and especially to the editor of this book, which is here dedicated to Walter's memory.

Preface

These selections from the first 3½ years of ABACUS, the computing professional's international quarterly, represent the best of what we have published. They are grouped into the magazine's established categories: Editorials, Articles, Departments, Reports from Correspondents, and Features. Letters to the Editor, ordinarily in a separate section, have been appended to their subjects or objects, as the case may be. The selection of our best has yielded samples from all these categories, including at least one contribution from every regular columnist. In short, what you see here is what an ABACUS subscriber gets.

To make room for the wide variety of material needed to truly represent ABACUS, some of the longer articles have been slightly shortened. In each case, the complete original article can be obtained by using the back-issue order information at the end of this book. Readers who want to continue the ABACUS experience may subscribe for future issues with the subscription information included with this book.

Contents

DEPARTMENTS

FEATURES

Introduction

It is all Tony Ralston's fault.

For years, he dreamt of starting a popular computer magazine comparable with *Scientific American* in editorial quality which, as he said, "would make explicit in clear and objective language the most important technical developments and events in computing." It would be aimed at the informed public, and it was to become a general and technical forum for the computing profession. Computing specialists would read it to keep up with what their peers were up to in other specialties. Computing generalists would read it for its insightful philosophical overviews. Important decision-makers in govement and industry would be readers and contributors.

In 1976, while president of the American Federation of Information Processing Societies (AFIPS), after a lot of high-level wrangling, he persuaded the leaders of that then financially bloated body to consider sponsoring such a public service magazine, dubbed ABACUS. AFIPS made a full-dress study, issued a prospectus, edited and printed copies of a colorful sample issue, and sought financial backing from the industry.

Then, as far as I, at the time an outside bemused observer, could see, the roof fell in. The AFIPS Board of Directors, stampeded into pusillanimous action by a notorious few shortsighted, cautious, and anti-everything representatives of the constituent AFIPS societies, ended its lukewarm support of Tony's dream. The excuse for abandonment was that since the myopic captains of our industry would not kick in, the magazine would cost AFIPS money that would reduce the flow of cash from the then golden National Computer Conference to the constituent societies. The AFIPS ABACUS had hit ABORT.

Tony kept the ABACUS vision alive in his mind until, in 1981, he laid the scheme on the late Walter Kaufmann-Bühler, the mathematician-editor of the *Mathematical Intelligencer*. He and Tony persuaded Walter's employer, Springer-Verlag, a privately owned German publishing house, to publish ABACUS as a quarterly magazine, starting in the fall of 1983. In this, its current manifestation, it is described below in an excerpt from Tony's first editorial and in its Aims and Scope.

Tony assembled some almost-volunteer editors to help him, and called on his vast army of writer-friends to contribute articles. Springer-Verlag handled the production and circulation.

ABACUS has become what its prospectus proposed, an international journal of quality and of generality for computing professionals who want to be informed beyond their specialties. You may judge this for yourself by reading the samples that follow.

Excerpt from Anthony Ralston's editorial in the first issue of ABACUS:

Today, there are no computing generalists. The body of knowledge about computing is so large—and growing so fast—that no one can be expert in more than a small part of it, and no one can be even very knowledgeable about much of it. This doesn't set us apart from any other discipline. But the rate of change in computing is probably more rapid than any other discipline has ever witnessed. And, although perhaps it just seems that way, people in computing appear so busy compared to most other professionals that the problem of keeping up with new applications, science, and technology is compounded.

ABACUS will be devoted to making some small dent in this problem. Its articles, its departments, and other features, such as these editorials, will be devoted to presenting a broad variety of subject matter on computer science, computer technology, and computer applications. And lest that sounds a shade too didactic, I hasten to add that we hope to be at least as entertaining as we are informative. Timely, too, and, on occasion, controversial, although not just for the sake of controversy.

Aims and Scope

ABACUS is a journal about computing, computer science, and computer technology, intended not only for professionals in these fields, but also for knowledgeable and interested amateurs. Besides containing articles about computer science and technology themselves and applications of computers, it will also contain articles about the profession and the people in it, and about the social, economic, political, and other impacts of computing. The articles and departments will generally have an informal style, and are intended to entertain as well as inform. Opinion and humor will be encouraged, and fiction may occasionally appear. Letters to the editor will also be welcome, and where appropriate, may be controversial (but not outrageous).

Eric A. Weiss
October 1987

Credits

Everybody who participated in editing or production and whose name has appeared on the ABACUS masthead is listed below.

Editor and Founder
Anthony Ralston
SUNY at Buffalo

EDITORIAL COORDINATOR
Caryl Ann Dahlin
SUNY at Buffalo

Associate Editors
Edwin D. Reilly, Jr.
SUNY at Albany

Eric A. Weiss
Consultant

Department Editors
BOOK REVIEWS
Eric A. Weiss

COMPUTERS AND THE LAW
Michael Gemignani
University of Maine

COMPUTING AND THE CITIZEN
Severo M. Ornstein
Computer Professionals for Social Responsibility

INTERRUPTS
Aaron Finerman
University of Michigan

PERSONAL COMPUTING
Lawrence I. Press
Small Systems Group

PROBLEMS AND PUZZLES
Richard V. Andree
University of Oklahoma

THE COMPUTER PRESS
Anne A. Armstrong
Langley Publications

Correspondents
WASHINGTON
Edith Holmes

EUROPE
Rex Malik
Andrew Lloyd

JAPAN
Tosiyasu Kunii

Editorials

The Editor and his associates write the editorials as circumstances and their spirits move them, choosing subjects and expressing themselves as they wish. The editorials are usually tutorial, critical, and opinionated, and are intended to provoke modest controversy. The following are characteristic.

Who Reads ABACUS?

Eric A. Weiss

The 120 ABACUS readers who returned the questionnaires bound into last fall's issue (Fall 1984) gave us our first reliable idea of the nature of our audience. I thought you might like to know what we found out.

The size of the response is good for a long, multipart questionnaire addressed to a few thousand readers. The sample is neither too small to have meaning nor so large as to make it impossible to consider every answer.

I have read and reread every return, and analyzed the results as far as my patience allowed and the law of small numbers justified. Although my analysis applies only to the somewhat unique and self-selected sample of respondents, with a little naive faith and trust the returns can be interpreted into a sketch of the average ABACUS reader. He is a 38-year-old, highly educated California programmer/professor with an annual personal income of $42 thousand; he knows and uses Basic and Pascal, and likes *Byte* and the *Communications of the ACM* in addition to ABACUS, which he finds interesting. His handwriting shows that penmanship, like long division, will soon be a lost art among computer professionals. He hates to damage his copy of ABACUS by tearing out a questionnaire which is not bound as the centerfold.

When asked whether they would renew their subscriptions, some 80% said they would. About 5% of the respondents made a characteristic academic equivocation. They said they couldn't decide about ABACUS be-

Eric A. Weiss is a free-lance writer and editor. He received his degree in electrical engineering from Lehigh University and for almost four decades guided the Sun Company in computer use. At the same time, he wrote or edited seven computing textbooks and participated in the publication programs of several technical societies. He was the first chairman of the ACM Publication Board, and is now Biographies Editor of the AFIPS *Annals of the History of Computing,* and Associate Editor of *Computing Reviews.*

Reprinted from ABACUS, Volume 2, Number 3, Spring 1985.

cause they had only seen a single issue. Since no one will remain indecisive about renewing after seeing the magnificent Winter issue, I have lumped their responses in with those of my real friends, the probable or definite renewers.

Let's get back to our average reader. He is extremely male; fewer than 10% of the respondents were female. The youngest respondent was 15, a nonsubscribing high school student, and the oldest was 66. The median age is almost the same as the average, 38, so the readership is clearly skewed toward the young.

All the respondents but the youth mentioned above have been to college. 90% graduated, 80% have done graduate work, 60% have advanced degrees, and 30% are Ph.D.'s. Only five reported personal incomes under $15K, and only three over $75K. The average household income is roughly $10K or $20K more than the personal average of $42K.

The respondents' principal occupations are:

Programmer/analyst	28%
Educator	25%
Engineer/scientist	20%
Manager/administrator	10%

All other jobs reported represented less than 5% each. No one chose the category "medicine" or "professional."

Half of the educators said "education" was their "principle [*sic*—several commented on the questionnaire's sick spelling] product." One said "real or artificial intelligence," one professor said "truth, wisdom, & knowledge," but an assistant professor produces "illiterates," and an instructor turns out "idiots."

Roughly a third of the respondents are in the five states bordering the Pacific, chiefly in California; a third are in the twenty-four states between the Mississippi and the Atlantic, and a third are in the remainder of the country. About 5% responded from Canada in spite of the fact that the questionnaire did not provide international postage. Although I am sure we have some European readers, we heard from none of them.

About thirty-nine computer magazines were mentioned as favorites, most of them only once. Those named more than ten times are, in the order of popularity:

□ *Byte*
□ ABACUS
□ *Communications of the Association for Computing Machinery*
□ *IEEE Computer* (listed in the questionnaire as *IEEE Computing,* but no one commented)
□ *InfoWorld*

Notably missing from the Top Five, although included in the questionnaire prompt list, are those old favorites *Datamation, ComputerWorld, Scientific American,* and *Creative Computing.*

In addition to the five languages suggested on the form, the respondents named twenty others that they knew or used. Of these twenty-five, ten were mentioned more than ten times. Everybody knows Basic, and almost everybody knows Pascal. More than half volunteered that they knew Fortran, and almost as many know C. Following these in descending order of mention are Modula-2, Ada, Cobol, assemblers of many kinds, PL/I, and Lisp.

Because they were asked, almost all respondents told what they liked best about ABACUS and made suggestions for changes. In spite of some ambiguity and contradictions, these comments give us important guidance. Thanks.

No single suggestion predominated, but we gather that readers like AB-ACUS because it is interesting, enjoyable, different, informative, and readable. Readers want it to be more frequent, cheaper, and bigger. They would like ABACUS to be even more attractive and easy to read than it already is. The rest of the readers' suggestions were too diverse and disparate to be easily summarized. When I have worked them over some more and interpreted them into advice for ABACUS editors, authors, and salesmen, I will do an article to feed the information back to you.

INTERRUPT

In a *New York Times* review of *The Culture of Technology* by Arnold Pacey (February 19, 1984), Lionel Tiger notes:

"In the Times Square movie house where I saw *The Right Stuff,* the audience applauded when the astronauts bested the scientists in an argument over whether the space capsules were going to have windows. Obviously, human beings want to see where they are going, however inconvenient or unnecessary this may be for their mission. . . .

"In the most rigorous and technically elegant structures, the weakest bit is still the softest and most familiar—people. One of Mr. Pacey's suggestions seems sadly correct, that the schools teaching people to produce and manage technology by and large continue to mismanage the problem of the window. An accurate little mirror wouldn't hurt either."

Faculty of computer science and engineering departments, please take note of the human element and mend your ways!

Star Wars: What Is the Professional Responsibility of Computer Scientists?

Anthony Ralston

In the issue of 19 April 1985, the "News and Comment" section of *Science* devoted a full page to the administration's Strategic Defense Initiative (SDI), the so-called Star Wars program. In that article the following passage appeared:

As many as 100 million lines of error-free software code must be written for a network of computers capable of up to 1 trillion operations per second. "We don't want to have a few lines of bad code mistakenly set off a nuclear weapon or cause something to miss a target," says Edward Wegman, chief of the mathematical sciences divisions at the Office of Naval Research and one of the program's primary research reviewers, only partly in jest.

In response to that passage and some quotations from engineering school deans about what a wonderful research opportunity SDI is for their institutions, I wrote a letter to *Science* which appeared in the issue of 31 May, and which is reproduced in the panel accompanying this editorial.

I wonder how many of you agree and how many disagree with my position. I do not pose as an expert in software technology generally, or software testing or verification in particular. But I have been a computing

ANTHONY RALSTON is Professor of Computer Science and Mathematics at the State University of New York at Buffalo, where he has been since 1965. Although in a previous incarnation he was a numerical analyst, his chief research interests now are in discrete mathematics and in mathematics and computer science education. He is a past president of both the Association for Computing Machinery and the American Federation of Information Processing Societies. Among the too many pies into which he has his fingers, he is editor of ABACUS, a member of the Board of Governors of the Mathematical Association of America, Chairman of the ACM Committee on Scientific Freedom and Human Rights, and Chairman of a National Research Council task force studying the kindergarten through high school mathematics curriculum.

Reprinted from ABACUS, Volume 3, Number 1, Fall 1985.

"Star Wars" Program

"Only partly in jest" is the way R. Jeffrey Smith describes the statement by Edward Wegman of the Office of Naval Research about the Strategic Defense Initiative (SDI) or "Star Wars" program that "we don't want to have a few lines of bad code mistakenly set off a nuclear weapon" (News and Comment, 19 Apr., p. 304). This quotation follows a statement that "100 million lines of error-free software code must be written for the SDI system. But whether 100 million is the correct estimate of the size of the program needed or not [an estimate of 10 million has appeared elsewhere (1, p. 87)], this is no joke. In no foreseeable future—and this certainly covers the 10- to 20-year period during which the SDI is to become operational—is there any valid prospect of writing 10 million or 100 million or anything approaching this number of correct lines of code. There is even less prospect of writing a program such as this that will work the first time it is used, as it must. No regimen of testing or simulation and no application of program verification techniques is even on the horizon that would not leave such a vast program with many bugs. Thus, quite aside from any other technical, political, or economic objections that might be raised about the Star Wars system, its computer software problems doom it to failure.

It is extremely distressing to see that prestigious engineering schools are rationalizing their participation in the Star Wars program. No one doubts that interesting research problems are posed by the attempt to develop this system. And let us accept that traditional standards of open publication of university research will be observed. Nevertheless, when enough money is at stake, unversities are all too ready to accept Pentagon largesse. But the project itself is intellectually dishonest. Is intellectual honesty one academic value that will succumb to the economic difficulties in which universities find themselves?

ANTHONY RALSTON

References

1. Economist 295, 85 (13 April 1985).

generalist for a long time, and think I am close enough to the current literature to be pretty sure of my ground. None of the reactions I have gotten to this letter gives me any reason to doubt my stand.

The only person who has told me that he disagreed (thus far) suggested that the software could be written so that, like the telephone system, although there would be bugs and it would sometimes fail, it could achieve a satisfactory level of performance. After all, even Star Wars' most vociferous proponents have backed off from suggesting that the system would be perfect, claiming that, if 90% or so of the missiles could be intercepted, this would be enough to deter a foe, or to make it prohibitively expensive to mount an effective attack.

Well, I just don't believe this argument. The Star Wars system must be designed to handle a problem which *cannot* be fully understood, in the sense that its designers cannot foresee *all* the possible threats which it would have to handle. No matter how thoroughly tested, any software system with 10 million lines of code (or any significant fraction of that number) designed for such an ill-structured task will crash helplessly the first—and only—time it has to be used. And while we might hope to develop software technology that would make such a statement false in the future, I believe the kind of breakthrough that would be required to make such vast systems essentially foolproof is extremely unlikely in the next two decades.

And I think the proponents of Star Wars know this. Why, then is the system being pushed so hard? Essentially, I believe, because there is so much money and power involved that, to put it kindly, judgment becomes warped, and credulous and scientifically naive people become too easily convinced of what they would like to believe.

If you agree with me and have no present or potential connection with SDI, then I hope you will express your opposition to this program in whatever forms are available to you. But what is your responsibility as computer scientists and technologists when presented with the opportunity to work on valid, interesting research or development related to Star Wars? Not an easy question. If your job or livelihood is on the line, whistle blowing is only for the very brave (or, perhaps, the very foolhardy). But for many computer scientists who might be involved, some bonuses may be at risk, but not their livelihood. Such people must consider not only the question of intellectual honesty, but whether the attempt to develop such a system may not also be economically idiotic and politically destabilizing.

INTERRUPT

Among the artifacts at the Computer Museum in Boston is "the first object produced by computer-aided design"—an aluminum ashtray. It was donated by Douglas Ross, who developed APT (the Automatic Programmed Tools program at MIT) in the late 1950s. At that time, the *San Francisco Chronicle* reported:

"The Air Force announced today that it has a machine that can receive instructions in English, figure out how to make whatever is wanted, and teach other machines how to make it. An Air Force general said it will enable the United States to 'build a war machine that nobody would want to tackle.' Today it made an ashtray."

Less than Meets the Eye

ANTHONY RALSTON

Readers of ABACUS undoubtedly are expecting early coverage of the Fifth Generation—as was, indeed, predicted in my preceding editorial (Fall 1983). But I had not anticipated that there would be so much so fast. The coverage of MCC (Microelectronics and Computer Technology Corporation)—a reaction of the Fifth Generation—in the WASHINGTON REPORT of the previous issue and the extensive coverage in the BOOK REVIEWS section of the present issue were initiated by the editors of those departments. I'm pleased that this gives me an excuse to make some observations on the Fifth Generation and related matters here.

There is a rhythm to the projects of Big Science, whether in high-energy physics or artificial intelligence or whatever. First something is launched in one country, and then another country (more often than not the United States) argues that it must do something better in order not to be left behind, scientifically, economically, or militarily. The present attempt by the U.S. physics community to get funding for the next gigantic particle accelerator, in response to the LEP (Large Electron-Positron Collider) at CERN in Geneva, is just the latest example of this.

With the corresponding attempt by the artificial intelligence community to persuade the federal government to support a response to the Japanese Fifth Generation Project, the computer science establishment is making its first substantial attempt to gorge itself at the public trough (although it might be argued that Illiac IV was a prior example). Although computer scientists do not have anything like the clout in Washington that physicists have assiduously cultivated since World War II, they do have one thing going for them that the high-energy physicists do not.

While there is plenty of money and power involved with building large accelerators, the arguments for embarking on such projects are essentially

Reprinted from ABACUS, Volume 1, Number 2, Winter 1984.

scientific, intellectual, and philosophical ones which revolve around the need for any society to justify its birthright by remaining in the forefront of scientific progress. There just are no economic benefits—direct or short-term ones, anyhow—which can reasonably be adduced to support high-energy physics research. Not so with computer science. Our technology and science are crucially important for the current, short-term and long-term economic prospects of the United States. Thus, if we lack the explicit clout of the physicists, we have plenty of implicit clout.

Hence all the activity connected with the American reaction to the Fifth Generation. If we do not respond, if there is not some massive infusion of federal funds to match or surpass the Japanese half-billion, so the argument goes, we may fall behind, not just in AI itself but also much more generally in hardware and software technology. So let's establish a National Center for Knowledge Technology or crank up a new federal (DoD?) research program. Anyhow, *something*.

Well, should we? Is the hand-wringing and doom-saying to be listened to or not? A definitive, unequivocal answer is not on, because the issue is too complex and depends upon too many fallible judgments. I was once an advocate of a National Computer Laboratory where computer scientists from small or poor universities could obtain access to facilities not available at their home institutions. This was an ill-timed idea just before the VAX explosion took place. Now almost everyone has access to good facilities on campuses or via networks such as CSNET. Currently there is an effort—with which I am sympathetic—to establish federally-supported regional computer centers allowing university researchers access to super-computer power too costly for individual universities to provide for the relatively few researchers who need it.

This latter example suggests the criterion that massive federal funding should be provided for research programs only when normal research funding channels won't be effective. I don't see this as being the case for the Fifth Generation. Nor do I see a National Center for Knowledge Technology providing anything that is not already widely available through standard channels. Indeed, there appears to be much less than meets the eye to the Fifth Generation project.

Let us give full credit to the Japanese for identifying an important area of computer science research and development, and for packaging their plans in such a way that they were able to obtain substantial amounts of governmental money for them. But the prospects for success—real success in the attainment of sophisticated knowledge-engineering systems, rather than smaller successes in such areas as chip technology, logic programming, natural-language processing, and expert systems—do not look very good. Most important, it is far from clear that even major success would give the Japanese an economic benefit not also available to others who are merely smart enough to adapt new science and technology for productive purposes. After all, as Eric Weiss points out in his book review column, this is just how the Japanese have achieved their present great economic success.

I have no doubts that the United States needs to continue to support basic research in all the sciences. But the main reason for doing so is not immediate or short-range economic benefit, but rather to maintain the general intellectual vitality of the nation—which does, of course, contribute essentially to our long-term economic health. We Americans should stop insisting that we must be first in everything in science in order to maintain our military or economic strength. It is sufficient to do enough to assure that other industrialized democracies will want the fruits of our research just as much as we want the fruits of theirs.

I conclude that all the ballyhoo about the Fifth Generation in the United States has much more to do with levers for prying loose government funds that it does with any profound national interest. By all means let us continue and increase government support of computer science research. But let us use traditional—and traditionally successful—means, through agencies like the National Science Foundation. Let's not be stampeded by scare talk about the Fifth Generation into supporting unnecessary and, perhaps, unwise Big Science projects.

INTERRUPT

Last year, Addison-Wesley published a book called *The Cognitive Computer* by Roger Schenk with Peter Childers. In the introduction to her discussion of it for the *New York Times Book Review*, Susan Chase quoted from "Artificial Intelligence," a 1961 poem by Adrienne Rich addressed to a chess-playing computer:

Still, when
they make you write your poems, later on,
who'd envy you, force-fed
on all those variorum
editions of our primitive endeavors
those frozen pemmican language-
rations
they'll cram you with? Denied
our luxury of nausea, you
forget nothing, have no dreams.

The fear and frustration—so eloquently expressed in this poem—that "sturdy, tireless and imperturbable silicon reasoning machines" may replace humans underlies the review:

"In 10 years, Mr. Schenk predicts, the machine will be able to explain why it came to the conclusions it did, what lines of reasoning it rejected and why it rejected them. But computers will never have empathy for human beings, he notes, because human 'output' at the level of empathy cannot easily be put into words or 'representations.' For example, what happens when the output is a kiss or a backrub, or a wonderfully cooked dinner, or a vase of flowers?"

Well said, indeed.

Babel and Newspeak in 1984

ANTHONY RALSTON

Two programming languages are enough to start a controversy about which is better. The hundreds we have now can be aptly represented by a modern Tower of Babel decorated with the names of high-level computer languages (see the January 1961 issue of the *Communications of the ACM* or the dust jacket of Jean Sammet's book, *Programming Languages: History and Fundamentals* [Prentice-Hall, 1969]). In the 1960s, in the 1970s, and still in the 1980's, programming languages have been a source of dispute and conflict among computer scientists and technologists.

On one level, there has always been the question of what language to use for a particular application. And whether we try to match the language to the application, or to the quality of the implementation on the machine on which it is going to run, or to the related software with which it will have to run, we seldom, if ever, *know* whether or not we have made the right decisions. With languages, as with so much of what we do in software, there are no metrics yet—perhaps there never will be—to give definite answers on what language is best (in any sense) for a particular application. Still, in most cases, accumulated experience and a variety of other factors usually point clearly to a particular language for a particular application.

Not so with teaching. Although there have been periodic fads in languages for teaching computer science, there has never been anything close to general agreement on this matter, nor can such a consensus be expected in the foreseeable future. The Summer 1984 ABACUS, Vol. 1, No. 4, features five articles on languages for a first course in computer science, which testify to this lack of agreement. And if it is true that Pascal today, like Fortran not so many years ago, is the language of choice in many leading departments of computer science, these articles attest to the fact that we are a long way from unanimity.

Reprinted from ABACUS, Volume 1, Number 4, Summer 1984.

How much does it really matter what language students are exposed to in their first course in computing? Various prophets of doom—some of them quoted in the articles—would have you believe that to be exposed to the wrong language is to be maimed for life, or nearly so. But is it really true that bad habits acquired from being taught to use bad languages just can't be overcome? I don't believe it. Like so many of my contemporaries, I was weaned on Fortran and learned to write GOTO-laden programs. Indeed, I had the distinction of having one such program immortalized by Kernighan and Plauger in *The Elements of Programming Style* (McGraw-Hill, 2nd edition, 1978) as an example of bad style. Nevertheless, I think I've outgrown my bad habits. Whatever language I use, I write better programs now than ever before. My early miseducation—extensive as it was—no longer haunts me.

Does it follow then that the language you learn first has no significance at all? Surely not. Bad habits learned early can be unlearned, but the process may be painful—very painful—and many bad programs may be written before good habits are fully learned. And yet, notwithstanding the articles in this issue, I continue to believe that the quality of the instructor in a first course in computer science is far more important than the quality of the language used as a vehicle. An instructor with a deep, broad understanding of computer science and programming methodology can teach a successful course with a bad language—take your pick—but an instructor without such perspective will not teach a good course even with the best language available—again, take your pick.

There can be no expectation of revealed truth about the relative quality of programming languages in any foreseeable future. Newspeak will be perennially with us, and the Tower of Babel is sure to grow substantially taller.

Don't Shoot, They Are Your Children!

Eric A. Weiss

Hacker, as computing rather than golfing or riding slang, now has a permanent place in the public consciousness (although the French, as yet, have no official word for it). It is used pejoratively, as defined in the panel at right, in the public press, on the nightly TV news, in movies, and in the halls of Congress. Hacking is the theme of frequent weekend feature articles, the basis for periodic panicking of the public and industry by opportunistic security merchants, the permanent object of state and federal legislation, and the repeated subject of thoughtful discussion panels, like a recent one reported on in the April 1986 *Communications of the ACM*.

Amid all the heavy breathing, viewing with alarm, breast beating, and hacking coughing over ethics, responsibilities, computer abuse, needed legislation, threats to the nation, and codes of responsible use, the ACM panel proceedings show what has long been evident—that the leading computing professionals are extremely ambivalent about hacking. They would rather not adopt the hard "lock 'em up and cut off their bytes" attitude of the enraged and bristling security Rambos, and instead are inclined to slide off into softer fantasies of special education and moral suasion for young people who might acquire the hacker viral deficiency. All those who remember their own youth can understand the reason for this ambivalence.

It seems that the brightest and best of our college-age young have always been energetic nonconformist rebels in some way: scoffing at authority and delighting in dangerous and mildly lawless acts of defiance; scaling university towers to display vulgar objects; testing the limits of faculty and administration tolerance in dress, language, and behavior; and perpetrating elaborate, ingenious, and often traditional practical jokes. Students with a technical and mechanical turn of mind have always felt chal-

Reprinted from ABACUS, Volume 4, Number 1, Fall 1986.

Hacker:
Some Pejorative
Definitions

ACM Panel:
"A person who utilizes computing talent to gain unauthorized access to software, systems, and data bases."

The Penguin Dictionary of Computers, Second Edition (Chandor, Graham, and Williamson; Penguin Books, 1977):
"One who invades a network's privacy"

The Hacker's Dictionary (Guy L. Steele, Jr., et al.; Harper & Row, 1983):
"A malicious or inquisitive meddler who tries to discover information by poking around. For example, a 'password hacker' is one who tries, possibly by deceptive or illegal means, to discover other people's computer passwords. A 'network hacker' is one who tries to learn about the computer network (possibly because he wants to interfere)—one can tell the difference only by context and tone of voice)."

lenged by vending machines, telephones, locks of every kind, codes, puzzles, and protective procedures, especially those that authority has assumed are impossible to defeat.

In a way, those students reflect the attitude toward truth, knowledge, and authority that they are being taught. Seek, think, experiment, find out for yourself. Accept nothing without proof. Accept nothing on the basis of authority alone. More importantly, the youngsters are displaying the same enthusiastic joy in searching, discovering, conquering obstacles, and exceeding old limits of knowledge and accomplishment that we hope for in our best scientists. Indeed, these are the basic mental characteristics of our heroes of science and technology, and from time to time such a hero reveals how this attitude was displayed in his or her own youthful escapades.

For example, Richard Feynman's book of stories about himself (*"Surely You're Joking, Mr. Feynman!" Adventures of a Curious Character*, one of the top ten in campus reading in 1986) tells how this Nobel-prize-winning genius of theoretical physics delighted in the illegal and potentially dangerous acts of circumventing wartime censorship, picking locks, and opening safes while at Los Alamos atom bomb works during World War II. Visible in all the stories is Feynman's clear antagonism to authority, coupled with his excitement and joy in exercising his powerful intellect to defeat physical and institutional barriers and to show up his ignorant, pretentious, and incompetent adversaries. Are this opposition to authority and this attraction to puzzles—mechanical, logical, or mathematical—the youthful manifestations of the mental approach that our most creative scientist adopt in examining the problems and puzzles of nature, or of computing systems?

Consider a complex and opaque system—natural or human—established by some authority—natural or human—and declared impregnable. It has an unbreakable lock. Can I understand the system, devise a key, open the lock, and solve the insoluble puzzle? Can I do this by cleverness and skill and thought and perseverence, rather than by brute force?

Aren't these the problems that the best teachers set their students, and that the best students set for themselves? Aren't these the motivations of the best hackers? And aren't hackers not only the children and disciples of the brightest and the best in computing now, but a source of the brightest and the best in future computing?

What does this say about the hacker problem? To me, it suggests that like all the important problems of life, death, taxes, and the preeminence of IBM, this problem will never be solved. Improvements in computer security will make the challenge to hackers even more interesting and attractive. More laws will increase their thrill of victory by increasing the threatened agony of defeat. Lectures, speeches, harangues, and codes of ethics and responsibilities will comfort the hand-wringers, but will merely add to the white-noise background on the screens of the hackers.

As long as there are computers, bright young people who are interested in them, and heroes and teachers who set examples, we will have hackers. Don't shoot, they are your children!

INTERRUPT

In the *New York Times*, May 31, 1984, David Sanger reports that the latest integrated software packages tax the limits of the capabilities of even the more powerful computers. When asked when the constantly rising user expectations of microcomputer capabilities would be satisfied, Darrell Miller of Digital Research replied, "When I can sit in front of the computer with my hands in my pockets, and it does exactly what I want."

The prospect of a completely hands-off access leaves us unhandily speechless.

Articles

The subjects of ABACUS articles are those the editors think are of importance to intelligent, curious, practicing computing professionals. Through solicitation of authors and selection of volunteered manuscripts, we try to provide a wide variety of subjects, writers, and approaches while insisting on a high quality of content and expression. Manuscripts presenting well thought-out analyses, summaries, overviews, or explanations are preferred, while those reporting new work, discoveries, novelties, or inventions are certainly not asked for and usually not accepted.

Authors are encouraged to include illustrative and decorative material of every kind; diagrams, figures, tables, charts, panels, boxes, photographs, whatever. Authors are paid a small fee per printed page on publication. No set writing style is prescribed other than being interesting and, if possible, entertaining. *Strunk and White* is often recommended to some highly educated but too often illiterate potential contributors. Editing is limited to ensuring clarity, accuracy, unity, coherence, and emphasis.

I should mention the only rigid sylistic rule. Masculine pronouns may not be used to indicate both sexes. It turns out not to be hard to word things in this nonsexist way without constantly resorting to "him or her."

As the following samples show, the aims of ABACUS as expressed in the Introduction have been achieved except in the total lack of overt fiction.

Who Invented the First Electronic Digital Computer?

How much did the invention of the ENIAC owe to a little-known professor of physics from Iowa?

NANCY STERN

The electronic digital computer was invented just over four decades ago, ushering in a series of technological changes which can only be compared to the Industrial Revolution in their scope, magnitude, and impact. Even though we are still in the infancy—if not the birth throes—of this so-called "computer revolution," its history has been the subject of considerable interest in recent years.

This article will address one fundamental issue in the history of computing: who should be credited with the invention of the first electronic digital computer? The issue is not as clear-cut as it may seem. Did J. Presper Eckert, Jr., John William Mauchly, and their associates at the Moore School of Electrical Engineering of the University of Pennsylvania invent the first electronic digital computer (called the ENIAC) during the years 1943–1946, or was the ENIAC based on the prior invention of a small, special-purpose vacuum tube device developed by John Vincent Atanasoff and his associate Clifford Berry at Iowa State College in 1939?

This priority issue first became controversial in 1971, as the result of a major court case which to some extent has shaped the direction of historical study and research on the early years of computing.

In 1950, Eckert and Mauchly assigned their rights to the ENIAC patent to the Remington Rand Corporation, which later became Sperry Rand.

NANCY STERN is Professor of Computer Information Systems at Hofstra University. She has written numerous articles on the history of computing, as well as a monograph, *From ENIAC to UNIVAC,* and she has lectured widely on the topic as well. She is on the Editorial Board of the *Annals of the History of Computing,* and is a member of the History of Computing Committee of the American Federation of Information Processing Societies. She is also the coauthor of six textbooks on computer information processing. She is currently undertaking research on John von Neumann's computing project at the Institute for Advanced Study, 1946–1952.
Reprinted from ABACUS, Volume 1, Number 1, Fall 1983.

The ENIAC patent, number 3,120,606, is huge. It starts with 91 sheets of drawings detailing the computer with circuit and block diagrams, and showing its physical arrangement and appearance. There are 104 pages of description, and 148 claims ranging from details of pulse generation to systems for data processing. Because of the broad scope and fundamental nature of the patent, Sperry could look forward to receiving royalties from companies building computers, once the patent was issued. Eckert and Mauchly applied for the patent on 26 June 1947. Under the law, a patent may be applied for up to a year after it has been placed in public use. The patent was not, however, actually issued until 4 February 1964; thus, beginning in 1964, Sperry received royalties which they believed would continue for seventeen years, the period during which the patent would be valid.

In 1970, however, Honeywell decided to challenge the validity of the ENIAC patent because they believed the royalties they would have to pay would be inordinate. They hired the law firm of Dorset, Windhorst, Whitney and Halladay to represent them, with Henry Halladay serving as chief counsel. When Honeywell failed to pay the required royalties in 1971, Sperry sued, charging patent infringement. Honeywell countersued, charging, among other things, that the ENIAC was based on the prior invention of John Vincent Atanasoff.

The trial, which lasted two years, generated 50,000 pages of transcript and used as evidence over 30,000 documents that were read into the record.

The decision was handed down by the presiding judge, Earl R. Larson, on 19 October 1973, in a 319-page document entitled "Findings of Fact, Conclusions of Law, and Order for Judgment." In his decision, the judge declared the ENIAC patent invalid, charging that "Eckert and Mauchly did not themselves first invent the automatic electronic digital computer, but instead derived the subject matter from one Dr. John Vincent Atanasoff."

This decision brought into question the whole issue of priority, but in a larger sense it also raised questions regarding the nature of invention, what constitutes an operational device, and whether legal assessments of priority should be viewed as objective, historical evaluations. In short, did Eckert and Mauchly really invent the first electronic digital computer or was it actually invented by Atanasoff, who until the trial was an obscure physicist and inventor whose work did not itself impact the development of computers in the 1940s?

After the decision in the Honeywell vs. Sperry trial was reached, considerable controversy arose over the issues raised during litigation. Initially, the controversy was generated by the participants themselves. In 1972, Herman Goldstine, who worked with Eckert and Mauchly on the ENIAC, wrote the first historical survey which addressed these issues, *The Computer From Pascal to von Neumann*. His book essentially portrays Mauchly as a disseminator of Atanasoff's ideas. Until his death in

1980, Mauchly wrote numerous informal papers and gave lectures and interviews in which he attempted to dispel this notion. Atanasoff has remained relatively noncommittal about the controversy until recently. An autobiographical account by Atanasoff, in which he focuses on the ideas Mauchly derived from him, appeared in the July 1984 issue of the *Annals of the History of Computing*.

In addition, Arthur W. Burks and his wife Alice R. Burks have written a detailed account of how the ENIAC derived its form from Atanasoff's computer. Kay Mauchly, John Mauchly's wife, has responded with evidence which suggests that Mauchly had conceived of his machine years before he even met Atanasoff.

In short, the controversy surrounding this priority issue remains heated, and continues to dominate much of the writing on the history of electronic digital computers. This paper will focus on the development of the ENIAC itself and the relationship between Mauchly and Atanasoff which may have influenced the ENIAC development.

The ENIAC

The ENIAC was a computer developed to fill a very specific wartime need. During World War II, the number of new artillery developed put a great strain on the Army's Ballistic Research Laboratory (BRL), which had primary responsibility for preparing range tables so that gunners could make effective use of new weapons. Even with 200 human "computers" (mostly female), the backlog at BRL rendered many of the new weapons virtually useless. It was this crisis situation that made the Army willing, indeed eager, to consider any new technology with the potential for solving their computational problem.

As far back as 1930, when he was a Ph.D. candidate in physics at Johns Hopkins University, John William Mauchly had a keen interest in building computational devices. After receiving his Ph.D. from Hopkins, as an instructor at Ursinus College near Philadelphia, he experimented with building high-speed counters, using first neon and then vacuum tubes.

Lacking formal education in electronics, Mauchly enrolled in a summer war-training course at the Moore School of Electrical Engineering at the University of Pennsylvania, where he learned of the Army's critical need. The Moore School had numerous contracts with the Army for R&D projects at the time. Mauchly continued to develop ideas for an electronic digital computer, and hoped to be in a position to present proposals for computational devices to the government. Mauchly discussed his ideas with J. Presper Eckert, Jr., a brilliant young graduate engineering student who taught some of the school's war-training courses. Eckert was immediately interested in building the kind of device envisioned by Mauchly.

Mauchly continued to discuss his ideas with Carl Chambers and John

John William Mauchly. (From *Encyclopedia of Computer Science and Engineering,* courtesy of Van Nostrand Reinhold Company, Inc.)

Grist Brainerd, two of the Moore School's administrators, and with the Army's technical liaison, Lt. Herman H. Goldstine. It was Goldstine who, along with Brainerd, brought Eckert and Mauchly's idea to the Army in April 1943; by June, a contract for an "Electronic Numerical Integrator and Computer" (ENIAC) at a development cost of $150,000 was signed. Brainerd was named project supervisor; Eckert, chief engineer; Mauchly, principal consultant; and Goldstine, technical liaison for BRL.

Despite a great deal of skepticism on the part of the government's old-line science advisors, the ENIAC project moved along smoothly. By the end of the first year, two out of 20 electronic accumulators, the arithmetic units of the ENIAC, were complete. By the fall of 1945 the major components of ENIAC were operational. These included a forty-panel system with 18,000 vacuum tubes and 1500 relays grouped into 30 units.

There were 20 accumulators for addition and subtraction, a multiplier and a divider/square-rooter.

A constant pulse transmitter enabled an IBM card reader to enter input, and an output unit enabled the ENIAC to punch cards as output.

A function table with switches was used to store functions, numbers, and, later, instructions. A master programmer provided a limited amount of centralized memory.

The initiating unit controlled the power and the initiating of computations. The cycling unit synchronized the machine.

On 15 February 1946, the ENIAC was dedicated in a much-publicized event that marked the Moore School's preeminence in electronic computers. The celebration made it clear that the ENIAC represented a major accomplishment not only for Eckert and Mauchly but for the dozens of other engineers who worked on the project.

The Legal Issue

During the development and construction of the ENIAC, Eckert and Mauchly were employed by the University of Pennsylvania, and were operating under a government-funded project. Typically the government required license-free rights to all its R&D projects, meaning that it would not be required to pay a royalty or license fee for use of an invention. Such rights would legally be granted by the organization or individual holding the patent. In 1944, the government sought to establish legally its license-free rights to the ENIAC. Since the law states that only the holder of a patent can issue a license-free right, a patent on the ENIAC had to be filed, and Eckert and Mauchly took the initiative. Some of the Moore School administrators were outraged at this attempt to obtain an independent patent, first because they believed the patent rightfully belonged to the University, and secondly because they regarded the pursuit of a patent as a violation of academic norms.

In March of 1945, the President of the University of Pennsylvania, George W. McClelland, eager to put the controversy and dissension to rest, granted Eckert and Mauchly permission to file for the ENIAC patent; but the issue remained a divisive one, ultimately leading to the resignation from the university of the two inventors.

In 1946 Eckert and Mauchly formed their own company to build the UNIVAC, an acronym for Universal Automatic Computer; although their company was under contract for several UNIVACs and for a smaller computer called the BINAC (Binary Automatic Computer), it remained on the brink of bankruptcy for much of its existence, and finally, in 1950, it was acquired by the Sperry Corporation.

Sperry acquired the Eckert-Mauchly Computer Corporation because they hoped to derive great benefit from the UNIVAC and to reap financial rewards from the ENIAC patent. They did not realize that Eckert and Mauchly had been overzealous in their claims for the patent; and Sperry was also unaware of Atanasoff's work. When the trial was over—twenty-three years after the Eckert-Mauchly Corporation had been acquired—Sperry chose not to challenge the decision.

An assessment of the legal and technical issues stemming from the trial clearly indicates that, had Eckert and Mauchly been more modest in their claims, the patent would not have been invalidated. By naively laying claim to virtually all aspects of electronic digital computer technology, the two inventors opened themselves to challenges regarding the validity of their patent. Even though it is common in patent applications to cast the net widely, care must be taken to lay claim only to components originating with the inventor.

The 1971 court case also brought to light the fact that before 1941, Mauchly did have prior contact with John Vincent Atanasoff, who was himself developing an electronic digital computational device. For most observers, and for most students of the history, the trial uncovered Atanasoff's work for the first time. Therefore, when one now studies the history of the electronic digital computer, the work of Atanasoff and his relationship to Mauchly become matters of considerable interest. When one now considers the revolutionary nature of the ENIAC, one must also consider what aspects, if any, were derived from Atanasoff.

Mauchly's Relationship to Atanasoff

Atanasoff received his Ph.D. in physics from the University of Wisconsin in 1930. He became a professor of physics and mathematics at Iowa State College (later Iowa State University), where he experimented with vacuum-tube circuits for solving computational problems digitally.

In 1939, Atanasoff and his graduate student Clifford Berry began construction of a prototype of their machine, later called ABC, an abreviation for Atanasoff-Berry Computer. This computer was developed specifically for solving systems of linear algebraic equations. A prototype or breadboard model without an input/output unit was completed in 1940, but the

John Vincent Atanasoff. (From *Encyclopedia of Computer Science and Engineering,* courtesy of Van Nostrand Reinhold Company, Inc.)

machine itself was never finished. A lack of adequate financial backing prevented further progress; moreover, when World War II began, Atanasoff was asked to serve at the U.S. Naval Ordnance Laboratory. It is interesting to note that he did not pursue his computational interests any further at the Laboratory, even though his government affiliation would have provided an excellent vehicle for doing so.

Because Atanasoff's prototype was successfully completed years before the ENIAC, many people regard him as the true inventor of the first electronic digital computer. Arthur Burks provides his full assessment of Atanasoff's work in the October 1981 issue of *Annals of the History of Computing:*

All of the parts had been completed, and the machine had been assembled and tested. Everything worked well, with the exception of the electric-spark method of punching holes in the binary cards. This had succeeded in preliminary tests in 1939, but now failed, though only rarely. Because the rate of failure was so low—perhaps one in 100,000 times—the computer could solve small sets of equations correctly; it could not solve large sets, however, on account of the great number of binary digits to be recorded and read in these.

Unfortunately, this difficulty had not been overcome by the fall of 1942, when both John Atanasoff and Clifford Berry had to leave Iowa State College, and their computer project, for war research. Neither returned after the war, no one else worked on their machine, and it was ultimately dismantled. Nor was a patent ever applied for, although Iowa State had agreed to finance a joint venture and Atanasoff prepared the necessary materials.

Nevertheless, Atanasoff had succeeded in designing and building an electronic computer whose computing system worked; the fact that its electromechanical input-output system was not perfected does not detract from the success of the invention in terms of electronic computation. Moreover, a functional input-output system was already in existence, but not available to Atanasoff, and was, as we shall see, used in the ENIAC.

So, clearly, Atanasoff had achieved a great deal in his pioneering efforts. He invented a novel form of serial store suitable for electronic computation. He also conceived, developed, and proved the fundamental principles of electronic switching for digital computation, principles encompassing arithmetic operations, control, base conversion, the transfer and restoration of data, and synchronization. He designed a well-balanced electronic computing machine utilizing this store and these principles and having a centralized architecture of store, arithmetic unit, control circuits, and input-output with base conversion. His was the first special-purpose electronic computer ever invented; indeed, it was the first electronic computer of any degree of generality ever invented.

Burks ignores the facts that Atanasoff's machine was never operational, that it was never used to solve any computational problems, and that it—unlike ENIAC—did not lead directly to further advances. To Burks, these points do not detract from the significance of the computer called the ABC.

Burks, however, goes beyond his claim that Atanasoff invented the first electronic digital computer. He further charges, as is also implicit in the

The ABC Computer

Photo courtesy of The Computer Museum, Boston, MA.

court decision, that Mauchly derived his ideas for the ENIAC from Atanasoff. Goldstine confirms this opinion in his book on the computer:

> During this period of Atanasoff's work on his linear equation solver, Mauchly
> was at Ursinus College. . . . Somehow he became aware of Atanasoff's project
> and visited him for a week in 1941. During the visit the two men apparently went
> into Atanasoff's ideas in considerable detail. The discussion greatly influenced
> Mauchly and through him the entire history of electronic computers. Just about
> at the time Atanasoff confided his ideas to Mauchly, the latter left Ursinus to take
> a post at the Moore School of Electrical Engineering at the University of Penn-
> sylvania. Atanasoff also apparently had ideas for a more general-purpose electronic
> digital computer and discussed his nascent ideas with Mauchly on this occasion.

Since Mauchly had prior knowledge of Atanasoff's work, the findings
of the court and the opinions of Goldstine, Burks, and others suggest that
he was not a true inventor, but rather a transmitter of ideas (''pirate'' was
the intemperate term used by the Honeywell attorneys). Moreover, since
Mauchly's role in the ENIAC project was as a consultant on existing computational techniques and technology rather than as an inventor or engineer
per se, others have questioned the significance of his contribution on this
level. Let us consider his precise relationship with Atanasoff.

In December 1940, Mauchly gave a lecture to the American Association
for the Advancement of Science on the application of harmonic analyzers
(a type of analog computer) to weather forecasting. At that meeting, he
met Atanasoff and discovered that he, like Mauchly himself, had been
influenced by Vannevar Bush's work on analog devices, and had been
working on an electronic digital computer which used vacuum tubes and
solved linear equations. Mauchly immediately saw the potential significance of the ABC, since he had previously considered the use of vacuum

The ENIAC

Photo courtesy of The Computer Museum, Boston, MA.

tubes in computational devices. During the next few months, Mauchly wrote to Atanasoff seeking more information: "I am wondering how your plans with regard to computing devices are working out. Need I say again that I await with some suspense the time when you will be able to let me have more information." Later in 1941 Mauchly visited Atanasoff and had the opportunity to see his ABC prototype first-hand. In that year, Mauchly brought his own ideas of a general-purpose computer—combined with his knowledge of Atanasoff's work on that small, special-purpose device for computing solutions to simultaneous equations—to the Moore School.

In 1976 Mauchly spoke at the Los Alamos conference on the history of computing and recalled:

My ideas about the feasibility of electronic calculation date back to the days in which I was teaching college physics at Ursinus, and reading the journals such as the *Review of Scientific Instruments,* in which circuits were published for "binary scalers". . . . At Ursinus College, some of the students remember my building small models of experimental digital circuits using some gas tubes as well as vacuum tubes. Some of these still exist and work. All of this predates a visit I made to Ames, Iowa, where I found it impossible to persuade Dr. Atanasoff that his projected machine did not realize the potential speeds of electronic calculation that I had in mind. He said he had not succeeded in making flip-flops reliable.

In a similar vein, Mauchly wrote the present author in January 1979:

I strongly maintain that I took no ideas whatsoever from Atanasoff. I tried to give him some, such as using the "scaling circuits" with which I was already acquainted to make his proposed device much faster, but JVA said that he couldn't get flip-flops to work reliably.

Indeed, until his death in 1980, Mauchly steadfastly claimed that he had formed his ideas for an electronic digital computer well before he ever met John Vincent Atanasoff. There is some evidence to support this claim but it is, however, sparse. For example, there is this excerpt from a 1940 letter from Mauchly to H. Helm Clayton:

In a week or two my academic work will not be quite so heavy, and I shall begin to give some time to the construction of computing devices. We have further simplified the design of our proposed 27-ordinate analyser. In addition, we are now considering the construction of an electrical computing machine to obtain sum of squares and cross-products as rapidly as the numbers can be punched into the machine. The machine would perform its operations in about 1/200 second, using vacuum tube relays, and yielding mathematically exact, not approximate, results. (*Annals*, July 1982)

In numerous interviews with the author, Mauchly has also claimed that his Ursinus students could attest to his electronic work in the 1930s.

Since his death, Mauchly's wife, Kay Mauchly, has actively sought to continue Mauchly's crusade to support his priority claims. Mrs. Mauchly was herself a programmer for the ENIAC project when it was nearing completion. In an *Annals* paper (April 1984), she states:

It was after Mauchly's death in 1980, while I was assembling the papers to be given to the Van Pelt Library [at the University of Pennsylvania] that I came across a letter file from the Ursinus period. This box had been sealed for nearly 40 years, and its contents had not been known at the time of the Honeywell-Sperry trial in Minneapolis. In the file were carbons of letters showing that Mauchly had been actively working on a computer at Ursinus—something John had claimed all along.

Besides these paper items, we have physical components of the electronic computer that Mauchly was building during the time he was teaching at Ursinus College. These components alone are evidence that Mauchly's concept of an electronic "computer-calculator" predated any association with John V. Atanasoff and led directly to the design of the ENIAC.

She goes on to cite correspondence such as the following, written by John Dewire:

During the period 1936–1938 I visited both the Bartol Foundation and DTM [Department of Terrestrial Magnetism] with John, certainly several times in the case of DTM. We saw counting devices being used in both laboratories. At Ursinus we had a Geiger counter and some type of counting circuit, perhaps the equipment you still have. In my senior year I took a course from John, in which he used the text Atomic Physics *by members of the physics staff at Pitt. In that text there are descriptions of coincidence circuits and other counting devices.*

What I remember most clearly was John's interest in flip-flops. I only did a little work on one, but quite a lot of work was done by another student whose identity I do not recall. All of us around John were fully aware that the motivation behind this work was to develop a device to do arithmetic calculations electronically using binary digits. John had many calculations under way and he was obsessed with finding ways to make these calculations less painful. One of my jobs was to solve some high-order simultaneous equations using a method called Synthetic Division. I spent many hours at an old Marchant doing this work and fully appreciated John's interest in finding a better way to do the job.

In his later years, Mauchly, sensitive to the priority issue raised at the trial, consistently took every opportunity to detail his early work with vacuum tubes:

Well, if they could use vacuum tubes for a million counts a second, as far as I was concerned, let's forget about the cosmic rays and let's get those counts counting whatever I wanted to count. Weather data. Of course, it doesn't take much imagination to see that if you can count weather data, you can also count money, dollars in the bank; you can do all kinds of business calculations, if you like. Even at that point, I had no reservations as to how limited this idea might be if it once got put into practice and carried out and people were really behind it. But nobody was really behind it then. You always have to demonstrate things.

So I started, again, buying my own vacuum tubes and putting things together in a laboratory—showing that you could generate counts and use these counting devices with vacuum tubes in them (not gears and wheels like all the traditional calculators had). You could do all this if you just had enough money.

There you have it. I don't have enough money, but I have at least an idea which, put together with money, ought to produce something that would be valuable not just for weather, but for other things.

[In 1939], I started, again, buying my own vacuum tubes and putting things together in a laboratory—showing that you could generate counts and use these counting devices with vacuum tube storage in them (not gears and wheels like all the traditional calculators had). (*Annals,* July 1982)

Mauchly was understandably bitter about accusations, insinuations, and judgments that denied him full credit:

Nor could I have surmised how completely Nancy Stern, in her thesis research, could have become convinced that I was an "innovator" who took J.V.A.'s ideas and improved them. [Reference is to my Ph.D. dissertation entitled *From ENIAC to UNIVAC,* completed in 1978.] Perhaps someone will be able to show her how completely different my ideas were from those of J.V.A. and that I had formed my ideas before I went to Ames—even before I had ever met J.V.A. She really should have interviewed John Dewire and Tay Hayashi (at Illinois Institute, but professor of biophysics at Columbia for a good many years) before she "bought" the judge's decision that I got useful ideas or inspiration from the "innovator" of Ames. (*Annals,* July 1982)

Thus, there is some tangible evidence that Mauchly did, indeed, conceive of an electronic digital computer prior to his meeting with Atanasoff. Clearly, however, his interaction with Atanasoff served, at the very least, to bolster his confidence and to provide him with evidence that he did indeed have an idea worth pursuing. Moreover, his failure to credit Atan-

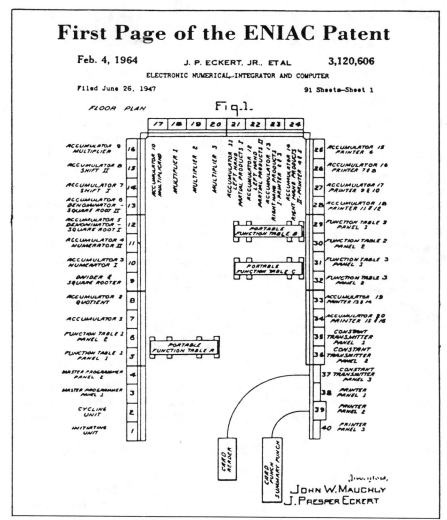

First Page of the ENIAC Patent

Feb. 4, 1964   J. P. ECKERT, JR., ET AL   3,120,606

ELECTRONIC NUMERICAL-INTEGRATOR AND COMPUTER

Filed June 26, 1947   91 Sheets—Sheet 1

Courtesy of The Computer Museum, Boston, MA

asoff in the patent application or even to reveal his knowledge of Atanasoff's work to the Moore School staff demonstrated poor judgment. There is, however, still one undeniable fact that tends to be clouded by the verdict: ENIAC was the first *operational* electronic digital computer developed in the United States.

But the quest for proper recognition for the development of the electronic computer goes beyond the allegations that John Mauchly derived all his ideas from Atanasoff. Several participants on the ENIAC project not only discount Mauchly's version of how he conceived of the ENIAC, but they also give him very little credit for actually making any contributions at all to the project. Goldstine states the following in his book:

At the beginning, at least, Mauchly was to continue to play a key role in the ENIAC project. He alone of the staff of the Moore School knew a lot about the design of the standard electromechanical IBM machines of the period and was able to suggest to the engineers how to handle various design problems by analogy to methods used by IBM. Then as time went on his involvement decreased until it became mainly one of writing up of patent applications. Mauchly was at his absolute best during the early days because his was a quick and restless mind best suited to coping with problems of the moment. He was fundamentally a great sprinter, whereas Eckert not only excelled at sprinting but was also a superb marathon runner.

Eckert was very fortunate in having a first-class engineering group associated with him largely composed of men whom Brainerd had assembled over the war period. It consisted of the following persons: Arthur Burks, Joseph Chedaker, Chuan Chu, James Cummings, John Davis, Harry Gail, Adele Goldstine, Harry Huskey, Hyman James, Edward Knobeloch, Robert Michael, Frank Mural, Kite Sharpless, and Robert Shaw.

The most vociferous voices in denigrating Mauchly's contributions and denouncing him for his claims are those of Arthur and Alice Burks. Arthur Burks served as an engineer on the ENIAC project, and in recent years has actively engaged in research to demonstrate that not only was ENIAC based largely on Atanasoff's machine, but that Mauchly's actual contributions to computing were minimal.

The following citation from a letter to the editor of the *Annals of the History of Computing* (July 1982) sums up the Burks' beliefs. The quote is in response to Mauchly's "Fireside Chat," which appeared in the same issue of the *Annals*. The "Fireside Chat" was delivered by Mauchly in a 1973 Sperry Univac gathering at its International Executive Centre at Villa Les Aigles near Rome, Italy. The Burks' letter is quoted at length because it details the authors' full opinions on the matter.

There are other recurring themes in these two pieces by Mauchly, more or less related to the major one we have been discussing. One, in the letter to [Henry] Tropp, is that Judge Larson unfairly dismissed Mauchly's work in digital computing prior to his visit to Atanasoff's laboratory, for which Mauchly's only "evidence" is that certain of his Ursinus students could have given supporting testimony if they had been called upon to do so. A judge, of course, must assume that the attorneys on each side have presented their best possible case. It also happens that the machine Mauchly did build in the late 1930s was an analog device, his electrical harmonic analyzer. It was this device, in fact, and the results he had obtained from it, that he presented in his December 1940 talk before the AAAS—a talk to which he here refers without identification. At least one member of his audience was responsive, too: Atanasoff; this is how Mauchly met Atanasoff.

Another theme is that Mauchly did not learn anything about electronic computing from Atanasoff—related with a note of bitterness over insinuations made from his brief contact with the Iowa scientist. We believe the case for John Atanasoff's original work in this area and its influence on the ENIAC through Mauchly will ultimately be understood and accepted as the true situation. Certainly no one has yet produced any solid counter-evidence to the findings of the court in the essentials of this case, or against the facts as we presented them in the *Annals*.

A final, and less important, theme is the one about money—or lack thereof. The depression years were indeed as Mauchly describes them, although it would seem he might have been able to design and build a low-speed counter with vacuum tubes while at Ursinus College. There seems no reason, however, that he could not have put his ideas for high-speed computation to work at the Moore School, by 1941–1942, where a laboratory with oscilloscopes was available to him. We believe he has extended the wherewithal excuse beyond its applicable period, rather than face the fact that the high-speed counter problem was not solved until the ENIAC was being designed in 1943, at which point it was solved primarily by Eckert.

Mauchly also commits serious errors of omission in these two works. Most striking is his failure to give the names of people whose roles he describes, or of corporations or projects he mentions. It must be said that, throughout, there is a pattern of insufficient detail, as well as incorrect detail, such that verification of his statements is rendered impossible. The historian is left with a rather grandiloquent picture of events and circumstances, unsupported by concrete evidence, against which must be weighed not just the word of other actors in the drama but an overwhelming amount of evidence and documentation.

The so-called fireside chat is especially strained in this regard. It is of course understandable that, after many years of adulation for one of the most far-reaching inventions in history, a person might tend to exaggerate in the glow of a "fireside" meeting with his corporate associates. We deem it less understandable that he could distort and mislead, with such equanimity, only 25 days after a federal court had ruled "his" invention derived from another, and his (joint) patent accordingly invalid—moreover, that he could do so without once mentioning either the court's decision or the person whose ideas he had wrongly appropriated.

We will close with a brief comment on Mauchly's letter to H. Helm Clayton, since it too is being published, confining ourselves to the paragraph on Mauchly's computing interests at the time (November 15, 1940). The first reference, to a "proposed 27-ordinate analyser," is to an analog device, the electrical harmonic analyzer we mentioned in Section 3 of our *Annals* article (and referred to in this Afterword). The second reference, to considering "construction of an electrical computing machine," is to a digital device, what we called in that same section a "keyboard-operated digital calculator based on electronic counters." We do not believe that Mauchly built any electronic counter that could be part of such a machine—certainly not before he visited Atanasoff and very probably not before the ENIAC project began.

It is clear that the Burkses are, at the very least, impatient with Mauchly's subjectivity, and believe that such subjectivity has led to clear distortions. Indeed, when reading comments written by participants, one must always be cognizant of possible misstatements that might be unconscious, as well as conscious distortions. This is particularly true when major issues of priority are involved. In fairness to the Mauchlys, however, it should be noted that Arthur Burks has always believed that he did not receive appropriate credit for his own contributions; and it is possible that this opinion has clouded his perception of Mauchly and prodded the attempt to discredit him.

In short, there is wide disparity in opinion regarding the relationship between Atanasoff and Mauchly. Mauchly's early work has not been well documented, and during his lifetime he was unable to demonstrate conclusively that he had in fact considered vacuum-tube technology for his electronic digital computer. As a result, his claims of priority are suspect. Moreover, until the court case, he did not actively attribute any of his work to Atanasoff; and indeed, even after the trial, he consistently claimed that he had learned nothing new from Atanasoff or his device.

In an historical sense, one aspect remains critical: the fact that the computer pioneers in the forefront of technology in the 1940s and 1950s were unaware of Atanasoff's early work and instead drew heavily on the Eckert-Mauchly inventions. Even if Atanasoff had been first, he had no direct impact at all on his contemporaries in the 1940s.

It should also be noted that, throughout history, there have always been antecedents to revolutionary inventions and discoveries. Aristarchus, for example, hypothesized about a heliocentric universe fifteen hundred years before Copernicus was credited with the discovery. What makes Copernicus's theme distinctive is that his hypothesis became the basis for a new paradigm which dominated scientific belief for hundreds of years, whereas Ptolemy's hypothesis was viewed as an interesting scientific theory.

Finally, it should be noted that attention to priority issues may be important, but they should not dominate historical studies. As Louis C. Hunter suggests in his study of the steamboat (in the book *Technology and Social Change in America*):

Historians have been too prone to compensate for the wide gaps in our knowledge by playing up the achievements of the few men whose names have come down to us. There is reason to believe that if the returns were all in, the accomplishments of a Fulton, a Shreve, an Evans or a French (inventors of steamboats) would assume a quite modest position beside the collective contribution of scores of master mechanics, ship carpenters, and shop foremen in whose hands the detailed work of construction, adaption and innovation largely rested.

Nonetheless, it must be stated that Mauchly and Eckert were a unique team—hybrid, in a sense. Mauchly was an innovator capable of conceiving numerous original ideas, inspiring others with his ideas, and bringing together the ideas and concepts of others to enhance his own work. Eckert was the consummate engineer, by all accounts, a genius in his ability to take an idea and bring it to practical fruition. The result of the efforts of these two men was the ENIAC, a machine which can stand on its own as the first truly operational electronic computer capable of solving a wide variety of real problems. In this author's opinion, Eckert and Mauchly are clearly the inventors of the first electronic digital computer.

References

Goldstine, Herman H. *The Computer from Pascal to von Neumann*. Princeton University Press, 1972.
Mauchly, John W. The ENIAC. In *A History of Computing in the Twentieth Century*, edited by Nicholas Metropolis et al. Academic Press, 1981.
Stern, Nancy. *From ENIAC to UNIVAC*. Digital Press, 1981.
Annals of the History of Computing, AFIPS Press.

LETTER

Who Owned the ENIAC/UNIVAC Interest in the 1950s?

Nancy Stern in "Who Invented the First Electronic Digital Computer" states that in 1950 "Sperry acquired the Eckert-Mauchly Computer Corporation . . .". This is not quite true. The Eckert-Mauchly Corporation was bought by the Remington Rand Corporation, which also bought Engineering Research Associates, Inc. about the same time, to get into the computer business. The two divisions then went on to build and market the UNIVAC and 1101 computers, respectively, for Remington Rand. It was not until 1956 that the Sperry Corporation merged with Remington Rand to form the Sperry Rand Corporation. (Only recently did that corporation drop the word "Rand" and revert to just "Sperry Corporation".) I remember the period well; I was in charge of Sperry's digital computer development at that time and designed Sperry's first digital computer, the SPEEDAC, beginning in 1950.

> *Herbert Freeman*
> *Director CA/P Centa*
> *Rutgers University*

Reprinted from ABACUS, Volume 1, Number 3, Spring 1984.

Editor's Note

The ever-changing name routine has looped again as "Sperry" and "Burroughs" merged into "Unisys."

Programmers: The Amateur vs. the Professional

Are many professional programmers really amateurs in disguise?

Henry Ledgard

This article is the first of four by Henry Ledgard on the practice of programming. The subsequent articles discussed "Human Factors—Misconceptions" (Fall 1985), "Is Pascal Too Large?" (Winter 1986), and "Programming Teams" (Spring 1986).

At the outset, it should be understood that no attempt to compare an amateur and a professional could describe the full hierarchy in programming or any other vocation or avocation. The complete spectrum might be: the *ignorant,* the *novice,* the *aficionado,* the *amateur,* the *professional,* and the *master.*

Music, specifically classical music, comes to mind if all six rankings are to be defined. Most teenagers are ignorant of classical music (no letters, please), and the spectrum from bottom to top is roughly parallel to age: The ignorant listener appreciates Tchaikovsky's *1812 Overture* every Fourth of July when the cannons go off along the Charles River in Boston. The novice learns the notes of the scale in order to play an instrument (usually the piano or guitar). The aficionado can tell the difference between Mozart and Mahler; the amateur can play the first two movements of the

HENRY LEDGARD operates a private consulting and writing practice in Leverett, Massachusetts. He is a well-known author of books on programming, and is editor of the "Human Aspects of Computing" section of the *Communications of the ACM.* He is currently writing a book on the practice of programming. Dr. Ledgard received a B.S. from Tufts University in 1964 and a Ph.D. from M.I.T. in 1969. He has taught at Johns Hopkins, at the University of Massachusetts, and for Philips Electronics.

Reprinted from ABACUS, Volume 2, Number 4, Summer 1985. This article has been published, in a slightly different form, as the first chapter of *Professional Software: Volume I, Software Engineering Concepts,* by Henry Ledgard with John Tauer, Addison-Wesley, Reading, Massachusetts, 1987, softbound, 219 pages (ISBN 0-201-12231-6).

"Moonlight" Sonata, and the professional can play all thirty-two Bee-thoven sonatas. The master writes the music that eventually finds its way into the repertoire.

The distinction between amateur and professional that we are making, however, is probably closer to an analogy with the golfer. Given some basic talent, capable instruction, and a good deal of practice, a youngster can approach playing close-to-par golf and decide to pursue a career as a professional. After a perfunctory declaration or surviving the qualification tournaments, the golfer may end up as a "club pro" or be invited to the Masters Tournament. But the status is clearly defined. What the individual can or cannot do in golf is limited by personal skill. Not so with pro-grammers.

In the past ten years there has been such a revolution in the computer industry that a politician could rightfully campaign for a computer in every home rather than a chicken in every pot. It would be difficult to speculate on how many new owners of computers either are ignorant of programming or are novices in the practice. But imagine the delight of the novice when, after writing a first program:

```
10 REM THIS IS AN ADDING MACHINE
20 LET A = 2
30 LET B = 3
40 LET Y = A + B
50 PRINT Y
```

. . . the answer comes out 5 and a new programmer is born!

This example is facetious. Perhaps our novice programmer is writing a paper on Pope Pius II, and eventually lights onto a program that determines the date of Easter in any year from 1415 to 2030. Imagine the delight to find that this humanist pope must have celebrated Easter Mass on 19 April in 1460, as calculated by the program. Now the novice programmer is almost an amateur.

If at first the computer was a fascination for the very few, it has created a romance that is now a fiber of both industry and academia. No major corporation with even the smallest industrial base can function without a staff of programmers. Computer courses continue to proliferate in colleges and universities across the country. Programming is now even an integral part of high school curricula. In sum, millions of people know how to program to some degree.

A generation of amateur programmers is afoot across the land. And that's all right. Many find programming useful as an addendum to a career in another field, perhaps in biology or management. Often they are good programmers who are not paid primarily for their programming skills. In-deed, they may be highly skilled in certain aspects of programming, and even consider themselves experts.

Those whom we call "professionals" are computer scientists, engineers,

---

Egoless Programming

To the best of my knowledge, this term was introduced in Jerry Weinberg's *The Psychology of Computer Programming*. It generally implies:

- Frequent exposure of work;
- A view of drafts, outlines, and sketches as part of the job;
- Acceptance of peer review;
- Seeking out criticism in an open and neutral manner;
- Daily activity.

Chief Programmer Teams

This concept relates to a method of organizing a group of programmers so that:

- The group acts as a unit.
- There is a highly skilled team leader.
- A back-up person supports the chief.
- Other programmers act in various support or design roles.

---

system developers, university teachers, or application specialists. They are paid for their computer expertise, which is their specialty. But something has happened. In my view, there are simply too many amateurs today in the professional ranks. Said another way, many so-called professionals are locked into a purely quantitative practice of programming. The purpose of this essay is to define "professionals" as those who have a grasp of the quantitative requirements of their duties along with an understanding of the qualitative demands that are necessary to this high calling.

Let us examine these two entities, the amateur and the professional, in their own idealized worlds.

The Amateur

The amateur programmer usually:

1. Writes programs only for a limited number of users:
   a. often only for the author,
   b. otherwise for a small number of colleagues.

2. Writes programs that:
   a. crash under varied and bizarre inputs;
   b. result in unusual but acceptable outputs.
3. Writes programs that only the author needs to be able to read.
4. Writes programs that need not be fully tested.
5. Writes programs that require little documentation.
6. Writes programs without regard to user requirements.
7. Writes programs without regard to a software lifecycle.
8. Writes programs without regard to integration with other, larger, or future systems.

This little taxonomy is not critical, only descriptive of the amateur programmer. The amateur programmer may be a hobbyist who writes programs to play games or draw pictures, a scientist who writes programs to analyze data, or a university student who writes a program to fulfill a course or thesis requirement. In each case, the programs are written without regard to anyone else having to understand, debug, or maintain them.

A number of issues are unimportant when programs are written for individual use. It doesn't matter if input formats are unwieldy or inconvenient or if the program doesn't work well or all of the time—as long as it works most of the time. These shortcomings are acceptable. What may seem to be bizarre and unusual inputs do not concern the amateur programmer. In writing a program for solving the roots of an equation, for instance, it matters little that someone might enter inputs consisting of carriage returns, people's names, or strange control codes. The amateur knows what the program is supposed to do, and these unreasonable inputs seem too unreasonable to worry about.

Likewise, the output for the amateur need not be satisfying or pleasing as to format, style, or screen layout. More often than not, the program is used only occasionally, and only the programmer needs to understand the output. For example, consider a program designed to compute areas. If measurements are given only to an accuracy of three decimal places, the program might be written using real arithmetic and the output displayed to ten decimal places. To another user of the program, this might be annoying—but it does not bother the author, who simply disregards the last seven decimals and presses forward.

For the amateur, the program itself need not be particularly readable. Matters like choosing appropriate names, organizing the program into simple logical units, or giving the program a well-spaced appearance are not of vital concern. Most programmers can read their own programs and fix or debug them when necessary. It's the other person's programs that are incomprehensible.

The amateur seldom has to test a program thoroughly. For the university student, too often the only requirement is to meet stated output criteria in order to pass a course. The fact that most of the control paths have never been exercised is not of much concern in either submitting or planning the program.

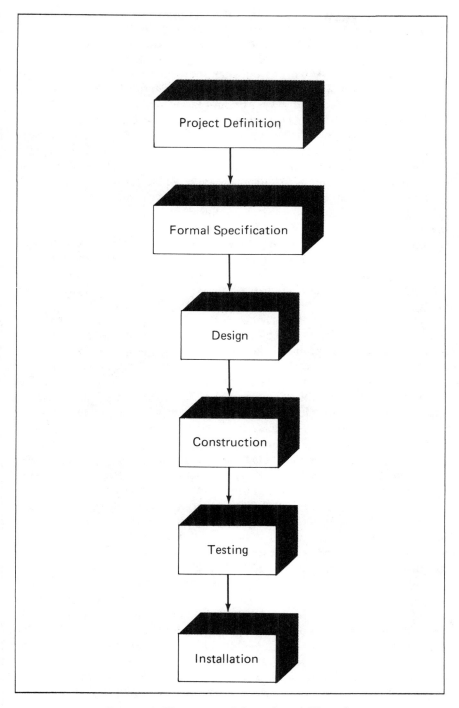

FIGURE 1. The stages of the software lifecycle.

Only a few decades ago, almost all programming was done using the direct machine codes of the hardware. Placed in the form of a program, these codes were extremely difficult to understand, so getting programs to work was a fairly sophisticated task in itself. Sometimes it was almost a miracle when they did work. And when they did, there was a great sense of accomplishment in achieving this simple objective. As a result, the early phase of programming was, by and large, reserved to the elite.

Programming is now widespread in all disciplines and business activities. The esoteric mysteries that were understood by a very few have disappeared as programming, in one form or another, has become more critical in our daily activities. Suppose that a corporation develops a piece of software to handle a payroll. This program must be written in such a way as to have a long lifespan; eventually hundreds of people will be involved in simply keeping the program up-to-date with current payroll requirements.

This is a different game from that played by an amateur who hardly sees what the implications of a program are, or how it affects anyone else. If the program "does the job," it's all right. If there is one habit that an amateur develops, it is a kind of tunnel vision for the end product: by God, it works! And if it works, that's it.

The amateur is not particularly concerned about documenting a program. If the program performs reasonably and the output is fairly consistent, no documentation is required, because the program works. Who cares? No one else has to learn the program, no one else has to maintain it.

And why would an amateur care about the lifecycle of software? The program belongs to the programmer alone. Any ideas about the functional specifications are not relevant. User requirements are not a consideration when writing a program because the programmer is the only user. The requirement is met when the program works, even if that program is fairly complicated. Whatever particular (and personal) needs are required or suggested along the way, the amateur programmer can change the behavior of the program to meet them. Features can be added or subtracted at any time; no one else will be affected. If it works out, it's all right.

Any commercially necessary program, such as the payroll program mentioned above, has another dimension that need not concern the amateur: estimating the resources needed to do the job and estimating the length of time the programming task will take. Of course, the professor meeting a research deadline at the university has some concern for a time schedule. However, the general software lifecycle (see Figure 1), which includes planning, specification, design, construction, testing, and actual user operation of the program, is hardly relevant.

Finally, there is the matter of integrating a program into the software of a larger system. Reasonably, the amateur never considers this in the program design. Creating a generalized sorting package for use inside an operating system or writing a general-purpose formatting program are tasks

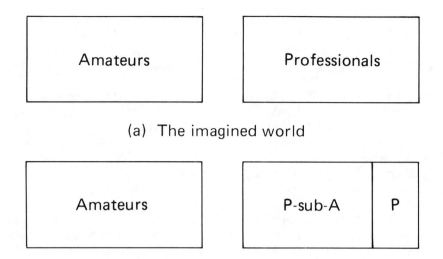

(a) The imagined world

(b) The likely reality

FIGURE 2. The programmer population.

beyond the desire of the amateur programmer. Such programs must interface with other programs and, in a general sort of way, with the conventions and protocols of the supporting environment. These are the type of considerations that describe the requirements for any kind of software that is needed; one can never ignore the kind of host for which a program is to be written.

If all this describes the idealized world of an amateur programmer, it is simply a world where the programmer is a lone ranger. What of the professional?

The Professional

I suggested earlier that there are many professionals who are amateurs in disguise. Paralleling our description of the amateur, additional shadings might be interjected into the spectrum so that we have:

ignorant;
novice;
aficionado;
amateur; .
amateur who claims to be a professional;
professional who is really an amateur;
professional;
master.

The italicized descriptions are interchangeable (choose the one that you prefer). If "P" is a professional, we could call this new ranking "P-sub-A"—something beneath a professional but above an amateur. Figure 2 depicts the situation as I have come to understand it. We think the programming world looks like Figure 2a, but my experience has led me to believe it looks like Figure 2b. Most "professionals" are amateurs in disguise. The true professional is rare.

Do not take this matter lightly: it is the substance of my arguments. Figure 3 will show you why. In comparing truly professional attitudes with those of the common counterfeit, you can see that we are defining our goal: the description of the professional.

Professionals write "real programs." What are "real programs?" They could be pieces of software that are commercially available: a program written for a microcomputer in a car or an orbiting satellite or a mobile telephone unit. These are the programs that are used to make monthly billings or to schedule courses at a university. The common characteristic of such programs is that other people make use of the software, directly or indirectly. Many, many people are affected by the programmer.

When other people are involved as users, new requirements and problems immediately come into play. Most users of software do not understand the inner workings. They become confused by its operation, and are apt to type all sorts of inputs into the program. In a word-processing program, if a user is unsure of how to get out of the text-editing mode, for instance, all kinds of consequences can occur. The user can type control codes, carriage returns, file names, and words like "help" or "quit." Even something apparently clear—like responding to a computer-prompted question—can lead to surprises. The professional takes account of these spurious cases in writing a program.

Many users demand nearly perfect implementations, and are generally impatient with faulty software. The first-time user of a program—especially one who was expecting a Christmas-night reward with the new "toy"— may be not only impatient but discouraged: the promises of the program were empty. This is the professional programmer's concern at the inception of the program. The technical requirements, the team composition and attitude toward egoless work [see panel on page 37], the tools, and the schedule all bear heavily on the ultimate reliability of the program.

In some software projects, outside evaluators are called upon to make an independent assessment. This can be a general-purpose walkthrough or, at a later stage, an exercise generally called "beta-testing." The professional welcomes these. A good beta-test is rigorous and thorough. Often the process is automated, in that predefined sets of data are fed to the software. Boundary conditions, spurious inputs, and exceptional cases are all tried.

An issue that the amateur almost never considers, but that is vital to the professional, is the matter of documentation. Documentation is the means by which other people can specify what the software is to accom-

Observable Attitudes

The "P-sub-A" programmer:

1. Perpetuates the mythical user (assumes the user is just like the programmer).

2. Lives in the "systems mentality" where dealing with anomalies is a way of life.

3. Considers work reading (that is, offering one's own work for open criticism) as a nuisance.

4. Keeps trashing out the bugs.

5. Deals with documentation later.

6. Is always "programming"—always developing some new feature on the terminal.

7. Doesn't see the software lifecycle slowly fall apart.

8. Gets on with the job.

Figure 3

The professional programmer:

1. Writes real programs for a large class of users (does *not* assume user knowledge).

2. Worries about "unusual" cases.

3. Writes programs that *anyone* can read.

4. Releases programs with *no* known errors or "strange" features.

5. Writes beautiful documentation *first.*

6. Negotiates and develops user requirements and functional specifications in great detail.

7. Has well-defined phases with hard benchmarks.

8. Writes programs with concern for future and larger systems.

plish: a job description, as it were. It is a means of describing one's work to others. The more important the software, the more important the documentation.

The need for documentation abounds during the lifetime of a software project. There are preliminary documents describing the intent of the system, project planning, sketches of the technical requirements, detailed requirements on the user interface behavior, user manuals, test-data specifications, training guides, and maintenance information. On most projects, these documents form the basis of the entire lifecycle of development. They are not superfluous. Often they are the cornerstones for defining and measuring progress. For the amateur, a few scruffy pages may seem adequate. For the professional, documentation may consume half of one's working hours.

It is a fallacy to think of documentation as neutral to software behavior. It is not (or at least should not be) an after-the-fact process. Documentation should precede implementation. The designers should spell out the general requirements of the software before any implementation is started. Written commitments may be needed for a given feature or a given style of behavior. Protocols for the user interface may need to be established. Performance requirements on the speed or use of resources may have to be spelled out. In some cases—the better ones—the entire input and output behavior for the software is defined before a line of final software is started. In this way, the documentation serves as a blueprint for the program, which must follow its dictates.

Professional software must often be integrated with other components of a software or hardware system. A program that handles the management of files in an operating system, for example, must be integrated with the text-editing facilities. This means that the software does not stand alone. In some cases, these concerns can be paramount. Things like protocol for input and output may dictate severe constraints on any supporting software. Often the programmer has no latitude in such matters, but must go to great detail to guarantee that the behavior of software is accurate.

Beyond these more-or-less technical requirements, there is another issue that *dramatically* distinguishes the professional from the amateur. A professional does not work in isolation. Most professional software projects are simply too big and too extensive for a single person to conceive, write, and maintain.

Projects of the professional dimension have given rise to a pattern of developing software with a team of participants. Like a professional football team, the professional programming team [see panel on page 37] is a collection of many people who combine many different skills working toward a single goal—the completed software project. Working with others involves many social and organizational aspects. In many cases, a piece of software may have to be read hundreds of times by many different people before it is publicly released. This puts a responsibility on the author of the program unit. Every minute wasted trying to understand what a particular construct means, every hour wasted wondering how a particular module works, and every day or week wasted when an error is discovered and corrected can result in setbacks for the entire project.

The viability of a general programming effort is hampered by individual idiosyncrasies. The ideas that one hides at first because of their supposed impotence might be the very ones that other team members need to solve a testy problem. Others may make bold talk of their own excellence, or may think that some completed sub-project is good when it is not. I have observed that such attitudes in software projects are the rule, not the exception. It is the role of the professional to set exceptionally high standards so that not only does the individual team member understand that all ideas are important, but no one single team programmer can consider his or her contribution immune from fault or criticism.

Professional software is often around for a long time, typically five to ten years. Compared to buying an automobile, the maintenance issue is far more pervasive. There used to be an adage that if you got a "lemon" from Detroit, it was probably a "Monday-morning" car, or was built just before new tooling was put on line. Different automobiles may have different maintenance problems, but the software maintenance problem grows over time.

For software, "maintenance" is really the wrong word. First of all, programs do not wear out. Instead, mistakes have to be fixed and changed, and new versions of programs are the norm. If the catalytic converter of an automobile malfunctions, it can be replaced, and the car will perform for its expected lifetime. But when software goes awry, or updates are needed, the authors may have forgotten what was really in the program, or they may have moved on to other projects. It may be absurd to think that one can find a good mechanic for a 1933 Essex, but one should expect that bugs or updates in a 1983 payroll program can be handled by any good software engineer. Actually, one should expect that there will be no bugs at all in the software.

The problem of software produced by our "P-sub-A" programmer is that maintenance is not a priority in design. Planning for maintenance was largely a token-homage issue. When things are not quite right, the user is often stuck with a lemon but has no warranty to exercise. On the one hand, most "P-sub-A" programmers *think* their software is maintainable; on the other, most of them complain about the "other person's" software they are assigned to maintain. Quite simply, maintainable software is seldom written.

The evidence of this difference can be seen in the fact that customers and users who buy software find a new version of it coming out every year or so. It's the software version of a Detroit recall of automobiles. "We found out something didn't work the first time—we hope you like it better the second time around." Why should a user want a new release of an old program? Why wasn't the software right in the first place? What does one do with the old manuals? These should be the responses of the user in greeting a new release.

Let us add a final comparative of our "P-sub-A" and the professional: *"P-sub-A" writes software for the computer. "P" writes software for the human reader.* For the "P-sub-A" programmer, the human reader is an aside. For the true professional, the computer is really just a necessary prerequisite; the human reader is paramount.

The worlds of the amateur and the professional are strikingly different. So, too, are the worlds of the assumed professional *(P-sub-A)* and the true professional. These differences are observable. Ultimately the differences are manifest in the *quality* of their work.

Acknowledgments

I am grateful to Allen Macro for providing me with the challenging opportunity to teach some of the senior software engineering courses at Philips Electronics; and to John Tauer, a man of many talents, who helped me understand the issues discussed here and provided splendid editorial assistance.

LETTER

On Software Development

Some comments are brought to mind by reading "Programmers: The Amateur vs. the Professional" (Summer 1985) by Henry Ledgard.

His Figure 1 does show the current conventional approach to developing software. There is, however, an alternative when one is able to use a more productive language such as APL. On the facing page, Figure 1 is modified in two respects which respond to the following three conditions:

1. The users may not know the precise definitions and specifications for their project.

2. The users may have thought they knew their precise definitions and specifications, but get better ideas as they work with the new input and output provided to them.

3. The definitions and specifications may actually change from outside forces after the project starts.

These are the two modifications of Figure 1:

1. At the Project Definition and Formal Specification stages there may be another step of Prototyping where one can quickly give the users an idea of what input screens and output reports will look like, correct as to format but not complete as to figures and calculations.

2. There can be a feedback loop from Testing and after Installation back to Design and Formal Specification based on any of the three conditions listed above. This starts with the users and comes to the programmers.

This approach then modifies the judgment that "in some cases—the better ones—the entire input and output behavior for the software is defined before a line of final software is started."

It also turns out that many professional software projects are not too big and extensive for a single person or a very few people to conceive, write, and maintain.

George Y. Cherlin
Philadelphia
Pennsylvania

Reprinted from ABACUS, Volume 3, Number 2, Winter 1986.

Author's Response

I agree with Mr. Cherlin. The idea of a prototype might be the subject of another essay.

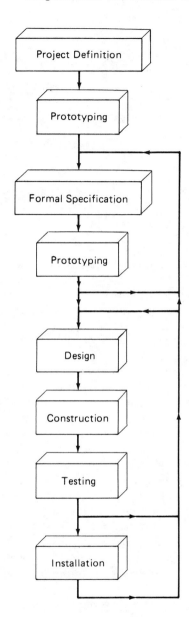

FIGURE 1. (modified). The stages of the software lifecycle (with additions by George Cherlin). Added feedback loop based on detection of user ignorance, better ideas, or changed conditions.

Japanese Word Processing: Interfacing with the Inscrutable

Word processing of ideographic languages will overcome their technology-induced disadvantages.

NEIL K. FRIEDMAN

For the past century, Western languages written with alphabets have had a distinct advantage over Oriental languages written with ideographs (the Chinese characters used in Chinese, Japanese, or Korean). Alphabetic languages could be written on typewriters—simple machines any writer could own and even carry around—and could also be transmitted by telex, then printed out at the receiving end by something like a typewriter.

Before this mechanical technology existed, when everything had to be written by hand, the merits of Western versus Oriental languages could have been debated inconclusively. Westerners could argue that Chinese characters were too difficult to master, while East Asians could counter that each character carried greater meaning at a glance. But the advent of the typewriter and telex seemed to tip the balance toward alphabetic languages as the rational means of communication in the modern world.

What happens, though, when we enter the computer age, and writing and transmitting equipment becomes fully capable of handling Chinese characters? Do Oriental languages lose their disadvantage as a means of modern communication over short and long distances? Considering how far the technology has come already and how fast it is developing, we can assume that by the twenty-first century a microcomputer with Chinese or Japanese software capable of displaying and printing characters will not be significantly more expensive than one designed for English word processing.

Similarly, we will have at our disposal high-resolution facsimile trans-

NEIL K. FRIEDMAN is Information Manager in the Corporate Planning department of Mitsui & Co. USA, Inc. He joined Mitsui in 1976 upon completing his Ph.D. in political science at Stanford University, with a specialty in contemporary Japanese politics. Several years of studying and working in Japan have made him aware of the difficulties of the language.
Reprinted from ABACUS, Volume 3, Number 2, Winter 1986.

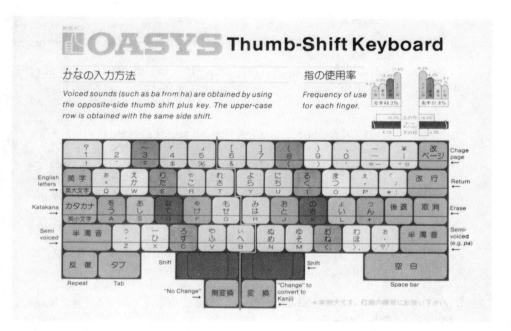

mission, invented originally to carry pictures and charts across distances, but just as able to carry complex Chinese characters. Meanwhile our daisywheel printers and other noisy devices that work by hitting alphabetic shapes against a ribbon and paper will be made obsolete by "letter-quality" printers that work by ink jet, laser, or other fast, quiet methods, and can integrate graphics with text.

Thus, within our lifetimes, technology will remove those advantages of alphabetic languages that technology created. For readers, text in any form of language will be available on affordable equipment. For writers, however, the problem of how to input the message conveniently will still remain. In this context, let us examine the nature of word processing in Oriental languages, taking Japanese as the primary example, with some comparisons to Chinese and Korean. It is for Japanese that the technology of ideographic word processing has been primarily developed and first put into widespread use.

The Japanese Written Language

Written Japanese is peculiar because of the way it developed historically. While the people of the Japanese islands were still illiterate, the Chinese had developed a highly sophisticated writing system and a civilization based on respect for the written word. The Japanese were exposed to writing only in the Chinese form, and so for ancient Japanese, to be literate meant to be literate in Chinese. At first it was not possible to write Japanese at all, and to read, you had to know Chinese. This was comparable to the situation that prevailed for centuries in Europe, where literacy meant literacy in Latin, not in one's native dialect.

By the ninth century A.D., the Japanese had begun to write Chinese and pronounce it in Japanese—awkward because sentence structure in the two languages is completely different. A Chinese sentence could not be read straight through from beginning to end; the Japanese reader had to skip ahead and back with the aid of tiny marginal symbols. Even when the Chinese characters were rearranged in a more Japanese order, there was a big gap between the resultant text and spoken Japanese, because the complexities of Japanese grammar could not be incorporated. Japanese inflects word endings to indicate tense, mood, voice, and degree of politeness. Thus the verb *taberu*, "to eat," becomes *tabemasu* in the next higher level of formality; in fact, the *-masu* ending can be attached to any verb stem. The past tense is *tabeta*, or more politely, *tabemashita*.

Edwin O. Reischauer, in his textbook *East Asia: The Great Tradition* (written with John K. Fairbank), concludes that "it was a major historical tragedy for both the Japanese and the Koreans that, because they were so far removed from the other centers of early writing, they did not learn about phonetic systems of transcription until after the use of Chinese characters had become firmly established." He further judges that "Japanese could not be adequately written with Chinese characters."

Eventually, the Japanese developed their own *phonetic* alphabets, which they used alongside Chinese characters to make sentences with the advantages of both worlds: combining the profundity of the Chinese ideographs and the manipulation of words through Japanese grammatical transformations. In this system, still in use today, a typical "word" is often a mixture of a Chinese ideograph—pronounced the Japanese way and called *Kanji*—and a few letters of the *Hiragana* alphabet.

The Japanese do not use as many characters as the Chinese use; about two thousand Kanji will do for newspapers and basic literacy, whereas a Chinese person with a comparable level of education might use twice as many in the same circumstances. But with their gift for overdoing things, the Japanese produced two different alphabets, each having fifty characters with exactly the same pronunciations: *ka, ki, ku, ke, ko*, etc. (see figure, *Japanese Alphabets*).

Today one alphabet, *Katakana*, is used almost entirely for transliterating foreign words and names into Japanese (although it can also be employed for emphasis, something like using italics in English), while the other, *Hiragana*, is used for adding the grammatical transformations needed to make Chinese characters into readable Japanese sentences. The absorption of foreign (especially English) words rendered phonetically, along with the possibility of writing whole words in an alphabet rather than with Kanji, means that Japanese does not need as many characters as Chinese. (All of this is summarized in the figure, *Japanese Writing Systems* on page 52.)

Japanese Alphabets

THE HIRAGANA A-I-U-E-O ARRANGEMENT

あ *a*	か *ka*	さ *sa*	た *ta*	な *na*	は *ha*	ま *ma*	や *ya* ¹	ら *ra*	わ *wa* ²	
い *i*	き *ki*	し *shi*	ち *chi*	に *ni*	ひ *hi*	み *mi*	い *(y)i*	り *ri*	ゐ *(w)i* ¹	
う *u*	く *ku*	す *su*	つ *tsu*	ぬ *nu*	ふ *fu*	む *mu*	ゆ *yu* ¹	る *ru*	う *(w)u* ²	
え *e*	け *ke*	せ *se*	て *te*	ね *ne*	へ *he*	め *me*	え *(y)e*	れ *re*	ゑ *(w)e* ³	
お *o*	こ *ko*	そ *so*	と *to*	の *no*	ほ *ho*	も *mo*	よ *yo*	ろ *ro*	を *(w)o*	ん *n*

THE KATAKANA A-I-U-E-O ARRANGEMENT

ア *a*	カ *ka*	サ *sa*	タ *ta*	ナ *na*	ハ *ha*	マ *ma*	ヤ *ya* ¹	ラ *ra*	ワ *wa* ²	
イ *i*	キ *ki*	シ *shi*	チ *chi*	ニ *ni*	ヒ *hi*	ミ *mi*	イ *(y)i*	リ *ri*	ヰ *(w)i* ¹	
ウ *u*	ク *ku*	ス *su*	ツ *tsu*	ヌ *nu*	フ *fu*	ム *mu*	ユ *yu* ¹	ル *ru*	ウ *(w)u* ²	
エ *e*	ケ *ke*	セ *se*	テ *te*	ネ *ne*	ヘ *he*	メ *me*	エ *(y)e*	レ *re*	エ *(w)e* ³	
オ *o*	コ *ko*	ソ *so*	ト *to*	ノ *no*	ホ *ho*	モ *mo*	ヨ *yo*	ロ *ro*	ヲ *(w)o*	ン *n*

These two phonetic alphabets have 50 characters each, both expressing the same sets of sounds. Along with other tables and individual characters used in this article, the above charts are reprinted by permission from *The Modern Reader's Japanese-English Character Dictionary* (Second Revised Edition) by Andrew N. Nelson; Tokyo, Japan, and Rutland, Vermont: Charles E. Tuttle Co., 1974.

From Keyboard to Kanji

How, then, does one "word-process" in Japanese? Do you need a keyboard with two thousand character keys plus fifty keys for each alphabet? Fortunately not. It is still not as easy as typing in English, with a mere twenty-six letters plus punctuation, but there is a way to do it with a keyboard no larger than an English one. You can enter words by their pronunciation.

Many Japanese word processors allow you to input with either the Japanese alphabet or the Roman alphabet. The latter is more convenient for people familiar with the touch system on an English keyboard; and many Japanese fit this category, having had to type in English while students in the West or while doing English correspondence for business. For an American trying to use a Japanese word processor, the *Romaji* (Roman letter) input is a godsend—no new keyboard to learn.

One minor obstacle is that there is not full agreement on how to Romanize Japanese. The Hepburn system (which the Japanese call *Hebon-shiki*) is supported by the Japanese government and taught officially, but there are alternatives to it. Thus the Hepburn phonetic series *ta, chi, tsu, te, to* can be rendered as *ta, ti, tu, te, to* in another convention. But never mind. You can get software that is user-friendly enough to accept input in either system or a mixture of the two: type *"c-h-i"* or *"t-i"* and you get the same result when you have the machine turn it into a Japanese alphabet or Kanji.

While the Roman-letter keyboard is convenient for those who already know how to type in English, Japanese people who plan to do much word

Japanese Writing Systems

The same Japanese word can often be rendered different ways. Pronunciation is not affected by the choice of writing system.

Romaji	TABERU	("to eat")
Katakana	タ ベ ル (ta) (be) (ru)	The letter *be* is one of the few that is the same in both alphabets
Hiragana	た べ る (ta) (be) (ru)	
Kanji	食 べ る (ta) (be) (ru)	The Hiragana letters *be* and *ru* are put after the Kanji to show the verb ending. Past tense would be 食 べ た, read *tabeta*.

The Japanese word for "a meal" is pronounced *shokuji* and written with two Kanji: 食事. The first character is the same one used in *taberu*, but in combination is read *shoku* instead of *ta*. The trouble with Japanese is that the same Kanji can have different readings depending on its context. What is worse for word processing, the same sound can apply to many different Kanji.

processing find it worthwhile to learn the Japanese alphabetic keyboard. Its main advantage is that a letter in Japanese can be entered with one keystroke (sometimes in combination with the shift key), whereas in *Romaji* two strokes are needed for most letters. Manufacturers have designed Japanese alphabet keyboards of various types, trying to put the most-used letters in the most convenient places (see *OASYS Thumb-Shift Keyboard* on page 49). In fact, some Japanese makers have even rearranged the Roman letters on their keyboards in patterns that make more apparent sense than the "QWERTY" system used in English; for example, they might put all the vowels together. In any case, the bottom line in marketing is that users prefer whatever keyboard they are used to.

Having entered the pronunciation of the desired word, you face the real inconvenience of Japanese word processing. Because Japanese has relatively few basic sounds (essentially the fifty represented in either Japanese alphabet), there are many, many homophones. If English spelling were perfectly phonetic and we typed the pronunciation *"new,"* it could also stand for *knew, gnu,* or even *nu.* Another example of English homophones often cited is *peek, peak,* and *pique;* and there are a good many cases involving two words (*shoot* and *chute*). But imagine the problem if *most* words had homophones like this, and in many cases more than three! This barrier is what stands in the way of making Japanese completely alphabetic.

A Question of Simplification

From time to time there have been suggestions that the Japanese abandon Kanji and write their language phonetically, either with Roman letters or one of their own alphabets. The last time such a proposal was taken up seriously was during the American occupation. During that period many reforms of Japanese education and society were carried out, and simplification of the language must have seemed eminently reasonable to any of the occupation officers who tried to learn Japanese. But this suggestion met with extreme resistance and did not get off the ground. Without Kanji, Japanese loses a lot of its semantic content.

A much less drastic strategy was taken: streamlining some characters (see figure, *Postwar Simplification* on the next page), limiting the number of Kanji characters taught in public schools to a basic list of approximately two thousand, and restricting newspapers to these characters. Even today some Japanese, when asked about efforts to restrict the use of Kanji, will say that the American occupiers were "trying to make us stupid, so we could not be a threat to them in the future." To understand how they could misconstrue the well-intentioned efforts of American reformers to "help" them, you have to realize that to an Oriental with a traditional education, the level of learning can virtually be measured by the number of characters one knows. To take away half of one's Kanji would be equivalent, in English, to taking away half of one's vocabulary (even though the Japanese words whose characters had been removed could still be spoken and written alphabetically).

In Korean, which has a wider variety of spoken sounds than Japanese and an alphabet considered the most rational in the world, it is possible to write everything phonetically. North Korea has gone over to writing virtually everything in the alphabet, and South Korea has gone far in that direction, but there is a lingering attachment to Chinese characters. And, of course, students are still taught the characters to be able to read older writings and appreciate their cultural heritage.

In the People's Republic of China, many characters in basic use were simplified, often by adopting for printing the abbreviations that were common in handwriting. A character previously written with twenty strokes might be reduced to five strokes of the pen (in an extreme example), but the shape is still vaguely recognizable. (The Nationalist regime on Taiwan refuses to countenance any simplification of characters, seeing itself as the preserver of Chinese traditions that are being desecrated on the main-

---

Postwar Simplification

Since World War II, some Kanji characters have been simplified. Usually an effort was made to keep the *radical*, the key element of a character which has to do with the meaning.

New	Old	
伝	傳	*Legend* or *to report*. Note how the *person* radical イ on the left was preserved.
囯	國	In the character for *country*, the radical is the enclosing box.
売	賣	In the character for *selling*, the top element was kept intact.
桜	櫻	In *cherry blossom*, the tree radical 木 was kept.
浜	濱	For *beach*, the water radical 氵 was kept on the left. Regrettably, a part meaning *shell* 貝 was lost. The old form of *cherry blossom* above also had two little shells in it; the ancient Chinese noticed the resemblance of blossoms to delicate shells.

land; the Nationalists also stood up for Confucius when the sage was being maligned during the Cultural Revolution.)

However, among all the radical experiments in mainland Chinese education and society since 1949, a transformation of the written language to a phonetic basis has not been seriously contemplated. There are good reasons to keep the characters. First, pronunciation differs greatly among different regions of China; all the people would have to be forced to speak Mandarin for a phonetic system to cover the whole country. Second, the four tones of Mandarin Chinese pronunciation (flat, rising, falling then rising, and falling) would have to be indicated in a phonetic system to avoid confusion; this can be done, but it complicates any proposed alphabet or spelling system. Third, even with these tones indicated, there would still be several homophones for most words. All in all, the Chinese are much better off keeping their characters, which have worked for thousands of years.

The Japanese simplification of Kanji did not go as far as that of the mainland Chinese. For one thing, the Japanese only turned their attention

Homophones

All these Kanji are pronounced *shin*:

晋申伸侵信真参呻娠　宸寝審心慎振搢斟新　晨森榛槙沁沈津浸清　深潯滲疹瞋矧神秦箴　簪糝紳絹臣芯蓁薪襯　親診請誠賑身鯵辛辰　唇脣蜃進針鍼震駸

to those characters in the basic list of under 2,000. Characters outside that list, but still printed in literary books, were left alone or left to printers to simplify along similar lines. More importantly, the degree of simplification was not as drastic as in China; where the Chinese may have reduced a twenty-stroke character to five strokes, the Japanese would be satisfied with something closer to the original—say ten strokes. More importance was placed on keeping the elements that make up a character and hint at its meaning or pronunciation.

Even the Japanese degree of simplification does make the characters easier to portray on a video display or to print in a dot matrix. But again, as the technology gets better, even the most complex character can be handled, so character simplification is not essential to word processing. The Chinese on Taiwan will be able to go electronic without making any concessions to simplified characters, if they use enough dots.

Choosing the Right Character

Now let us sit back down at our Japanese word processor. Having input the pronunciation of the character on the keyboard in either Japanese or Roman alphabet, we now punch the Kanji key (a sort of function key) to get the character on the screen. As mentioned, however, there are a limited number of sounds in Japanese, and often one pronunciation has to cover a number of characters. (To make matters worse, the same character can have different pronunciations in different contexts.) For example, over fifty Kanji in common use have the pronunciation *"shin"* (see figure, *Homophones* on the previous page). The word processor could show you all fifty on the screen, and you could move the cursor to the proper one or type a number from 1 to 50 to make your choice, but this would be quite an awkward process.

The software therefore takes advantage of the fact that most words are made up of more than one syllable, and most commonly of two characters. So let us type in the two syllables *"shinkei"* and then ask the machine for the word written in Kanji. In this case there is only one Japanese word in common use, and accordingly the characters for the word *nerve* appear on the screen. Satisfied with this, we hit another function key to place it in our sentence.

Many multisyllabic words do have homophones, however, and if we should type in *"shinkoo"* (the double *o* being used to indicate a long *o* in pronunciation) and ask for the Kanji rendition, we must be aware of the alternatives: *pickled vegetables, invasion, promotion, friendship, faith, advance, newly-rising,* and *late at night.* All these are written with different Kanji.

Japanese word-processing software usually deals with this problem in one of two ways. It can show you a numbered list of the possible choices on the screen, allowing you to hit the number for the desired one. Or it can first give you the most commonly used one and, if you do not want that, let you hit a key to get the second-most-common, then the third-most common, and so on, until you come to the right one to input into your sentence. In some versions of the latter software, an added convenience is that once you make a certain choice, the next time you input the same pronunciation, your choice will be put at the top of the list and presented first (the "last-in, first-out" system), under the reasonable assumption that you will be on the same topic and using the same vocabulary repeatedly.

The next big breakthrough happening in Japanese word processors is one that allows you to type phonetically a whole phrase or sentence, then uses the combination of words to determine which vocabulary you are using, and automatically puts what you have written into the normal combination of Kanji and alphabet. This is a major step toward the level of technology that would allow a translation machine. In fact, it amounts to a machine to translate from spoken Japanese to written Japanese, in effect making some of the same inferences that the human mind makes when listening to someone speak. Such a machine, if perfected, could be enhanced with a device to recognize voice input—one of the goals of current "artificial intelligence" programs.

Such advanced software is under development in Japan, but difficult obstacles have to be surmounted before it becomes reliable. For one thing, it will require more computer power than ordinary Japanese word processors. One problem is that in Japanese sentences the words are not separated by spaces; in fact, it is debatable exactly where a "word" begins and ends in Japanese. Therefore, the machine has to solve a more difficult parsing problem than in English: it must determine where to break the sentence before it classifies its component parts, and it must determine what units to compare to its dictionary. Then the machine has to choose among the possible homophones. Using an analogy to English, imagine the difficulty of programming a computer to correct our spelling automatically if we typed *peek* when we meant *peak*.

Even when such sophisticated software is perfected, it will not completely satisfy conscientious Japanese writers, particularly literary people. That is because the Japanese author retains a certain discretion about which words to render in Kanji and which in the two alphabets. And when using Kanji, there is sometimes a choice among alternative characters with different nuances of meaning but the same pronunciation. For example, the verb *omou,* "to think," can be rendered with several different Kanji depending on the type of thinking suggested. So Japan's literary class might not want word processors that were too "intelligent." But the secretary or student would welcome all the help the software could give.

While the approximately two thousand Kanji designated by the Ministry of Education for basic and secondary education are enough for minimal literacy, in Japanese literature there is no such limit to the number of

Kanji that can be used. Nelson's Japanese/English character dictionary, the standard one used by foreign students of the Japanese language, gives over 5,000 Kanji and is adequate for looking up almost everything in contemporary Japanese. But there are Japanese dictionaries with thousands more Kanji than that.

Therefore, a good Japanese word processor has to have more than the minimum two thousand Kanji built in. It might have four thousand or five thousand. Besides that, there is a backup system to custom-make further characters to specification. This is necessary, for example, because some Japanese personal and place names use rare Kanji. The most versatile word-processing software lets you design new Kanji from scratch with a dot matrix blown up on the screen; you literally place every dot where you want it, then ask the machine to record the character you have just designed for future use.

The steps of Japanese word processing thus may be summarized as follows. First, input the pronunciation of the word in either Japanese alphabet or Roman alphabet. Second, hit the choice for rendition, specifying one of the two Japanese alphabets or Kanji (or even Roman-letter type, which may be inserted in a Japanese sentence to show the spelling of a

Steps in Kanji Input

Because many characters can have the same pronunciation, it is more practical to input two-Kanji words at once.

Step	Keyboard	Screen
1.	Type SHINKEI.	し ん け い appears boldface (in Hiragana).
2.	Press *Kanji* conversion key.	神 経 replaces its alphabetic equivalent.
3.	Press *Kanji* key again if the word that appeared was the wrong homophone.	Not necessary in this case, since no other common word is pronounced *shinkei*.
4.	Press the function key to accept the choice.	神 経 enters into the next place in the sentence you are writing, and boldface fades to ordinary text.

foreign word). Third, if you are putting it in Kanji, pick the correct Kanji from the available choices (or, in extreme cases, create a new character). Finally, hit one more function key to place the word next in line in your sentence. (See the figure, *Steps in Kanji Input.*)

Chinese and Japanese

Chinese word processing is evolving similar procedures, except that the second step may be skipped because the language is written entirely with ideographs (except where Western words are inserted in their original alphabetical spelling, as is done often in scientific and educational texts). As in Japanese, different schemes for the Romanization of Chinese exist, but the Beijing government has settled on Pinyin as the one to teach nationwide.

Yet Chinese has more of a problem than Japanese with phonetic input in two respects. First, it is a tonal language, so the software either has to provide for indication of the four tones, or has to offer more choices of characters when the tones are not indicated (to distinguish among words that sound alike except for tonal inflection). However, where the conversion from phonetics to ideographs usually takes place at the level of two-character words or longer units, it is feasible without input of tones. At this level, Chinese (omitting tones) and Japanese face approximately the same frequency of occurrence of homophones.

The second problem is that regional differences in pronunciation are much greater in China than in Japan—to the point of mutual noncomprehension. Gradually, though, public education and mass media are making the Chinese people universally able to understand the standard Mandarin form of the spoken language. Of course, software can be designed for speakers of Cantonese and other dialects if necessary.

Because of these features of Chinese, another major approach in Chinese word processing is to create characters from their component parts. (The key elements—usually forming the left side or bottom of a character and helping to determine the meaning—are called ''radicals,'' by analogy with the radicals making up molecules in chemistry; see chart on the next two pages). The number of elements that are the building blocks of Chinese characters is finite: a couple of hundred. Each one can be coded with a letter or two on an English keyboard. A Chinese typist will quickly learn the codes for the common ones, and can refer to a chart for the rare ones.

The simplest characters are made of just one radical; or, more properly speaking, they are the sources of the radicals. Most of the characters are composed of two elements, left and right or upper and lower. The most complex characters may have three or four elements as their component parts. For example, most names of trees in Chinese are single characters with the tree radical on the left and another element on the right. To input

THE 214 HISTORICAL RADICALS			**1**	一 1	一 (1)	｜ 2	｜ (2)	、 3	ノ 4	′ (4)	一 (4)
乙 5	L (5)	L (5)	｣ 6	**2**	二 7	二 (7)	亠 8	亠 (8)			
人 9	亻 (9)	𠆢 (9)	儿 10	入 11	𠓥 (11)	八 12	丷 (12)	丷 (12)	冂 13	冖 (13)	刂 (13)	刀 (13)
冖 14	冫 15	几 16	几 (16)	凵 17	刀 18	刂 (18)	力 19	勹 20	匕 21	匕 (21)	匚 22	匚 (22)
匸 23	十 24	忄 (24)	艹 (24)	卜 25	卜 (25)	⺊ (25)	卩 26	卩 (26)	厂 27	厶 28	又 29	又 (29)
辶 [162]	阝 [163]	阝 [170]	**3**	口 30	囗 31	土 32	士 (32)	⺍ (32)	士 (32)	夂 33	夂 (34)	夊 (34)
攵 35	夕 36	大 37	大 (37)	女 38	子 39	宀 40	寸 41	小 42	⺌ (42)	尢 43	尸 44	屮 45
屯 (45)	⺍ (45)	山 46	川 47	巛 (47)	工 48	工 (48)	己 49	已 (49)	巳 (49)	巾 50	干 51	幺 52
广 53	廴 54	廾 55	廿 (55)	弋 56	弓 57	ヨ 58	彐 (58)	彑 (58)	彑 (58)	彡 59	彳 60	⺗ [61]
扌 [64]	氵 [85]	丬 [90]	犭 [94]	艹 [140]	辶 [162]	**4**	心 61	小 (61)	忄 [61]	戈 62	戈 (62)	戸 63
戶 (63)	手 64	手 (64)	扌 [64]	支 65	攴 (65)	攴 66	攵 (66)	文 67	斗 68	斤 69	方 70	无 71
无 (71)	旡 [71]	旡 [71]	日 72	曰 (72)	曰 73	月 74	木 75	欠 76	止 77	⺊ (77)	歹 78	歹 (78)
殳 79	毋 80	母 [80]	比 81	毛 82	毛 (82)	氏 83	气 84	水 85	氵 [85]	米 [85]	火 86	灬 (86)
爪 87	爪 (87)	爫 (87)	𤓰 (87)	父 88	爻 89	⽊ (89)	爿 90	丬 [90]	片 91	牙 92	牙 [92]	牛 93
牛 (93)	犬 94	犭 [94]	王 96	王 (96)	壬 (96)	正 [103]	礻 [113]	内 [114]	屮 [125]	月 [130]	月 [130]	艹 [140]
5	旡 [71]	旡 [71]	母 [80]	比 [81]	米 [85]	牙 [92]	玄 95	玉 96	王 [96]	壬 [96]	瓜 97
瓦 98	瓦 (98)	甘 99	生 100	用 101	田 102	⻊ 103	正 (103)	疒 104	癶 105	白 106	皮 107	皿 108

All Chinese characters are built from these 214 radicals. Software designers have tried to give each a short letter or number code, so that input could be done by putting the parts together. However, it turns out (for Japanese, and probably for Chinese as well) that input by pronunciation of the word or phrase is easier.

such a character, one can hit the letter code for *tree* (say, *T,* although the makers of Chinese word processors are not this kind to their English-speaking users), then another letter key or two for the right-hand element, then a function key to put them together. In this way any Chinese character can be created with from two to five or six strokes on the keyboard.

Sophisticated Japanese word processors may offer this Chinese-style option as an accessory to create unusual characters. Thus, the tasks in Chinese and Japanese word processing overlap to some extent, and the learning curve in developing software for one language benefits those writing software for the other. Japanese hardware and software companies

are aiming at the potentially vast Chinese market, and hope to be a step ahead of the American companies thanks to their familiarity with Chinese characters. At the same time, major American hardware and software designers have employed people fluent in Oriental languages to help open up the East Asian market, and the Japanese firms can by no means take their advantage for granted. At some point, Korean, Taiwanese, and mainland Chinese makers will also become competitive.

Consequences of Japanese Word Processing

Japanese word processing will never be as easy as English typing, due to the nature of the language. The limited number of sounds in spoken Japanese relative to the rich vocabulary available from the three major sources of modern Japanese—Chinese, Western languages, and traditional Japanese—means that there are inevitably many homophones.

If there is any development of the Japanese language influenced by technology in the coming decades, it should be in the direction of reducing the number of homophones by letting the least-used disappear from normal writing. At the same time, the number of different allowable readings (pronunciations) of each character will probably erode. It is less useful to limit the number of characters in normal use, as was tried half-heartedly and inconsistently after World War II.

In other words, what is "wrong" with Japanese is not the use of Chinese characters per se, or even the number of characters employed, but the loose fit between the written and the spoken language. This fault will be pointed up more and more by word-processing technology. Unfortunately, Japan's Ministry of Education is the kind of bureaucracy that is incapable of anticipating this sort of problem and guiding the educational system toward a solution. Not that any government can or should control a country's language (though within our own century, the Soviets modernized the old Russian orthography, and more recently, the Fraktur tradition has fallen into disuse among the Germans). But there is a need for the Japanese to review the limited, half-useless language reforms undertaken after 1945, and to realize that reform efforts could be redirected so that future generations using the new technology will not be unduly burdened by the language itself.

We see then that Japanese word processing is feasible, although it presents some difficulties for the writer. The greatest benefits are clearly for the reader. Until the advent of the word processor, Japanese offices were—and still are to a large extent—dependent on handwritten documents. The analogous situation in America would be an office with no typewriters, as we had until about a century ago. In that setting, you have two choices for a document: have it written by hand, or send it to the printer. You need a slew of secretaries to recopy executives' statements into legible form for distribution. Or you have to wait until a professional printer—who represents an occupational specialization—sets type and prints copies. Obviously only the documents deemed most important are going to be sent to the printer.

In a busy organization, the appearance of memos and documents is sacrificed to speed. Most Japanese middle managers today write many memos in their own hand. How easily these can be read depends on the handwriting. It also seems that the higher the executive, the more he (almost never *she*) has the right to scribble to subordinates. In the Japanese trading company where I work, I am sometimes asked to translate memos or notes into English for the other American staff. It is not surprising that often I cannot decipher the handwriting, since my experience with handwritten Japanese is limited. But what shocks me is that sometimes, when I show such memos to native speakers, they have to squint and scowl in trying to make out what is written. Clearly the equivalent of the type-

Japanese Word Processors

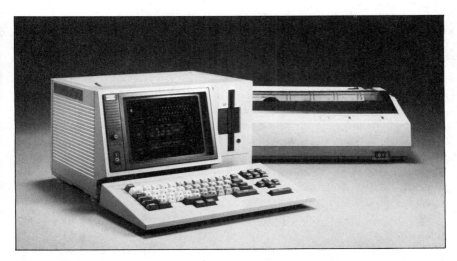

Top: The Fujitsu *OASYS lite* is a Japanese word processor with built-in thermal printer. It is roughly 13″ × 12½″ × 3″ and weighs less than 8 pounds, yet can store 2 pages of text, or up to 40 pages when augmented by an optional bubble memory; information can also be downloaded onto a standard audio tape. Bottom: Fujitsu's *MyOASYS* is a more elaborate wordprocessing system. Both of these products make use of the *OASYS Thumb-Shift Keyboard* designed by Yasunori Kanda (see page 49), which facilitates the conversion of Hiragana input to Kanji output.

writer—a Japanese word processor that every employee can use at his or her desk—is needed.

It will still be some years before the Japanese word processor gains the same acceptance as the English typewriter for office and home use. Slowness of acceptance is due to the difficulties on both the input and output sides. Even for an experienced operator, input in Japanese is more tedious than typing in English. In my company we find that even when middle-level Japanese managers are trained on the latest word processors, they resist using them except for the most important memos or letters (such as those intended to be seen by top executives), because of time pressures. In English, a decent typist can type faster than writing by hand, but this is not the case in Japanese.

On the output side, the fact that a dot matrix printer is needed for Japanese means that the appearance of documents is not as good as that of English documents done on an electric typewriter or letter-quality printer. Except for top-of-the-line equipment, Japanese printers are not yet "letter quality"; they yield the aesthetic equivalent of English printed by dot matrix (see facing figure, *Sample Japanese Word-Processor Output*). However, improvements in laser printers will result in lower-cost "letter-quality" Japanese output in due time.

In international transmission of Japanese messages, there are still major inconveniences. The telex is the most economical and most widely used means of transmission for multinational companies. The huge trading companies such as Mitsui & Co. and Mitsubishi Corporation have computerized, global telex networks using dedicated lines. Mitsui, for example, estimates that its telex system handles an average of eighty thousand messages a day, and can connect any two of its two hundred offices in the world within minutes. However, the limitation of the telex is its restriction to the Roman alphabet plus numbers and punctuation. Only in recent years has facsimile transmission (usually over long-distance telephone lines at a much higher cost than telex) gained a substantial share of business transmission.

When the Japanese international businessman sits down at his desk in the morning, he is faced with a pile of telexes. These are his first priority of the day. If he is working in America or Europe, the telexes are from Japan the same day, because the telex room has been working overnight to take in the messages sent during the Japanese working day. If he is working at headquarters in Tokyo, he gets the messages from the West dated the previous day. In either case, the telexes are written entirely in capital letters, either in English or in Japanese *Romaji*. Which of the two is more troublesome to read will depend on the businessman's facility in English; but neither can hold a candle to Japanese printed in Japanese for ease of comprehension.

The highest executives have the privilege of having Japanese secretaries transcribe in a neat hand the *Romaji* telexes that have been addressed to

Sample Japanese Word Processor Output

Japan Society

JAPAN SOCIETY, INC. 333 EAST 47TH STREET, NEW YORK, NY 10017 (212) 832-1155 TELEX: 234450 JSNY

１９８５年夏期英会話教室
(1985 Summer English Class)

ジャパン・ソサエティでは５月１４日（火曜日）から12週間にわたり英会話教室を開きます
講師は (Mrs.)Hazel R. Jarvisさん。英国生まれ，英米両国で教育を受けられ，
University of Sussexの英語学 及び 美術史を優等で卒業されたのち，約二年半 日本で
英会話の先生の経験を積まれました。生徒とのコミュニケーションを大切にしながら，正確で格調
高い本場の英語を教えることを心がけていられます。

クラス　Ａ（初心者 又は 基礎から復習したい方のクラス）

　　　　日常生活に必要な実用的な英会話を中心に，最も基本的な文法・慣用句を学び
ながら，まず聞きとること，喋ることの練習に力を入れます。

週　二　回：　　　火曜日・木曜日　　５月１４日 － ８月６日（7月4日休講）

時　　間：　　　午前１０時１５分－１１時４５分

クラス　Ｂ（基礎的な会話力のある方を対象）

　　　　正しい発音と理解力の練習，より豊富なボキャブラリー，慣用句を身につけ，
正確に自由に話せるようにするためのクラスです。詩や短かいストーリーなどを
作ったり，新聞記事を教材に使うこともあります。

週　二　回：　　　火曜日・木曜日　　５月１４日 － ８月６日（7月4日休講）

時　　間：　　　午後１時 － ２時３０分

（注）
１．　クラスは１０人前後。（先着順）
２．　申し込み締め切りは５月１０日。
３．　授業料：　ジャパン・ソサエティ会員　$220，　非会員　$270。
４．　会員費　$45（学生は$20）をお払いいただければ会員になることが出来ます
５．　法人会員の団体に所属する本人及び配偶者は会員として受付けます。

お問い合わせはLanguage Proguram 佐々　までどうぞ。

An announcement from the Japan Society of their English classes for Japanese
residents in the New York area, printed by a word processor on the Society's
letterhead. A few English words and names are mixed right into the Japanese
text. The title is printed in expanded-width Kanji.

them. Most middle-management staff, however, read their messages as they are printed right off the telex machine—in capital Roman letters. They often mutter the words to themselves quietly as if someone were reading the telex to them, mentally translating the phonetics into Kanji visualized in their heads. Sometimes they jot key Kanji in the margin for ease of reference.

Some Japanese homophones are particularly inconvenient: *konshuu* can mean either "this week" or "this autumn." Here the Japanese find it easiest just to substitute an English word in a Japanese sentence; after all, English is compulsory in Japanese schools, and every Japanese reader should know at least what "this week" means. Another inconvenience is when a Japanese name or other key word has to be transmitted, but it can be written with alternative Kanji having the same pronunciation. For example, the family name *Sakamoto* has at least half a dozen renderings in Kanji. To make sure it is transcribed correctly at the other end, companies have standard dictionaries with the characters all numbered. They could telex "Sakamoto (1124-2432)" to eliminate guesswork.

That is the state of technology up to now. With word processors and lower-cost facsimile transmission, the situation suddenly improves. Either the sending side prints out its message and sends it by facsimile, or the sending system reads the signals off the sender's word-processor terminal into a central computer, then routes the message, and the receiving computer decodes it and prints it out on a Kanji printer. It is not clear yet which of these alternatives will come to dominate long-distance transmission of Japanese. We might judge that the direct computer-link version will prove more effective than the print/facsimile version in the long run for quality of image and reliability. On the other hand, the facsimile allows you to send already-printed documents such as newspaper articles along with your message.

It is not too much to expect that within a reasonable time, Japanese word processing and communications hardware/software will be integrated so that the same terminals can be used for both purposes. The Japanese "office of the future" then will allow every employee to have a desktop machine combining typewriter and telex functions, except that this will operate with the full richness of the Japanese writing system, including its alphabets and ideographs. At that stage, it will be possible to say that the technology-induced disadvantage of Japanese has been overcome.

Future Evolution of the Language

Looking further into the future, we might ask what evolutionary consequences Japanese word processing could have. This does not refer to physical evolution of the human species—although through natural selection the Japanese might eventually evolve longer fingers to reach all the keys on computer terminals. More important is the evolution of language, the cornerstone of human social behavior.

Natural languages such as Japanese and English continually evolve, and the process is accelerated by technology such as mass media and word processing. Perhaps we have entered an era when the computer will be the dominant influence on linguistic development. We already see signs of it in expressions that achieved currency in the computer field but later became common in ordinary discourse, both in English and in Japanese: *input, feedback,* and so forth.

Besides the new popular terms and analogies from computerese to daily life, what will probably happen to natural languages such as Japanese is that they will gradually become more "logical" or "rational." If and when artificial intelligence gives us machines that use natural language for input and output, there will be a premium put on clear, concise, logical use of the natural language in education and training, so that people can interface smoothly with the machines.

The Japanese object when outsiders characterize their language as "less logical" than English; they argue that Japanese logic is just different—perhaps more subtle—than Western explicit rationality. Perhaps this is the case, but both Japanese and foreigners familiar with Japan would agree that the Japanese have a higher tolerance for ambiguity in their linguistic behavior. In Japan's homogeneous society there is more implicit understanding between people, and too much explicitness is considered rude.

Such linguistic customs do not lend themselves to human/machine interaction. No matter how well the software is designed, computers cannot tolerate much ambiguity. It has been noted that living abroad or experiencing prolonged exposure to foreign languages influences the use of their own language by the Japanese, to the point where Japanese citizens returning from long stays overseas find it difficult to be as politely ambiguous as traditional Japanese society demands. In all likelihood, interaction with computers will have a comparable effect.

With rapid diffusion of personal computers among the population, from elementary-school children to corporate executives, the influence of "computerese" on the Japanese language could be profound in the next decades. In fact, educational efforts might be needed to maintain an appreciation for traditional literary Japanese in the face of this onslaught. The older generation already laments that the postwar generation has lowered linguistic standards. The challenge for the Japanese (and also for the Koreans and Chinese) will be to preserve the best of their linguistic heritage while adapting current usage to the computer age.

LETTER

Should the Japanese Language Be Reformed?

We are writing to commend ABACUS on the article "Japanese Word Processing" by Neil Friedman in the Winter 1986 issue. Of several articles that we've seen recently on similar themes, it was by far the best in providing a clear description of the relevant features of the written Japanese language and of the operation of Japanese word processors. Moreover, perhaps because of the author's obvious acquaintance with Japanese customs and language, the treatment was much more culturally even-handed than we are accustomed to reading.

So we found it all the more striking to notice that the article evidenced a bias which is universal in popular discussions about computers as well as in most writings on technology: the belief that the perceived direction of technological development is both desirable and inevitable. This belief set the tone of Friedman's discussion, influenced his choice of topics (e.g., "Future Evolution of the Language"), and was stated explicitly:

But there is a need for the Japanese . . . to realize that reform efforts could be redirected so that future generations using the new technology will not be unduly burdened by the language itself.

The challenge for the Japanese . . . will be to preserve the best of their linguistic heritage while adapting current usage to the computer age.

Having concluded that Japanese writing and communication habits would be improved through the introduction of word processors, Friedman makes the startling claim that the relation of the written to the spoken language is basically flawed:

In other words, what is "wrong" with Japanese is . . . the loose fit between the written and the spoken language. This fault will be pointed up more and more by word-processing technology.

What does Friedman mean by the "loose fit" of spoken and written Japanese? Does English exhibit a "tight fit"? It seems that Friedman assumes that it does. But wouldn't this mean that one can move back and forth between the written and spoken language with more ease? If so, how are we to explain a very high rate of functional illiteracy in the U.S. as compared to Japan with its "loosely fitting" written and spoken language? It seems to us that as used in this article the term "loose fit" has no clear meaning but merely reflects Friedman's unstated presumptions. For example, when he refers to the large number of homophones in spoken Japanese as a factor contributing to that language's disadvantageous "loose fit," Friedman tacitly assumes that it is the spoken language which is of first importance, with the written language primarily serving to record the former accurately. Whatever the case with English, this is not the situation with Japanese. There the form of the written language provides not only an art form but affects speech. Many Japanese create Chinese characters mentally as they speak to each other and this influences what is said.

But let us assume with Friedman that the spoken language is *the* language and further, as he seems to imply, that it is not affected by the written language to an appreciable degree. Even then one could argue that the increased use of word processors would result in more rather than fewer Chinese characters being used in the written language, and hence in the homophonically induced "loose fit" between written and spoken language becoming still "worse." Keep in mind that it is the written language which is transcribed by a word processor and not the spoken language. At present, because most Japanese' passive recognition of Chinese characters is better than their active ability to write them, the range of such characters that they use in writing is rather restricted. But word processors relieve the user of the need to write characters themselves and hence leave him or her free to use even more in documents. (Consider, by way of analogy, how people are using machines like the Macintosh to increase the variety of fonts with which they decorate their written productions.)

It is clear that the relationship between the written and spoken language in any culture is a complicated matter that has evolved over time in a complex manner and whose form probably influences and is influenced by other social structures. To be willing nevertheless to induce change in this relationship simply because it doesn't fit comfortably on a particular technological Procrustean bed is to act fanatically. Friedman might object to this criticism by saying that he was not being prescriptive in his comments—not saying what should be—but simply being descriptive—i.e., saying what will be. But in the situation under discussion this division is illusory: there is no objective future but only a subjective interpretation of trends. Hence his "description"—once accepted by enough people— becomes a "prescription." After all, it is probably not the case that people or even businesses have adopted word processors in the United States solely on the basis of "obvious" advantages, but because they have been persuaded to buy them. Business doesn't spend billions on advertising for nothing.

Once his rather narrow (from our viewpoint) technical yardstick has persuaded the author that there is something organically wrong with the relation of written to spoken Japanese, he is in a position to indulge in what seem to us to be very far-fetched analyses. Thus, in the section on "Future Evolution of the Language," Friedman suggests that the (imputed) difficulty which Japanese who spend a long time in other (English-speaking?) countries have in readapting to life in Japan when they come home, can be explained by the fact that their "logic" or "rationality" has become more clear-cut and less ambiguous while living abroad. Presumably this is because foreign languages have fewer of those ambiguity-causing homophones. This strikes us as absurd. More simply, one can suppose that they may simply have gotten out of the habit of practicing what we call "social graces," some of which are linguistic but most of which are not.

Clearly cultural changes as massive as the author predicts should be compensated for by equally massive benefits to be conferred by the technology. As far as we can tell, the author only discusses these benefits in the section "Consequences of Japanese Word Processing" and even there only mentions a few questionable gains: elimination of certain job categories (is that a gain?), and improving the legibility of internal memos in business organizations. The latter would be nice, yes, but is the communication situation really any better in a highly automated American office? Not only has the point not been made, but one could argue simply on the basis of the current trade imbalance between the two nations that the Japanese should stick with their old-fashioned handwritten memos. Besides, who knows what might be lost as the ability to write Chinese characters atrophied with the adoption of word processors? Many Japanese feel that in the style of handwriting of even a memo there is information that the uniform font of a word processor would destroy. Even more intriguing (and on just as solid ground as the author's own speculations) is the possibility that because the Japanese had to be careful in scribing complicated characters all the time, the entire culture learned to pay attention to minute details. Perhaps this trait carries over into the care the Japanese exhibit in manufacturing high-technology goods and marketing them around the world. Nor should we overlook the possibility that because everyone has had to communicate via handwritten messages, the communal bond between people has been strengthened and the crime rate has been kept low!

We do not mean to be merely facetious with the last suggestions. What we want to do is to ask that when writing about the social effects of technology, writers try to lay bare their own preconceptions. Thus Friedman argues that something (English a few years ago, Japanese soon) has an advantage just because it can utilize a certain technology. One might as well argue that farming has an advantage over painting because the farmer uses a plow and the painter doesn't. In what does the advantage consist— and at what price is it gained? In the case with which Friedman deals— word processors for Japanese—the lack of convincing advantages (and in view of their purported effects, these advantages should be overwhelming) suggests what the real story is: the author is emotionally wedded to the view that word processors are the wave of the future—everywhere—and has to shape his rationalizations to that end. One does not have to be a Luddite to be sceptical of this kind of argument.

David Isles and
Tadatoshi Akiba
Norbert Wiener Forum
Tufts University
Medford, Massachusetts

Reprinted from ABACUS,
Volume 4, Number 1, Fall
1986.

Author's Response

Akiba and Isles raise important issues, which I hope are being discussed in Japan's educational establishment with the same seriousness they are in the pages of ABACUS.

   While my article did come across as endorsing changes in the language to suit technology, that was not my real motivation. I am not one who thinks society must adapt to scientific advances rather than the other way around. I'm not for giving ground to the gasoline engine, the nuclear industry, or even computerization when it threatens rights of privacy or other values.

   Partly, I was expressing the frustrations of all students of Japanese: not being able to find words in the dictionary because they could be pronounced several ways; not knowing how to read names; wallowing in the ambiguity that Japanese intellectuals write. I knew that the complaints of a few thousand foreign students would never be heeded. But when I began to play with Japanese word processors I said, "Aha! The same problems that annoy us are going to plague a hundred million Japanese computer users eventually, so maybe we will get some serious language reform."

   What I called "the loose fit between the written and spoken language" does not imply that English has a perfect fit. English spelling is highly irregular and should be fixed. Every natural language can stand improvement. On the whole, however, there is a better "fit" between the written and spoken forms of the language in Chinese (and in most phonetically-written languages) than in Japanese, for historical reasons explained in my article.

   When I talk about a "loose fit" in Japanese I mean not just that there are many homophones, but that there is not even agreement as to how many readings there are for many characters, or on how to render certain words in Kanji, because dictionaries (all by reputable publishers) vary. Japanese has not evolved the level of standardization that English, for example, has.

   The Japanese government itself opened the door to language reform with its list of some 2000 basic Kanji and its character simplifications. Akiba and Isles seem to agree with me that limiting the number of characters was a misconceived policy. Their argument that word processors will encourage the use of more *Kanji is absolutely right. Similarly, in English, an on-line thesaurus fosters the use of a greater vocabulary.*

   It is not clear whether Akiba and Isles oppose any *deliberate reform of the language, or whether they object to doing it for the sake of computerization. My position is that certain reforms are desirable on their own merits, but that the exigencies of computerization make them more urgent. Even if the Japanese government fails to act, computerization and international communication will force the language to evolve more rapidly in the direction it is already going: toward a "tighter fit" of accepted readings for each Kanji and more explicitness in expression.*

The benefits of Japanese word processing go far beyond the narrow ones Akiba and Isles cite (legibility of memos and such). There are vast implications for communications, information retrieval, expert systems, and everything that comes under "artificial intelligence."

The relationship between language and society is truly complex, as Akiba and Isles indicate with suggestive examples. Maybe constant drill in writing Kanji makes the Japanese meticulous in their work, aiding economic success. Likewise, it is said that Chinese students are especially good at chemistry, because the structure of molecules is analogous to that of Chinese characters.

We should be extremely cautious about advocating drastic language reforms, since the consequences are incalculable. Yet, as Akiba and Isles perceptively point out, description tends to become prescription. They say I am "emotionally wedded to the view that word processors are the wave of the future—everywhere." Perhaps not everywhere; but in Japan, definitely.

INTERRUPT

The rash of reports about computer hackers puts us in mind of a story (perhaps apocryphal) about project MAC in the early 1960s. MAC—an acronym for Multiple Access Computer or Machine-Aided Cognition, depending on which expert you asked—was MIT's seminal effort to develop an interactive, time-shared computing environment.

As might be expected, MAC was a challenge to MIT students. Indeed, many thought it their duty to gain unauthorized access to the system and perform all sorts of mischief; it was practically a rite of passage. Dr. Robert Fano, the articulate but volatile first director of project MAC, became increasingly incensed at the mounting transgressions of these hackers. At length he put a message on the system, for all to read when signing on. The message, "Attention Project MAC," informed the hackers that their day of judgment was near at hand. Dr. Fano was through being Mr. Nice Guy; from here on in, unless the hackers ceased and desisted, he would have them relentlessly tracked down and punished for their wayward ways.

The story goes that within twenty minutes or so, the on-line message had been hacked. Its new title? "Attention Project HACK."

Living with a New Mathematical Species

Computing and computer science prove again that mathematics is a living part of human culture.

Lynn Arthur Steen

In 1985 the International Commission on Mathematical Instruction (ICMI) convened a meeting in France of mathematicians, computer scientists, and mathematics educators from around the world to discuss the impact of "informatics" (the common European term for computer science) on mathematics—specifically, on mathematical research, on the mathematical curriculum, and on mathematical pedagogy.

Prior to the 1985 conference, an ICMI Steering Committee prepared a draft paper on "the influence of computers and informatics on mathematics and its teaching." This paper was circulated worldwide to interested mathematics educators, and served as the focal point for the meeting.

This ABACUS article is adapted from one of the responses to that ICMI discussion document. A formal report from the ICMI study, including several responses, has been published by Cambridge University Press [The Influence of Computers and Informatics on Mathematics and Its Teaching].

In this article, a dagger [†] indicates an expression defined in the glossary on the next page.

Lynn Arthur Steen is a professor of mathematics at St. Olaf College in Northfield, Minnesota, and president of the Mathematical Association of America. He is editor or author of seven books, including *Mathematics Today* and *Mathematics Tomorrow,* a pair of volumes that survey the state of contemporary mathematics for the general reader. He has written numerous articles about mathematics and computer science for such periodicals as *Scientific American, Science News,* and *Science,* and for five years was coeditor of *Mathematics Magazine.* Steen is Secretary of Section A, Mathematics, of the American Association for the Advancement of Science, and is a member of the Executive Committee of the Mathematical Sciences Education Board of the National Research Council. He received a Ph.D. in mathematics from M.I.T. in 1965.
Reprinted from ABACUS, Volume 3, Number 3, Spring 1986.

Glossary

Category theory	A general theory of mathematical structures, emphasizing similarity of form by means of mappings (called *functors*) from one structure to another.
Feigenbaum constant	The number 4.669196223 . . . , calculated as the limit of the ratio of differences between successive values of a parameter α at bifurcation points of iterations of a map $x \rightarrow f_\alpha(x)$. This constant arises experimentally in many contexts; M. Feigenbaum showed that it is independent of the particular family of functions involved in the iteration.
Fixed-point argument	A method of proof derived from topology which, under certain circumstances, guarantees a solution to an equation of the form $f(x) = x$.
Ising model	A simple model for magnetization strength in permanent magnets based on tiny abstract magnets or "spins" arranged in a regular lattice.
Stochastic process	A sequence or continual process of random events.

Computers are both the creature and the creator of mathematics. They are, in the apt phrase of Seymour Papert, "mathematics-speaking beings." More recently, J. David Bolter, in his stimulating book *Turing's Man,* calls computers "embodied mathematics." Computers shape and enhance the power of mathematics, while mathematics shapes and enhances the power of computers. Each forces the other to grow and change, creating—in Thomas Kuhn's language—a new mathematical paradigm.

Until recently, mathematics was a strictly human endeavor. It evolved with human society, achieving a degree of universality equalled by few other aspects of human culture. Its ecology was a human ecology, linked closely to science and language, evolving as human science and language changed.

But suddenly, in a brief instant on the time scale of mathematics, a new species has entered the mathematical ecosystem. Computers speak mathematics, but in a dialect that is difficult for some humans to understand. Their number systems are finite rather than infinite; their addition is not commutative; and they don't really understand "zero," not to speak of "infinity." Nonetheless, they do embody mathematics.

Many features of the new computer mathematics appear superficial: notation such as $\wedge$ and ** for exponentiation; linearized expressions for formulas traditionally represented by a two-dimensional layout; a preference for binary, octal, or hexadecimal representations of numbers; and in early languages, a new action-oriented meaning to the equals sign. Some variances are more significant, and more difficult to assimilate into traditional mathematics: finite number systems, interval arithmetic, roundoff errors, or computational intractability.

As mathematics goes, linguistic and notational changes are truly superficial—it really is the same subject modulo an isomorphism. These differences can be very confusing to students learning mathematics and computing, although perhaps no more so than the differences in vocabulary and perspective between an engineer and a mathematician. The blend of computer language and traditional mathematics produces a kind of Franglais, decried by purists yet employed by everyone.

The core of mathematics, however, is also changing under the ecological onslaught of mathematics-speaking computers. New specialties in computational complexity, theory of algorithms, graph theory, and formal logic attest to the impact that computing is having on mathematical research. As Harvard physicist Arthur Jaffe has argued so well in his recent essay "Ordering the Universe," the computer revolution *is* a mathematical revolution. The intruder has changed the ecosystem of mathematics, profoundly and permanently.

New Mathematics for a New Age

Computers are discrete, finite machines. Unlike a Turing machine with an infinite tape, real machines have limits of both time and space. Theirs is not an idealistic Platonic mathematics, but a mathematics of limited resources. The goal is not just to get a result, but to get the best result for the least effort. Optimization, efficiency, speed, productivity—these are essential objectives of modern computer mathematics. Questions of optimization lead to the study of graphs, of operations research, of computational complexity.

Computers are also logic machines. They embody the fundamental engine of mathematics—rigorous propositional calculus. So it comes as no surprise that computer programs can become full partners in the process of mathematical proof. The first celebrated computer proof was that of the four-color theorem: the computer served there as a sophisticated accountant, checking out thousands of cases of reductions. Despite philosophical alarms that computer-based proofs would change mathematics from an *a priori* to a contingent, fallible subject, careful analysis reveals that nothing much had really changed. The human practice of mathematics has always been fallible; now it has a partner in fallibility.

Recent work on the mysterious Feigenbaum constant† reveals just how far this evolution has progressed in just eight years: computer-assisted investigations of families of periodic maps suggested the presence of a mysterious universal limit, apparently independent of the particular family of maps. Subsequent theoretical investigations led to proofs that are true hybrids of classical analysis and computer programming: the crucial step in a fixed-point argument† requires a tight estimate on the norm of a high-degree polynomial. This estimate is made by a computer program, carefully crafted using interval arithmetic to account in advance for all possible inaccuracies introduced by roundoff error. Thus computer-assisted proofs are possible not just in graph theory, but also in that bastion of classical mathematics, functional analysis.

Computers are also computing machines. By absorbing, transforming, and summarizing massive quantities of data, computers can simulate reality. No longer need the scientist build an elaborate wind tunnel or a scale-model refinery in order to test engineering designs. Wherever basic science is well understood, computer models can emulate physical processes by carrying out instead the process implied by mathematical equations. Mathematical models used to be primarily tools used by theoretical scientists to formulate general theories; now they are practical tools of enormous value in the everyday world of engineering and economics. They focus mathematical attention on the relation between data and theory, on stochastic processes† and differential equations, on data analysis and mathematical statistics.

In many respects mathematics has become the creature of the computer: by providing compelling tools in combinatorics, logic, and calculation, the computer has made an offer of intellectual adventure that mathematicians cannot refuse. But in a very real sense, mathematics is also the creator of the computer. David Hilbert's struggle with the foundations of mathematics—itself precipitated by the paradoxes of set theory elucidated by Frege and Russell—led directly to Alan Turing's proposal for a universal machine of mathematics.

It has been fifty years since Turing developed his scheme of computability, in which he argued that machines could do whatever humans might hope to do. His was a formal, abstract system, devoid of hardware and real machines. It took two decades of engineering effort to turn Turing's abstractions into productive real machines.

During that same period, abstract mathematics flourished, led by Bourbaki, symbolized by the "generalized abstract nonsense" of category theory†. But with abstraction came power; with rigor came certainty. Once real computers emerged, the complexity of programs quickly overwhelmed the informal techniques of backyard programmers. Formal methods became *de rigueur;* even the once-maligned category theory is now enlisted to represent finite automata and recursive functions. Once again, as happened before with physics, mathematics became more efficacious by becoming more abstract.

Changing the Mathematics Curriculum

Twenty years ago, in the United States, the Committee on the Undergraduate Program in Mathematics (CUPM) issued a series of reports that led to a gradual standardization of curricula among undergraduate mathematics departments. Yet the circumstances that make computing a force for rapid evolution in the notation and practice of mathematics also put pressure on the mathematics curriculum in colleges and universities. This pressure is not new, but has been building in intensity throughout the past decade.

In 1971, Garrett Birkhoff and J. Barkley Rosser presented papers at a meeting of the Mathematical Association of America concerning their predictions for undergraduate mathematics in 1984. Birkhoff urged increased emphasis on modelling, numerical algebra, scientific computing, and discrete mathematics. He also advocated increased use of computer methods in pure mathematics: "Far from muddying the limpid waters of clear mathematical thinking, they make them more transparent by filtering out most of the messy drudgery which would otherwise accompany the working out of specific illustrations." Rosser emphasized many of the same points, and warned of impending disaster to undergraduate mathematics if their advice went unheeded: "Unless we revise [mathematics courses] so as to embody much use of computers, most of the clientele for these courses will instead be taking computer courses in 1984."

In the decade since these words were written, U.S. undergraduate and graduate degrees in mathematics have declined by 50%. New courses in modelling, discrete mathematics, and data analysis are emerging in every college and university. The clientele for traditional mathematics has indeed migrated to computer science. The former CUPM consensus is all but shattered. Five years ago CUPM issued a new report, this one on the Undergraduate Program in Mathematical Sciences. Beyond calculus and linear algebra, they could agree on no specific content for the core of a mathematics major: "There is no longer a common body of pure mathematical information that every student should know."

The symbol of reformation has become discrete mathematics. Several years ago Anthony Ralston argued forcefully the need for change before both the mathematics community and the computer science community. Discrete mathematics, in Ralston's view, is the central link between the fields. College mathematics must introduce discrete methods early and in depth; computer science curricula must, in turn, require and utilize mathematical concepts and techniques. The advocacy of discrete mathematics rapidly became quite vigorous, and the Sloan Foundation funded experimental curricula at six institutions to encourage development of discrete-based alternatives to standard freshman calculus.

The niche of mathematics in the university ecosystem has been radically transformed by the presence of computer science in the undergraduate curriculum. The strongest mathematics departments continue to offer the traditional CUPM major, oftentimes for a declining number of students. Many smaller departments, however, have been forced to drop regular offerings of such former core courses as topology, analysis, and algebra. In such institutions, where resources do not permit full majors in mathematics and computer science, the mathematics program often becomes a hybrid major consisting of some computer science, some mathematics, and some statistics—introductions to everything, mastery of nothing.

The need for consensus on the contents of undergraduate mathematics is perhaps the most important issue facing American college and university mathematics departments. On the one hand, departments that have a strong traditional major often fail to provide their students with the robust background required to survive the evolutionary turmoil in the mathematical sciences. Like the Giant Panda, they depend for survival on a dwindling supply of bamboo—strong students interested in pure mathematics. On the other hand, departments offering flabby composite majors run a different risk: by avoiding advanced, abstract requirements, they often misrepresent the true source of mathematical knowledge and power. Like zoo-bred animals unable to forage in the wild, students who have never been required to master a deep theorem are ill-equipped to master the significant theoretical complications of real-world computing and mathematics.

Computer Literacy

Mathematical scientists at American institutions of higher education are responsible not only for the technical training of future scientists and engineers, but also for the quantitative literacy of lay people—of future lawyers, politicians, doctors, educators, and clergy. Public demand that college graduates be prepared to live and work in a computer age has caused many institutions to introduce requirements in quantitative or computer literacy. Many educators are calling for a total reform of liberal education.

In 1981 the Alfred P. Sloan foundation initiated curricular exploration of "the new liberal arts," the role of applied mathematical and computer sciences in the education of students outside technical fields: "The ability to cast one's thoughts in a form that makes possible mathematical manipulation and to perform that manipulation [has] become essential in higher education, and above all in liberal education." In November 1982, University of California President David Saxon wrote in a *Science* editorial that liberal education "will continue to be a failed idea as long as our students are shut out from, or only superficially acquainted with, knowledge of the kinds of questions science can answer and those it cannot."

Too often these days the general public views computer literacy as the appropriate modern substitute for mathematical knowledge. Unfortunately, this often leads students to superficial courses that emphasize vocabulary and experiences over concepts and principles. The advocates of computer literacy conjure images of an electronic society dominated by the information industries. Their slogan of "literacy" echoes traditional educational values, conferring the aura but not the logic of legitimacy.

Typical courses in computer literacy, however, are filled with ephemeral details whose intellectual life will barely survive the students' school years. A best-selling textbook in the United States for courses introducing computing to nonspecialists is full of glossy color pictures, but does not even mention the word "algorithm." These courses contain neither a Shakespeare nor a Newton, neither a Faulkner nor a Darwin; they convey no fundamental principles nor enduring truths.

Computer literacy is more like driver education than like calculus. It teaches students the prevailing rules of the road concerning computers: how to create and save files, how to use word processors and spreadsheets, how to program in Basic. One can be confident only that most students finishing such a course will not injure themselves or others in their first encounter with a real computer in the workplace. But such courses do not leave students well prepared for a lifetime of work in the information age.

Algorithms and data structures are to computer science what functions and matrices are to mathematics. As much of the traditional mathematics curriculum is devoted to elementary functions and matrices, so beginning courses in computing—by whatever name—should stress standard algorithms and typical data structures.

For example, as early as students study linear equations they could also learn about stacks and queues; when they move on to conic sections and quadratic equations, they could in a parallel course investigate linked lists and binary trees. The algorithms for sorting and searching, while not part of traditional mathematics, convey the power of abstract ideas in diverse applications every bit as much as do conic sections or derivatives.

Computer languages can (and should) be studied for the concepts they represent—procedures in Pascal, recursion and lists for Lisp—rather than for the syntactic details of semicolons and line numbers. They should not be undersold as mere technical devices for encoding problems for a dumb machine, nor oversold as exemplars of a new form of literacy. Computer languages are not modern equivalents of Latin or French; they do not deal in nuance and emotion, nor are they capable of persuasion, conviction, or humor. Although computer languages do represent a new and powerful way to think about problems, they are not a new form of literacy.

Computer Science

The confusion evident in university mathematics departments is an order of magnitude less severe than that which operates in university computer science programs. In the United States, these programs cover an enormous spectrum, from business-oriented data-processing curricula through management information science to theoretical computer science. All of these intersect with the mathematics curriculum, each in different ways. The computer science community is now struggling with this chaos, and has a process in place for identifying exemplary programs of different types as a first step towards an accreditation system for college computer science departments.

Several computer science curricula have been developed by the professional societies ACM and IEEE, for both large universities and small colleges. Recently Mary Shaw of Carnegie-Mellon University put together a composite report on the undergraduate computer science curriculum. This report is quite forceful about the contribution mathematics makes to the study of computer science: "The most important contribution a mathematics curriculum can make to computer science is the one least likely to be encapsulated as an individual course: a deep appreciation of the modes of thought that characterize mathematics."

The converse is equally true: one of the more important contributions that computer science can make to the study of mathematics is to develop in students an appreciation for the power of abstract methods when applied to concrete situations. Students of traditional mathematics used to study a subject called "Real and Abstract Analysis"; students of computer science now can take a course titled "Real and Abstract Machines." In the former "new math," as well as in modern algebra, students learned about relations, abstract versions of functions; today, business students study "relational data structures" in their computer courses, and advertisers tout "fully relational" as the latest innovation in business software. The abstract theories of finite-state machines and deterministic automata are reflections in the mirror of computer science of well-established mathematical structures from abstract algebra and mathematical logic.

An interesting and pedagogically attractive example of the power of abstraction made concrete can be seen in the popular electronic spreadsheets that are marketed under such trade names as Lotus and VisiCalc. Originally designed for accounting, they can equally well emulate cellular automata or the Ising model for ferromagnetic materials†. They can also be "programmed" to carry out most standard mathematical algorithms: the Euclidean algorithm, the simplex method, Euler's method for solving differential equations. An electronic spreadsheet—the archetype of applied computing—is a structured form for recursive procedures—the fundamental tool of algorithmic mathematics. It is, to echo David Bolter, mathematics embodied in a computer.

Computers in the Classroom

Computers are mathematics machines, as calculators are arithmetic machines. Just as the introduction of calculators upset the comfortable paradigm of primary-school arithmetic, so the spread of sophisticated computers will upset the centuries-old-tradition of college and university mathematics. This year, long division is passe; next year, integration will be under attack.

Reactions to machines in the mathematics classroom are entirely predictable. Committee oracles and curriculum visionaries proclaim a utopia in which students concentrate on problem solving and machines perform the mindless calculations (long division and integration). Yet many teachers, secure in their authoritarian rule-dominated world, banish calculators (and computers) from ordinary mathematics instruction, using them if at all for separate curricular units where different ground rules apply. The recent International Assessment of Mathematics documented that in the United States calculators are never permitted in one-third of the 8th grade classes, and rarely used in all but 5% of the rest.

The large gap between theory and practice in the use of computers and calculators for mathematics instruction is due in part to a pedagogical assumption that pits teacher against machine. If the teacher's role is to help (or force) students to learn the rules of arithmetic (or calculus), then any machine that makes such learning unnecessary is more a threat than an aid. Debates continue without end: Should calculators be used on exams? Should we expect less mastery of complex algorithms like long division or integration? Will diminished practice with computation undermine subsequent courses that require these skills?

The impact of computing on secondary-school mathematics has been the subject of many recent discussions in the United States. University of Maryland mathematician Jim Fey, coordinator of two of the most recent assessments, described these efforts as "an unequivocal dissent from the spirit and substance of efforts to improve school mathematics that seek broad agreement on conservative curricula. Many mathematics educators working with emerging electronic technology see neither stability nor consensus in the future of school mathematics."

The technology wars are just beginning to spread to the college classroom. Lap-size computers are now common—they cost about as much as ten textbooks, but take up only the space of one. Herb Wilf, editor-elect of the *American Mathematical Monthly,* argues that it is only a matter of time before students will carry with them a device to perform all the algorithms of undergraduate mathematics. A recent survey of applied research based on symbolic algebra asserts that "it will not be long before computer algebra is as common to engineering students as the now obsolete slide rule once was."

John Kemeny tells a story about calculus instruction that sheds interesting new light on the debate about manipulating symbols. He asks for the value of $\int_0^{13} e^x \, dx$. A moment's thought reveals the answer to be $e^{13} - 1$. That's the exact answer. Kemeny's first question is this: What is its value to *one* significant digit? With just paper and pencil, that's hard to do—beyond the likely skills of typical calculus students. (The answer:

400,000.) Now comes the second question: What's the difference between the original question and the traditional exact answer? They are both exact expressions for the value we seek, equally unenlightening. So the proper question is not to find an exact value, but to choose which of many possible exact values is more suitable to the purpose at hand.

The challenges of computers in the classroom are exactly analogous to those of calculators. The computer will do for the teaching of calculus algorithms just what calculators did for arithmetic computations—it will make them redundant. In so doing, it will challenge rigid teachers to find new ways to reassert authority. Good teachers, however, should respond to the computer as a blessing in disguise—as a *deus ex machina* to rescue teaching from the morass of rules and templates that generations of texts and tests have produced.

Following the Rules

Mathematics students, just like any other students, like to get correct answers. Computers, for the most part, reinforce the student's desire for answers. Their school uses have been largely extensions of the old "teaching machines": programmed drill with predetermined branches for all possible answers, right or wrong. In colleges and universities, computers are still used most often as blackbox calculators, spewing out numbers in answer to questions both asked and unasked.

Core mathematics courses continue this long-standing tradition, reinforcing the emphasis on rules and answers. Traditional calculus textbooks bear an uncanny resemblance to the first calculus text ever published: l'Hopital's 1699 classic. They present rules of differentiation and integration, with or without proof: linearity, product and quotient rules, chain rule, substitution, and so forth. After each rule are exercises to practice on. At the end of the chapter are mixed exercises, where the challenge is to use all the rules at the same time.

Most students of even modest ability can master these rules. If there is one thing that school does well, it is training students to learn rules. Strong students master them quickly, and yearn for tough problems that extend the rules (for instance, to x^x). Weak students work by rote, carefully adhering to template examples. Students of all types flounder when presented with "word problems" to "apply" their skills on: "A farmer has 200 meters of fence with which to. . . ." Too often, such problems are merely mathematical crossword puzzles—stylized enigmas whose solutions depend in large part on recognizing the unstated problem pattern. Indeed, recent research in problem solving suggests that many students learn to solve such problems by establishing mental categories of problem-type, and of course many instructors teach students to identify such types.

The confluence of research on learning with symbolic algebra has produced a rich new territory for imaginative pedagogy. Symbolic algebra packages linked to so-called "expert systems" on computers of sufficient power (with high-resolution graphics, mouse-like pointers, and multiple windows) can provide an effective intelligent tutor for learning algebraic skills. Computers can manipulate algebraic and numerical expressions as well as students can, usually better. However, they cannot recognize, parse, or model a word problem except in the narrowest sense—by matching templates to canonical forms.

It is commonplace now to debate the value of teaching skills such as differentiation that computers can do as well or better than humans. Is it really worth spending one month of every year teaching half of a country's 18-year-old students how to imitate a computer? What is not yet so common is to examine critically the effect of applying to mathematics pedagogy computer systems that are only capable of following rules or matching templates. Is it really worth the time and resources to devise sophisticated computer systems for efficiently teaching precisely those skills that computers can do better than humans, particularly those skills that make the computer tutor possible? The basic question is this: since computers can now do algebra and calculus algorithms, should we use this power to reduce the curricular emphasis on calculations, or as a means of teaching calculations more efficiently? This is a new question, with a very old answer.

Let Us Teach Guessing

Thirty-five years ago, George Pólya wrote a brief paper with the memorable title "Let Us Teach Guessing." Too few teachers actually do that: most teachers—the overwhelming number—are authoritarian. Teachers set the problems; students solve them. Good students soon learn that the key to school mathematics is to discern the right answer; poor students soon give up.

But Pólya says: let us teach guessing. It is not differentiation that our students need to learn, but the art of guessing. A month spent learning the rules of differentiation reinforces a student's ability to learn (and live by) the rules. In contrast, time spent making conjectures about derivatives will teach a student something about the art of mathematics and the science of order.

With the aid of a mathematics-speaking computer, students can for the first time learn college mathematics by discovery. This is an opportunity for pedagogy that mathematics educators cannot afford to pass up. Mathematics is, after all, the science of order and pattern, not just a mechanism for grinding out formulas. Students discovering mathematics gain insight into the discovery of pattern, and slowly build confidence in their own ability to understand mathematics.

Formerly, only students of sufficient genius to forge ahead on their own could have the experience of discovery. Now, with computers as an aid, the majority of students can experience the joy of discovery for themselves. Only when the computer is used as an instrument of discovery will it truly aid the learning of mathematics.

Metaphors for Mathematics

Two metaphors from science are useful for understanding the relation between computer science and mathematics in education. Cosmologists long debated two theories for the origin of the universe—the Big Bang theory, and the theory of Continuous Creation. Current evidence tilts the cosmology debate in favor of the Big Bang. Unfortunately, this is all too often the public image of mathematics as well, even though in mathematics the evidence favors Continuous Creation.

The impact of computer science on mathematics and of mathematics on computer science is the most powerful evidence available to beginning students that mathematics is not just the product of an original Euclidean big bang, but is continually created in response to challenges both internal and external. Students today, even beginning students, can learn things that were simply not known twenty years ago. We must not only teach new mathematics and new computer science, but we must also teach the fact that this mathematics and computer science is new. That's a very important lesson for laymen to learn.

The other apt metaphor for mathematics comes from the history of the theory of evolution. Prior to Darwin, the educated public believed that forms of life were static, just as the educated public of today assumes that the forms of mathematics are static, laid down by Euclid, Newton, and Einstein. Students learning mathematics from contemporary textbooks are like the pupils of Linnaeus, the great eighteenth-century Swedish botanist: they see a static, pre-Darwinian discipline that is neither growing nor evolving. For most students, learning mathematics is an exercise in classification and memorization, in labelling notations, definitions, theorems, and techniques that are laid out in textbooks like so much flora in a wonderous if somewhat abstract Platonic universe.

Students rarely realize that mathematics continually evolves in response to both internal and external pressures. Notations change; conjectures emerge; theorems are proved; counterexamples are discovered. Indeed, the passion for intellectual order combined with the pressure of new problems—especially those posed by the computer—force researchers to be continually creating new mathematics and archiving old theories.

The practice of computing and the theory of computer science combine to change mathematics in ways that are highly visible and attractive to students. This continual change reveals to students and laymen the living character of mathematics, restoring to the educated public some of what the experts have always known—that mathematics is a living, evolving component of human culture.

References

Bolter, J. David. *Turing's Man: Western Culture in the Computer Age*. Chapel Hill: University of North Carolina Press, 1984.

Committee on the Undergraduate Program in Mathematics. *Recommendations for a General Mathematical Sciences Program*. Mathematical Association of America, 1980.

Fey, James T., et al., eds. *Computing and Mathematics: The Impact on Secondary School Curricula*. National Council of Teachers of Mathematics, 1984.

Jaffe, Arthur. "Ordering the Universe: The Role of Mathematics." In: *Renewing U.S. Mathematics*. Washington, DC: National Academy Press, 1984.

Koerner, James D., ed. *The New Liberal Arts: An Exchange of Views*. Alfred P. Sloan Foundation, 1981.

Ralston, Anthony. "Computer Science, Mathematics, and the Undergraduate Curricula in Both." *American Mathematical Monthly* **88** (1981):472–85.

Ralston, Anthony, and Young, Gail S. *The Future of College Mathematics*. New York: Springer-Verlag, 1983.

Shaw, Mary, ed. *The Carnegie-Mellon Curriculum for Undergraduate Computer Science*. New York: Springer-Verlag, 1985.

Steen, Lynn Arthur. "1 + 1 = 0: New Math for a New Age." *Science* **225** (1984):981.

Wilf, Herbert. "The Disk with the College Education." *American Mathematical Monthly* **89** (1982):4–8.

Foretelling the Future by Adaptive Modeling

Dynamic Markov models can compress data to 2.2 bits per character or 0.18 bits per pixel.

IAN H. WITTEN AND JOHN G. CLEARY

Foretelling the future is a pastime that all of us enjoy, but is not normally viewed as a scientific activity. We would all like to be able to predict which horse will win a particular race or which stock will double next week. If *we* knew how to do that, we would not be writing this article. Yet it is often quite possible to predict the future—in a limited way—and to put the prediction to good use. By describing an expected, "normal" course of events, a good prediction focuses attention on how an unfolding event differs from the norm. In many cases this is more interesting than the events themselves.

For example, suppose one computer is sending a stream of numbers to another. If it is possible to predict exactly what the next number is going

JOHN G. CLEARY received a Ph.D. from the University of Canterbury, New Zealand, in 1980. Prior to this, he spent five years working in commercial data processing. In 1982 he joined the Department of Computer Science at the University of Calgary, where he is now an associate professor. He has published a number of papers on adaptive and learning systems, distributed systems and algorithms, and logic programming.

IAN H. WITTEN received a Ph.D. in Electrical Engineering from Essex University, England, in 1976. He is currently a professor in the Department of Computer Science, University of Calgary. His research interests span the field of man/machine systems, and he has specialized in fundamental problems of human and machine learning, in computational phonetics (the science of speech synthesis by computer), in signal processing and, recently, in document preparation systems and documentation graphics. He is the author or coauthor of about eighty publications, including three books: *Communicating with Microcomputers* (Academic Press, 1980), *Principles of Computer Speech* (Academic Press, 1982), and *Talking with Computers* (Prentice Hall, 1986).

Reprinted from ABACUS, Volume 3, Number 3, Spring 1986.

Glossary

Arithmetic coding	A method of data compression that utilizes the probability of occurrence of symbols to provide extremely effective compression. The probability of each symbol must be known beforehand. It does not encode each symbol into a fixed pattern of bits, but instead encodes the message as a whole. Any particular symbol will in general affect all the remainder of the coded message.
Data compression	The encoding of a string of symbols into a sequence of bits in such a way that the sequence can be decoded uniquely to reproduce the original string. The smaller the encoded sequence of bits, the more effective the compression is.
Entropy	A measure of the disorder of a system. The entropy of a set of messages with respect to a model measures how disordered the messages are. For example, if the model predicts them exactly, then the entropy is zero; the less successful the prediction, the greater the entropy.
Grey scale	The range of intensities between black and white to which each point (pixel) on a display screen can be set. For example, there might be 256 values in the grey scale, from 0 (pure black) to 255 (pure white).
Huffman coding	A data compression technique which, like arithmetic coding, utilizes the probability of occurrence of symbols. Again, the probability of each symbol must be known beforehand. However, in Huffman coding each symbol is encoded into a fixed pattern of bits. This constraint generally degrades the compression performance, because symbols cannot be represented in fractional numbers of bits.
Markov model	A model that assumes each symbol in a sequence is affected by a fixed number of directly preceding symbols. For example, a first-order Markov model uses one symbol of prior context for prediction, a second-order Markov model two, and so on.
Model	A stylized representation used to analyze or explain a certain sequence, or (in the case of models considered in this article) to predict what follows.
Pixel	A tiny point on a display screen; every screen is divided into an array of pixels. Each pixel can take on an intensity in some set of values (the grey scale) between black and white.
Progressive transmission	A method of picture transmission that results in the image being built up gradually in successive whole-screen sweeps. The entire picture goes from a first

rough representation through intermediate stages to its final detailed state. This is in contrast to transmission methods in which the final detailed image is built up bit by bit in a slow, single screen sweep.

Robustness   Refers to a modeling system that does not just abort if predetermined assumptions about the input sequence turn out not to be justified.

---

to be, there is no point in sending it at all! But suppose the guesses are not quite so reliable. Then it may be advantageous to send only those numbers which differ from the predicted ones, or to use some more sophisticated way of coding the discrepancies between predictions and observations. The receiver—if it can make identical guesses—will be able to reconstruct the correct number from the portion that is sent. If the guesses are good, this scheme will reduce the amount of information that needs to be sent. In fact, the reduction achieved is a quantitative measure of success at guessing; in this light, the act of *data compression* is inextricably bound up with foretelling the future.

As an example of your predictive ability, cover the following paragraph with a slip of paper, moving it down slowly to reveal one line at a time. You should have a response in mind by the time you reach the end of the third line.

Now: What kind of character will follow the last word in this sentence, according to your best guess? Of course! It was a question mark. (And this in turn was followed by a space.) Your knowledge of punctuation, vocabulary, grammar, and sentence formation makes you remarkably accurate in predicting what characters come next. Any prediction is based on a model of the events being predicted. In this case, the model is your personal one of the behavior of English—a very complex model built up over many years of experience.

You could try to program your "intuitive" models into a computer so that it could make the same predictions as you. In this case, the accuracy of the predictions would depend on your cleverness and diligence in formulating and expressing the model. But there is an alternative: having the model constructed automatically by the computer from observation of past events. Then it can change dynamically, adapting itself to the course of events. Naturally the model will have to be an unsophisticated one, probably much simpler than any you might construct by hand. Nevertheless, the machine's untiring accuracy in keeping it updated may lead to quite useful predictions once it has been exposed to a long behavior sequence. Although a static model of English may fail completely if used to predict French, an adaptive modeler that based its predictions on the observed text would stand some chance of success.

Using Prediction Techniques

Before looking at methods of modeling discrete sequences, let's get acquainted with a few applications.

Figure 1 on the next page shows the *reactive keyboard,* a way of entering text into a computer without a conventional keyboard. At all times, a display on the computer's screen shows what the computer thinks you will type next. It does this by building its own model of what you are typing from what you have typed so far. The most likely strings are shown at the top of the screen, and the less likely ones further down. If your computer has a mouse (or other pointing device), you select what you want to enter by pointing at the prediction which is correct. In this way it may be possible to enter a number of characters (for example, a sequence of words that almost always go together) in one operation. If you don't have a mouse, a very simple keypad will suffice; for example, a pushbutton telephone with ten keys can be used. This can only select the first character of each prediction. Even so, after a little experience, the computer is able to ensure that the character sought is almost always among the first ten predictions displayed.

You may wonder why on earth anyone would want to enter text in this way, rather than having a trained typist key it in. Some people, such as those who are physically handicapped, are only able to select from a small number of keys at a time. Also, in some applications, such as accessing remote databases using only a home television set and telephone handset, only ten or twelve keys are available for input. In both of these cases the reactive keyboard allows fast access to the full alphabet. In essence, it substitutes the cognitive skill of selecting from a menu for the mechanical skill of typing.

Another application of modeling is in programming itself. The idea is that, if a computer is shown the steps to perform a task a number of times, it can build a model of the sequence of steps. The different input data provided each time will usually cause the task to be executed in different ways, adding new paths to the model. Once the model is good enough, it can predict the next step at all times, and be left to run its "program" all by itself! Completely automating the programming process in this way is something of a utopian dream (utopian for all but professional computer programmers!). However, it can be done in simple enough situations. In some of our work, we have used as a test case the simple, nonprogrammable pocket calculator shown in Figure 2 on page 92. By arranging for a model-building system to "look over your shoulder" while you use it for a repetitive task, it is possible after a while to predict the keys that will be pressed next. Any that cannot be predicted correspond to "input." Thus the device can eventually behave as though it had been explicitly programmed for the task at hand, waiting for the user to enter a number,

Typing Without a Keyboard

FIGURE 1. The "reactive keyboard," currently under development, allows text to be typed without any conventional keyboard. Instead, a menu display shows predicted character strings that are likely to appear in the current context. Here is a sample menu.

context	prediction
operating	much slower than s
	with compute
	prompts the
	of system)
	separately
	is through
	known word
	disregards
	to pronoun
	☞

The last few characters which have been entered are shown as the "context" string on the left. The ten menu items represent alternative pieces of text from which you can choose the next character. If you wish to enter, for example, "prompts the", you point at the end of the third menu item. In that case, eleven characters will be entered at a single selection. If instead the characters "pr" are correct, but the remaining ones are not, you point between the second and third character of the third menu item. If the next character is "p" but the "r" is incorrect, the first character alone of the third menu item should be selected.

The menu items are displayed from most to least likely, in terms of the predictive model of the text. Here, the most likely next character (according to the model) is "m", so the first menu item begins with this. The next letters, "uch slower than s", show the most likely future prediction following "m". Predictions become significantly less reliable as you go further into the future.

Of course, in some cases more than one page of the menu will have to be examined because the required character is not predicted at the head of any menu item. A special page-turning selection shows the next page. Simulations show that this will not often be necessary.

In the event that a pointing device is not available for indicating the selection, a simpler display is used:

context	prediction	
operating	0	m
	1	w
	2	p
	3	o
	4	s
	5	l
	6	k
	7	d
	8	t
	9	☞

In this mode the user types the appropriate number, and only one letter can be
entered at a time.

---

and simulating the appropriate sequence of keypresses to come up with
the answer. Using a calculator (rather than a programming language like
Basic) sidesteps some of the more difficult problems of automatic programming, for the calculator is suited only to simple jobs.

Picture Compression is another interesting problem. A picture is represented in the computer by a two-dimensional matrix of grey-scale values,
each giving the blackness (or whiteness) of one tiny picture element or
pixel. For example, a monochromatic TV-quality picture might have 300
pixels horizontally and 250 vertically, each with a 6-bit grey-scale value;
this adds up to 75,000 pixels, or a total of 450,000 bits. In text, as we have
seen, a character is best predicted from the context of characters that
immediately precede it. What should you use as the "context" for predictions in picture coding? The easiest thing is the pixels to the left and
above the one being encoded, for a television generates pictures one line
at a time with a horizontal scan. However, there seems to be no intrinsic
reason to prefer the left context to the right context, or the top context
to the bottom context. It would be nice to use all eight surrounding pixels
as the context, but then it's hard to see how the picture could be drawn—
you've got to start somewhere!

One way to resolve this problem is to use a binary image tree (see Figure
3 on page 96). Although the tree is built from the picture bottom-up, it is
best transmitted top-down, starting from the root. The picture will build
up gradually over the whole screen, instead of being painted from top to
bottom. This in itself is a nice feature. The progressive transmission gives
you a rough representation very early on, and most of the time is spent
refining it to full detail.

For the purpose of coding, the binary image tree makes it easy to construct contexts for the grey-scale values that are being sent. For example,
the level of the tree above the current one will have been completely sent
already. The value of a particular pixel in the current level will be strongly
dependent on neighboring ones in the level above, and these can be used
as context in exactly the same way that prior characters are used as context
for text compression. Apart from this difference in context, coding can
proceed exactly as for "one-dimensional" text.

Making a Model of Text

How can you build models of discrete sequences such as the letters in
text? We will first describe one way which is notable for its simplicity
and generality, although the resulting models can be very large. Later we

An Autoprinting Calculator

FIGURE 2. Adaptive modeling has been used to investigate an autoprogramming feature on an electronic calculator. The model predicts the key that will be pressed next. If the prediction is sufficiently firm, the modeler will press that key. Thus, some keystrokes are made for the user. Sometimes the prediction will be wrong, and an *undo* allows the user to correct errors.

The calculator looks like this:

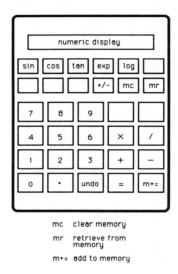

mc   clear memory

mr   retrieve from memory

m+=   add to memory

As the user presses keys, an adaptive model is made of the sequence of keystrokes. If the task is repetitive (like calculating a simple function for various argument values), the modeler will soon catch on to the sequence and begin to activate the key functions itself. Shortly, the device will behave as if explicitly programmed for the calculation.

Here are some examples of the operation of this "self-programming" calculator. The first sequence below shows the evaluation of xe^{1-x} for a range of values of x. The keys pressed by the operator are in normal type; those supplied by the system are in outline characters.

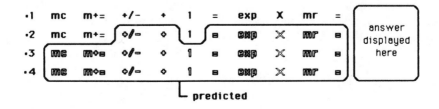

From halfway through the second iteration onwards, the device behaves as though it had been explicitly programmed for the calculation. It waits for the user to enter a number, and displays the answer. It takes slightly longer for the constant *1* to be predicted than the preceding operators because numbers in a sequence are more likely to change than operators. Therefore, they system requires an additional confirmation before venturing to predict a number.

Below is the evaluation of

$$1 + \frac{\log x}{8 \log 2}$$

for various values of *x*. The first line stores the constant log 2 in memory.

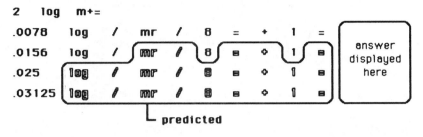

will look at an equally general but more economical method of modeling. To simplify the matter, suppose that you are asked to predict the next letter of the sequence

A   B   A   B   A   B   A

B would seem to be a reasonable guess. Of course it may be wrong. The letters might, for example, represent notes in a tune that continued differently on the eighth note, or digits in the binary expansion of a number that just happened to begin that way. But *B* is a natural default value for the next letter. It would be mildly surprising if it turned out wrong. If it did, and the next letter was, say, *Q,* one could hardly resist asking why.

This prediction would be suggested by a predecessor-based scheme which remembered, for each letter, what its successor was. But this is hopelessly simplistic, for it fails when the successor to a letter is not unique. For example, if the sequence was

A   B   A   C   A   B   A   B   A   C   A   B
A   C   A   C   A   C   A   B   A

it seems likely that the next letter will be either *B* or *C*—although it is not clear which. In this case, a frequency-based scheme which accumulates the frequency of each letter pair will do the trick. This is the same as maintaining a set of letter frequencies depending on the preceding letter. For the above sequence this would produce these probabilities:

Next letter				
Previous letter	A	B	C	D ...
A	0%	50%	50%	0% ...
B	100%	0%	0%	0% ...
C	100%	0%	0%	0% ...
D	?	?	?	? ...
.	.	.	.	.
.	.	.	.	.
.	.	.	.	.

This model predicts that following an *A* will come either *B* or *C*, with a 50% probability for each, and that the letter following either *B* or *C* will definitely be *A*. It is termed a *first-order Markov model*, "first-order" because one character of prior context is used for prediction, and "Markov" after the mathematician A. A. Markov (1856–1922).

A first-order Markov model cannot account for some very simple dependencies. In the sequence

$$A \quad B \quad A \quad C \quad A \quad B \quad A \quad C \quad A \quad B \quad A \quad C \quad A$$

it seems clear that *B*'s and *C*'s alternately follow *A*, so that *B* is expected next. But the first-order model above cannot tell this because it only uses one letter of prior context. A second-order model is necessary, which maintains frequencies of each letter following each letter *pair*. For example, the pair *"B A"* is always followed by *C*, while *"C A"* is always followed by *B*. Higher-order models are needed to capture more complicated effects of this type.

A serious drawback to the use of high-order Markov models is that not only do they consume a great deal of space but, more important, they have to see inordinately long stretches of behavior before they can form accurate models. We will return to this problem shortly. First, however, we will examine a more pressing issue. Suppose we have a suitable model. How can it be used for data compression?

Coding a Message with Respect to a Model

Given that we have some model which provides us with probabilities for the next character, how can it be used to compress a message? Assume that the text to be compressed has first been prepared by translating it into a sequence of 0's and 1's. These are the simplest units in which a message can be sent, and any other type of message can be reduced to such a sequence.

Huffman Coding

The first general solution to the compression problem was discovered by D. A. Huffman in 1952. He reasoned that common characters should be translated to short sequences of bits and rare characters to longer ones. Figure 4 on page 101 shows some translations of messages and how they can be made shorter by adjusting the lengths of the translations for individual characters. Not only did Huffman show that this was possible; he also gave a formula for calculating the length of the translation for each character. The length according to this formula is the negative of the logarithm to base 2 of the probability that the character will occur. If p is the probability, then this is written as $-\log_2 p$. For example, if a character is predicted with probability $\frac{1}{2}$, it should be translated to 1 bit; with probability $\frac{1}{4}$, to 2 bits; with probability $\frac{1}{8}$, to 3 bits; and so on.

The compression achieved by a particular translation of the characters is measured by the average number of bits needed whenever a character is translated. A small average gives a short translation, and a large average a longer one. If the character probabilities remain constant throughout the message, the expected compression can be calculated from the probabilities alone. This is done by averaging over a long message. The number of times any given character occurs will be approximately the length of the message multiplied by the character's probability. Each occurrence of the character adds the same number of bits to the translation. Thus the number of bits contributed to the translation by the character is *the length of the message* times *the probability of the character* times *the length of its translation*. By adding together the contributions of all characters, the total expected length of the translation is obtained in bits. This can then be divided by the message length to give the average number of bits per character:

$$\sum_{\text{all characters } C} \text{Probability } [C] \times \text{length}$$

of translation of C.

Applying this to Huffman codes, where the lengths are determined by the formula $-\log_2 p$, the average number of bits is given by

$$\sum_{\text{all characters } C} - p(C) \log_2 p(C),$$

$p(C)$ being the probability of character C. For example, if there are three characters with probabilities $\frac{1}{2}$, $\frac{1}{4}$, and $\frac{1}{4}$, the average number of bits per character in a translation is

$$- \tfrac{1}{2} \log_2 \tfrac{1}{2} - \tfrac{1}{4} \log_2 \tfrac{1}{4} - \tfrac{1}{4} \log_2 \tfrac{1}{4},$$

which equals 2.

Levels of Resolution

FIGURE 3. Each level in the binary image tree to the right has twice as many rectangles as the level above. At the very bottom is the full picture, and each square represents a picture element or *pixel* with a certain numeric grey-scale value. At the top is the average grey-scale value over the whole picture. At the next level, the picture is split into halves in one direction, and the tree records the average grey-scale value of each half. Next, each half is split again, this time in the other direction, forming four quadrants out of the original picture. This level of the tree holds the four corresponding grey-level values. And so it proceeds, until finally the full pixel resolution is achieved at the bottom. In fact, the method only works if the picture is square and the sides are a power of two, but any picture can be padded out to meet this requirement.

The photographs below show selected levels from a picture of a girl. It has 256×256 pixels, which is $2^8 \times 2^8$. This gives a total of 17 levels, which we number from 0 (at the top) to 16 (the final picture). The first version shown, at level 10, is 32×32, and has 1024 pixels—only 1.6% of the 65,500 pixels in the full picture. Although it is obviously not very good, it is clearly recognizable as a girl's face. By the time you get to level 14, the picture is quite clear, even though only 25% of the information is present.

Level 10 (0.9 secs)

Level 12 (3.5 secs)

Level 14 (14 secs)

Level 16 (final level—55 secs)

If this picture is transmitted at 1200 bits/sec, it will take 55 secs to be transmitted. the quite recognizable picture at level 12 will arrive in only 3.5 secs.

The photographs on the next page show a picture of text, with 512×512 pixels. The form and layout are visible by level 12, a 64×64 version, and the text is legible by level 16 (256×256).

Binary Image Tree

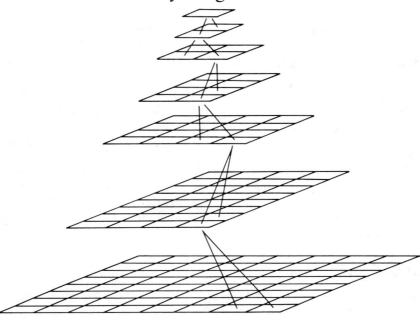

USINGADAPTIVE MODELL
"Abstract"

The quad tree is becoming a sta
& Rosenfeld, 1980; Hunter & Stei
images at successively higher re
and its higher-resolution neighbo
provides a very natural way of
refinement, where the receiver p
approximation Because of the log
medium resolution version is buil
is consumed in refining it to full
applications like teleconferencin
representation independent of th

Level 12

Level 14

Level 16

Level 18 (final level)

This sum has been studied extensively, and is called the *entropy* of the set of probabilities. Entropy is a measure of the disorder of a system. In this case, it measures how disordered the messages are (at least as seen by the particular model). For example, if there is only one character that can possibly occur, then the entropy is $-1 \log_2 1 = 0$, and there is only one possible message and no disorder at all. If there are two possible characters, each with a probability of $\frac{1}{2}$, then more disorder is expected; the entropy is 1 bit per character. It was shown by the mathematician C. A. Shannon in 1950 that the best possible compression that could be obtained with any message was measured by the entropy. It follows that provided all the probabilities are powers of $\frac{1}{2}$, Huffman codes achieve this best possible compression. Unfortunately, if we are not blessed with such a set of probabilities, Huffman codes do not achieve optimum compression.

Arithmetic Coding

Since 1976 a number of workers—R. Pasco, M. Guazzo, G. B. Jones, J. J. Rissanen, and G. G. Langdon—have developed a new coding scheme called *arithmetic coding,* which can always achieve Shannon's entropy limit no matter what probabilities are involved. However, it abandons certain simple features of Huffman codes. Huffman codes always make a fixed translation for each character: if there is an *A* in the message in more than one place, the pattern of bits standing for *A* can be found in all corresponding places of the translation. The pattern of bits produced by arithmetic coding bears no obvious relationship to the message being encoded. The reason for this can be seen by considering a character with probability, say, $\frac{3}{4}$. Taking its logarithm, it should have a translated length of 0.415—less than one bit! Obviously no fixed translation can do this.

Arithmetic coding is most easily described if we assume that the length of the message to be sent is known by both sender and receiver before transmission begins. It works by making the rather curious assumption that the translated message is a fraction between 0 and 1. Thus, a fraction such as 0.375 would be transmitted as the number 375. The receiver assumes that the decimal point is at the left-hand end. In fact, in keeping with our earlier practice we will send this as a sequence of bits. To do this, we represent the fraction in base 2. For example, 0.375 is $\frac{3}{8}$, which in base 2 is 0.011.

Say two characters *A* and *B* occur, with probabilities $\frac{3}{4}$ and $\frac{1}{4}$. If we are going to send a one-character message, *A* can be translated into any fraction from 0 up to (but not including) $\frac{3}{4}$, and *B* into any fraction from $\frac{3}{4}$ up to (but not including) 1. Successive binary digits of the translation need only be sent until it is clear in which range the fraction lies. For example, if a 1 is sent, the largest possible fraction that might follow is 0.111111 . . . , which is in the range $\frac{3}{4}$ to 1. The smallest that might follow is 0.10000 . . . , which is less than $\frac{3}{4}$. So after seeing just the 1, we still cannot identify the character. If the next bit transmitted is a 1, then the largest possible fraction is 0.1111111 . . . (just less than 1) and the smallest is 0.11000 . . . (equal to ¾). No matter what follows, the fraction must be in the range ¾ to 1, and so the message must be a translation of *B*. This means that no more need be sent; the sequence 11 is sufficient to identify the message. Similarly, a sequence of bits 10 has largest and smallest fractions 0.1011111 . . . (just less than ¾) and 0.10000 . . . (equal to ½). These are both in the range 0 to ¾, and so 10 must be a translation of *A*. However, 0 is a shorter translation, as then the largest and smallest values are 0.01111 . . . (just less than ½) and 0.0000 . . . (equal to 0), both in the range 0 to ¾. Given a range of fractions to choose from, it is easy to produce rules that yield the shortest translation and select 10 and 0 as the proper translations in this example. These rules guarantee that the number of bits in a translation will never exceed the length computed from the entropy of the message. Actually, a small overhead of at most two bits is incurred, but as most messages between computers are thousands of bits long, the extra two are negligible.

To translate a long message using arithmetic coding, a range of fractions must be associated with each possible message. Consider messages with two characters. A range for the message *BA* is computed as follows. The initial character *B* restricts the range to ¾ through 1. The second character *A* divides this interval in the same proportions as the probabilities ¾ and ¼. Since ¾ × ¼ = ³⁄₁₆, the message *BA* is allocated the range ¾ to ¹⁵⁄₁₆ = ¾ + ³⁄₁₆. The shortest fraction such that all of its extensions are in this range is 0.110, so a correct translation of *BA* is 110. The process can be continued for messages of any length. At each step, the range of allowed fractions is divided in proportion to the probabilities of the possible characters, and the correct subrange selected. Figure 5 shows the ranges of all possible sequences up to 3 characters for this example, and some examples of their best translations.

Arithmetic coding may seem to be a very complicated and obscure way of compressing a message. Computers, however, find it very easy, and it has significant advantages over Huffman codes. Huffman codes require prior tabulation of the translations of each character, and while Huffman showed how to do this in the best possible way, it can still take a long time. When adaptive or complex models of the sequence are being used, the frequencies of characters keep changing during the message. As these frequencies change, so does the Huffman code, and the table of translations must be computed afresh at each step, or a lot of computer memory used to store many different tables. In contrast, arithmetic coding requires only a small number of additions and multiplications to recalculate the range of fractions as each new character is seen. This is very fast on computers (which, after all, are very good at binary arithmetic). The result is that arithmetic coding is significantly faster than Huffman coding, and needs no computer memory to store tables. It is also guaranteed to produce the optimum coding, as given by the entropy.

Some thought about the process described above might lead to the conclusion that it is necessary to store fractions with many thousands of bits and to perform arithmetic on these very long numbers. This would be unfortunate, as most computers today can do arithmetic only on short numbers (16 and 32 bits are common lengths). Arithmetic coding avoids very long numbers by two techniques. Firstly, if the range of fractions partway through encoding a message is such that the first few bits in the highest fraction and the lowest fraction are the same, these bits can be sent immediately and discarded, leaving only the remainder of the fractions. For example, suppose after encoding the fourth character that the highest fraction is 0.10110111 and the lowest is 0.10110010. Then the initial sequence 10110 can be sent, and the highest and lowest fractions set to the remainders 0.111 and 0.010, before proceeding to encode the fifth and subsequent characters. Secondly, these remaining fractions need not be stored to arbitrarily high precision. Truncating them to a fixed precision sacrifices some compression efficiency, but increases the effectiveness of the implementation by speeding up arithmetic operations. We have found that using 16-bit fractions causes messages to be no more than 0.5% longer than if infinite accuracy were used!

Variable-Length Matching

Now let's return to the drawback of Markov models which we alluded to earlier, that large amounts of storage are apparently needed for models of only moderate order. With 27 symbols (26 letters and the space), a tenth-order Markov model contains 5.6×10^{15} frequencies, since this is the number of possible 11-character sequences. If a small number—say a thousand—characters of a sequence have been seen, only 1000 of these frequencies at most (and generally less because of repetitions) can have nonzero values. This is an exceedingly small proportion of the total number of frequencies in the model. It is therefore highly likely that the next character has never before been encountered in its present context, which is the sequence of the last ten characters. If this is the case, the prediction has to be based on a previous frequency of zero. In other words, a higher-order model will only work well after an enormous amount of text has been used to "prime" it.

On the other hand, a low-order model reduces the incidence of zero frequencies. The lowest possible order is zero. A zero-order Markov model uses single-letter frequencies as the basis for prediction. In this case, with 27 symbols, the zero-frequency problem will be encountered (at most) 27 times in any sequence, regardless of its length. The disadvantage is that zero-order models employ no contextual information for prediction.

A good way out of the dilemma is to use variable-length matching, where models of different orders are used together. A maximum value can be imposed on the order to ensure that the length of contexts stored does not grow indefinitely. However, there is no best way of combining the probabilities from the different levels to give an overall probability. One way that we have found works well in a wide range of circumstances is to ignore the predictions of all models except for the longest context actually making a prediction. The calculation of the probability of a letter is done in sequence. If a maximum order of, say, 3 is being used, then the order-3 model is consulted to see if it predicts the character. If it does, the probability predicted by that model alone is used. If it does not, the order-2 model is used to compute the probabilities of all letters not predicted by the order-3 model, and so on, until the letter which actually occurs next has been predicted. So that the receiver knows which model was used, a special pseudo-character "DOWN" is used to say that the model of next-lower order should be used.

Figure 4. Huffman codes.

Huffman codes translate each character to a fixed sequence of bits. Huffman showed that, for best compression, the length of a character's translation should be governed by its probability. The best length is equal to minus the logarithm to base 2 of the probability. If this is a whole number for all characters, then the Huffman code achieves the best compression possible for any code. The best possible compression is given by the entropy of the character probabilities.

The top half of the diagram on the next page shows a set of characters for which the entropy indicates that 1.75 bits are needed, on the average, for each character. The Huffman code allocates one bit for the A (0), two bits for B (10), and three bits for C (110) and D (111). You may wonder why B is encoded as 10 instead of simply 1. This is because the characters must be uniquely decodable from the transmitted message. If B were encoded as 1, any sequence of 0's and 1's could be decoded into just A's and B's, leaving

no possibility of transmitting C or D. Encoding A as 0 does not cause this problem, because it is the *only* code which begins with a 0. The code shown is more effective than the normal binary code, which would use two bits for each of the four symbols (00, 01, 10, 11), since then the expected number of bits per character transmitted would be 2. The code shown achieves an average of 1.75 bits per transmitted character, which is the same as the entropy. As an example, the translation of the message ABADCAAABB into the bits 01001111100001010 is shown.

The lower half of the diagram gives an example where the best Huffman code requires 2 bits per character, while the entropy indicates that 1.918 bits per character is achievable. In this case, the normal binary coding scheme 00, 01, 10, 11 is used; however, the same performance of 2 bits per character would in fact be achieved by the code 0, 10, 110, 111 used previously. Using the code shown, the message translates into 00010011100000000101.

Figure continued

Figure continued

Character	Probability p	$-\log p$	Entropy $-p \log p$	Huffman code	Expected bits/char ($p \times$ code length)
A	0.5	1	0.5	0	0.5
B	0.25	2	0.5	10	0.5
C	0.125	3	0.375	110	0.375
D	0.125	3	0.375	111	0.375
			1.75		1.75

Sample message: A   B   A   D   C   A   A   A   B   B
Character translation: 0   10   0   111   110   0   0   0   10   10
Translated message: 01001111100001010

A	0.333	1.585	0.528	00	0.667
B	0.333	1.585	0.528	01	0.667
C	0.167	2.585	0.431	10	0.333
D	0.167	2.585	0.431	11	0.333
			1.918		2.0

Sample message: A   B   A   D   C   A   A   A   B   B
Character translation: 00   01   00   11   10   00   00   00   01   01
Translated message: 0001001110000000101

As an example of how this might work in practice, suppose the maximum order is 3, and the sequence so far is

$$\cdots A\ B\ C$$

Then an order-3 model with context "*ABC*", an order-2 model with context "*BC*", an order-1 model with context "*C*", and an order-0 model are all used. If the only time *D* had occurred previously was in the sequence "*X Y Z C D*", then a *D* would be predicted by the order-0 and order-1 models but not by the order-2 or order-3 models. The order-3 model does not predict "*D*", so a DOWN is transmitted. The order-2 model does not predict "*D*", so another DOWN is transmitted. Finally the order-1 model predicts "*D*", and it is transmitted using the probability predicted by that model. So that it can be transmitted, each DOWN must be assigned a probability, and we assign it a small probability on a rather arbitrary basis. Figure 6 shows another example of the working of the coding scheme.

Using this scheme, all characters will almost always have been seen before—if only by the order-0 model. Although more than one model is used, no extra information need be stored. It turns out that the order-0, 1, and 2 models are implicit in the order-3 model. Curiously, the tree structure needed to store more than one model at a time dramatically reduces the amount of storage needed for the model. Only the sequences actually seen take up room in the computer's memory, rather than all potential sequences.

Assessing the Success of Prediction

Now that we have seen how you can make adaptive models of discrete sequences, let's return to the applications and examine how well they work in practice. One of the best ways of evaluating the quality of predictions is to use them for data compression. Then it is easy to get a quantitative indication of the success of the predictions; any reduction in the amount of data transmitted corresponds to more accurate predictions by the model. Compression is also an extremely useful application in its own right, mainly for increasing effective transmission speed over communications lines, and also for storing information on disk or tape. In the first case, the encoder and decoder work together, separated by the transmission line. They both build the same model of the text stream. The encoder encodes the next character to be sent according to the model, and then updates the model to incorporate that character. The decoder decodes the character according to its model, and then updates its model. In the second application, the computer builds a model as the file is written and uses that to do compression. The model is forgotten: it is no longer needed, for it can be reconstructed from the file just as the decoder can reconstruct it in the case of data transmission. When the file is needed, the model is reconstructed and at the same time used for decoding as the file is read back.

We have experimented with coding

□ English text;
□ bibliography files;
□ computer programs in various source languages;
□ binary machine-language computer programs;
□ conversations between an interactive computer terminal and the computer;
□ numeric data in a geophysical application;
□ black-and-white pictures;
□ gray-scale pictures.

Text Results

One sample text was a complete eleven-chapter book containing over half a million characters. It included both upper- and lowercase letters, and a good assortment of special characters. There were a significant number of tables, formatted using tabs and spaces. The whole book was coded in exactly the way depicted in Figure 6, and occupied an average of 2.2 bits per character. (Compare this with the 7 bits that are normally used.) Two bits is the quantity of information needed to select one particular member of a set containing four elements. So coding each character in 2.2 bits is like using an alphabet of about 5 different letters in the book instead of the 94 symbols that actually occurred!

Arithmetic Coding

FIGURE 5. Arithmetic coding works by dividing the fractions from 0 to 1 into ranges, one for each possible message. The length of the range is equal to the probability that the message will occur. The top diagram shows ranges as binary fractions (with their equivalents as proper fractions underneath in brackets). The ranges shown are for messages of 1, 2, and 3 characters, composed of A's which occur with probability ¾ and B's which occur with probability ¼.

It is possible to read off the translation of each message from this diagram. For example, the message AB lies in the range 0.1001 to 0.11. The shortest fraction whose extensions all lie in this range is 0.101. So the translation of AB is 101. A receiver, having seen 101, knows that the only possible two-character message starting this way is AB. (Both sender and receiver need to know beforehand that a two-character message is being sent, because there are many 3, 4 ... -character messages which start this way.) The message ABA lies in the range 0.1001 to 0.101101; the shortest fraction in this range is 0.1010, so the translation of ABA is 1010.

In practice, the computer does not remember a table of ranges in this way but calculates them "on the fly." The bottom diagrams show such a calculation of an arithmetic code for the two messages BAB (above) and ABA (below). At each step, the highest and lowest possible fractions for the message so far are remembered, and are shown in binary notation. As each character is encoded, the range is divided in proportion to the probabilities of the characters, and the appropriate subrange is chosen for the character. For example, when the first character B of BAB in the upper part is encoded, it confines the code space to the region from 0.11 to 1.00. The next character, A, confines it further to the bottom three-quarters of this region, namely from 0.1100 to 0.1111. The final character, B, confines it to the upper part of this new range, 0.111001 to 0.1111.

In practice, not all of the bits in the fractions need be remembered or transmitted as part of the final translation. The sender need only transmit a binary fraction that uniquely identifies the final range. In the BAB example it could transmit, for example, 0.111001—but not 0.1111, since there are numbers lying above the range that begin this way. A clever encoder will transmit the shortest fraction that uniquely identifies the range—in this case, 0.11101. Of course, it need not transmit the initial "0.". Moreover, as soon as the first bits of the high and low fractions are equal, they can be transmitted immediately as part of the translation and forgotten by the sender. The bits transmitted at each step are shown in italic; only the remaining nonitalic bits are retained.

1.0
0.111111 (63/64) BBB
BB BBA
0.1111 (15/16) BAB
B
BA 0.111001 (57/64) BAA

0.11 (3/4)
ABB
AB 0.101101 (45/64)
ABA
0.1001 (9/16)

A AAB

0.011011 (27/64)
AA
AAA

0

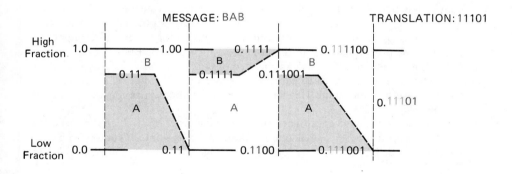

MESSAGE: BAB   TRANSLATION: 11101

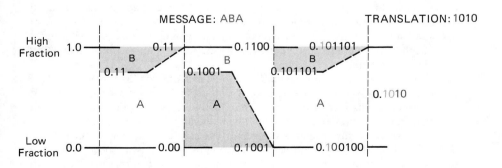

MESSAGE: ABA   TRANSLATION: 1010

One reason for such excellent compression is that the book was long enough for an accurate model to be formed by the time the end was reached. However, significant gains are also achieved in shorter texts. A single chapter (45,000 characters from a 76-letter alphabet) was coded with 2.8 bits per character, and a short abstract (3,600 characters from a 61-letter alphabet) required 3.8 bits.

Similar coding efficiencies are achieved with other kinds of text, such as computer programs in source form. However, binary machine-language programs and binary numeric data cannot be encoded so efficiently. They generally contain much less redundancy than languages designed for use by people.

Picture Results

When we use the same methods to encode two-dimensional data in the form of black-and-white and grey-scale pictures, the best way of providing

Compressing a Snippet from *Hamlet*

$\triangleright$

FIGURE 6. Here is an example of the compression method in action. Hamlet's famous soliloquy on existentialism is being transmitted (in lowercase only). The next letter to be processed is the second *b*.

The diagram depicts the state of the encoder. It is working with a maximum context length of four characters preceding the one to be transmitted. The second *b* has not yet been encountered in its order-4 context, so the order-3 context is used. An escape code is transmitted first to suppress the order-4 interpretation, and then the probability of *b* in the order-3 context is sent. Both of these values are arithmetically encoded into a sequence of bits. Since *b* is the only character yet to have been encountered in this particular order-3 context, its probability will be close to 1 (not quite 1 because room in the code space must be reserved for the escape code).

The decoder will have constructed the same dictionary. The first bits are decoded into the escape code, which tells it not to attempt order-4 interpretation. The next bits are decoded, and the result looked up against the order-3 context to recover the *b*.

Now both encoder and decoder update their dictionaries. In this case, the prediction *b* should be inserted with the current order-4 context; and frequency counts associated with order-0, order-1, order-2, order-3, and order-4 contexts should be updated. In other cases, only a frequency update would be required. Although it looks as though the model will require a large amount of storage, since all contexts must be remembered.

Although it is easiest to conceptualize first the escape code, and then the order-3 probability being transmitted, one after the other, in fact they cannot necessarily be discerned as distinct sequences of bits in the coded output. The arithmetic coding method does not treat each symbol independently, but accumulates a code for the message so far, which is extended to a greater or lesser extent by each new symbol. In this way, high-probability symbols (such as the occurrence of *b* in this context in the order-3 model) may consume less than one bit of the code space.

next character

to□be□or□not□to□be,□that□ ...

add □to□b →

model

context

string	prob
...	...
to□b	...
o□b	...
□b	...
□o	...
□n	...
□t	...
...	...

□to□
to□
o□
□

←— longest match —→

probability of DOWN (skip order-4 context)
probability of b   (from longest match)

arithmetic
coding

sequence of bits
for transmission

context for the model-builder is to use a binary image tree and transmit the tree from the top down. This gives the advantage that images are built up progressively over the whole screen.

Typical pictures with 8-bit grey levels can be coded with 65% of the number of bits in the original picture, while the corresponding figure for 4-bit grey levels is below 50%. Greater gains are achievable for pictures which are only black or white, like text or line drawings. Then each pixel can be coded in about 0.18 bits, instead of the 1 bit which is necessary to distinguish black from white. It is remarkable that the convenience of progressive transmission can be combined with significant compression in this way. Note that in all cases the coding is *exact:* the reconstructed picture is identical, bit for bit, with the original. There is absolutely no degradation in the pictures. Of course, any noise in the original is faithfully transmitted too, which accounts for the relatively poor results with 8-bit grey levels. The low-order bit or two is probably effectively random, and the encoder and decoder go to great pains to reproduce this useless data correctly!

Retrospect

Looking back, what have we learned? Prediction of discrete sequences like the characters of text is quite possible for a machine, just as it is for a person. All predictions are based on a mode of the sequence of events. People draw on a vast store of knowledge to accomplish prediction; their models are copious and diffuse, replete with structure of all kinds. More-over, people are adaptable, and can easily accumulate new information from experience. Machines are not so well equipped. The most useful kind of model we have found for prediction is a variant of the Markov model, which incorporates variable-length matching. Relying on purely lexical information, such a relatively narrow-minded model is impotent compared with those used by people. But it can adapt quite successfully to the character of the sequences it sees, "learning" from experience by stashing away stretches of the sequence in a tree structure.

The easiest way to measure the success of a machine that foretells the future by adaptive modeling is to test its efficiency at data compression. In order to do this, we were compelled to review some results in coding theory; in particular, the superior performance of the recently-developed method of arithmetic coding as compared with traditional Huffman coding. This technique gives virtually optimal coding (in terms of entropy), and so focuses attention on the effectiveness of the adaptive modeling method used for prediction.

When arithmetic coding is combined with variable-length modeling, the results are pretty impressive—ordinary mixed-case text coded in 2.2 bits per character, for example, or black-and-white pictures coded in 0.18 bits per pixel. This is even more startling when one considers that in each case the machine begins with an empty memory, with no prior knowledge at all about the sort of sequences to expect—it learns everything it knows on the job, so to speak. This is a fine illustration that adaptive modeling really does accomplish prediction successfully. On text, for example, the 2.2 bits that on the average are needed to encode each character are equivalent to selecting the character from an alphabet of five instead of the 100-odd symbols that actually occur.

But data compression is by no means the only application for adaptive modeling techniques. You can model *users* of an interactive computer system, and predict their actions—to a limited extent. The reactive keyboard predicts what characters will be typed next, and uses this to form a menu display, thereby dispensing with a conventional keyboard. This does not rival traditional keyboard input, but can complement it in some special situations. The self-programming calculator models the sequence of keystrokes involved in a computation, and allows repetitive operations to be programmed "by example." Again, this does not supersede traditional computer programming, but could replace it in certain kinds of tasks.

Unless they are unusually insightful and prophetic, people foretelling the future tend to forecast a "default" or expected sequence of events, based on an extrapolation of history. So do our machines: they lack creativity and real inspiration. Perhaps that is why we are writing this article instead of living it up in Las Vegas.

Further Reading

Huffman, D.A. "A Method for the Construction of Minimum-Redundancy Codes." *Proceedings of the Institute of Radio Engineers* **40** (1952):1698.

Shannon, C.E., and Weaver, W. *The Mathematical Theory of Communication.* Urbana, IL: The University of Illinois Press, 1949.

Wiener, N. *Extrapolation, Interpolation and Smoothing of Stationary Time Series.* Cambridge, MA: M.I.T. Press, 1947.

Automating Reasoning

How to use a computer to help solve problems requiring logical reasoning.

Larry Wos

How can a single computer program correctly solve the following problems and puzzles? How can you determine whether its answers are correct or not? How would you correctly solve each of the problems and puzzles?

☐ The first problem concerns computer programs and their reliability. You are given a subroutine for finding the maximum element of any given array. You must give a proof that the code performs as claimed, or find a counterexample and thus demonstrate that the code contains a bug.

☐ For the second problem, you are given three checkerboards missing various squares (see Figures 1, 2, and 3). You are also given an adequate supply of one-square by two-square dominoes. The problem is to determine which, if any, of the checkerboards can be precisely covered with dominoes. (Puzzles of this type are reminiscent of layout problems.)

☐ In the third problem, you are given the design of a circuit that supposedly meets certain specifications (see Figure 4). It is required to take as input x and y (with x above y) and yield as output y and x (with y above x), and without any crossing wires. The goal is to prove that the design meets the specifications. (Avoiding crossing wires is often important in layout problems.)

☐ The fourth problem—sometimes known as the "fruit puzzle"—is one

---

LARRY WOS is a senior mathematician in the Mathematics and Computer Science Division at Argonne National Laboratory. He has written numerous articles on automated theorem proving and automated reasoning, and lectured extensively on both topics. He recently coauthored the book *Automated Reasoning: Introduction and Applications,* and has written a companion to this book, *Automated Reasoning: 33 Basic Research Problems,* which will be published in 1987; he is also editor-in-chief of the *Journal of Automated Reasoning,* and president of the Association for Automated Reasoning. Dr. Wos is currently conducting research at Argonne National Laboratory on the formulation of more effective inference rules and more powerful strategies for automated reasoning.
Reprinted from ABACUS, Volume 2, Number 3, Spring 1985.

that Sherlock Holmes would have solved with a flourish. There are three boxes, respectively labeled APPLES, ORANGES, and BANANAS (see Figure 5). Unfortunately, each box is mislabeled. You are correctly told that each box contains exactly one of the three kinds of fruit, and no two boxes contain the same kind. You are also correctly told that box 2— the one labeled ORANGES—actually contains apples. You are asked to determine the contents of boxes 1 and 3, and then, just as important, prove that your answer is correct. (This problem will be used later to illustrate various concepts in automated reasoning.)

□ The fifth and final problem can be viewed as a problem in circuit design or a problem in computer programming. From the viewpoint of circuit design, you are asked to design a circuit that will return the signals *not(x)*, *not(y)*, and *not(z)*, when *x*, *y*, and *z* are input to it (see Figure 6). The task would be trivial were it not for one important constraint. You can use as many AND and OR gates as you like, but you cannot use more than two NOT gates. From the viewpoint of assembly language programming, you are asked to write a program that will store in locations *U*, *V*, and *W* the 1s complement of locations *x*, *y*, and *z*. You can use as many COPY, OR, and AND instructions as you like, but you cannot use more than two COMP (1s complement) instructions.

The way a single computer program can correctly solve the five problems, and the way you can also, is by using reasoning—logical reasoning. The way to determine whether the answers given by a program using logical reasoning are correct is by "asking" it for a "proof." When such a request is made, a reasoning program can explicitly give every step used in its reasoning, and also cite precisely which facts were used to reach each conclusion. You can then check any step you question. (A detailed discussion of all but the first of the five problems, as well as an expanded treatment of the concepts and applications of automated reasoning discussed in this article, can be found in the book *Automated Reasoning: Introduction and Applications* by Wos, Overbeek, Lusk, and Boyle, published by Prentice-Hall.)

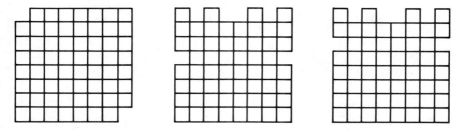

FIGURES 1, 2, and 3. Which of these checkerboards can be precisely covered with dominoes? [*Automated Reasoning Programs* by L. Wos, July 1984. Reprinted with permission of SIAM. Copyright 1984 by SIAM.]

Since you may have already solved some or all of the five problems, you might be curious about how well reasoning programs do when given those same problems. Some of them do very well. For example, each of the five problems has been solved by a single program—the automated reasoning program AURA (AUtomated Reasoning Assistant). But what is automated reasoning—and what are the answers to the five problems?

What Automated Reasoning Is

Automated reasoning is the study of how the computer can be programmed to assist in that part of problem solving that requires reasoning. *Reasoning* as used here means logical reasoning, not probabilistic or common-sense reasoning. Each conclusion that is reached must follow inevitably from the facts from which it is drawn. If a conclusion is false but obtained with logical reasoning, then at least one of the facts from which it is obtained is false. Using a computer program that reasons logically thus assures you of obtaining totally accurate information, providing you give it totally accurate information to begin with. Such a program, if it gives you access to an appropriate array of choices, can be used effectively as an automated reasoning assistant.

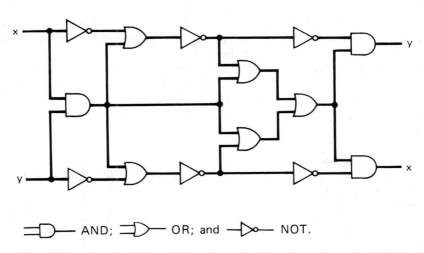

FIGURE 4. The circuit design puzzle. Does the circuit produce the outputs as shown? [Wos/Overbeek/Lusk/Boyle, *Automated Reasoning: Introduction & Applications,* © 1984, p. 244. Reprinted by permission of Prentice-Hall, Inc., Englewood Cliffs, New Jersey.]

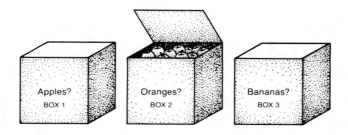

FIGURE 5. Mislabeled boxes of fruit. [*Automated Reasoning Programs* by L. Wos, September 1984. Reprinted with permission of SIAM. Copyright 1984 by SIAM.]

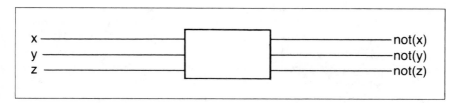

FIGURE 6. The inverter problem. Can you design it with no more than two NOTs? [*Automated Reasoning Programs* by L. Wos, July 1984. Reprinted with permission of SIAM. Copyright 1984 by SIAM.]

History of Automated Reasoning

From one viewpoint, the challenging and exciting field of automated reasoning was invented, evolved, or simply identified in 1980. (For those interested in the precise history of terms, the term *automated reasoning* was introduced by the author in 1980 in a discussion at Argonne National Laboratory.) From another viewpoint, the field can be traced to the work in automated theorem proving, a field in which the first significant research occurred in the early 1960s. That research immediately led to programs that could prove some simple theorems in mathematics. Although those programs were not very powerful, especially compared to those in existence now, they provided an important beginning. In fact, were it not for those programs and the concepts that were formulated based on experiments with them, the entire field of automated reasoning might not exist today.

The main difference between automated theorem proving and automated reasoning is the way in which the corresponding computer programs are used. In most cases, a theorem-proving program is used to find proofs of purported theorems. An automated reasoning program, on the other hand, is often used simply to find information of various kinds. While one use of automated reasoning is in fact proving theorems, other uses include finding models and counterexamples, assisting in formulating conjectures, and simply drawing conclusions from some set of hypotheses. Applications include designing logic circuits, proving properties of computer programs, writing computer programs, and conducting research in mathematics.

In contrast to the early 1960s, surprisingly powerful automated reasoning programs now exist. The general-purpose reasoning program AURA has provided invaluable assistance in answering various previously open questions in mathematics and in formal logic. Boyer and Moore's program-verification system has been used to verify an encryption algorithm currently in use. Good's program-verification system has verified a 4200-line Gypsy program that is an encryption packet interface to the ARPANET.

In addition to these three programs, one other program deserves mention, especially in view of its use. That program is LMA (Logic Machine Architecture). While each of the three previously mentioned programs is employed to "reason" about some situation, LMA is employed to "produce" reasoning programs tailored to given specifications. LMA offers mechanisms at the subroutine level that encode the various processes you will learn about in this article. It is portable (written in Pascal) and modular in design, and it and the reasoning program ITP produced with it have been ported to various machines including the VAX, PERQ, Apollo, Ridge, and IBM 3033. To use LMA or ITP requires approximately one megabyte of memory. (LMA was designed and implemented by Overbeek, Lusk, and McCune; AURA was designed and implemented by Overbeek, with contributions from Lusk, Winker, and Smith. Overbeek, Lusk, McCune, and Smith are currently active as members of the Argonne National Laboratory automated reasoning group.)

The Basic Elements of Automated Reasoning

For an automated reasoning program to assist you, you need a language (of the type to be illustrated shortly) for communicating with the program. After selecting the problem or question to study, you must have a means for telling the program what the problem is about. Ordinary language does not suffice. It is too ambiguous, and too often relies on connotation and implicit information. What is needed is a language that removes ambiguity, and forces the user to state the required information explicitly rather than trusting to connotation. Since reasoning programs have little or no knowledge on their own, you must adequately describe the concepts and relationships involved in the problem under attack, and you must follow the conventions required by the particular reasoning program you are using. As you will see later, you are sometimes forced to include mundane and obvious facts.

While the burden of describing the problem in detail rests with you, the burden of drawing conclusions rests with the program. The better reasoning programs offer a variety of ways of reasoning, some of which will be illustrated later. For example, one type takes very small reasoning steps, another takes moderate-size steps, and a third automatically substitutes one term for another when they are known to be equal. You can either choose the way(s) of reasoning you deem best for the problem at hand, or you can rely on the program's default choice. Since the type of reasoning used in solving one problem is often not effective in solving the next problem being studied, access to a number of ways of reasoning—inference rules—is very advantageous.

Even with effective inference rules, still more is needed. Neither you nor an automated reasoning program should be turned loose to draw conclusions without regard to their relevance to the question being investigated. Such uncontrolled reasoning will prevent you or a reasoning program from reaching the goal, for entirely too many irrelevant conclusions will be drawn. What is needed is strategy—strategy to *direct* the search for information and, even more important, strategy to *restrict* the search. Both types of strategy will be illustrated.

In addition to a precise language, effective ways of reasoning, and powerful strategies, two additional components are essential for a reasoning program to be very useful. First, a means for automatically rephrasing and rewriting information into a normal (standard) form must be available. In many cases, there are far too many ways to express the same fact or relationship. For example, facts about "my father's father's brother's son" can be rephrased as facts about "my second cousin." Similarly, $"-(-a)"$ can be replaced by $"a,"$ $"b + 0"$ by $"b,"$ and $"c(d + e)"$ by $"cd + ce."$ The normal form to be used, as the last example shows, is not necessarily the simplest possible form. The user of the program can decide which, if any, normal forms are preferred. Although retention of information in more than one form provides alternative paths from which to reason, many of those paths often lead to the same conclusion. Such duplication can sharply interfere with the effectiveness of a reasoning program—or with your effectiveness—when trying to solve some problem or answer some question.

However, even with a means for automatically rephrasing information into a normal form and thus enhancing the effectiveness of reasoning programs, a second procedure is needed for automatically removing both redundant and less general information. For example, drawing and retaining the conclusion that "Sheila is a teacher" once is sufficient; retention of additional copies of that fact serves no purpose. Such redundancy obviously should be avoided—by a reasoning program or by a person attempting to solve some given problem. Also to be avoided is retention of a new fact when some already-known fact is more general—contains the same information that the new fact does, and more. For example, knowing that "all people are female or male" should cause a reasoning program to discard the conclusion that "Kim is female or male." For a somewhat different example, if a program "knows" that "Sheila is a teacher," the conclusion that "Sheila is a teacher or a nurse" should be discarded because it contains less information. Given either of these examples of *more general* versus *less general* information, you and your reasoning program would usually prefer keeping the more informative. Retaining more general information in preference to less general contributes to effective problem solving. Just as the presence of the same information in a number of different forms can interfere markedly with a reasoning program's (or your) attempt to solve a problem, so also can the presence of either redundant or less general information interfere markedly.

A Language Some Reasoning Programs Understand

If you have ever written a computer program, you know that you cannot simply tell a computer in everyday language what you wish it to do. Similarly, you cannot use everyday language to present the problem under attack to an automated reasoning program. What you must do is observe certain conventions of the language your particular reasoning program "understands." Of the various languages "understood" by reasoning programs, perhaps the most common is the *language of clauses*—a language that is, for example, understood by AURA and by ITP. Rather than giving a formal discussion of that language, various examples will suffice.

The following pairs of statements—first in everyday language, and then in a language acceptable to many automated reasoning programs—show how various information is translated into "clauses." In the "clause language," "not" can be represented with " ¬ ", and "or" with " | ". (A convention observed by AURA and ITP is to write predicates such as "married" in uppercase and functions such as "sum" in lowercase. Both programs treat EQUAL as a built-in predicate, a predicate that does not require inclusion of such axioms as symmetry, transitivity, and substitutivity.)

> Nan is pretty
> PRETTY(Nan)

> Nan is married
> MARRIED(Nan)

> Shiela is a teacher
> HASAJOB(Sheila,teacher)

Sheila is not a boxer
¬ HASAJOB(Sheila,boxer)

Sheila is a teacher or a nurse
HASAJOB(Sheila,teacher)
 | HASAJOB(Sheila,nurse)

$c(d + e) = cd + ce$
EQUAL(prod(c,sum(d,e)),
  sum(prod(c,d),prod(c,e)))

Just as you can easily convey specific information with clauses, you can also convey general information.

all people are female or male
FEMALE(x) | MALE(x)

The "variable" x is automatically interpreted by the program as "for all", for any value that is substituted for x. In fact, in the language of clauses, all variables are treated as meaning "for all". The program "knows" that a well-formed expression is a variable by observing the convention that all well-formed expressions beginning with (lowercase) u through z are variables, and any variable must begin with (lowercase) u through z. (Although variables could be declared, the given convention is one currently observed by various reasoning programs such as AURA and ITP.) The ability to represent general information by simply writing the appropriate clause(s) has a variety of uses. For example, it is far preferable simply to write the general form for distributing product over sum

$x(y + z) = xy + xz$
(for all x, y, and z)

as

EQUAL(prod(x,sum(y,z)),
  sum(prod(x,y),prod(x,z)))

than to write some instance of it involving c, d, and e. (Directly using mathematical notation rather than using equivalent statements in clause form is acceptable to many reasoning programs as well.)

Three additional conventions are present in this language—one for "and", one for "if-then", and one for "there exists". The operator "and" is used, but only implicitly. For example, to translate the fact that

Nan is pretty "and" intelligent

requires two clauses. The clauses

PRETTY(Nan)
INTELLIGENT(Nan)

will do. The program automatically "understands" that between each pair of clauses there is an implicit occurrence of "and".

As for "if-then", it is replaced by using "not" and "or". Instead of translating (directly) "if x is female, then x is not male," you translate "x is not female, or x is not male."

for all x, x is not female or x is not male
$$\neg \, \text{FEMALE}(x) \mid \neg \, \text{MALE}(x)$$

No information is lost—and this is one point that sometimes presents some difficulty—since "if P, then Q" is logically equivalent to "not P, or Q" (see the truth table in Figure 7).

P	Q	not P	(not P) or Q	if P then Q
true	true	false	true	true
true	false	false	false	false
false	true	true	true	true
false	false	true	true	true

FIGURE 7. Truth table for equivalence of *if-then* with *not-or*.

Finally, to express the "existence" of something, you introduce an appropriate *constant* or *function*. If you wish to write a clause for the statement

there exists some kind of fruit in box 2

the clause

CONTAINS(box2,a)

suffices. The constant a is the name of the kind of fruit that exists in box 2; you "name" the kind of fruit. In other words, you use names with the reasoning program as you frequently do with a co-worker. For example, you give the "name" 7 to the integer that exists (strictly) between 6 and 8; you use an appropriate constant. On the other hand, some facts about existence require use of an appropriate *function:*

for all integers x, there exists a number greater than x and a number less than x

GREATERTHAN(f(x),x)
LESSTHAN(g(x),x)

Two clauses are required because of the "and" in the statement: two different functions, $f(x)$ and $g(x)$, are required to express the two existences.

How might you translate into clauses the following statement? Given arrays a, b, and c, for every pair x, y such that x is in a and x is an integer and y is in b and y is an integer, there exists an element z in c, (strictly) between x and y, such that z is an integer. Since this translation illustrates what you might be required to do to use an automated reasoning program, you might wish to attempt it before looking at the answer that follows immediately.

for every integer pair x, y with x in a and y in b, there is an element $h(x,y)$ in c

$\neg$ EL(x,a) | $\neg$ INT(x) | $\neg$ EL(y,b) | $\neg$ INT(y) | EL(h(x,y),c)

for every integer pair x, y with x in a and y in b, $h(x,y)$ is greater than x

$\neg$ EL(x,a) | $\neg$ INT(x) | $\neg$ EL(y,b) | $\neg$ INT(y)
| GREATERTHAN(h(x,y),x)

for every integer pair x,y with x in a and y in b, $h(x,y)$ is less than y

$\neg$ EL(x,a) | $\neg$ INT(x) | $\neg$ EL(y,b) | $\neg$ INT(y)
| LESSTHAN(h(x,y),y)

for every integer pair x,y with x in a and y in b, $h(x,y)$ is an integer

$\neg$ EL(x,a) | $\neg$ INT(x) | $\neg$ EL(y,b) | $\neg$ INT(y) | INT(h(x,y))

The language of clauses is richer than it might appear; the set of clauses just given is not the only acceptable answer (see Figure 8). As in writing any program—or, for that matter, in language in general—you have some freedom in how you express information. However, you must observe the requirements of using variables to replace "for every" or "for all" statements, using constants or functions to replace "exists" statements, and relying on the explicit use of "not" and "or" within a clause and the implicit use of "and" between clauses. By doing so, as you will

---

for every integer pair x,y with x in a and y in b, there is an element $h(xa,x,yb,y)$ in c
$\neg$EQUAL(EVAL(a,xa),x) | $\neg$ INT(x) | $\neg$ EQUAL(EVAL(b, yb),y) | $\neg$ INT(y)
| EQUAL(EVAL(c,j(xa,x,yb,y)),h(xa,x,yb,y))

for every integer pair x,y with x in a and y in b, $h(xa,x,yb,y)$ is greater than x
$\neg$EQUAL(EVAL(a,xa),x) | $\neg$ INT(x) | $\neg$ EQUAL(EVAL(b,yb),y) | $\neg$ INT(y)
| GREATERTHAN(h(xa,x,yb,y),x)

for every integer pair x,y with x in a and y in b, $h(xa,x,yb,y)$ is less than y
$\neg$EQUAL(EVAL(z,xa),x) | $\neg$ INT(x) | $\neg$ EQUAL(EVAL(b,yb),y) | $\neg$ INT(y)
| LESSTHAN(h(xa,x,yb,y),y)

for every integer pair x,y with x in a and y in b, $h(xa,x,yb,y)$ is an integer
$\neg$ EQUAL(EVAL(a,xa),x) | $\neg$ INT(x) | $\neg$ EQUAL(EVAL(b,yb),y) | $\neg$ INT(y)
| INT(h(xa,x,yb,y))

FIGURE 8. Translation of program verification statements into automated reasoning clauses.

shortly see, you can have a reasoning program provide flawless assistance for solving a number of different problems requiring (logical) reasoning.

How Such Programs Reason

An automated reasoning program usually offers you a variety of ways of reasoning, called "inference rules," from which to choose. Almost all of the inference rules are based on just two operations, *canceling* one part of a clause against a part of another clause, and *substituting* expressions for variables in a clause.

As an example of *canceling*, the two clauses

$$\text{FEMALE(Kim)}$$
$$\neg \text{FEMALE(Kim)} \mid \neg \text{MALE(Kim)}$$

together (logically) imply the conclusion

$$\neg \text{MALE(Kim)}$$

by canceling FEMALE(Kim) with ¬ FEMALE(Kim). For, if you know that "Kim is female" and that "Kim is not female or not male," then it follows logically that "Kim is not male." (You cannot conclude from "Kim is female" alone that "Kim is not male"; as Sherlock Holmes or Mr. Spock of "Star Trek" would say, "The conclusion does not follow logically." Here you have an example of the kind of implicit information that is often used by *people* but that must be given explicitly to a reasoning program, namely, that "all people are not female or not male." As you will see later, while being forced to supply such information is a nuisance, it does have some advantages.)

To see how substituting for variables comes into play, two clauses closely related to the preceding two will suffice. The two clauses

$$\text{FEMALE(Kim)}$$
$$\neg \text{FEMALE}(x) \mid \neg \text{MALE}(x)$$

together (logically) imply the conclusion

$$\neg \text{MALE(Kim)}$$

by first substituting Kim for the variable x in the second clause to obtain temporarily a new second clause   [¬ FEMALE(Kim) | ¬ MALE(Kim)], and then applying cancellation to the new pair of clauses. To see that the conclusion is valid, first note that the second clause can be read as "for all x, x is not female or not male." Then note that "Kim is not female or not male" follows trivially from the second clause by merely substituting *Kim* for x. By applying the kind of reasoning used in the preceding paragraph to explain "canceling," the validity of the conclusion is established.

Both examples, that illustrating "canceling" and that illustrating "substituting," are covered by one inference rule, *binary resolution*. A two-step explanation provides an intuitive justification for the name of this inference rule. First, the rule always simultaneously considers two clauses from which to attempt to draw a conclusion, hence "binary." Second, the rule attempts to resolve the question of what is the maximum common ground covered by obvious consequences of the two clauses, hence "resolution." In the first of the two examples of this section, no effort is required to find the common ground; no substitution for variables is necessary to permit an obvious cancellation. In the second example, however, to find the common ground requires substituting *Kim* for the variable x in the second clause. The conclusions yielded by applying binary resolution always follow logically from the pairs of statements to which it is applied. Of course, if one of the statements is false, then the conclusion may (but still might not) be false. What inference rules used by an automated reasoning program promise is "logical soundness"—the conclusions that are drawn follow inevitably from the statements from which they are drawn.

In addition to this vital logical property of being "sound," the rules draw as general a conclusion as possible, which is why the word *maximum* was used when discussing "common ground." For example, binary resolution applied to the two clauses

$\neg$ HASAJOB(x,nurse) | MALE(x)
(for all x, x is not a nurse or x is male)

$\neg$ FEMALE(y) | $\neg$ MALE(y)
(for all y, y is not female or y is not male)

yields the clause

$\neg$ HASAJOB(x,nurse) | $\neg$ FEMALE(x)
(for all x, x is not a nurse or x is not female)

as the conclusion. It does not yield

$\neg$ HASAJOB(Kim,nurse) | $\neg$ FEMALE(Kim)
(Kim is not a nurse or Kim is not female)

which also follows logically from the two given clauses. This last conclusion simply lacks the generality required by the kind of inference rules employed by automated reasoning programs.

Unfortunately, binary resolution is not ordinarily effective enough, for its use usually yields too many conclusions, each representing too small a step of reasoning. As you will see when the puzzle about boxes of fruit is solved by a reasoning program, refinements of binary solution exist that yield larger reasoning steps because they can be applied to clauses taken two at a time, three at a time, and more.

A Reasoning Program Solves the Fruit Puzzle

In the fourth problem—the "fruit puzzle"—given at the beginning of this article, you are asked to determine the contents of two of the three boxes of fruit. (You are correctly told that box 2 contains apples.) Perhaps more interesting, you are also asked to "prove" your answer correct. Of the various types of proof, *proof by contradiction* will be the choice, for that is the usual form of proof found by an automated reasoning program. A proof by contradiction consists of a sequence of steps of reasoning that starts with statements taken from the problem under study, together with the additional assumption of the falseness of what you are trying to prove, and ends with a statement that contradicts some earlier statement in the sequence. One reason for seeking this form of proof is that it provides a means for a reasoning program to "know" that it has succeeded in completing the assigned task. For the fruit puzzle, for example, the search for such a proof could begin by first adding a "false" assumption about the contents of, say, box 1, with the object of eventually finding a contradiction. If a contradiction is found, then the falseness of the assumption will have been discovered, and the actual contents of box 1 will be known.

In particular, you might begin with the "false" assumption that box 1 does not contain bananas. You could then reason to a contradiction in this way:

□ First, box 1 does not contain apples, for box 2 does.

□ Second, box 1 must then contain oranges, from the preceding conclusion and the false assumption.

□ Third, by arguing as in drawing the first conclusion, box 3 does not contain apples.

□ Fourth, from the second conclusion, box 3 does not contain oranges.

□ Fifth, box 3 must then contain bananas.

□ Since, according to the puzzle, every box is mislabeled, and therefore its label cannot match its contents, your sixth conclusion might be that box 3 is not labeled BANANAS. But box 3 is, in fact, labeled BANANAS, and you have completed a proof by contradiction.

(Although giving such an argument can be tedious, explicit and detailed reasoning, supplied by a person or by a reasoning program, has the advantage of permitting the argument to be totally checked for validity.)

An automated reasoning program, given an appropriate inference rule, can find a proof (expressed in clauses) identical to the one just completed. To give the steps of that proof, the description of the puzzle must first be translated into an appropriate set of clauses, as is done immediately. If some of the clauses seem unclear, the comments that precede them may help.

box 2 contains apples
(1) CONTAINS(box2, apples)

boxes 1, 2, and 3 are respectively labeled APPLES, ORANGES, BANANAS
(2) LABEL(box1,apples)
(3) LABEL(box2,oranges)
(4) LABEL(box3,bananas)

each of the boxes contains apples, bananas, or oranges
(5) CONTAINS(xbox,apples) | CONTAINS(xbox,bananas)
    | CONTAINS(xbox,oranges)

each box is mislabeled
(6) ¬ LABEL(xbox,yfruit) | ¬ CONTAINS(xbox,yfruit)

no fruit is contained in more than one box
(7) EQUAL(xbox,ybox) | ¬ CONTAINS(xbox,zfruit)
    | ¬ CONTAINS(ybox,zfruit)

there are three (distinct) boxes
(8) ¬ EQUAL(box1,box2)
(9) ¬ EQUAL(box2,box3)
(10) ¬ EQUAL(box1,box3)

box 1 does not contain bananas
(11) ¬ CONTAINS(box1,bananas)

Before giving a proof that an automated reasoning program might give, a few comments about the clauses will fill in some gaps and provide a review of what has already been discussed. Clause 11 is not part of the puzzle description; it corresponds to denying the true situation; its purpose is to enable the program to seek a contradiction and, if one is found, provide a means for the program to "know" it has succeeded. Clauses 1 through 10 are sufficient for solving the puzzle, but they provide no means for the program to "know" when the puzzle has been solved. Without a clause such as clause 11 and the proof by contradiction it leads to, a typical reasoning program would most likely continue reasoning even after the solution had been found. The presence of clause 11 does not mean that you need to know the correct answer about the contents of box 1; clause 11 merely represents denying one of the possibilities being true. (What happens when clause 11 is replaced by a clause that denies the other obvious possibility—the possibility that box 1 contains oranges—is discussed in the next paragraph.) In clause 5, the variable *xbox* implicitly ranges over all possible boxes. By convention, all well-formed expressions beginning with u through z are automatically treated as variables meaning "for all."

In clause 6, the variable *xbox* implicitly ranges over all boxes, while the variable *yfruit* implicitly ranges over all types of fruit in the puzzle. It is obtained by translating the corresponding clue in the puzzle first into "if a box *x* is labeled *y,* then it cannot contain *y,*" and then translating the *if-then* into clause form using the fact that "if *P,* then *Q*" is logically equivalent to "not *P,* or *Q.*" Clause 7 can be obtained by taking actions similar to those taken to obtain clause 6, and using the fact that "not(not(*P*))" is logically equivalent to "*P*." Clauses 8, 9, and 10 are examples of the kind of mundane information, as commented earlier, you are sometimes forced to include. Finally, for those who wish to know the whole story, clauses 1 through 10—although sufficient for illustrative purposes—do not capture all of the information in the puzzle. For example, no clause is given for the fact that each box contains exactly one kind of fruit. You might give your representation in clause form for this fact.

In place of clause 11 denying that box 1 contains bananas, you could give the reasoning program

$$(11') \neg \text{CONTAINS(box1,oranges)}$$

denying the possibility that box 1 contains oranges. Since, as it turns out, clause 11' does not represent false information, a program reasoning from 11' together with clauses 1 through 10 could never find a proof by contradiction. Among other effects, the program would not "know" when the task had been completed. In such a situation—when given a set of clauses from which no proof by contradiction can be obtained—a reasoning program will run out of time, or run out of memory, or run out of conclusions to draw. In the case under discussion, the program will run out of conclusions to draw. Although among the conclusions drawn from clause 11' together with clauses 1 through 10 will be the statements (true, as it turns out) that box 1 contains bananas and box 3 contains oranges, you cannot simply consider the problem solved. The truth of deduced statements depends on the truth of the statements in the history of the deduction of the corresponding clauses.

Conclusions drawn from false statements, as remarked earlier, may be false. In particular, if clause 11' is in the history of some deduced clause, the "truth" of that clause is in doubt, since 11' represents an assumption that may be false. Since using clause 11' in place of clause 11 does not lead to a proof by contradiction, the truth or falseness of 11' remains in doubt. On the other hand, since using clause 11 can lead to a proof by contradiction, the falseness of 11 can be established. In short, when trying to solve this problem, you do not know whether to use 11 or 11'. If you try the latter first, the result will be inconclusive, and you would then naturally try the former and obtain a solution. To understand more fully what can happen when clause 11 is replaced with clause 11', you might write down a proof that parallels the following one.

The following proof by contradiction, equivalent to the one cited earlier, does establish that box 1 contains bananas. Rather than using binary resolution (discussed in the preceding section) as the rule for drawing conclusions, the rule to be used will be *UR-resolution*. UR-resolution is a more powerful inference rule than binary resolution: it is not constrained to consider only two clauses at a time; it is required to draw simple conclusions—clauses that contain no occurrence of " | " ("or") and contain at least one symbol. For example, simultaneous consideration by UR-resolution of the three clauses

FEMALE(Gail)

(Gail is female)

HASCHILDREN(Gail)

(Gail has children)

¬ FEMALE(x) | ¬ HASCHILDREN(x) | MOTHER(x)

(females who have children are mothers)

yields

MOTHER(Gail)

(Gail is a mother)

as the conclusion. If the second of these three clauses is replaced by

¬ MOTHER(Gail)

(Gail is not a mother)

UR-resolution applied to the new set of three clauses yields

¬ HASCHILDREN(Gail)

(Gail has no children)

as the conclusion. The two conclusions are examples of *unit clauses*. UR-resolution (unit-resulting) derives its name from the requirement of yielding unit clauses as conclusions.

Here is the promised proof.

From clauses 8, 1, and 7:
(12) ¬ CONTAINS(box1,apples)

From clauses 12, 11, and 5:
(13) CONTAINS(box1,oranges)

From clauses 9, 1, and 7:
(14) ¬ CONTAINS(box3,apples)

From clauses 10, 13, and 7:
(15) ¬ CONTAINS(box3,oranges)

From clauses 14, 15, and 5:
(16) CONTAINS(box3,bananas)

From clauses 16 and 6:
(17) ¬ LABEL(box3,bananas)

Since clauses 17 and 4 contradict each other, a "proof by contradiction" has been found (see Figure 9). The assumption, clause 11, that box 1 does not contain bananas is proved false—the other 10 clauses come from the puzzle description—so box 1 does, in fact, contain that fruit.

If you are puzzled by the fact that various clauses—such as clause 13—in the proof are actually "false," the explanation lies with the rigor of logical reasoning. The program is simply drawing conclusions that follow logically from the given information. Since clause 11 is "false," it is not surprising that some clauses having clause 11 in their ancestry are also "false." Clauses representing false information are to be expected, for here the program is, after all, seeking a "proof by contradiction."

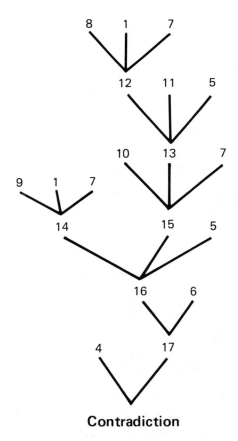

Contradiction

FIGURE 9. Proof by contradiction: a "proof tree" for the fruit puzzle (see Figure 5).

Strategy for Controlling Reasoning

Just as you will usually fail if you try to solve a problem or answer a question without using strategy, so too will an automated reasoning program usually fail without it. Without strategy—for a person or an automated reasoning program—it is simply too easy to get lost, to draw too many irrelevant conclusions, and to fail to focus on the problem under attack. When you, for example, give a hint or suggestion to a co-worker about how to attack some problem, you are trying to give that co-worker an advantage by using a strategy based on your knowledge or intuition. To provide a reasoning program with the same advantage, you may use a strategy called the "weighting strategy." With "weighting," you instruct the program about the priorities (weights) to be assigned to the concepts, properties, and symbols that occur in the problem under study. In the fruit puzzle, for example, you could tell the program to concentrate on any information that mentions apples. Equally, you could instead tell it to delay reasoning from any information mentioning apples. By using the "weighting strategy," you can use your knowledge and intuition to "direct" the program's search for information toward or away from an area. With that strategy, you can even tell the program to discard all information of some given type whenever it is found.

Of potentially greater value than strategies that *direct* the reasoning program's search are strategies that *restrict* its search. For example, in the proof in clause form that was just given, no conclusion depends on clauses 2 through 10 alone; each (deduced) step can be traced back to clause 1. By prohibiting the program from drawing conclusions involving clauses 2 through 10 only—and thus restricting its search for information—the number of possible conclusions to be examined can be sharply reduced. Such a restriction of the program's reasoning can be achieved by using a strategy called the "set of support strategy" (see Figure 10). Using that strategy, an automated reasoning program can be restricted to reasoning from certain clauses only, using the remaining clauses merely to complete the application of some inference rule.

The most common use of the "set of support strategy" relegates the general information in a problem to that which is used only to complete applications of inference rules. When it is used this way, you are taking advantage of the fact that you are asking the program to seek a proof by contradiction, knowing that reasoning from the general information (ordinarily) simply adds more self-consistent information. In particular, you are using the known consistency of certain information to increase the effectiveness of the reasoning program. You are providing a means for the reasoning program to concentrate on the specific problem at hand rather than on exploring the entire theory underlying the problem. Use of strategies that *direct* and strategies that *restrict* a reasoning program's actions is required if such a program is to provide much assistance in solving problems and in answering questions.

No Strategy

Information

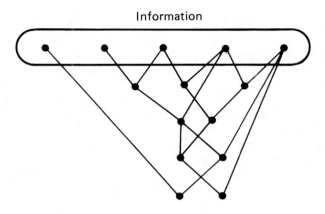

Set of Support Strategy

Key Information   Auxiliary Information

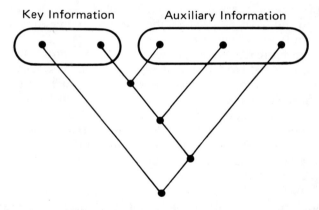

FIGURE 10. The intuitive notion of the "set of support" strategy, used in restricting a search. [*Automated Reasoning Programs* by L. Wos, September 1984. Reprinted with permission of SIAM. Copyright 1984 by SIAM.]

Using an Automated Reasoning Program

An automated reasoning program can be used in three ways. You can submit the problem to it for study and disappear for some time, hoping on your return to find a solution *(batch mode)*. You can sit at a terminal and have a dialogue with the program, asking it to execute each instruction you issue *(interactive mode)*. You can submit the problem to it with some chosen constraint on the time it is allowed or on the amount of new information to be found, and then examine the results to see how the next run should be modified *(graduate assistant mode)*.

Of these three ways to use an automated reasoning program, the way that has yielded the most significant achievements is the graduate assistant mode. In that mode, you play an integral role in the attempt to solve each given problem, but you do not have to issue the detailed instructions usually required in the interactive mode. Based on the results of earlier runs, you decide whether or not to change the inference rule or strategy to be employed in later runs. Each run takes the form of an experiment or a small investigation, often yielding a substantial amount of information. The graduate assistant mode has the advantage—over the batch mode—of not limiting the possible outcome to complete failure or total success, and—over the interactive mode—of avoiding the usual dialogue that occurs in that mode. In such a dialogue, you might, for example, begin by asking the program to draw three conclusions; it might respond with three new facts or relationships. You might then instruct it to discard the second of the three; it would respond by signifying that the second was purged. You might next ask it to draw two additional conclusions from the first; it might then display two additional statements. Although the dialogue that usually occurs in the interactive mode can be very profitable, often the preferred choice is to use the program as an assistant. On the other hand, although seeking an answer in a single attempt (as occurs in the batch mode) sometimes meets with success, for many problems the graduate assistant mode works best. By using your knowledge and intuition to direct your automated reasoning assistant, you might solve problems that neither you nor it could solve alone.

Given the problem or question to be attacked with the assistance of your reasoning program, you decide on which of the three modes of operation to use. Next, you translate the problem or question into an appropriate set of clauses, being careful to include explicitly whatever information you suspect is needed to pin down the various concepts that are involved in the problem. You must also pick the inference rule(s) that seem suited to the problem and the strategy (or strategies) that reflect the attack you wish made. Although it may be far from obvious, the three choices—representation, inference rule, and strategy—should be made simultaneously, for the effects of the three are tightly coupled. (Guidelines, in the form of proverbs, for making such choices are discussed in Chapter 16 of *Automated Reasoning: Introduction and Applications*.) Finally, since the most effective way to use an automated reasoning program is to have it seek a contradiction, you usually assume the result false, the goal unreachable, or the fact not deducible. You might also add clauses that permit the program to rephrase all information into a normal form. If you are not sure which clauses to add but conjecture that normal forms would help, the reasoning program can be asked to find candidates.

As with any co-worker or colleague, the program's attempt at solving the given problem or answering the given question can lead to utter failure, some help, or total success. Failure to complete the assignment is not always a disaster, and, in fact, the run may provide some help. In particular, examination of the program's output after a failure often reveals the key to the answer you are seeking. Sometimes the information you desire is obtained only after a sequence of runs, each influenced by the results of the preceding run. And, of course, sometimes you must accept defeat, deciding that the problem is simply too difficult or the program not powerful enough. However, before deciding that the power of the program is inadequate to the task, you should examine the conclusions it has drawn to see if some mundane information is missing from the input. For example, both clauses

$$\text{FEMALE(x)} \mid \text{MALE(x)} \quad \neg\,\text{FEMALE(x)} \mid \neg\,\text{MALE(x)}$$

are required to pin down the relationship of people to gender—in particular, to state that every person is either female or male. Regardless of what happens when submitting any given problem or question to an automated reasoning program, the advantages of using such a program often outweigh the disadvantages.

Disadvantages of Automated Reasoning

Most of the disadvantages of using a reasoning program can be traced to questions of language. To be required to learn yet another language is often annoying or, for some, not worth the effort. To be forced to include obvious and mundane information of the type you tell to the totally uninitiated is boring at best. Finally, to have to look for information that is implicitly present is tedious. In short, automated reasoning programs "understand" very little at the beginning of any completely new endeavor.

As for mastering the use of a reasoning program—learning which inference rules work best where, and which strategies are most effective in which situations, for example—it is like acquiring any complex skill. No real substitute exists for practice and experience. That is clearly a disadvantage.

Advantages of Automated Reasoning

One of the most important advantages of using an automated reasoning program is its reliability. Such programs do not make errors—well, hardly ever. If a bug exists, then of course they can err. However, if you are suspicious of any result, you can check its validity by simply applying the same algorithm the program was intended to use. After all, a reasoning program can list every step of its reasoning, and provide the justification for each step. Flaws in the information given to such a program to describe the problem are in fact often discovered by finding obvious nonsense among the conclusions drawn by it. What is missing and needed can often be discovered with such an examination.

Perhaps equal in value to reliability is a reasoning program's ability to complete assignments that might be extremely difficult if not impossible for a person. For example, a 297-step proof validating the correctness of the design of a 16-bit adder was obtained in less than 20 seconds of CPU time on an IBM 3033 by the reasoning program AURA. That proof would have been tedious—and perhaps out of reach—for a person to find. Equally, the 162-step proof that settled a previously open question in formal logic might never have been found without the assistance of a program like AURA, especially since some of the formulas that occur in that proof contain 103 symbols exclusive of commas and grouping symbols. The formula

$$E(E(E(x0,E(E(x1,x2),E(E(x2,x0),x1))),$$
$$E(E(x3,x4),E(E(x4,E(x5,E(E(x6,x7),$$
$$E(E(x7,x5),x6)))),x3))),E(E(E(E(E(x8,$$
$$E(x9,x10),E(E(x10,x8),x9))),x11),$$
$$E(E(x12,E(x13,E(E(x13,x12),E(x14,$$
$$E(E(x15,x16),E(E(x16,x14),x15)))))),$$
$$E(x17,E(E(x18,x19),E(E(x19,x17),x18))))),$$
$$E(x11,E(x20,E(E(x21,x22),E(E(x22,x20),x21))))),$$
$$E(x23,E(E(x24,x25),E(E(x25,x23),x24)))))$$

illustrates the complexity of that proof, and also illustrates the kind of expressions that an automated reasoning program easily handles.

The third advantage of using a reasoning program concerns the wish to "prove" that your answer to some given problem or question is correct. You might, for example, wish to know that a piece of code is free of bugs, that a circuit is correctly designed, or that a statement from mathematics is true. An automated reasoning program can sometimes provide that knowledge. In particular, if you have wished for a way to examine an argument for flaws, find inconsistencies, or discover hidden and invalid assumptions, use of a reasoning program may get you your wish.

The fourth advantage of using an automated reasoning program is that it makes no implicit assumptions. You are forced to state in an unambiguous manner precisely what the problem is about. Though often painful, the result can be the discovery of invalid assumptions and subtle but useful distinctions.

The last and perhaps most obvious advantage of using an automated reasoning program is simply to have access to logical reasoning—to have an automated assistant that can draw conclusions that follow logically from some given set of hypotheses.

Summary: Applications for Automated Reasoning

Automated reasoning is a young and challenging field whose long-term objective is to design and implement computer programs each of which functions as an automated reasoning assistant. The object is for one single program to provide assistance that ranges from that offered by an individual with much experience and intelligence to that offered by an untrained individual, where the choice of the level is at the user's control. You and your automated reasoning assistant form a partnership, where, for each given problem, the distribution of work is your choice. At one end of the spectrum, your choice might be to issue very specific instructions: draw three conclusions; discard the second; save the third to be used with other facts later; draw two additional conclusions from the first of the three; . . . . At the opposite end of the spectrum—if the current research succeeds—your choice might be simply to describe the problem, and then rely on your assistant to choose the rules for reasoning, to pick the strategy for controlling the reasoning, and self-analytically to redirect the attack if necessary. Between these two points, your choice might be to make a series of computer runs, each modified according to what you find in the preceding runs—in effect, a dialogue between you and your assistant. Having access to a computer program that functions as a reasoning assistant may make it possible to solve many difficult problems that are currently beyond those that can now be solved by a computer alone or by a person alone.

A computer program of the type just discussed reflects one of the differences between automated reasoning (AR) and that part of (classical) artificial intelligence (AI) that focuses on reasoning. In AR you are combining the power of the computer with the control of the user in a fashion that permits and even encourages you to play an active role. In AI you are often using a "black box" approach, an approach in which your function is essentially to submit the problem. While the use of an AR program can produce results that lie at various points between success and failure, the use of an AI program usually produces either one or the other.

A second difference between AR and AI concerns the nature of the reasoning and approach to problem solving that is employed. In AR, the reasoning and approach are not necessarily designed to imitate the way a person would attack a problem; in fact, they are often designed to rely on a combination of the computer's ability to manipulate symbols and to match patterns, enabling it to use procedures (such as paramodulation and subsumption) that a person would not use. (*Paramodulation* is an inference rule that enables a reasoning program to "build in" equality substitution, and *subsumption* is the procedure used to remove both redundant and less general information automatically.) In AR, the inference rules, strategies, and language for representing the problem are general-purpose rather than being tuned to a specific problem or problem domain. The inference rules are designed to yield (the most) general conclusions, and the strategies are designed to give you (the most) general control over the rules. Of course, when using an automated reasoning program, you must describe the problem to be solved by that program; but, when that is done, you are permitted the use of a wide variety of inference rules and strategies and related procedures that enable you to give varying amounts of guidance to the program. In AI, the approach often is special-purpose, oriented to a specific problem or problem domain, imitating a person's method, and guided by heuristics that a person might use. While the emphasis in AR is on reasoning that yields conclusions that follow logically and inevitably, in much of AI the reasoning is probabilistic or common-sense. As discussed here, both AR and AI approaches have their advantages and disadvantages, and it remains to be seen which is best for which applications. Until more is known, research in automated reasoning will continue to aim at producing a general-purpose high-level reasoning assistant.

To reach the goal of making available a high-level automated reasoning assistant will require first answering various theoretical questions about more useful representations of information, more effective inference rules for drawing conclusions, and more powerful strategies for controlling the inference rules. As those questions are being studied—in fact, in order to study them—computer programs are needed to conduct numerous experiments. Only through extensive experimentation can the needed theory be developed, tested, and evaluated. The more useful programs, therefore, must offer a variety of inference rules and strategies from which to choose, but also offer certain other necessary features. For example, they should offer a procedure for automatically rephrasing information, and a procedure for automatically removing both redundant and less general information.

Effective and useful automated reasoning programs do exist. The general-purpose reasoning program AURA, the program verification system of Boyer and Moore, and the program verification system of Good are three programs that have a number of successes to their credit. Of a somewhat different nature, the system LMA (Logic Machine Architecture) has been successfully used to produce effective reasoning programs tailored to given specifications. In particular, the portable reasoning program ITP produced with LMA is now in use by many people throughout the world. Some of the users of ITP are studying circuit design, some studying circuit validation, some conducting research in mathematics, some exploring the application to chemical synthesis, some exploring the application to program verification, and some employing it as a teaching aid.

Although most reasoning programs have been available only for a few years—and in fact the field of automated reasoning itself is very young— a number of applications of automated reasoning already exist. Computer

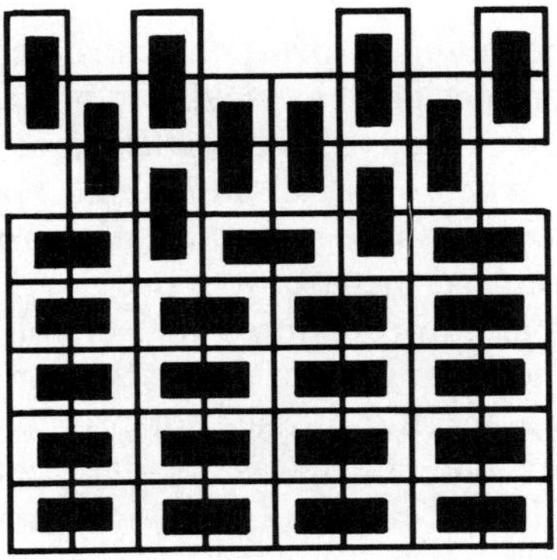

FIGURE 11. A pattern of dominoes showing the solution for the checkerboard puzzle in Figure 3.

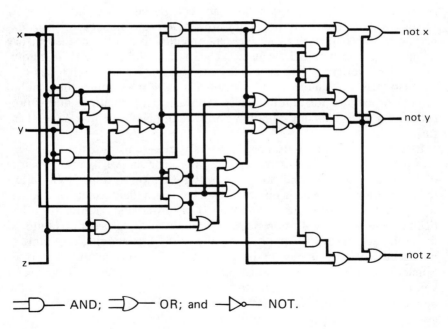

AND; OR; and NOT.

FIGURE 12. Solution to the inverter problem (Figure 6). [Wos/Overbeek/Lusk/Boyle, *Automated Reasoning: Introduction & Applications,* © 1984, p. 215. Reprinted by permission of Prentice-Hall, Inc., Englewood Cliffs, New Jersey.]

Answers to Problems and Puzzles

• The first problem is merely an example of what can be done, and therefore does not admit of an answer other than that such subroutines have been verified.

• Of the three checkerboards shown in Figures 1, 2, and 3, as proved by the reasoning programs AURA and ITP, no placement of dominoes exists that covers precisely either of the first two, while the third can in fact be covered precisely (see Figure 11).

• The circuit shown in Figure 4 does in fact satisfy the requirements.

• A solution of the fourth problem—one you might give, and its equivalent in clauses—was given earlier (see Figure 9) to illustrate various concepts.

• The circuit design in Figure 12 is a solution to the fifth and final problem, if viewed as a problem in circuit design. If viewed as a problem in computer programming, then Figure 12 provides a solution by replacing the NOT gates by 1s complement instructions, the OR gates by OR instructions, and the AND gates by AND instructions, and using the appropriate COPY instructions.

---

programs actually in use have been verified, superior logic circuits designed, other existing circuits validated, and previously open questions in mathematics and in formal logic answered. Some of the results were obtained by people far from expert in automated reasoning itself, demonstrating that, with effort, reasoning programs can be used without substantial expertise in automated reasoning.

The reliability of reasoning programs makes them very attractive as assistants. The results obtained with them can be generally accepted without question. Such programs provide a needed complement to those used for numerical computation and for data processing. Learning to use a reasoning program can require substantial effort, especially when exploring a new application. However, once the database of facts and relationships describing the application is in place, it can be used repeatedly.

The mastery of the use of a reasoning program is in part made easier because many of its functions correspond somewhat to ordinary actions (see Figure 13). People often use normal (standard) forms, discard trivial consequences of known information, remove duplicate information, and occasionally keep track of which facts lead to which conclusions. Those who are more successful at solving problems and answering questions use strategy, even though they do not always do so explicitly. After all, to play chess well, to win at poker, to score well at most games, strategy is indispensable. Thus, in view of the variety of problems that can be solved with a reasoning program, becoming familiar with the explicit use of strategy is not very taxing.

The future is very exciting, offering many opportunities for using, im-

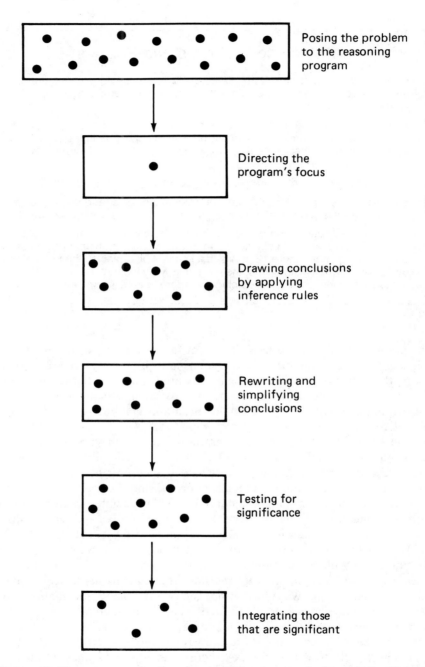

FIGURE 13. The sequence of actions in a reasoning program is shown in the diagram at left. [*Automated Reasoning Programs* by L. Wos, September 1984. Reprinted with permission of SIAM. Copyright 1984 by SIAM.]

plementing, and conducting research in automated reasoning. Some of the programs that will be developed will use extensive amounts of parallelism, some will incorporate a logic programming component, some will be tailored to a given application. Soon it may be commonplace for all kinds of applications and research to rely on a program that functions as a high-level automated reasoning assistant.

References

Bledsoe, W.W., and Loveland, D., eds. *Automated Theorem Proving: After 25 Years*. Contemporary Mathematics, Vol. 29. Providence, RI: AMS, 1984.

Boyer, R.S., and Moore, J. Strother. *A Computational Logic*. New York: Academic Press, 1979.

Chang, C., and Lee, R. *Symbolic Logic and Mechanical Theorem Proving*. New York: Academic Press, 1973.

Kowalski, R. *Logic for Problem Solving*. New York: Elsevier North-Holland, 1979.

Loveland, D. *Automated Theorem Proving: A Logical Basis*. New York: North-Holland, 1978.

Siekmann, J.H., and Wrightson, G., eds. *The Automation of Reasoning, Vols. I and II*. Classical Papers on Computational Logic. New York: Springer-Verlag, 1983.

Wos, L.; Overbeek, R.; Lusk, E.; and Boyle, J. *Automated Reasoning: Introduction and Applications*. Englewood Cliffs, NJ: Prentice-Hall, 1984.

INTERRUPT

Joan Rivers recently spoke with the *Chicago Tribune* about the difficulty of coming up with all those jokes.

"One thing that helps is that I have a filing system. . . . All the jokes are on cards, and I back that up with computers, which I hate because if the power goes off, they lose things. I don't like computers and I think they're the Devil's tool. I have three of them in my house—Damien I, Damien II and Damien III."

We believe that His Santanic Majesty, the angel of the bottomless pit, is getting a bum rap. He probably has problems keeping up with his Apple or PC just like everyone else.

The Composer and the Computer

The history and development of music composition on computers, with emphasis on the system used by the author.

LEJAREN HILLER

Perhaps it comes as no surprise that computers are having a profound effect in the world of music, just as in so many other fields of human endeavor. Computers are being applied to many practical aspects of music-making; consider, for example, the recent introduction of digital recording techniques to replace conventional tape recording in making the masters for commercial records and cassettes. Scholastic activities are also being affected: musicological research, music library management, and pedagogy. Since such activities have analogs in other fields of work, they are readily perceived as natural applications for digital processing.

However, computers are also finding ever more widespread use as tools for musical invention. Even today, this strikes many people as controversial because it impinges upon a process that is often labelled "creative" and hence is supposed to be beyond rational analysis. Nevertheless, composers are becoming increasingly involved in the use of computers, and are beginning to speak in language that takes on more and more attributes

LEJAREN HILLER received his Ph.D. in Chemistry in 1947 at Princeton University and his M.Mus. in 1958 at the University of Illinois, having studied composition with Roger Sessions and Milton Babbitt at Princeton. He was a research chemist at E. I. du Pont de Nemours from 1947 to 1952, and from 1952 to 1958 was a member of the Department of Chemistry at the University of Illinois. From 1958 until 1968, he was Professor of Music there, where he designed and built the Experimental Music Studio. Since 1968, Dr. Hiller has been at the State University of New York at Buffalo, where he is currently Birge-Cary Professor of Composition. Until 1975 he was also codirector, with Lukas Foss, of the Buffalo Center of the Creative and Performing Arts. He is the author of three books and numerous scientific articles, as well as being the composer of some seventy scores for instruments, voice, eelectronics, computers, theater, film, and TV.

This version has been shortened by the editor from the original article that appeared in ABACUS, Volume 1, Number 4, Summer 1984.

of technology. Note that today there is an active Computer Music Association with a substantial membership; there is a quarterly *Computer Music Journal* published by M.I.T. Press; and there are annual "International Computer Music Conferences" with invited lecturers, numerous papers (often quite technical in nature), and concerts devoted exclusively to computer music.

At this point it is convenient, though not entirely accurate, to compartmentalize computer music into two broad categories. The first consists of music composed—or at least thoroughly sketched out—in a more-or-less conventional fashion, and then converted into electronic sound by means of computer processing (specifically by digital-to-analog conversion). This variety of computer music, by far the more prevalent type, is the successor to so-called "electronic music" made with analog equipment—oscillators, filters, reverberators, synthesizers, and so on.

The second type of computer music is composed directly with compositional algorithms so that note choices are made (to a greater or lesser extent) by the computer itself. It is this form of composition with which I shall deal here, illustrating my remarks mainly with my own music.

Composition with Computers

The process of computer-assisted composition does not differ greatly from what one does when composing music in the "normal" way. It is as essential as ever that the composer have an idea, a vision, an image of what to create. However, it is highly likely that this image will be influenced by both the resources and the obstacles a computer provides—as it certainly ought to be. When a composer writes a piece for piano, for example, the fact that a piano possesses a keyboard that permits polyphony and chords certainly affects compositional choices. With a computer, these resources are not just expanded; they are markedly different in that the composer must think in a new language—the language of algorithms—rather than the language of music notation. The composer is forced to concentrate on composition as *process* because it is process, not end result, that is encoded into the statements that a computer can accept and act upon. By one stratagem or another, a composer must design a process that produces a result that is acceptable as music.

Note that I am discussing two different types of activities. The first is the writing of the composition program itself, and the second is its exploitation to produce a piece of music. In computer sound synthesis, these activities have become quite separate, because in many music centers standardized software is now available, inspired by MUSIC 5 and written by computer experts. Composers use these programs to produce music. All they need to know is how to start them up and how to introduce data; they do not need to know how the programs operate. In computer-assisted

Glossary of Musical Terms

Arco	Bowing a string, e.g., on a violin.
Beat	One basic rhythmic pulse, e.g., a quarter note in ¼ meter.
Cadence	Musical progression which ends a composition or section; generally, a harmonic resolution.
Cantus firmus	A given melodic line, often traditionally taken from liturgical chant.
Chromatic	Pertaining to all twelve notes of the ordinary equal-tempered scale.
Counterpoint	Interdependent functioning of two or more simultaneous melodic lines.
Fugue	Polyphonic form characterized by successive imitative entries of individual melodic lines.
Harmony	Chordal structure which supports a melody.
Interval	Distance between two pitches, either simultaneous or consecutive.
Microtonal	Possessing more than twelve notes per octave.
Monody	Music consisting of a single melodic line.
Modulation	Shift from one key to another.
Pizzicato	Plucking a string.
Polyphonic	Possessing several simultaneous melodic lines.
Serial	Note parameters chosen in accord with an arbitrary list of integers.
Stretto	Overlapping of theme and imitation in a fugue.
Temperament	Adjustment made by tuning away from the natural overtone series; in equal temperament, each successive pitch is $\sqrt[12]{2}\ \times$ the previous pitch.
Tonal	Adhering to a standard key system, e.g., C major.
Transposition	Shift of pitch level or tonality.
Trill	Rapid alternation between two pitches.
Twelve-note	Serial process applied only to pitch choices.

composition the situation is less advanced. Most composers who attempt this sort of work still do their own programming.

Perhaps my own approach to this over the years is not atypical. I start by defining a set of compositional algorithms which, I hope, express a set of musical ideas that reflect my own musical biases. I then write the composition program (or, these days, refine and expand part of a substantial catalog of programs which I have used repeatedly over recent years). To test the program, I write a piece of music—a composition that is a product of the program. I also see to it that the music is performed, because hearing it is the ultimate test. I note its strengths and weaknesses, and then return to the computer to refine and improve the compositional process and move on to plan the next piece. At all stages, I set realistic goals and do not attempt to create global, all-encompassing models. Incremental advances do work in practice to produce better and more sophisticated pieces. One must realize that music, like any language, is not a closed system; there is always more to be said.

I do more than this, however. I am not just interested in turning out one piece after another, expressing only my own idiosyncratic compositional desires. I also evaluate each process I encode in terms of how it might be used by the composing community at large. I accept, refine, expand, or reject each compositional operation not only in relation to my own needs, but also in terms of its general applicability. Thus, assuming that my choices of what to program are generally reasonable ones, I am building up a library of what one might call "compositional modules." Even at this early stage, the programs I will be discussing below can be used to produce music strikingly different from my own. Thus, these programs, along with those written by other composers, are beginning to form a repertory of resources which soon should permit user-composers not expert in programming to utilize computers for composition just as they now do for sound synthesis.

For the present, however, a composer normally writes a computer program that embodies a compositional process; it may be simple, or complex enough to take over compositional chores. In addition to the program itself, both reference and input data files are normally needed. The reference files contain rudimentary but essential statements defining things such as the playing ranges of instruments, minimal rhythmic durations, performance style limitations (e.g., a trumpet cannot play pizzicato). These data remain invariant no matter what kind of music is intended. Input data, on the other hand, define the shape and style of a particular piece (or pieces) being composed (see Table 1). Here, some data are global parameters that define larger aspects of the composition, such as how long it lasts, how many sections it has, and whether it utilizes a structure derived from a classical form such as a fugue. My input data files also supply negations of performance options defined in the reference files (it is important to delete undesired possibilities), and finally contain many parameters required by programs utilizing probabilistic or statistical models for composing—a point I shall consider in some detail later on. The result of executing the composition program with this data is output convertible to a musical score or to electronic sound on tape.

By now there have been a number of approaches to the design of compositional systems that can be programmed for computer processing. I particularly like the way these systems have been classified by Otto Laske,

TABLE 1. Simplified Sample Input Data File for Composition Program

(a)   Overall data for piece:

TITLE   PARTS 1 TO 4 OF PARTS, WITH NVOICES = 12

	LIMIT	BAR	PHRASE	ROW	KEY	MODULATION	METER	TEMPO
PART 1	384	32	20	12	C$_\#$	G$_\#$	4/4	1/4 = 96

	MINPCH	MAXPCH	QUOTE
FLUTE	C_4	C_7	0
OBOE	B♭3	G_6	41
PERCN.	F_3	F_4	0

384 denotes the maximum number of beats in Part 1, 32 is the number of beats in a bar, 20 is the maximum number of notes in a phrase, and 12 is the length of the tone row. G$_\#$ represents a shift in keys (for example, K$_2$ in Figure 1). 96 represents the number of quarter-note beats per minute. C_4 represents middle C and is the minimum pitch for the flute; C_7 denotes 3 octaves higher than C_4. The oboe "quote" of 41 denotes that 41 notes will be quoted from another piece of music.

(b)   Typical choice functions for process options for individual instruments:

Y1	0.20	0.50	0.60	Chance for choosing free flow
Y2	0.20	0.50	0.40	Chance for choosing phrase assembly*
Y3	0.90	0.90	0.90	Chance for continuing a phrase
Y4	0.60	0.60	0.60	Chance for free-flow play versus rest
Y5	1.00	0.00	1.00	Chance for phrase-assembly play versus rest
Y6	0.33	0.33	0.33	Chance for long versus short rhythms

*Chance for imitation = 1.00 (Y1 + Y2)
The 3 columns represent the probabilities for flute, oboe, and percussion, respectively.

(c)   Typical data for note parameter choices for each instrument, using values defined by program (e.g., for pitch, 1 = C, 2 = C$_\#$, etc.):

			FLUTE					2	2	2	2	2	Stochastic order
1	2	3	4	5	6	7	8	9	10	11	12		Available rhythm choices
1	2	3	4	5	6	7	8	9	10	11	12		Available pitch choices per octave
1	−1	−1	−1	−1	−1	7	−1	9	−1	−1	−1		Available dynamic level choices
1	2	3	4	−1	−1	−1	−1	−1	−1	−1	−1		Available timbre choices
1	2	3	4	5	6	−1	8	9	−1	−1	12		Available style choices

			OBOE					2	2	2	2	2	Stochastic order
1	2	3	4	5	6	7	8	9	10	11	12		Available rhythm choices
1	2	3	4	5	6	7	8	9	10	11	12		Available pitch choice per octave
1	−1	−1	−1	−1	−1	7	−1	9	−1	−1	−1		Available dynamic level choices
1	−1	−1	4	−1	−1	−1	−1	−1	−1	−1	−1		Available timbre choices
1	2	3	4	5	6	−1	8	9	−1	−1	12		Available style choices

			PERCN.					2	2	2	2	2	Stochastic order
1	2	3	4	5	6	7	8	9	10	11	12		Available rhythm choices
1	2	3	4	5	6	7	8	9	10	11	12		Available pitch choices per octave
1	−1	−1	−1	−1	−1	7	−1	9	−1	−1	−1		Available dynamic level choices
1	2	3	4	5	6	7	8	9	10	11	12		Available timbre choices
1	2	3	4	−1	−1	7	8	9	−1	−1	12		Available style choices

The five 2s represent the stochastic order as described in the text for the five parameters which follow. 1 through 12 represent the normal choices available in the program (e.g., the twelve notes on the chromatic scale). An entry of − 1 indicates that this choice is not available.

a composer of computer music who is also much concerned with theoretical aspects of this whole development. Before going on to my own ideas, I should like to summarize Laske's concepts, including some of his terminology and examples. In order of increasing complexity, his four categories of compositional programming are: (1) non-hierarchic, (2) opportunistic, (3) script-based, and (4) hierarchic.

Non-hierarchic design involves an arbitrary linear ordering of goals, all of which are assumed to be of substantially equal significance. A one-way tunnel might serve as a homely analog. This imposes severe limits because the scheme breaks down once any sort of music is planned other than elementary material such as nursery tunes or textbook chorales. The process operates in one pass, and there is really only one valid goal—reaching the end. Non-hierarchic programming is useful, however, in sound synthesis because normally such programs can only transform data; they do not create it. Stereotyped representations of note parameters (frequency, duration, amplitude envelopes, etc.) are read and converted to audible output. Material is rejected only for technical flaws, and evaluation only occurs at the listening end.

Opportunistic processes are more complex because they involve "asynchronous" or "parallel" operations that are not always causally related. In ordinary music, collages of disjunct materials, such as one finds, for example, in compositions by Charles Ives, illustrate one feature of this type of structure. Opportunistic systems can also be triggered by events (even random ones) to produce long streams of further events without impediment. Event streams of this sort are commonplace in analog electronic music, because trigger circuits are normal components of the hardware used to produce such music.

Script-based designs are more sophisticated because they utilize two stages of planning: the selection of a skeletal plan and the writing of a matching musical sequence which to some degree approximates the model. For centuries, skeletal plans have been taken from the most diverse sources; recent examples include much of the music of John Cage. Examples of computer music essentially planned this way include a number of compositions written in the early 1960s by Xenakis, with titles like "ST-4," "ST-10," and "Atrées." Xenakis used a Poisson distribution to allocate note parameters to graphical representations of all these scores. More recent examples include Larry Austin's "Canadian Coastlines," derived from Canadian maps and dependent on the use of fractal distributions for making choices, and Klarenz Barlow's "Bus Journey to Parametron." This last work (which exists in two versions, for keyboard or for electronic sound) consists of four "streams" of musical events, tightly constrained to conform to an elaborate set of controls divided into three categories: "material," "texture," and "form."

Hierarchic design is the most complex approach because it involves defining levels of significance for all the various decisions which must be faced, and arranging the temporal ordering of these decisions. It is also the most popular design for computer-assisted composition because it seems to have the greatest historical validity. I am concentrating on this approach in the present article, if only because it is my own preference. I can cite other composers' work as well; for example, Koenig's programs PROJECT I, PROJECT II, and PROJECT III, and Barbaud's programs ALGOM I to ALGOM7. There also exist more recent programs written by Charles Ames (also of Buffalo), which he has used to compose compositions with titles like "Crystals" and "Undulant." Although all these composing schemes have hierarchic design built into them, their design details can be widely different, illustrating the point that none of them (including mine) does more than scratch the surface of an extremely complicated problem space.

Let's explore why most of the composing done so far with computers has been hierarchic and why so much of it has been governed by time-dependent chance elements, i.e., by stochastic processes. First, hierarchic structure is a frequently recurring concept in contemporary music theory, just as it is in computer science. A musical message is no longer considered to be a linear string of events resembling beads on a chain; instead, these events are said to be tied together by complex networks which subordinate some events to others.

A simple diagram which clearly lays out a hierarchic scheme is shown in Figure 1. This diagram is not only an image of hierarchic structure, but also the trajectory of a process of composition. The composer does not (at least I don't) compose in a linear fashion, adding one note to the next, one bar after the other, by stringing the beads on the chain mentioned above. Rather, the composer jumps about conceptually, sometimes leaping ahead to define an important goal such as a cadence or an iteration of an important theme, and other times backtracking to fill in details. In general, the way the composer moves about in a projected time continuum does not have a one-to-one relationship to the finished composition as experienced in real time by the listener.

In Figure 1, I have chosen a hypothetical scheme that might be employed by a composer designing a piece of tonal music containing key centers and traditional harmonies. The K's represent relatively stable key areas, and the H's, individual harmonies as they will appear in the final score. The arrows suggest successive paths of process used by the composer. For example, at the start, a key for the composition (K_1) is chosen. The next concern is the key of the first major cadence, well into the composition, so the composer thinks ahead and chooses K_2, and then backtracks to insert the key (K_3) of an intermediate passage in a contrasting tonality. At this point, the composer might well decide to begin filling in various harmonies, moving back and forth and skipping about, selecting first the harmonies that relate most directly to the chosen keys, following this by inserting others of lesser and lesser significance. When this is done, the

Key (K) and Harmony (H) Choice Process

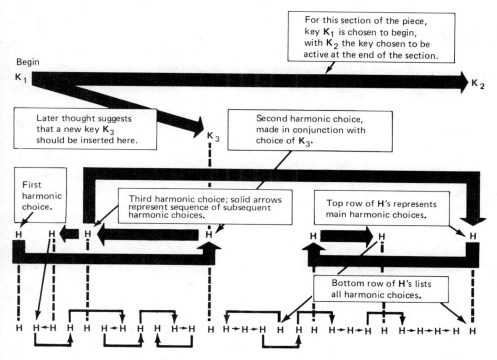

FIGURE 1. A typical hierarchic scheme for a process of musical composition involving keys and harmonies.

composer moves on to the next section of the score and continues in a comparable fashion.

The other important aspect of writing compositional algorithms, use of the chance factor, is derived rather directly from studies of how to apply statistics and information theory to music analysis. I can trace this aspect of my own compositional practice back to comments such as those made in 1940 by Stravinsky in his *Poetics of Music:* "We feel the necessity to bring order out of chaos, to extricate the straight line of our operation from the tangle of possibilities; . . . to proceed by elimination—to know how to discard . . . that is the great technique of selection." These thoughts are hardly novel today, especially since the ideas of composers like John Cage have taken firm root in the new music; but forty years ago this kind of thinking was regarded by the musical establishment with considerable hostility.

From such considerations, it follows that one practical way of writing music with a computer involves using a stochastic process in which elements are chosen sequentially according to a probability distribution, and throwing away unwanted choices. This is a departure from the idea that a musical structure must always be some sort of deterministically conceived entity. We can even specify compositional systems in which a particular composition is but one example taken from a large class of essentially similar compositions. For example, if some changes, perhaps even minor ones, are made in a chance-dependent compositional process, a composition may be produced which is different in terms of fine detail but not necessarily new in its overall structure.

The response of the listener to this should depend on what type of variance is incorporated into the compositional system at each particular hierarchic level. One can speculate that the lower the hierarchic level at which the variance is being applied, the less subjective attention it attracts. Evidence from psychoacoustical investigations suggests that subjective response, or "affect" as estheticians call it, depends substantially on hierarchic level. A high level (i.e., a macrostructure) attracts attention and reveals to the listener the logical plan of the work being played. Material of low hierarchic significance tends to be supportive filler and is absorbed into larger perceptive units (*Gestalten* is the term often used for these). Such material is also readily convertible to computer algorithms. Note that if we use a computer to produce a variance of some sort in a compositional process and its result, we also retain a precise record of how the variance was produced and what its limits were.

The general set of paradigms for incorporating chance into a compositional process is as follows. First, generate stochastic integers and associate each with some particular musical element. These elements can be the usual ones of pitch, rhythm, loudness, and playing instructions such as pizzicato and arco for ordinary instruments or acoustical parameters for electronic sounds. Moreover, in sophisticated programs, we can associate such integers with whole groups of elements already arranged into particular patterns such as themes, harmonic sequences, and so on.

Second, we subject the chosen integers to long series of tests that resemble sieves through which they must be strained. These tests might reflect the constraints of the usual compositional rules, "a priori" rules which merely strike one's fancy, the results of statistical analyses of existing music, or even self-generating heuristic rules produced in the computer (in this process, a structure is generated and then investigated in order to extend it by means of modified rules extrapolated from the original set of constraints imposed upon the system).

Third, we assemble our results into units of music, if not complete compositions, and then print them out or convert them to recorded sound. We are thus applying some of the ideas of information theory in an operational and practical way. We generate a system of high information content—which might even be a random music-generating process of maximum information content—and then reduce the information content to whatever degree we desire or can formulate.

This brings up some further points regarding the use of chance operations in composing music. For example, why shouldn't compositional algorithms be explicitly deterministic in concept and operation? My own reluctance to proceed this way has been motivated by several factors. First, it involves establishing a priority schedule according to which things get done. The advantage of having stochastic and chance-dependent operations at the heart of a system is that it eliminates procedural bias. Second, if a system is rigidly defined, one really knows the outcome in advance, and reduces the composing program to a mere data translation device as in non-hierarchic systems—eliminating the element of surprise, which serves as a sort of surrogate for the "creative" element. One learns nothing about composing as *process* that one did not know already.

Last, I have thought for some time that a composer, whether using a computer or not, is always confronted by a full spectrum of possibilities in terms of order and disorder. Even the traditional treatment of consonance and dissonance is just a slice out of this spectrum. Thus, the compositional method of inserting constraints really involves moving through this spectrum, starting at the "disordered" end and then shifting across it as more compositional algorithms are entered into the operation. The more redundancy is introduced, the more the structure becomes precisely defined and the more the music takes on the aspect of having been conceptualized in detail in advance. This is more a matter of degree than of kind. Also, having a stochastic note generator is advantageous because it is always there as a final resource; it provides a fail-safe fallback, the last resort if nothing else works. It produces note parameters that statistically relate to the compositional environment in which they are called upon to fulfill a role. They may not be the only possible choices; but they are at least compatible, or even—one might say—agreeable ones.

Stochastic Processes

A stochastic process has been defined as a "probability process whose outcomes are functions of time." Stochastic processes make use of transition probabilities which define the chance that each given state of a system proceeds to some new given state. It is convenient to use frequency distributions to express transition probabilities, and to build up tables of counts of selected items as representations of frequency distributions. These tables become increasingly complex as more attention is paid to elapsed time. What then are the items being counted? I selected seven for my own programming: duration, rhythmic extender for long durations, pitch within the octave, octave, dynamic level, timbre, and style. These last two note parameters relate to ways various instruments may be played or to acoustic attributes assigned to electronic sounds. Each of these seven

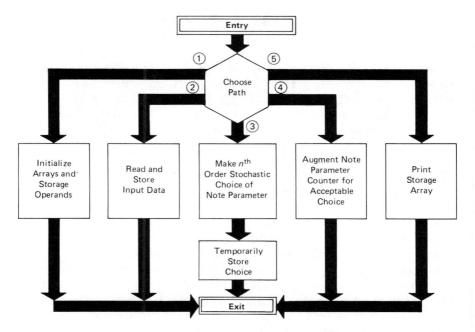

FIGURE 2. Block diagram for a subroutine which selects and stores stochastic note parameters.

parameters has a gamut of twelve items. The division of the octave into twelve notes of the scale suggested this plan.

When defining stochastic processes, one can start with two simpler situations in which time dependency does not exist, and one can then design a note parameter generator based upon n^{th}-order stochastic processes defined as follows:

☐ $n = 0$: A zeroth-order process makes random choices because all available choices are equiprobable.

☐ $n = 1$: A first-order process makes choices from a time-independent frequency distribution. Throwing a pair of dice is an example of this. The distribution is binomial, not equiprobable.

☐ $n = 2$: A second-order process depends upon choices just made; e.g., having just chosen a $C^{\#}$, what is the chance of choosing a $G^{\#}$?

☐ $n > 2$: The previous $n - 1$ choices determine what the new one will be; however, $n > 4$ yields diminishing returns, not only because increasing amounts of computer memory must be allocated to frequency distribution arrays, but also because note count data become so scattered as to be statistically meaningless. In addition, it is around the fourth-order level that hierarchic groupings of elements become more and more dominant. A simple analogy is ordinary language: letters become grouped into words, words into sentences, sentences into paragraphs, and so on.

The structure of a stochastic note parameter generator is shown in Figure 2. Path 1 is self-explanatory. Path 2 is provided for users who wish to enter data obtained from some external source such as a statistical analysis of a known piece of music. Path 3 is the major part of the subroutine—where new choices are made. Path 4 is separated from this, because note choices are provisional until they are accepted by other portions of a complete composition program. Only if a choice is satisfactory is it stored for future use. Once a composition is complete, Path 5 prints out stored choices in order to provide documentation.

The array shown in Figure 3a provides four stochastic levels of storage, from first to fourth-order (zeroth-order is not needed because its distribution is known and invariant). Note that the arrays become larger as the order goes up. These arrays were compressed by taking advantage of the sixty-bit words of a Cyber 730, the machine on which this work was done. Five-bit cells in each sixty-bit word were allocated to each item in a parameter set. This sets an upper limit of 30 to the count of each item (not 31 because a full set of 31s—sixty 1s in a row—clears to zero by complementation). Storage of choices is made in all the arrays (save the first) no matter which stochastic order is used to make the choice. This means that one can change the stochastic order at any time during a process of composition, because all the accumulated history of previous selections is documented at every order level. Provision is also made for augmenting the order level automatically once a word in this array becomes saturated, i.e., each of its cells reaches the value of thirty. This prevents a process from reverting automatically to zeroth-order.

Program PHRASE

My current program for computer-assisted composition consists of a set of subroutines, mostly written in Fortran, organized into a program called PHRASE. It has become my main program for composition. It is the master program and all else is subsumed under it, the main reason being the one cited above: hierarchic structural layering had to be assigned a primary role in the composition process and not buried somewhere inside. Program PHRASE consists of five distinct sets of routines:

☐ The first contains the main program plus several closely related subroutines.

☐ The second contains three types of subroutines: those that move or locate data; those that provide frequency distributions of various sorts; and those which handle crucial choice processes (for example, choosing

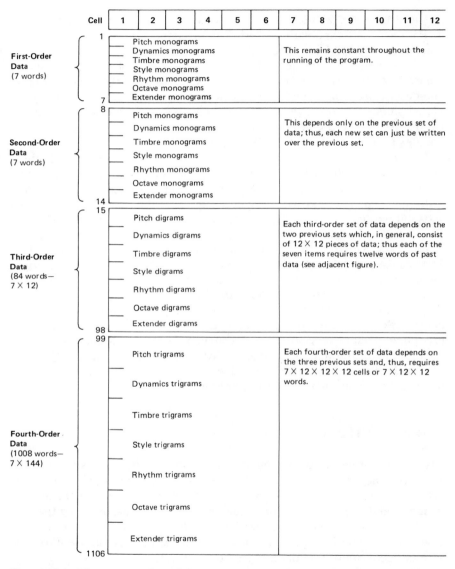

FIGURE 3A. The storage plan of the KFREQ array in subroutine STOCH. This array is suitable for storing stochastic note counts, designed for a memory made up of sixty-bit words.

B   **Third-Order Data for Pitch**

Pitch data consists of values for the probabilities of each of twelve notes stored in 5-bit cells in one 60-bit word:

C	C$^\#$	D	E^b	E	F	F$^\#$	G	A^b	A	B^b	B

For third-order data all possible combinations of probabilities at the previous two times need to be stored:

Word 1	C_1C_2	$C_1C^\#_2$										C_1Bb_2

Word 2	$C^\#_1C_2$	$C^\#_1C^\#_2$										$C^\#_1B_2$

⋮

Word 12	B_1C_2	$B_1C^\#_2$										B_1B_2

Subscript 1 represents the value at the previous time, and subscript 2 represents the value two time intervals previously.

FIGURE 3B. A "close-up view" showing the arrangement of pitch diagrams stored among third-order data in Figure 3A.

a compositional path in the main program, choosing whether a phrase should continue, choosing between play and rest, or deciding whether there should be rhythmic correlations between lines of the score).

□ The third consists of hierarchically organized compositional modules which set boundary conditions within which note parameter choices must be made. The most important module organizes the sequence in which note parameters are chosen.

□ The fourth contains more service subroutines which do such chores as printing the score, storing and recovering incomplete compositions, and extracting any parts of the score destined for sound synthesis on audio tape by D/A conversion.

□ The fifth set is normally not run until the compositional results obtained from all of the above routines satisfy the composer, for it is not sensible to use up computer time preparing sound files until the composing part of the process is working properly. However, once it is ready, we convert compositional output directly into note statements that sound synthesis programs can accept. Our own program for sound synthesis, modelled on MUSIC 5 and written by Charles Ames, can convert these note statements into a sound file of up to 40 KHz. The file is written on digital tape by the Cyber and then transferred to a sound-processing computer

152   Lejaren Hiller

From Computer to Audio Tape

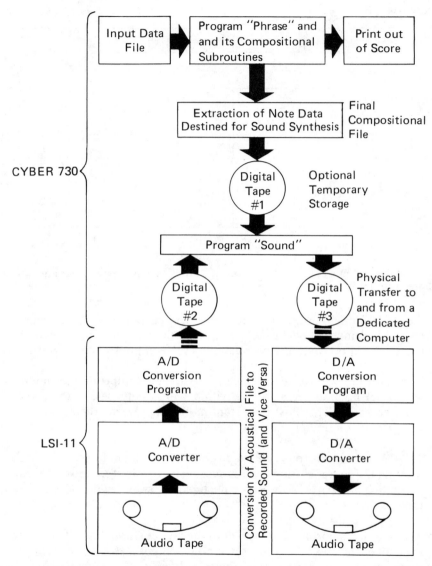

FIGURE 4. Block diagram showing the path which converts the output of a computer composition into recorded electronic sound.

(an LSI-11 plus peripherals), and thence converted to audio tape. The block diagram shown in Figure 4 summarizes this operation.

When assembled, the total package of composition routines (exclusive of sound synthesis) requires about 130K of memory, even though most of the larger important arrays are tightly packed like the one shown in Figures 3a and 3b. To produce, say, 100 bars of music for twelve instruments takes twenty to thirty minutes of central processor time. I cite these figures mainly to point out that composing is a laborious affair, even for a machine as fast as this one.

Let us now examine several parts of the composing system, starting with the main program. This contains three basic composing paths which I call "free flow," "phrase assembly," and "imitation." In Figure 5, I show a much condensed block diagram of this main program.

Free flow can be used for any sort of compositional operation that does not involve phrase manipulation. As this is composition at a low hierarchic level, it most nearly reflects the stochastic background lying behind the whole process; in fact, it often provides filler and other relatively neutral material against which more sophisticated operations may be highlighted.

Phrase assembly generates significant thematic material, material which is to be manipulated in various ways but which, in principle, must be identifiable. Familiar examples in conventional music would be the main themes of a symphony, the subject of a fugue, or the refrain of a song. Phrase assembly codifies the relationships between notes deemed to be especially significant, and tags them for future reference. At present, I provide three basic sources for phrases: (a) self-generated ones that are produced by the computer itself; (b) a special operation that produces serial structures such as twelve-note rows; and (c) quotation, which permits the user to read in thematic material as an alternative to themes produced internally (in conventional music, "Variations on a Theme by Composer X" would involve analogous ideas).

Imitation is the most complex of the three compositional paths. It simulates many of the operations a composer normally uses while writing music: repetition, transposition, permutation, ornamentation, transformation, and so on. One can tabulate a long list of such processes. So far, I have provided at least the most essential ones: imitation, imitation with either pitch or rhythm being newly chosen, and various kinds of permutation—a theme can be reproduced without change, upside down (inversion), backwards (retrograde), or both (retrograde inversion); phrases or imitations may overlap (imitation overlap occurs, for example, in fugal writing, forming what is called stretto).

Note that everything presented so far, except perhaps the production of serial music, says nothing whatsoever regarding musical style. It is my contention that the main program provides a compositional process, isolated and generalized, and that it can be adapted (at least in theory) to any musical style. It is the rest of the system that narrows down the range

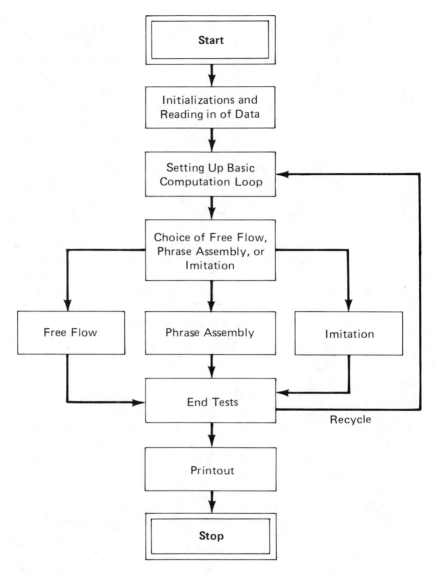

FIGURE 5. Condensed flow chart for the main program, PHRASE, currently being used for music composition.

of possibilities by throwing away undesired choices so as to impart structure, or in fact redundancy. We now must move to a lower hierarchic level and start to define constraints, both statistical and determinate.

Let us now look briefly at a typical distribution subroutine from the second portion of PHRASE. This is an embodiment of an idea proposed a number of years ago by G. K. Zipf that the frequency of occurrence of words in English is inversely proportional to rank order. He postulated that if $f(i)$ is the frequency of occurrence of the ith most common word, then $i \cdot f(i)$ is approximately a constant. Others have tested this so-called Zipf's Law against foreign languages and even music—specifically, pitch choices in Mozart's Bassoon Concerto, K. 191—and have found it surprisingly accurate.

Zipf's Law provides a particularly attractive distribution to work with because it is highly selective compared to many distributions, which is to say that it is highly prejudiced in favor of the recurrence of common events. That it works well in conjunction with choice subroutines seems reasonable to me because it builds up a meaningful collection of data more rapidly than a distribution that is less skewed toward favored choices. To date, I have used it more frequently than any other distribution for weighting choices of successive note parameters.

The most important of the composing subroutines is called FILL. Its flow chart and its interfaces with subordinate compositional modules are shown in Figure 6. It is basically a sequence of calls to subroutines which select note parameters. All this is modulated by the stochastic sequence, which obtains choices for note parameters from the stochastic note parameter generator described earlier. We determine whether each choice falls within the limits imposed by RHYTHM, PITCH, VOLUME, TIMBRE, and STYLE and the various subroutines they call in turn. If it does, we accept the choice; if not, we reject the choice and try again.

Until recently, the order of selection in FILL was different from that shown in Figure 6, because pitch was the first item on the list and rhythm the last. This arrangement resulted from traditional thinking on my part—stressing pitch relationships at the expense of time relationships. This is the way music theory has traditionally been taught; and I fell into the trap of getting the melodic and harmonic relationships in order and then supplying rhythms that support these structures. In the last half century, there has been a growing awareness that rhythm and time are just as crucial as pitch, if not more so, especially since Western tonal music has been supplemented by musical styles in which tonal relations are redefined, submerged, or negated. With pitch first and rhythm last, I began to run into more and more problems that required more and more programming patches as I persisted with this set of priorities. This taught me that my priorities were wrong. Once I made the decision to change, many of these complications simply disappeared.

The moral is this: I learned something about composing as process—something I should have known, but ignored until I was forced to think about it logically in terms of writing programs that are tight, logical, and efficient. For example, STYLE (in Figure 6) chooses whether a trill can be assigned to a given note. Trills, however, cannot be assigned to notes of minimum duration. Therefore, if the duration of the note is still unchosen, only backing and filling will serve to test whether this instruction is legitimate. This example may seem trivial, but it nevertheless illustrates how careful one must be in providing instructions that are both logical and in accord with performance practice.

Early Compositions

The list of compositions shown in Table 2 breaks rather neatly into two halves: early compositions written at the University of Illinois up through 1968, and compositions written since then in Buffalo. It is not just geography that separates these compositions, but also the thinking and programming.

The very first computer music composition, the "Illiac Suite for String Quartet," was composed in collaboration with Leonard Isaacson from 1955 to 1957. Nowadays I also call it my "String Quartet No. 4" because

TABLE 2. Lejaren Hiller: Computer Music Compositions

Illinois

Illiac Suite for String Quartet (1957) (cowritten with Leonard Isaacson).

"The Flying Lesson" from music for *The Birds* (1958).

Computer Cantata (1963) (cowritten with Robert Baker).

An Avalanche for Pitchman, Prima Donna, Player Piano, Percussionist and Pre-recorded Playback (1968).

HPSCHD for 1 to 7 Harpsichords and 1 to 51 Tapes (1968) (cowritten with John Cage).

Algorithms I for 9 Instruments and Tape (Versions 1 to 4) (1968).

Computer Music for Percussion and Tape (1968) (cowritten with G. Allan O'Connor).

Buffalo

Algorithms II for 10 instruments and Tape (Versions 1 to 4) (1972) (cowritten with Ravi Kumra).

A Preview of Coming Attractions for Orchestra (1975).

Persiflage for Flute, Oboe and Percussion (1977).

Computer Music for Voice, Piccolo, Percussion and Tape (1981).

Algorithms III for 9 Instruments and Tape (Versions 1 to 4) (work in progress).

Processing Note Parameters

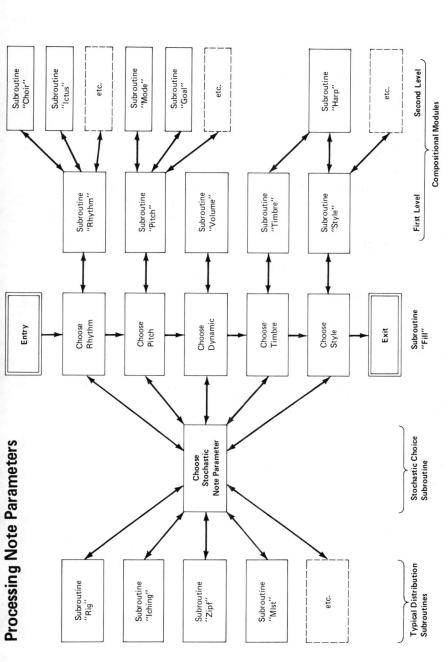

FIGURE 6. Block diagram showing how subroutine FILL sets on the far right represent typical subroutines which impose up the hierarchic processing of note parameters. The boxes stylistic constraints upon choices of rhythms, pitches, and on the left represent typical distribution subroutines used to other note parameters. The boxes influence choices of stochastic note parameters. The boxes

I decided, after many hearings, that it is better music than I had originally thought. More than just the innovative novelty it was at the time of its creation, it holds up as listenable music as well.

Full details on how this project was carried out are contained in the book *Experimental Music,* which Leonard Isaacson and I wrote in 1959.

Because of other commitments, some six years elapsed before I completed the next substantial computer music composition, the "Computer Cantata" of 1963, in collaboration with Robert Baker. It is the end product of experiments used to implement the MUSICOMP language used to compose the Illiac Suite.

In "An Avalanche for Pitchman, Prima Donna, Player Piano, Percussionist and Prerecorded Playback" (1968), I took a break from the rather academic composing discussed so far in order to apply computer processing to the production of a piece of musical theater. Actually, in this piece only the player piano roll represents computer music, but there is no reason why a composition must be purely one thing or another. The music on the player piano roll, composed or rather arranged via computer, consists of ninety themes taken from the standard symphonic repertoire, transformed into an increasingly complex melange which only a player piano, not a human pianist, could play.

In 1967, when John Cage was appointed a visiting professor at the University of Illinois, he and I decided to produce a huge computer-processed multi-media work called "HPSCHD." How all this came about has been documented by Stephen Husarik in a recent article in the new journal *American Music.* Most significantly, "HPSCHD" was the first major demonstration that the whole process of both composition and sound synthesis could be arranged in a sequential string from beginning to end, and that the two operations complement one another. The composer starts with compositional algorithms, and ends with a finished product on audio tape.

"Computer Music for Percussion and Tape" (1968) and its later scoring for piccolo, voice, percussion, and tape (1981) are really just arrangements of portions of the earlier "Computer Cantata."

This leaves one more work from this earlier period, "Algorithms I for Nine Instruments and Tape" of 1968. However, I will defer discussion of it because, even though it was written in assembly language at Illinois, it belongs conceptually with two more recent works, "Algorithms II" and "Algorithms III."

Recent Compositions

I should now call attention to an important difference between these compositions and more recent ones. Formerly, the counting of events was done by beats; that is, composing was done linearly in relation to the finished score, beat by beat, moving from top to bottom line. This is, of course, an easy way to keep track of what happens because we are composing music just as we later hear it in the concert hall. The procedure is orderly and regular, easy to index, and seems, at first glance, the obvious way to proceed. And it works—up to a point. But this is not how a composer creates music, if the scheme shown in Figure 1 is accepted as a realistic model.

As I said before, I do not believe that compositional ideas flow in a one-to-one relationship to performance time. This is true even of such affairs as "free improvisation," because memory and anticipation have their roles even here. The image created by the beat-by-beat approach resembles the image of a platoon of soldiers marching in a parade. This indexing also creates a bias in the composing process because the first line logged in at each new beat is normally the top one. The top line (e.g., flute, violin I, or soprano, depending on the score) possesses more degrees of freedom than the one at the bottom (e.g., double bass). This bottom line has fewer options because available choices are limited by what has already occurred on the beat in question.

In recent music, I have replaced this rigid bookkeeping with a more fluid form of indexing. This is note count, not beat count. Since notes are of variable length, each line of a score proceeds at its own pace and extends beyond or lags behind the pack depending on how many notes have already been assigned to it and how many beats each note contains. This permits a composer to place events such as goals far ahead and to place entire themes, imitations of themes, harmonic resolutions, and all sorts of more sophisticated structures into any location. Even retrospective improvement or replacement of already composed material becomes possible. Beat count is, of course, still needed; but it becomes a subsidiary index, not a controlling one. The difference between these two methods of keeping track of what is being composed is illustrated in Figure 7. The main loop in program PHRASE augments the note count each time it recycles, always operating first on the laggard in the pack (See Table 3).

The principal composition that remains to be discussed is the large "Algorithms" cycle, the structure of which is shown in Table 4. The complete cycle consists of seven movements, symmetrically organized into a plan that sets timings to read the same way in either direction. The even-numbered movements are all slow movements; they exploit specialized

FIGURE 7. Two methods for logging compositional events: (a) beat count, (b) note count.

TABLE 3. Structure of Program "PHRASE"

(1) Main program and three closely related subroutines	(3) Composing subroutines
	(4) Results subroutines
(2) Control and choice subroutines	(5) Sound synthesis subroutines

algorithms for producing scores which are not intimately related to the progressive development of compositional modules that is the main feature of the odd-numbered faster movements. These faster movements move progressively from disorder and high information in the first movement to a rather highly determinate structure in the final movement.

These works are even more complex structurally, because each movement exists in four "versions." In effect, there exist twenty-eight movements, four sets of seven movements with parallel structures but different internal contents. Each "version" reflects small but important changes of input data or instructions inserted into the various compositional algorithms. They demonstrate that such changes drastically affect the impression of a given musical structure; and this demonstration is made in a controlled way, permitting the identification of the specific variance of input data or composing instructions. This realizes in concrete terms the ideas expressed earlier regarding variance in compositional procedure and end result.

"Persiflage for Flute, Oboe and Percussion" utilized a program in which many more controls were in place. "Persiflage" required twenty sets of input data defining limits on pitch and rhythm choices, proportions of play versus rest or of phrase assembly versus imitation, and so on. This imposed a gradual change of texture from very sparse and quiet to congested and loud. This can be seen in the two examples from the score shown in Figure 8. All of the phrase material in "Persiflage" was self-generated; there was no use of quotations, nor of serial processes. One motivation in writing this piece was finding out how one might build to a climax, because I felt such a study would be rewarding in terms of how one might later delegate

TABLE 4. The Complete Set of "Algorithms" Compositions

	Duration (minutes)
Algorithms I	
I. The Decay of Information	2
II. Icosahedron	3
III. The Incorporation of Constraints	4
Algorithms II	
IV. Campanology	5
Algorithms III	
V. Refinements	4
VI. Quotations and Phraseology	3
VII. Synthesis	2

such processes to a computer. In fact, what is consistent throughout all my work starting with "Algorithms I" is the search for ways of reducing the amount of composer-supplied input data and converting operations dependent upon such input to self-generating internal operations.

The first movement of "Algorithms I" introduced an evolving plan of stochastic order from zeroth to fourth order. This reduces the information content of the movement as it progresses; hence the title. The only variance permitted was the proportion of play to rest. "Version 1" is the emptiest, "Version 4" the fullest in terms of the number of notes played. Even this elementary variance provides striking contrasts among the four "versions."

The second movement is an integrated serial composition derived from a single tone row and all its transpositions and permutations, 576 notes

FIGURE 8. Two excerpts from "Persiflage for Flute, Oboe and Percussion." [Reproduced by permission of the publisher, Waterloo Music Company Limited, Box 250, Waterloo, Ontario N2J 4A5, Canada.]

TABLE 5. Basic Change-Ringing
Process for an Even Number of Bells

Row 1 (lead-end)	12345678
Row 2	21436587
Row 3	24163857
Row 4	42618375
Row 5	46281735
Row 6	64827153
Row 7	68472513
Row 8	86745231
Row 9	87654321
Row 10	78563412
Row 11	75836142
Row 12	57381624
Row 13	53718264
Row 14	35172846
Row 15	31527486
Row 16	13254768
- - - - - - - - -	
Row 17 (lead-end repeats)	12345678

in all. One subroutine also sorted out 576 randomly produced rhythms such that rhythmic simultaneities would be concentrated near the center of the movement. If rewritten (since this is one subroutine not yet updated), this subroutine could profitably be generalized so that sorting and comparing of rhythms in different voices could be adapted to many kinds of musical structures. The variance among the four "versions" of this movement involved the use of different tone rows, different limits on melodic leaps, and different assignments of playing instructions.

In each of the ten sections of the third movement, "The Incorporation of Constraints," there were introduced controls upon harmonic processes, melodic motion, and rhythmic choices. For its final section, I programmed an elementary cadence. The constraints put into each section were not retained for later use, but were inserted one by one and then set aside. (This is in sharp contrast to "Algorithms III," where the same idea of introducing controls was examined again; but this time they were retained, so that their effect was cumulative.) The variance among the four "versions" was restricted to play/rest ratios and stochastic order levels so that the constraints being imposed could be easily perceived.

"Algorithms II," composed in collaboration with Ravi Kumra, was completed four years later. This piece exploited change-ringing, a permutational compositional technique for producing nonrepeating melodic sequences, used by the English over many centuries for the ringing of church bells. Change-ringing involves flipping pairs of integers in a list like the one shown in Table 5. This is only the first stage of the whole process, which can extend to enormous lengths if the number of bells is large. A complete peal of twelve bells, for example, would require the playing of 12! (479,001,600) lines of the type shown above—a rather long melody, one might say. In ringing bells, the integers in Table 5 represent bells of different sizes and pitches.

In the four "versions" of "Algorithms II," we did something more substantial in terms of variance than in "Algorithms I." The four "versions" became more complex in structure from "Version 1" to "Version 4," because we made increasing use of change-ringing to control more and more of the structure of the movement. In "Version 1," no use was made of change-ringing; in "Version 2," it controlled pitch; in "Version 3," it controlled both pitch and rhythm; in "Version 4," it controlled pitch in four out of five simultaneously performed polyphonic textures.

"Algorithms III," is the culmination of all this work (including "A Preview . . ." and "Persiflage"). Like "Algorithms I," it contains three movements, but these are presented in reverse order.

The first movement, "Refinements," takes up where the last movement of "Algorithms I" leaves off. I have also imposed a consistent style variance among the four "versions" that persists throughout the composition. In "Version 1," all the phrase material is generated by the PHRASE system itself. In "Version 2," all thematic material consists of twelve-note rows, which means that all imitations are twelve-note rows as well. "Version 3" is restricted to the use of quotations of various other compositions as thematic material. Finally, "Version 4" combines all three of these options, and serves as the severest test that all the various components of the program are meshing together properly.

The second movement, "Quotations and Phraseology," continues this pattern, but applies it to a structure reminiscent of the middle movement of "Algorithms I." It resembles that earlier movement in that it too has a musical structure of maximum density and complexity located in its middle.

The final movement is a summarizing one. The four "versions" retain the stylistic biases already described. Not a great deal of new programming was done except to impose upon the four "versions" rudimentary formats resembling familiar structures such as sonata form and fugue. The idea, I should emphasize, is not the slavish pursuit of classical forms, but the abstraction of their underlying logic as a guide to programming that would enhance form-generating algorithms in the most general sense.

Future Prospects

The completion of "Algorithms III" represents the conclusion of a long-sustained research project in computer-assisted composition. Now it might be worthwhile to conclude with some broader thoughts about how we may reasonably expect computer-assisted composition to develop in the next decade or so.

First, the interest in computer-assisted composition is certain to grow—

not just in a narrow sense along the lines I have outlined here in my own work, but much more generally. Algorithmic rhetoric for expressing compositional concepts can be expected to replace much of what is now considered standard music theory. Composers will increasingly formulate their ideas in terms of algorithms, and this will have a profound effect on the evolution of musical style. This will also have its effect on the teaching of composition. Our offerings at SUNY Buffalo, which are by no means unique, involve two semesters of graduate coursework, one in composition, one in sound synthesis. Familiarity with analog electronic music is a prerequisite.

Second, the boundary between composition and sound synthesis will become more and more fuzzy. This will markedly expand the repertory of compositional resources. At present, the most important decision a composer makes when planning a piece of computer music is the first one: Should it be for conventional musical instruments (i.e., scores of the type I have been discussing)? If so, the limitations of these instruments must be accepted, including their tuning systems—which normally means equal temperament. All the programming I have discussed here has implicitly assumed equal temperament, programs for portions of "HPSCHD" being the notable exception. So far, it has been valuable to use traditional and current compositional practice as a guideline for programming. Fortunately, since the well-tempered chromatic scale sets pitch relationships only, other parameters are not affected by this limitation.

On the other hand, once a composer chooses to compose for a purely electronic medium—and this includes digital synthesizers oriented toward performance as well as studio-type digital-to-analog conversion—then far fewer restrictions on the gamut of possibilities exist, because we now deal with a continuum. This is in sharp contrast to the use of normal musical instruments, where many real restrictions exist: not only technical ones imposed by performance realities, but also conceptual ones imposed by a vocabulary of discrete elements. In this situation, there seems to be a trade-off. Using familiar instruments, the loss of generality is substantial; on the other hand, the gain is also substantial because all the resources of both historical and current compositional craft become available.

Third, one important feature of the programming I have been describing has been the forging of an efficient link between composition programs and sound synthesis programs. This, indeed, is the first practical step toward merging the two significant developments into one integrated whole, a direct flow from input into an algorithmic compositional process to produce output to a system which converts such intentions directly into sound. All the necessary components already exist, so for me the next step is simply to tie them all together. Once this is done, there is no reason why much of what I have described here cannot be generalized so that it applies to a musical continuum as well as to an assemblage of discrete events.

Fourth, it is already a fact that digital synthesizers (Synclavier II is one example) are rapidly replacing equivalent analog synthesizers. This domain includes synthesizers designed for performance as well as for studio installation. Their advantages are all the obvious ones: precision, versatility, compactness, memory, price. Although most research attention is currently being directed toward their acoustical properties (how to achieve effective sound at a realistic cost), some attention is being paid to building at least some compositional power into them. My guess is that compositional options to be built into digital synthesizers initially will be rather elementary, both for technical reasons (computing time, memory allocation, etc.) and sales concerns (the domination of the market by commercial music).

Finally, digital synthesizers like the Synclavier II and William Buxton's system open up, at last, the possibility of meaningful interactive composing via computers. Thus far, almost all computer-assisted composition of any complexity, including my own, has had to be done by batch processing, with all the delays and inconveniences that such processing often entails. I imagine, however, that the transition to interactive composition can only come by gradual stages for reasons which this article has examined, reasons which arise from the elusive nature of the problem being addressed.

Author's Postscript

Since this article was published, I have completed the composition, "Algorithms III" which was described as the culminating work of the "Algorithms Cycle." Moreover, both "Version 1" and "Version 3" of this composition have been performed and recorded, and "Version 2" and "Version 4" are scheduled for performance in April 1987. Also, the recording for Wergo Records mentioned in the Discography has been released as Wergo 60128, but with a somewhat different content which starts off with a new composition prepared for "Expo '85" in Tsukuba, Japan, namely, "Expo '85 for Multiple Synthesizers." The record also includes older compositions mentioned in the article, namely, "Illiac Suite for String Quartet," "Persiflage for Flute, Oboe and Percussion," "Computer Music for Percussion and Tape," and "An Avalanche . . .".

References

Cherry, C. *On Human Communication.* 3rd Edition. New York: John Wiley and Sons, 1978.
Ernst, D. *The Evolution of Electronic Music.* New York: Schirmer Books, 1977.

Hiller, L.A., and Isaacson, L.M. *Experimental Music*. New York: McGraw-Hill, 1959; Westport, CT: Greenwood Press, 1979.

Lincoln, H., ed. *The Computer and Music*. Ithaca: Cornell University Press, 1970.

Mathews, M.V., et al. *The Technology of Computer Music*. Cambridge: M.I.T. Press, 1969.

Peterson, D. *Genesis II: Creation and Recreation with Computers*. Reston, VA: Reston Publishing Co. (Prentice-Hall), 1983.

Discography

In the discography which follows, I have limited the listings to records which contain examples of computer-assisted composition. Because records have an unpredictable way of appearing, disappearing, and occasionally reappearing, I have listed several important out-of-print releases. Deleted items also have a way of turning up in discount bins in certain record shops.

Larry Austin: "Canadian Coastlines." Folkways FTS 37475.

*Pierre Barbaud and Roger Blanchard: "Imprévisibles Nouveautés—Algorithme I." Critère Productions R. Douette CRD-430A.

Klarenz Barlow: "Çoğluotobüsişletmisi" ("Bus Journey to Parametron"). Wergo 60098.

Herbert Brun: "Sonoriferous Loops," "Non-Sequitur VI," "Algol Rhythms," along with other compositions. Non-Sequitur 301056/8 (available from composer).

John Cage and Lejaren Hiller: "HPSCHD." Nonesuch H71224.

*Lejaren Hiller: "Algorithms I (Versions 1 and 4)." Deutsche Grammophon 2543005.

Lejaren Hiller: "Avalanche. . . ." Capra 1206.

Lejaren Hiller: "Illiac Suite," "Computer Music," "Algorithms II," "Persiflage" (new record currently in preparation, see Author's Postcript, Wergo Records).

Lejaren Hiller and Robert Baker: "Computer Cantata." CRI SD310.

*Yannis Xenakis: "ST/4," "Atrées," "Morsima-Amorsima." Angel S36560.

*"Music from Mathematics," including James Tenney's "Noise Study." Decca DL9103.

*"Voice of the Computer," including Tenney's "Stochastic String Quartet." Decca 710180.

* = out of print.

Mathematical Modeling with Spreadsheets*

Commercial spreadsheet programs can be used to create and manipulate a variety of mathematical models.

DEANE E. ARGANBRIGHT

The electronic spreadsheet, most often thought of as a tool for business and economics, is being applied increasingly for modeling, teaching, and problem solving in a much wider range of disciplines. This article will illustrate how a spreadsheet can be a creative tool for both mathematics and mathematical modeling. A spreadsheet's concrete matrix format allows us to construct our mathematical models and algorithms on a computer in essentially the same natural manner that we do "by hand." Moreover, spreadsheets provide us with an easy way to interact with our models, allowing us to see quickly and visually the effects of changes in parameters or hypotheses.

We have chosen examples which, though concise, give an indication of the variety of topics that can be modeled on a spreadsheet and present techniques that can be adapted readily to more sophisticated models. While our examples will be described using VisiCalc, their translation into the format of other spreadsheet programs is straightforward.

A spreadsheet program employs a rectangular array, or matrix, a portion of which is displayed on the computer screen. The dimensions of the array vary with the program; standard VisiCalc employs 254 rows and 63 columns. The size of a computer's memory may prevent us from using the

---

*Additional examples in population migration and number theory may be found in the original article in the Summer 1986 ABACUS.

DEANE E. ARGANBRIGHT is currently a professor of mathematics and computer science at Whitworth College. He has a Ph.D. in finite group theory from the University of Washington. In recent years he has developed a wide range of mathematically oriented applications of electronic spreadsheets, and has presented addresses on this topic at national meetings of the Mathematical Association of America. He spent 1985 as the first Visiting Fellow at Bendigo College of Advanced Education in Australia.

Reprinted from ABACUS, Volume 3, Number 4, Summer 1986.

entire array. Columns of the array are usually denoted by letters (A, B, C, . . .), and rows by positive integers (1, 2, 3, . . .). A location or *cell* in the spreadsheet is given by its column and row (for instance, B4 is the cell at Column B, Row 4). A screen cursor points to one cell of the spreadsheet. After we position the cursor on a particular cell, we can then enter either a descriptive label, a number, or an algebraic expression into that cell. An algebraic expression, or formula, obtains its value from the cells that it references, and this value is displayed on the screen. If we change the entry in a cell, the value of each cell in the spreadsheet is recalculated, and values of the updated spreadsheet appear on the screen.

Figure 1 illustrates these concepts. The formulas that we have entered are shown on the left, and the resulting screen display in the center. In many spreadsheet programs we must choose the order in which the spreadsheet is calculated, either row by row (R) or column by column (C), and then arrange our model accordingly. In the formula heading we will indicate the order to be selected.

In Figure 1 we have created a spreadsheet version of the classical Newton-Raphson algorithm to approximate the square root of a number x. We enter x into Cell B1, and an estimate for its square root into Cell B2. The formula $+$B2 in Cell B5 copies this estimate as an initial approximation a_0. The next approximation a_1 of the square root is found in Cell B6 as the mean of the previous approximation a_0 ($+$B5) and the quotient x/a_0 (B1/B5). Subsequent approximations are computed similarly, using the recurrence relation

$$a_0 = \text{estimate},$$
$$a_{i+1} = .5(a_i + x/a_i).$$

The indicated formulas can be entered either individually, or by replicating (or copying) the formulas in Row 6.

To replicate the formula in Cell B6 down Column B using VisiCalc, we first place the cursor on Cell B6 and enter the command to replicate (/**R**). After receiving a prompt to enter the range of replication, we enter

B6 . . . B6:B7 . . . B20

to indicate that the formula in Cell B6 (literally, the formulas in Cells B6 through B6) is to be replicated into Cells B7 through B20. Finally, on receiving prompts asking whether the three variables in Cell B6 are to be treated as no-change (N) or relative (R) locations, we reply with **RNR**, indicating that each B5 is treated as a relative (R) location (that is, as the "cell immediately above the one containing the formula"), and B1 as a no-change (N) or constant location. The indicated formulas of Figure 1 will then be generated in Column B. We can generate formulas to count

Square-Root Algorithm

	Formulas (R)			Output (B2 = 7)			Output (B2 = 10)	
	A	B		A	B		A	B
1	NUM =	45.678	1	NUM =	45.678	1	NUM =	45.678
2	EST =	7	2	EST =	7	2	EST =	10
3			3			3		
4	ITER	APPROXIMATION	4	ITER	APPROX	4	ITER	APPROX
5	0	+B2	5	0	7	5	0	10
6	1+A5	.5*(B5+(B1/B5))	6	1	6.762714	6	1	7.283900
7	1+A6	.5*(B6+(B1/B6))	7	2	6.758551	7	2	6.777496
8	1+A7	.5*(B7+(B1/B7))	8	3	6.758550	8	3	6.758577
:	Rep.	Replicate	9	4	6.758550	9	4	6.758550
	↓ [R]	↓ [RNR]						

FIGURE 1

iterations in Column A similarly, by replicating the expression in Cell A6 with the variable A5 relative (R). Replication is indicated in our spreadsheet descriptions by arrows and the symbols [N] and [R].

After entering the model of Figure 1, we can easily investigate the consequences of changing the value of x (Cell B1) or the initial estimate a_0 (Cell B2). For example, if we change the value of Cell B2 to 10 (or even to 100 or 1000) the spreadsheet is recalculated, as in Figure 1, giving us rapid, visual indication that this algorithm is not very sensitive to the initial approximation.

Most spreadsheet programs permit us to employ circular references. A circular reference occurs when a formula refers to the cell that contains it, either directly or through a series of formulas in other cells. We will exploit this feature in some of our examples. Since each spreadsheet program handles this topic differently, a user's guide should be consulted for details.

We illustrate the use of circular references in Figure 2 by computing the growth of a given principal at compound annual interest. The formula @IF(B1 = 0,0,1 + D2) in Cell D2 is interpreted as: "If B1 = 0, then 0, else 1 + D2" (VisiCalc identifies library functions by @). Cell B1 is used to initialize the model. When the value of B1 is 0, a 0 is entered for the year in Cell D2, and the initial principal B3 is copied into Cell D3. When Cell B1 is set to a nonzero value, the value of Cell D2 is increased by 1, and the value of Cell D3 is multiplied by the factor (1 + rate) to compute the value after one year. Each time we press the recalculation key (usually "!") the spreadsheet will be recalculated. The first few iterations are shown in the figure.

Throughout this article, our spreadsheet descriptions are presented in the general format of Figures 1 and 2. Occasionally we will display long formulas and replication details beyond the spreadsheet description. For

Compound Interest

Formulas (R)

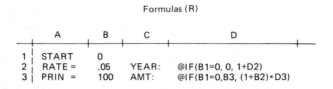

	A	B	C	D
1	START	0		
2	RATE =	.05	YEAR:	@IF(B1=0, 0, 1+D2)
3	PRIN =	100	AMT:	@IF(B1=0,B3, (1+B2)*D3)

Output

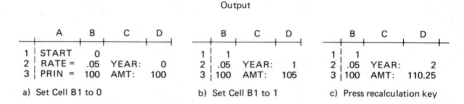

	A	B	C	D
1	START	0		
2	RATE =	.05	YEAR:	0
3	PRIN =	100	AMT:	100

a) Set Cell B1 to 0

	B	C	D
1	1		
2	.05	YEAR:	1
3	100	AMT:	105

b) Set Cell B1 to 1

	B	C	D
1	1		
2	.05	YEAR:	2
3	100	AMT:	110.25

c) Press recalculation key

FIGURE 2

example, in Figure 5, the notation <**B8**> indicates that the formula entered in Cell B8,

$$@SUM (B3 \ldots B6),$$

can be found below.

A Mathematical Algorithm: Binomial Probability

An extensive range of mathematical algorithms can be implemented on a spreadsheet. We will present an algorithm to generate binomial probability distributions as one example. A binomial event is one that has two possible outcomes, often denoted by success (S) and failure (F). For example, when a coin is flipped we might call obtaining a head a success, and a tail a failure. If the coin is fair, the probabilities of these events are P(S) = 0.5, P(F) = 0.5. In general, the probability of obtaining i successes (for $i = 0, 1, \ldots, n$), in n repetitions of a binomial event for which P(S) = p, is given by $P[i] = C(n, i)p^i (1 - p)^{n-i}$, where $C(n, i) = n!/[i!(n - i)!]$. The probabilities $P[i]$ can be generated by the recurrence relation:

$$P[0] = (1 - p)^n,$$

$$P[i + 1] = \frac{(n - i)P[i]p}{(i + 1)(1 - p)}$$

We use this relation in Column B of our spreadsheet model in Figure 3. In Column C, the probabilities of Column B are multiplied by a scaling factor (Cell C2), with the results displayed using the "*" format. In this format a cell's value is shown on the screen as k *s, where k is the largest integer not exceeding that value (some spreadsheets round). For example, Cell C4's value of 2.3 appears as **. Thus, our model not only calculates the binomial distribution for the given n and p, but also generates a picture of it. To see both the numeric and graphic effects of changing n or p, we only need change the values of Cells B1 and B2. Most spreadsheet programs allow us to increase the display width of Column C, perhaps by using a split-screen format, for even more effective display.

Legislative Apportionment

Challenging mathematical problems frequently arise in deceptively simple-looking settings. One such problem, which has generated interest for many years, is that of devising a fair method for legislative apportionment. To illustrate the problem, suppose that a country with three states, X, Y, and Z, has a population of 100 (million), and that we wish to apportion to each state an equitable number of seats in the country's legislature. If the legislature has n seats, how should we apportion these among the states?

One possible method is to award each state a fraction of seats in the legislature proportional to its percentage of the country's population. This portion is called the state's quota. If $n = 10$ and the populations of the states are 50, 30, and 20, respectively, then we can do this (Figure 4a), since each state's quota is an integer. However, since this will seldom be the case, as for example with $n = 10$ and populations of 53, 33, and 14

Binomial Probability

Formulas (R)

	A	B	C
1	N =	8	SCALE
2	P =	.3	40
3	I	P(I)	
4	0	(1−B2)^B1	+C2*B4
5	1+A4	+(B1−A4)*B4*B2/(A5*(1−B2))	+C2*B5
6	1+A5	+(B1−A5)*B5*B2/(A6*(1−B2))	+C2*B6
7	1+A6	+(B1−A6)*B6*B2/(A7*(1−B2))	+C2*B7
:	Rep.	Replicate	Rep.
	↓ [R]	↓ [NRRNRN]	↓ [NR]

Output

	A	B	C
1	N =	8	SCALE
2	P =	.3	40
3	I	P(I)	
4	0	.058	**
5	1	.198	*******
6	2	.296	***********
7	3	.254	**********
8	4	.136	*****
9	5	.047	*

FIGURE 3

Apportionment using Hamilton's Method

	Pop	%	Quo	Seats			Pop	%	Quo	I	R	Seats			Pop	%	Quo	I	R	Seats
X	50	.50	5.0	5		X	53	.53	5.3	5	.3	5		X	53	.53	5.8	5	.8	6
Y	30	.30	3.0	3		Y	33	.33	3.3	3	.3	3		Y	33	.33	3.6	3	.6	4
Z	20	.20	2.0	2		Z	14	.14	1.4	1	.4	2		Z	14	.14	1.5	1	.5	1
	100		10.0	10			100		10.0	9		10			100		11.0	9		11

a) n = 10 seats   b) n = 10 seats   c) n = 11 seats

FIGURE 4

(Figure 4b), and because we cannot allocate to a state a fractional number of seats, we must employ a more sophisticated method.

Hamilton's Method is a traditional apportionment scheme once used for the United States House of Representatives. Using this method, as illustrated in Figure 4b with $n = 10$, we first award to each state the integer part of its quota (5, 3, 1). We then award additional seats, if necessary, to the states having the largest remaining fractions. In Figure 4b, State Z, with a remainder of 0.4, receives the additional seat. However, this method gives rise to many unexpected difficulties. For example, suppose that the size of the legislature is increased to $n = 11$ seats. Surprisingly, as we see in Figure 4c, Z actually loses a seat, even though there are now more seats to allocate! This phenomenon, called the Alabama Paradox, is discussed from both historical and mathematical perspectives by Balinsky and Young.

Our spreadsheet model for Hamilton's Method is shown in Figure 5. It uses $n = 21$ seats and four states. A state's quota is calculated in Column C. When the value of Cell F1 is set to 0, the integer part of each state's quota is calculated in Column D and the remaining fraction in Column E, with the largest fraction found in Cell E8 using the library function @MAX to calculate the maximum value in the range E3 . . . E6. The library function @SUM is used similarly elsewhere in Row 8. The formulas in Column F add one seat to a state whose remainder is the maximum. If more seats must be awarded, we set Cell F1 to a nonzero value. Then, and each time we press the recalculation key thereafter, the values from Column F are copied into Column D, and the process is repeated. We continue this recalculation until all n seats have been awarded in Column F. We can modify our model to insure that we never assign more than n seats by changing the expression in Cell F3 to @IF(@AND(D8<B1,E3 = E8), 1 + D3,D3) and replicating it down Column F.

The output is shown for the three iterations needed. By changing the value of n (Cell B1) to 20 and repeating the process, we can see that this example also gives rise to the Alabama Paradox. We can use this spreadsheet to generate the results of Figure 4 by changing Cell B1 to 10 and entering the populations of Figure 4 into Column B, using 0 as the pop-

Hamilton's Method

Formulas (C)

	A	B	C	D	E	F
1	N =	21			START>	0
2	STATE	POP	QUOTA	INTEGER	FRACTION	SEATS
3	X	51	+B1*(B3/B8)	@IF(F1=0, @INT(C3), F3)	+C3-D3	@IF(E3=E8, 1+D3, D3)
4	Y	32	+B1*(B4/B8)	@IF(F1=0, @INT(C4), F4)	+C4-D4	@IF(E4=E8, 1+D4, D4)
5	Z	8	+B1*(B5/B8)	@IF(F1=0, @INT(C5), F5)	+C5-D5	@IF(E5=E8, 1+D5, D5)
6	W	9	+B1*(B6/B8)	@IF(F1=0, @INT(C6), F6)	+C6-D6	@IF(E6=E8, 1+D6, D6)
7						
8	TOT	<B8>	@SUM(C3...C6)	@SUM(D3...D6)	<E8>	@SUM(F3...F6)

B8: @SUM(B3...B6); E8: @MAX(E3...E6)
Replicate: From: C3 To : C4...C6 [NRN] ; From:D3 To : D4...D6 [NRR];
From: E3 To : E4...E6 [RR] ;   From:F3 To : F4...F6 [RNRR]

Output

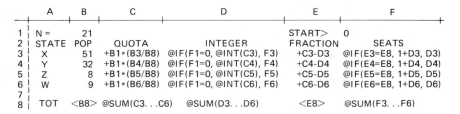

	A	B	C	D	E	F
1	N=	21			ST>	0
2	ST	POP	QUOTA	IN	FR	SE
3	X	51	10.71	10	.71	10
4	Y	32	6.72	6	.72	6
5	Z	8	1.68	1	.68	1
6	W	9	1.89	1	.89	2
7						
8	TO	100	21.00	18	.89	19

a) Set Cell F1 to 0

	B	C	D	E	F
1	21			ST>	1
2	POP	QUOTA	IN	FR	SE
3	51	10.71	10	.71	10
4	32	6.72	6	.72	7
5	8	1.68	1	.6	1
6	9	1.89	2	−.11	2
7					
8	100	21.00	19	.72	20

b) Set Cell F1 to 1

	B	C	D	E	F
1	21			ST>	1
2	POP	QUOTA	IN	FR	SE
3	51	10.71	10	.71	11
4	32	6.72	7	−.28	7
5	8	1.68	1	.68	1
6	9	1.89	2	−.11	2
7					
8	100	21.00	20	.71	21

c) Press recalculation key

FIGURE 5

ulation of State W. It is easy to modify the model to incorporate more states, and to insure that each state will have at least one seat.

Hamilton's Method gives rise to other "paradoxes" as well. One, the Population Paradox, is illustrated in Figure 6. In this example, using four states and $n = 435$, we can see that between the 1970 and 1980 reapportionments Y has gained the most population, but has lost a seat, while X has lost population but has gained a seat!

Hamilton's Method and the Population Paradox

	1970 Apportionment		1980 Apportionment		Change 1970-1980	
State	Population	Seats	Population	Seats	Population	Seats
W	1001	77	1036	78	+35(+3.5%)	+1
X	111	8	110	9	− 1(−0.9%)	+1
Y	4000	307	4060	306	+60(+1.5%)	−1
Z	555	43	560	42	+ 5(+0.9%)	−1
	5667	435	5766	435		

FIGURE 6

Webster's Method

Formulas (R)

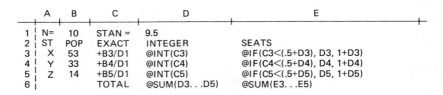

	A	B	C	D	E
1	N=	10	STAN =	9.5	
2	ST	POP	EXACT	INTEGER	SEATS
3	X	53	+B3/D1	@INT(C3)	@IF(C3<(.5+D3), D3, 1+D3)
4	Y	33	+B4/D1	@INT(C4)	@IF(C4<(.5+D4), D4, 1+D4)
5	Z	14	+B5/D1	@INT(C5)	@IF(C5<(.5+D5), D5, 1+D5)
6			TOTAL	@SUM(D3...D5)	@SUM(E3...E5)

Replicate: From: C3 To : C4...C5 [RN] ; From: D3 To : D4...D5 [R] ;
From: E3 To : E4...E5 [RRRR]

Output

	A	B	C	D	E
1	N=	10	STAN=	10	
2	ST	Pop	EXACT	INT	SEATS
3	X	53	5.3	5	5
4	Y	33	3.3	3	3
5	Z	14	1.4	1	1
6			TOTAL	9	9

	A	B	C	D	E
1	N=	10	STAN=	9	
2	ST	Pop	EXACT	INT	SEATS
3	X	53	5.889	5	6
4	Y	33	3.667	3	4
5	Z	14	1.556	1	2
6			TOTAL	9	12

	A	B	C	D	E
1	N=	10	STAN=	9.5	
2	ST	POP	EXACT	INT	SEATS
3	X	53	5.579	5	6
4	Y	33	3.474	3	3
5	Z	14	1.474	1	1
6			TOTAL	9	10

FIGURE 7

In order to overcome the difficulties presented by Hamilton's Method, a number of other apportionment schemes have been employed or proposed. One of the best-known is Webster's Method. To use it, we first estimate the size of a standard legislative district, that is, the number of people to be represented by one legislator. We then divide this number into each state's population to find the number of seats to allocate to the state, rounding each of the results to the nearest integer. If this process results in the allocation of more than n seats, we increase the standard district size; if fewer than n seats are allocated, we decrease it. By continually adjusting the standard district size, we eventually obtain an allocation of n seats. It has been shown that Webster's Method eliminates the "paradoxes" of Hamilton's Method, although it introduces others.

Webster's Method fits naturally into a spreadsheet format. Our model is shown in Figure 7. We enter an estimate of the standard district size into Cell D1 and find the resulting number of allocated seats in Cell E6. We adjust the value of Cell D1 until $E6 = n$. The greatest integer function, @INT, is used in Column D. The method of rounding can be seen in Cell E3. If X's exact entitlement (Cell C3) is less than the arithmetic mean $(.5 + D3)$ of the integers immediately above and below it (D3, D3 + 1), we round down (D3); otherwise we round up (1 + D3).

A number of other related divisor methods have been proposed. Each uses a different criteria for rounding in Column E, shown here for Cell E3:

☐ Hill (use geometric mean): @IF(C3<@SQRT(D3*(1+D3)), D3, 1+D3)
☐ Dean (use harmonic mean): @IF(C3<(2*D3*(1+D3)/(2*D3+1)), D3, 1+D3)
☐ Jefferson (round down): +D3
☐ Adams (round up): 1+D3

Genetic Modeling: The Hardy–Weinberg Law

A genetic characteristic in an individual diploid organism typically is determined by a pair of genes. Let us suppose that a gene for a certain characteristic (such as eye color) can be one of two forms, or *alleles*, A (let's say brown) or B (blue). In this case each individual will have a pair of genes for the characteristic of one of three genotypes: AA, AB, or BB. One of the fundamental principles of elementary genetics concerning proportions of alleles and genotypes in a population is the Hardy–Weinberg Law:

Suppose that the alleles of a genetic characteristic are A and B, and that, of the total number of genes for this characteristic in a large population, the proportion of allele A is $P(A) = p$, and the proportion of allele B is $P(B) = q$, where $p + q = 1$. Then, if mating is random within the population and all individuals have identical reproductive rates, the allele and genotype proportions in the population will remain constant in the future.

Our construction of a spreadsheet model illustrating this principle is based on a standard derivation. If a gene is selected at random from the population, the probabilities of its being of given alleles are $P(A) = p$, $P(B) = q$, respectively. Since mating is random, the probability of an A allele from one parent uniting with an A allele from another to produce an AA offspring is $P(AA) = P(A)P(A) = p^2$. The probabilities of producing an offspring of the other genotypes are similarly $P(AB) = pq + qp = 2pq$ and $P(BB) = q^2$. Thus, in the succeeding generation, the proportion of allele A in the population will be $p^2 + (2pq)/2$ (all of the genes from AA individuals and half of the genes from AB individuals). Since $p^2 + (2pq)/2 = p(p + q) = p$, the proportion of allele A—and therefore of B also—remains constant.

Our spreadsheet model and its output are given in Figure 8. Allele proportions p and q for each generation are calculated in Columns B and C. The genotype proportions are calculated in Columns D–F, using the expressions p^2, $2pq$, and q^2. Allele proportions are found using the genotype proportions of the previous generation and $.5P(AB) + P(AA)$ and $.5P(AB) + P(BB)$.

Once we have constructed our basic model, it is then easy to modify it in order to illustrate other genetic concepts that arise from changing the Hardy–Weinberg assumptions. As one example, we examine the concept of selection. Suppose that the fraction of AA individuals able to re-

Hardy-Weinberg Law

Formulas (R)   Output

	A	B	C	D	E	F		A	B	C	D	E	F
1	P =	.6	HARDY-WEINBERG				1	P = .6 HARDY- WEINBERG					
2							2						
3	GEN	A	B	AA	AB	BB	3	GEN	A	B	AA	AB	BB
4	0	+B1	1−B1	+B4*B4	2*B4*C4	+C4*C4	4	0	.6	.4	.36	.48	.16
5	1+ A4	.5*E4+D4	.5*E4+F4	+B5*B5	2*B5*C5	+C5*C5	5	1	.6	.4	.36	.48	.16
6	I1+ A5	.5*E5+D5	.5*E5+F5	+B6*B6	2*B6*C6	+C6*C6	6	2	.6	.4	.36	.48	.16
:	Rep.	Rep.	Rep.	Rep.	Rep.	Rep.	7	3	.6	.4	.36	.48	.16
	↓[R]	↓[R]	↓[RR]	↓[RR]	↓[RR]	↓[RR]							

FIGURE 8

produce is x, $0 \le x \le 1$, while the corresponding fractions for AB and BB individuals are y and z, respectively, with $0 \le y,z \le 1$. If one of these fitness coefficients x, y, z is less than the others, we say that there has been selection against that characteristic. If x, y, z are not equal, allele and genotype proportions in successive generations will no longer remain constant.

Figure 9 presents a spreadsheet model for selection. The fitness coefficients x, y, z for genotypes AA, AB, BB are entered into cells D2–F2. Population genotype proportions are calculated as before in Columns D–F. Next, in Columns G–I we multiply these proportions by the reproduction rates, and use the resulting values in Columns K–M to find genotype proportions among the reproducing individuals. These proportions in turn are used in the next row of Columns B and C to compute allele proportions for the succeeding generation. Output for the case $x = y = 1$, $z = .8$ is shown. Our output format indicates that the segment for screen display consists of the population proportions of Columns A–F.

Our model now allows us to investigate the effects of relative or complete selection against a certain genotype by simply changing the values of Cells D2–F2. Similar models can be constructed to examine topics such as mutation or migration.

Advantages and Drawbacks

The examples discussed here represent a brief sample of the variety of mathematical topics that can be implemented on a spreadsheet. In our presentation we have concentrated on using elementary features that are available on most spreadsheet programs. However, some programs have additional features that can greatly increase both the scope of the modeling capability and the effectiveness of the displays. Such features include random number generation, sorting, multiple windows for displaying different sections of the spreadsheet simultaneously, and the ability to define var-

Hardy-Weinberg Law with Selection

Formulas (R)

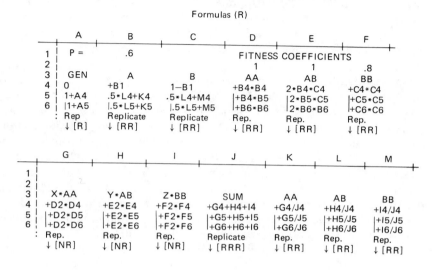

Output

FIGURE 9

iable names for use in formulas. Integrated programs, like Lotus 1-2-3, also offer the possibility of combining graphics and data-management capabilities with spreadsheet models.

Since it is also possible to implement examples like ours using programs written in high-level languages such as Pascal or Fortran, it is natural to compare features of the two approaches. In such a comparison, certain shortcomings of spreadsheets are apparent.

First, spreadsheet programs are not designed to handle truly large models efficiently. The recalculation of a large spreadsheet is a relatively slow process, and the number of calculations that can be performed in an algorithm is effectively limited, since each computation must be carried out either in a separate cell or through the use of circular references and recalculation.

Second, spreadsheet programs generally do not allow us to use the same structured approach possible in programs written in high-level languages, and currently do not permit user-defined functions or procedures. Consequently, spreadsheet descriptions for complex models can be more difficult to read than structured programs. Furthermore, some standard mathematical operations, such as the pivoting techniques used in linear algebra and linear programming, are not easy to implement on a spreadsheet.

On the other hand, in such a comparison, many strengths of the spreadsheet approach also become apparent. The spreadsheet matrix immediately gives us a convenient visual format in which to design, implement, and analyze mathematical algorithms and models. Moreover, spreadsheet implementation is often conceptually closer to the way we normally think about and do mathematics. Algorithms that are iterative or recursive, or that can be presented in a table format, generally can be implemented on a spreadsheet essentially as we describe and present them with pencil and paper. In fact, were we to work the examples in this article by hand, we would probably adopt the same layouts and computational procedures that we have used in our spreadsheet implementations.

The spreadsheet format and recalculation features also provide us with a concrete and graphic way to interact with an algorithm or model. We can quickly see the effects of changes in the parameters or formulas of a model by modifying entries directly in the output display.

Finally, much less time is required to become proficient at spreadsheet operation, and to be able to implement reasonably sophisticated models, than is needed to become equally proficient in programming. This can provide new opportunities in computing, especially for those with little or no programming background.

Thus, each approach has its advantages. While standard programming languages are superior for use with algorithms that require computational efficiency, spreadsheets offer many conceptual and interactive advantages. Their size limitations do not present difficulties for many algorithms and models. Even when they do, we can often construct smaller spreadsheet models to gain insight into the mathematical concepts involved before designing more efficient high-level-language programs. Moreover, the usefulness of spreadsheets in mathematics may well be further enhanced in the future by the development of spreadsheet programs that incorporate user-defined functions and built-in procedures for such operations as pivoting.

For Further Reading

Arganbright, Deane E. "The Electronic Spreadsheet and Mathematical Algorithms." *The College Mathematics Journal* **15**, 2(1984):148–57.

———. "Mathematical Applications of an Electronic Spreadsheet." In: *Computers in Mathematics Education: The 1984 Yearbook of the National Council of Teachers of Mathematics*. Reston, VA, 1984, 184–93.

———. "Mathematical Modeling with Spreadsheets." ABACUS **3**, 4(1986):18–31.

———. "Spreadsheet Solutions for Mathematical Modeling Problems." ABACUS **4**, 1(1986):24–27.

———. *Mathematical Applications of Electronic Spreadsheets*. New York: McGraw-Hill, 1985.

Balinsky, Michael L., and Young, H. Peyton. *Fair Representation*. New Haven, CT: Yale University Press, 1982.

Brams, Steven J.; Lucas, William F.; and Straffin, Philip D. Jr., eds. *Political and Related Models*. New York: Springer-Verlag, 1983.

Smith, J. Maynard. *Models in Ecology*. Cambridge: Cambridge University Press, 1974.

Wilson, Edward G., and Bossert, William H. *A Primer of Population Biology*. Sunderland, MA: Sinauer Associates Inc., 1971.

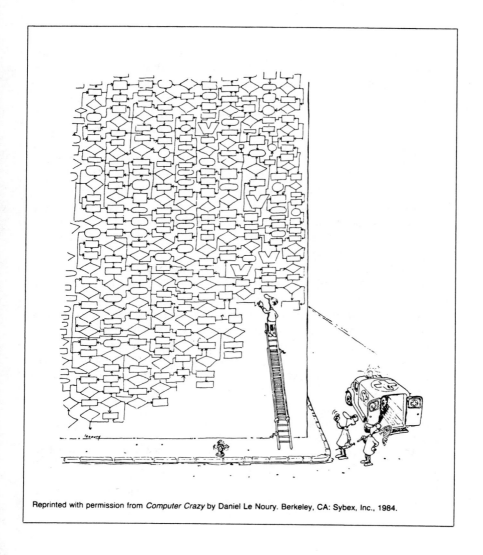

Reprinted with permission from *Computer Crazy* by Daniel Le Noury. Berkeley, CA: Sybex, Inc., 1984.

U.S. Versus *IBM:* An Exercise in Futility?

The longest-running antitrust suit in U.S. history petered out two years ago. What did it accomplish?

Robert P. Bigelow

As the administration of Lyndon Johnson wound to a close, Attorney General Ramsey Clark had to decide what to do about his investigation of possible antitrust violations by International Business Machines Corporation, then (and now) the world's largest computer manufacturer. Should he leave the matter for further action by Nixon's Attorney General, or should he file suit to make sure that the efforts of the Johnson administration had not gone to waste? He decided to file.

On 17 January 1969, the last business day of the Johnson administration, the Department of Justice filed a civil antitrust action against IBM alleging violation of Section 2 of the *Sherman Act,* 15 USC Section 2, the basic federal antimonopoly law [see *Glossary*]. Thirteen years later, on 8 January 1982, Reagan's Assistant Attorney General William Baxter, following an extensive review of the case, announced that the Department had decided to drop the case entirely.

Between these two events, David N. Edelstein, Chief Judge of the Federal Court for the Southern District of New York (who had sat on an earlier IBM antitrust suit which began in 1952 and ended in 1956), assigned this case to himself in 1972, in an effort to expedite its conclusion, since very little had happened in the preceding three years. Thereafter, he made a number of orders of a controversial nature, but still the trial did not begin until 19 May 1975. Three years later, on 27 April 1978, the government concluded its case; IBM's defense followed and lasted another three

ROBERT P. BIGELOW is counsel to the Boston law firm of Warner & Stockpole. He has written numerous articles on the legal aspects of computers; he also edits the monthly "Computer Law Newsletter," and has served as a columnist for American and Canadian computer periodicals. He is a Fellow of the British Computer Society.

This version has been shortened by the editor from the original article that appeared in ABACUS, Volume 1, Number 2, Winter 1984.

Glossary

Complaint	The document in which the plaintiff (in this case the government) sets out the facts it claims entitle it to relief by the court.
Consent decree	An agreement between the government and the defendant in which the defendant does not admit that it violated the law, but agrees that it will follow stated rules of conduct in the future.
Court of Appeals	There are twelve Federal Courts of Appeal covering the entire United States. The Second Circuit hears appeals from federal district (trial) courts in Connecticut, New York, and Vermont.
Discovery	Procedures during the pretrial stage in which each side tries to find out all it can about the other side's case. The purpose of discovery is to avoid surprise.
Sherman Act	The basic antitrust law of the United States, enacted in 1890. Section 2, which the Justice Department claimed IBM violated, says, "Every person who shall monopolize, or attempt to monopolize, or combine or conspire with any other person or persons, to monopolize any part of the trade or commerce among the several States, or with foreign nations, shall be deemed guilty of a misdemeanor. . . ."
Tunney Act	A federal law which requires, when a consent decree is entered in antitrust case, that the proposed decree be published and open for comment by the public.

years until the spring of 1981. Along the way, some new law was made, particularly regarding the right of the government to call expert witnesses without paying their standard fee, and establishing that apparent bias on the part of a judge is not necessarily grounds for forcing the judge off the case.

A Brief History of the Litigation

The lawsuit was filed under Section 4 of the Sherman Act, authorizing the federal government to bring suit to prevent and restrain monopolies. The government's *complaint* [see *Glossary*] charged that IBM "has attempted to monopolize and has monopolized [the market] . . . in general purpose digital computers." The general-purpose digital computer was defined as "one which has general commercial applications and is offered for sale or lease in standard model configurations;" it was thus distinguished from special-purpose computers designed for particularized needs and produced for a limited number of customers.

The Earlier Suit

In 1952 the United States had filed suit alleging that the Sherman Act had been violated by IBM's actions in the tabulating card industry. The government alleged that IBM owned more than 90% of all the tabulating machines in the United States and manufactured and sold about 90% of the cards therefor. The suit was terminated in January 1956 by a *consent decree* [see *Glossary*].

Under the consent decree, IBM was required to offer for sale all machines that it offered for lease, at a reasonable price schedule; to offer like services to purchasers and lessees; to maintain machines that it sold; to stay out of the service bureau business and to transfer all such business to the Service Bureau Corporation (subsequently transferred to Control Data as part of the settlement of an antitrust case which Control Data filed against IBM); and to grant patent licenses and furnish certain technical information. The court retained jurisdiction to enforce compliance with the decree.

While this old lawsuit may seem irrelevant now, it is not, because this consent decree is still in force, with minor modifications. When the Department of Justice ended the 1969 case in 1982, it did not release IBM from the commitments made in 1956, except for those which had expired because of the passage of time.

The 1969 Complaint

The complaint filed by the government in the 1969 suit alleged that IBM had prevented

competing manufacturers of general purpose digital computers from having adequate opportunity effectively to compete for business in the general purpose digital computer market and [had] . . .

(1) maintained a pricing policy under which hardware, software and related support is sold at a single price [the so-called 'bundled procedure' which was officially abandoned by IBM on 23 June 1969];

(2) used its accumulated software support and related facilities to preclude competitors from effectively competing for customer accounts;

(3) restrained entry by competitors to the general purpose digital computer market by premature announcement of new models and the introduction of selected computers with unusually low-profit expectations in markets where competitors were likely to have unusual competitive success; and

(4) dominated the educational market by exceptionally discriminatory allowances in favor of educational institutions.

What the Government Wanted

The government requested: (1) that the court find IBM had attempted to and did monopolize interstate trade and commerce, and that the company be enjoined from engaging in, carrying out, or renewing any contract agreement or understanding that violates the Sherman Act; (2) that IBM be required to price its computer products and services separately, and offer to sell or lease them separately; (3) that IBM be required to refrain from using special allowances when the purpose is to inhibit entry or growth of competitors; (4) that the company be prohibited from making premature announcements of new computer systems; and finally (5) that there be such divorcement, divestiture and reorganization of IBM as necessary to dissipate the effect of the defendant's unlawful activities and to restore competitive conditions in the general-purpose digital computer industry.

IBM, of course, denied any offense and further claimed that the government's definition of the general-purpose computer market was too ambiguous. The company subsequently requested a separate trial on this issue. Judge Edelstein decided that the outcome of a trial on this definitional issue would not resolve any major portion of the litigation, and denied such a separate trial. IBM also claimed that the alleged offenses were covered by the 1956 consent decree and were therefore barred by res judicata (a legal doctrine which says that once an issue has been tried by a court, it is settled and cannot be tried again; this is somewhat analogous to the criminal rule of double jeopardy).

Essential to each of the actions proscribed by the antitrust law invoked by the government is the offense of "monopoly power:" "(1) the possession of monopoly power in the relevant market and (2) the willful acquisition or maintenance of that power as distinguished from growth or development as a consequence of a superior product, business acumen, or historic accident." Monopoly power is generally defined as the power or ability to fix or control prices in a market, or to exclude competition from a market. The relevant market may be defined geographically, or by product or service.

If the defendant can show that, in the relevant market in which it sells, the products are reasonably interchangeable, and that it has only a relatively small percentage of that market, its position is much improved. However, in the years before the case began, there was a definite tendency to find a lack of interchangeability, and thus to make many small markets rather than one large. For example, championship boxing (as opposed to professional boxing in general) had been found to constitute a "relevant market" for Sherman Act purposes.

How much of the market must a defendant control to be guilty of monopoly? The test is "whether a defendant controls the price and competition of the market for such part of trade or commerce as it is charged with monopolizing." In the boxing case, this was 81%. The Justice Department claimed that IBM's total revenues in the general-purpose digital computer market varied from 69% to 80% in the period 1961–1967, and that in this market its total 1967 revenues were 74%, and its shipments 76%. But in order to prove a monopoly, it has also been necessary historically to show a "willful acquisition or maintenance of" monopoly power. The philosophy that monopoly power might be achieved lawfully but used illegally pervaded government antitrust thinking for many years; however, Assistant Attorney General William Baxter appeared to accept a more lenient approach to the question of what is illegal use, a factor that probably accounts in large part for his ultimate decision to dismiss the case.

Pretrial Maneuvering

For three years little happened in the federal case, though action was occurring in private antitrust cases against IBM—the Control Data and Greyhound cases. In late January 1972, Chief Judge Edelstein assigned himself to handle the case with all its ramifications. On 17 March of that year he entered the first of a continuing series of sometimes controversial pretrial orders, some of which are discussed later in the Sidelight Section. The first order was very brief, saying, in toto:

It is hereby ordered that both plaintiff and defendant shall henceforth preserve and secure from destruction all documents, writings, recordings or other records of any kind whatsoever which relate in any way to electronic data processing or to any electronic data processing product or service until further Order of this Court.

The quantity of paper that this order required both parties to keep is beyond comprehension. Unless either party could show a specific exemption, it was required to retain *all* documents dealing with data processing in any of its forms.

This, of course, made for a field day in the *discovery* area [see *Glossary*]. In any large case the amount of legal time and money consumed by discovery is enormous. In this case, the costs were extraordinary, since IBM attempted to discover not only practically all the information the federal government had about data processing, but also lots of records from other data processing manufacturers—its competitors—that might in any way show that there was competition and no monopolization. It was able to find out about competition because parties in litigation are allowed to discover all "relevant" information and the past sales of IBM competitors were relevant to IBM's share of the market.

The Trial

After more than six years of preparation, the first phase of the actual trial began on 19 May 1975 in the United States Courthouse in New York City before Judge Edelstein, presiding without a jury. The first several days were devoted to opening statements by the parties. The Department of Justice statement contended that IBM had monopoly power in the general-purpose digital computer market, which included IBM and seven competitors: Univac, Honeywell, Burroughs, NCR, Control Data, General

David N. Edelstein. Chief Judge of the Federal Court for the Southern District of New York; he was the trial judge of *U.S. v. IBM*.

Electric, and RCA (the latter two were included because the suit focused on violations during the period 1962 through 1970 when these companies were in the computer business).

IBM's opening statement said that it would try to prove that the industry was substantially broader, and more competitive and dynamic than the Department of Justice contended. The company pointed out that, due in part to IBM research and leadership, the industry provided increased computing power at decreased prices to all users. It also argued that the industry had played an instrumental role in space exploration, increased productivity in other industries, and aided the national defense effort. IBM also planned to meet the government's allegations head-on by arguing:

1. the government's market definition was unrealistic;
2. within any realistic market, IBM lacked the power to control entry or price; and
3. each of the challenged IBM practices was legally and competitively justified, and usually resulted in substantial benefit to data processing industry users.

From 26 May through 10 July, the Department of Justice introduced evidence to establish its definition of the "general purpose market" through expert testimony from Dr. Frederick Scherer, Director of the Bureau of Economics of the Federal Trade Commission; R.E. McDonald, President of the Sperry Rand Corporation; Max Palevsky, Founder and

Past Chairman of Scientific Data Systems (which was sold to Xerox); and the depositions (oral examinations and cross-examinations outside the courtroom before trial) of numerous IBM officers, managers, and employees. This was supplemented by thousands of pages of documentary evidence consisting of IBM memoranda, correspondence, business records, competitive analyses, and statistics, as well as reports and numerous documents from companies other than IBM.

Woven through the testimony, exhibits, and arguments presented by the Justice Department was the theme that not only did other members of the industry and their consultants view the general-purpose, mainframe market (as defined by the Department of Justice) as a *relevant, realistic* and *practical* market within which to measure competitive progress, to plan pricing and marketing strategy, and to determine respective market shares, but IBM did so as well.

Two months after the trial began, Judge Edelstein reluctantly agreed to requests by both parties for more time to prepare their cases. Despite the more than six years already consumed in trial preparation, the parties really did require additional time. One principal reason was that the government amended its complaint in January 1975 by adding claims that (1) the IBM antitrust violations continued after the complaint was first filed in 1969, and (2) the price reductions, long-term lease plans, and other IBM practices complained of in antitrust cases against IBM (notably Greyhound and Telex) violated the antitrust laws. Neither the Department of Justice nor IBM were ready to try these issues in the spring of 1975, and they were expressly excluded from consideration during the first phase of the trial. However, when the trial reconvened in the autumn of 1975, these issues were included.

Frank T. Cary. Chairman of the Board of IBM from 1973 to 1983, and IBM's Chief Executive Officer from 1973 to 1981.

On 26 April 1978, the Department of Justice completed its presentation of evidence and witnesses in the case. At that time, few of the government lawyers who had started the case were still active in its presentation, and most of the IBM executives responsible for framing and implementing the policies challenged by the Department were retired or dead. None of the products marketed by IBM in alleged violation of the antitrust law were still being marketed, or economically significant.

The Justice Department's Case: How Did the Antitrust Division Try to Prove Its Case?

Market Power

Within the markets as defined by the Justice Department, IBM was alleged to have consistently maintained a market share of 70% or more, and to have had the power to control prices within the market and to control entry into the market.

THE EVIDENCE. The Department of Justice's statistical evidence from IBM's own competitive analysis files, from the published reports of Arthur D. Little, Inc. and International Data Corporation, and from IBM's competitors, constituted a plethora of evidence corroborating an IBM market share of 70% in the general-purpose systems market, and at least that large a percentage in the submarkets from 1960 through 1976. While this was an extremely high market share, statistical evidence of market power is not so legally significant as evidence of power to control prices and power to control entry.

To establish IBM's control over pricing, the government used industry and competitor witnesses who said that even performance-superior equipment could only be marketed successfully against IBM with a price discount of approximately 15%, and virtually never at a price premium.

The Department of Justice tried to prove IBM's control over entry into the market by using government-orchestrated accounts of the failed entries of GE, RCA, Xerox, and Singer. Each of these companies possessed substantial financial resources, nationwide marketing and service facilities, and capable management. The enormous operating losses and ultimate write-offs by such companies were said to have solidly established IBM's control over entry into the general-purpose systems market. The experience of third-party leasing companies which had enjoyed considerable success in the IBM 360 market, and then faced virtual exclusion from the IBM 370 market, was also used to establish IBM's ability to control entry to serve its own interests.

Within the submarkets, it was argued that the demise or virtual demise of a host of once-strong peripheral suppliers, dramatically confirmed IBM control over entry, even though a few exceptions like Storage Technology Corp., AMS, and Memorex then remained relatively strong competitors.

Monopoly Intent

IBM was alleged to have deliberately and intentionally maintained and exercised its monopoly power through a series of practices, proof of which constituted the bulk of the evidence in the government case.

THE GOVERNMENT'S EVIDENCE. Reduced to its most fundamental terms, the government case tried to establish in several ways that there were deliberate IBM management decisions to maintain or increase market share at the cost of current profits, a classic way of proving intent to attain or maintain a monopoly within a market. This evidence involved several matters:

☐ The IBM "fighting machines" directed successively and successfully against GE, RCA, Control Data, and Memorex always anticipated lower-than-usual profit margins, and sometimes losses. The results frequently exceeded even the most pessimistic projections of loss, although virtually all achieved the objective of holding market share.
☐ Reduced-price peripheral products almost uniformly represented a sacrifice of current profits for market share, even to the point of prematurely obsoleting entire systems like the 155 and 165 to maintain IBM domination of a submarket (in this example, the IBM add-on memory market).
☐ The "explicit intent" documents introduced by the government, although substantively only frosting on the cake, summarized the government evidence better than any advocate could hope. In one, T.J. Watson, Jr., IBM's Chairman, told his brother that the company must maintain market share regardless of the impact upon profits.

The government concluded its case in April 1978, after 504 days of trial, having called 52 witnesses, read into evidence the testimony of many others, and introduced 7,461 exhibits. The transcript of all this testimony, with examinations, cross-examinations, and lawyers' arguments, totalled 72,038 pages.

IBM's Defense

On 26 April 1978, IBM began its defense. During over 200 trial days, IBM presented 30 live witnesses, 18 more by written narrative, and the testimony of still another 72 in writing by agreement with the government as to what they would say. In addition, IBM put 12,280 exhibits into evidence, plus written discovery proceedings, other testimony and narratives. This defense consumed some 32,350 additional pages of court transcript. Its objective was to prove to Judge Edelstein, who was to decide the case without a jury, that the evidence presented by the government in the preceding three years did not add up to a violation of the Sherman Act.

IBM finally stopped presenting evidence on 1 June 1981; the government presented a rebuttal, and both sides "rested." (To *rest* in legalese means to end the presentation of your case; here it probably was literally true also.) Judge Edelstein offered, as he had before, to help the parties settle the case. He set a 10 June meeting with both sides and asked newly appointed Assistant Attorney General William F. Baxter to attend, meanwhile establishing a timetable for post-trial proceedings running from 10 October to 5 January 1982 to wrap up the case before he began to make his decision. Mr. Baxter asked that the beginning of these post-trial proceedings be delayed from 1 October to 1 December so that he could educate himself about the case. This in turn led to a series of seven meetings, beginning in September and ending in December, in which attorneys for the Antitrust Division and for IBM met with Mr. Baxter to explain their respective views of the evidence. Prior to each of these meetings, both sides submitted written materials for his review; extensive reports were also prepared by an internal Antitrust Division task force assigned to study the case during the Carter administration.

Baxter's review convinced him that, weighing "the financial and social costs of continuing the litigation, the government's likelihood of success, and the potential benefits to be obtained if the government should win," the case should be dismissed without any attempt to obtain the relief that the government had requested.

William Baxter. Assistant Attorney General of the U.S., who decided to drop the government suit against IBM.

Prominent among the factors that to Baxter's mind compelled this decision were:

1. Even if IBM was a monopolist and controlled some segment of the computer market, IBM had not achieved that position illegally.

2. Even if the government prevailed at trial, its likelihood of success on an appeal would be small. Mr. Baxter cited a recent decision in the Second Circuit Court of Appeals (which would hear any appeal of the IBM case) in which that Court "defined the offense of monopolization in a manner which indicates it may be unreceptive to the theory of this case. . . . Also, the sheer length of the trial and the large number of pretrial and trial rulings involved make it possible that there were errors at trial which may in themselves warrant reversal."

3. As a third point, he said:

even assuming that the government could prove IBM's liability, there is no insurance that appropriate relief could be obtained. Where illegal acts have been proven, the purpose of relief is to remove the defendant's ability and incentive to engage in similar acts in the future. This can be done by injunction or divestiture. . . . In this case, injunctions are likely to be ineffective [since] it is impossible to fashion injunctions to prevent similar future violations that are neither so specific that they would be meaningless outside those now-extinct circumstances, nor so general that they would simply echo the language in the antitrust laws themselves. . . .

On the question of divestiture, Mr. Baxter said:

structural relief in this case would be totally disproportionate to the nature and scope of the violations that we might be able to prove.

Although the least controversial course of action would be to continue the litigation, he said that, in his view, it was the least appropriate option, since

. . . continuing the case would commit the government to years of additional litigation with little prospect of victory or meaningful remedy. The cost to the government of further litigation is expected to be between $1 million and $2 million per year for the foreseeable future. One cannot ignore the significance of these costs in the current fiscal climate.

4. And he concluded:

In sum, the government is not likely to win this case. Even if it did, there is no relief I could recommend in good conscience. I am convinced that continuing the case would be an expensive and ultimately futile endeavor. I cannot and would not wish to speak for those of my predecessors whose decisions to continue this litigation have brought us to this point. I am certain that they acted in the public interest based on the best information then available. Based upon the information available to me, I can see only one responsible course of action: to terminate this litigation as rapidly as possible.

And so, on 8 January 1982, the case came to an end.

Milestones in *U.S. versus IBM*

1967: The U.S. Department of Justice initiates an investigation of the DP industry.

17 January 1969: On the last business day of the Johnson administration, just before 4:30 P.M., Attorney General Ramsey Clark files the 12-page *U.S. v. IBM* suit in the Federal District Court of the Southern District of New York. The suit charges IBM with monopolizing the general-purpose computer market. Requested relief includes breaking up IBM into smaller companies.

January 1972: David N. Edelstein, Chief Judge of the Southern District, who had sat on an earlier IBM antitrust suit which began in 1952 and concluded in 1956, assigns the newer case to himself. Judge Edelstein pressures the parties to get on with the case and complete their discovery of each other's files. During the discovery period, he makes a number of orders, some of which are very controversial.

17 March 1972: Both the U.S. government and IBM are ordered to keep "all documents, writings, recordings, or other records" that in any way relate to electronic data processing until the judge says they can be destroyed. The amount of paper preserved under this order staggers the imagination.

12 May 1972: Judge Edelstein prohibits the government and IBM from disseminating information about the case "by press release, press conference or interview with the press, without the consent of the Court." The order is later modified, and finally revoked.

October 1972: IBM proposes that a separate trial be held on the issue of market definition. The Department of Justice objects and is upheld by Edelstein.

1 August 1973: IBM refuses to comply with Judge Edelstein's order to dislcose certain information. Judge Edelstein holds IBM in contempt of court and imposes a fine of $150,000 a day until it obeys. The fine is suspended while IBM appeals. When the U.S. Supreme Court refuses to change the order, on 13 May 1974, IBM gives in.

July 1974: Both sides inform Edelstein they have completed depositions from all witnesses.

1 November 1974: Over IBM's objections, the Justice Department's Antitrust Division enlarges the scope of its complaint, adding charges from the *Telex Corp. v. IBM* suit in which Telex was awarded $352 million in September 1973.

24 January 1975: The Court of Appeals in Denver reverses the Telex decision and rules in IBM's favor, but Telex claims remain the the *U.S. v. IBM* case.

19 May 1975: Over six years after the case was entered in the court, the trial starts. The government calls many witnesses, some of whom testify for days on end. The government also summons two experts—a management consultant and a certified public accountant—against their will. Judge Edelstein supports the government.

20 April 1976: The Court of Appeals affirms Judge Edelstein's decision.

April 1977: The Justice Department names a new lead counsel, its third in the suit.

22 June 1977: The Department of Justice petitions Edelstein to reopen discovery and redepose 28 of IBM's
continued

Continued

witnesses. Edelstein grants its petition.

20 December 1977: IBM moves for a mistrial, contending that the testimony of government witness Dr. Alan K. McAdams included changes in definitions of the relevant market that were serious and fundamental. Edelstein denies IBM's motion.

26 April 1978: The government concludes its case after 504 full or partial days of trial, having called 52 witnesses and read into evidence the testimony of many others. The transcript of all this testimony, with examinations, cross-examinations, and lawyers' arguments, totals 72,038 pages. IBM then begins its defense.

February 1979: With Edelstein's consent, the Justice Department subpoenas IBM Chairman Frank T. Cary (already questioned for 35 days at depositions and 3 days on the stand in other trials).

March 1979: The Cary subpoena is withdrawn. The Justice Department agrees to take Cary's testimony by deposition and his previous testimony given in other cases. IBM agrees Cary's testimony will deal only with pre-1974 matters.

June 1979: IBM is ordered to make more documents available. It responds with the claim that compliance would cost too much in time and money.

17 July 1979: IBM asks Edelstein to remove himself from the case because of bias and prejudice against IBM.

11 September 1979: Edelstein issues a ruling in which he refuses to remove himself. IBM goes to the Court of Appeals.

February 1980: The Second Circuit Court of Appeals denies IBM's petition saying, among other things, that too much time has already gone by in the trial.

10 March 1980: IBM asks the Court of Appeals to reconsider its rejected motion to remove Edelstein.

23 April 1980: The Court of Appeals denies IBM's requests for a rehearing.

April 1980: IBM says it will negotiate no further unless the Justice Department drops the precondition that the government will not settle the case for anything less than structural relief, which would change the makeup of the industry. Attorney General Benjamin Civiletti says the department's position has never been that divestiture was a precondition. IBM and Justice Department negotiators meet to discuss additional procedural aspects of the settlement talks.

9 April 1981: IBM moves for dismissal or mistrial on the grounds that "the proceedings have been incurably tainted and IBM thereby prejudiced by the wrongful and plainly erroneous access plaintiff sought and was granted to documents subject to attorney-client privilege and work production protection." IBM cites the Superior Court ruling in *Upjohn Co. v. U.S.,* which expanded the privilege of confidentiality between lawyers and their clients.

April 1981: Edelstein sets a June 1 deadline for the end of the trial, his first such public declaration. At the same same, Edelstein denies IBM's motion for dismissal or mistrial. The judge offers his services to both parties in efforts to make an out-of-court settlement.

1 June 1981: IBM and the Justice
continued

Continued

Department rest their cases. IBM accepts Edelstein's offer to help settle the case. Edelstein set a June 10 date for meeting with both sides and invites U.S. Assistant Attorney General William F. Baxter to attend.

June 1981: Baxter asks for a 60-day delay for the start of post-trial proceedings, from 1 October to 1 December, to allow for his self-education about the trial.

8 January 1982: Government drops case.

[Abridged and combined from *Computerworld,* January 18, 1982, page 6 (Copyright 1982 by CW/Communications, Inc., Framingham, MA 01701), and *Encyclopedia of Computer Science and Engineering,* 2d edition, page 843 (Copyright 1983 by Van Nostrand Reinhold, Inc.).]

After the Case Was Over

Several times during the trial, IBM appealed to the Second Circuit Court of Appeals for relief from certain orders and actions of Judge Edelstein and, indeed, at one point, objected to his having jurisdiction over the case at all. In each instance, IBM was turned down. (See Milestones panel). Finally, in the summer of 1982, after the suit was dismissed in a hearing on whether Judge Edelstein should reopen the case, the Court of Appeals looked at the new facts presented and also reviewed Edelstein's conduct during the trial. It concluded, "We think he has clearly abused his power by taking such a substantial amount of time to resolve what we have shown

Nicholas Katzenbach. IBM's Chief Legal Officer during almost all of the suit.

to be a clearcut issue [referring particularly to the Tunney Act and conflict questions]. He has been presented repeatedly with several factors which emphasize the importance of a prompt disposition of this matter and of the litigation. Foremost is that the parties are expending enormous sums of money—approximately $100,000 per week—to store superfluous documents pursuant to pretrial orders which Judge Edelstein refuses to vacate. . . . IBM has already incurred over $2 million storage costs since the 8 January stipulation was presented to Judge Edelstein." The court therefore ordered Judge Edelstein to stop his consideration of the case and "to dispose promptly of any matters presented by the parties necessary to effect the conclusion of this litigation, especially with respect to the needless storage of documents."

As late as April 1983, over a million documents relating to the case were still being stored at the U.S. Courthouse in Manhattan! Judge Edelstein would not release them until they were microfilmed, at an estimated cost of $112,000. The government refused to pay this cost.

THE PRESS RELATIONS ORDER. On 12 May 1972, Judge Edelstein entered Pretrial Order No. 4, one of the more controversial orders ever entered by an American court. Its two most significant paragraphs (from a total of five) are these:

It is hereby ordered that plaintiff and defendant are restricted from disseminating news of any proceedings before this Court or of any matters relating to this action by press release, press conference or interview with the press, without the consent of the Court.

Plaintiff and defendant may make available to the press or to the public a copy of any document, or permit the inspection of any transcript, which is on file with this Court, and may advise the press or the public of the existence of such materials, but are prohibited from commenting on or characterizing such documents or transcripts, or the information contained therein, without the permission of the Court. It is the intent of this provision that the documents and transcripts on file in the office of the Clerk of this Court shall speak for themselves with respect to all proceedings in this action, and it is also the intent of this provision that neither party shall initiate contacts with the press or volunteer information with respect to this action.

This order provoked considerable adverse comment, particularly in the computer trade press, and on 20 July 1972 the Association of Data Processing Organizations (ADAPSO), one of its members—United Data Centers—and the member organization's president, Bernard Goldstein (who was also the president of ADAPSO), filed a petition urging the withdrawal of Pretrial Order No. 4. ADAPSO argued that, as a practical matter, the public and the press were precluded from attending proceedings and hearings because they were unable to get advance notice, that the files of the court were in such poor shape that copies could not be obtained, that practically all persons in the computer industry were unable to make any comment on the case as they might be potential witnesses, and therefore the order violated the First Amendment rights of free speech and free press, Article III of the Constitution with respect to notice of court proceedings, the Publicity in Taking Evidence Act, and the rights of the public under the Tunney Act.

Although Judge Edelstein denied the standing of ADAPSO and the other petitioners, he did amend Pretrial Order No. 4 to require the filing of an agenda concerning matters to be discussed at pretrial conferences and a notice of any depositions being taken, and ordered that "a telephone contact should be designated by Department of Justice and by IBM, from whom any representative of the press may obtain answers to questions as to deposition schedules and schedule changes, and places of such depositions." However, both parties were still prohibited from making any comment on the documents.

After the entry of the amended order, it became much easier to obtain copies of the documents in this litigation, but press comment, over the years, was surprisingly small in view of the importance of the case. Finally, during the three year presentation of the government's case at trial, and at the request of both parties, Judge Edelstein vacated the gag order.

COMPELLING EXPERT WITNESSES TO TESTIFY. Another interesting sidelight on the IBM case was the successful effort by the government to require two experts to testify. The individuals involved were Felix Kaufman, a partner in the international accounting firm of Coopers & Lybrand, and Frederick G. (Ted) Withington, a senior staff member of the well-known management consulting firm of Arthur D. Little, Inc. The question was whether Messrs. Kaufman and Withington were entitled to be excused from responding to the government's subpoenas because the government was seeking to interrogate them on the basis of their expert knowledge of the computer industry.

When this question reached the Court of Appeals in 1976, the Antitrust Division made it clear that it would not ask them to state their current opinions, but rather the opinions they had expressed between 1960 and 1972, to explain the nature of their duties as computer systems consultants, and "especially to recount the advice which they gave to various users and potential users of computer systems." The government said it would not ask for an evaluation of the government's evidence nor ask either witness or his employer to conduct examinations or undertake any special studies in preparation for the trial. It also agreed that it would pay both witnesses as experts for their services in an amount to be negotiated between them and the government, rather than the statutory witness rate of $30 per day. But, as Mr. Withington put it in his affidavit opposing the subpoena, "the government is seeking the very core of my expertise which I do not wish to provide and which I consider to be a proprietary asset available solely to my employer or to those for whom I wish to work."

In affirming Judge Edelstein's denial of their motion to quash the subpoenas, the court concluded that neither expert had a general constitutional or statutory privilege against being forced to testify, especially since expertise was necessary to resolve the complex issues in the case. It pointed out that there were scores of experts in the various fields—everything from builders to tugboat captains. "To clothe all such expert testimony with privilege solely on the basis that the expert 'owns' his knowledge . . . would be to seal off too much evidence important to the just determination of disputes."

The final resolution was that Judge Edelstein ordered the government to pay Kaufman and Withington not as experts, but at the standard rates charged by their employers for their services when consulting to the government. In Withington's case, this was $900 a day. As for Kaufman, the government, after interviewing him, decided it did not want him as a witness.

Some Comments on the Implications of this Litigation

United States v. IBM was the longest and probably the most expensive lawsuit ever tried in the United States. According to figures released by the Justice Department, it cost the taxpayers over $17 million. IBM declined to release its figures, although it is clear that this case cost the company tens of thousands of hours and many millions. As a basis for comparison, it may be noted that the legal costs in the *U.S. v. AT&T* case were $13.8 million for the Antitrust Division and $360 million for AT&T. It is likely that IBM's costs were similar in proportion.

After many years of litigation, millions of dollars, and thousands of hours of labor, the case ended "not with a bang but a whimper." Generations of government lawyers had come and gone. Dozens of young lawyers working for IBM and Cravath, Swaine & Moore, its outside attorneys, had been involved with the case (even though Thomas D. Barr quarterbacked the case all the way through for Cravath). As early as 1979, Yale law professor Robert Bork, formerly U.S. Solicitor General, called the case "the Antitrust Division's Vietnam."

Paul Hoffman, in an article on the case (*Lions of the Eighties,* Chapter 1, Doubleday, 1982), called it "Cravath's Verdun." He reported that the case "drained the firm's manpower and sapped its ability to campaign on other fronts. At times, as many as eighty lawyers were tied up on IBM matters, forcing the firm to farm out litigation to other firms." The effect on Cravath's recruiting and junior lawyer morale was, says Hoffman, "devastating. . . . Most young lawyers regarded assignment to the antitrust actions [Cravath, as IBM's chief outside counsel, was involved in many of these cases] as a one-way ticket to oblivion. They feared that three or four years of paper-shuffling at Cravath's outpost in White Plains—convenient to IBM's headquarters in suburban Armonk—was an 'exile' that denied them the most important element of Cravath's training: resale val-

Thomas Barr. Head of the legal team for IBM's defense, from the law firm Cravath, Swaine & Moore.

ue. . . . As a result, Cravath had to offer inducements to attract law school graduates. . . . Associates who worked on *IBM* were paid bonuses of up to $10,000 a year and given year-round rent-free use of summer houses in suburban Westchester County and the free use of firm-leased autos.''

Why did the case end with a whimper? In my opinion, because of three factors. First, the enormous costs, which were projected to continue for a number of years as Judge Edelstein went on to render his opinion on the merits and this was appealed by the loser, first to the Court of Appeals and then to the Supreme Court. Second, a changing philosophy in the Department of Justice resulting from Reagan's election in 1980: being big was no longer automatically bad. And third, the march of computer technology and marketing techniques had left the IBM actions that allegedly violated the Sherman Act as anachronisms of the past.

IBM had unbundled hardware and software a few months after the case began. Computer companies like Digital Equipment, Data General, and Prime fueled the mini-computer revolution. By 1982, the IBM 360 series, which in January 1969 had been IBM's leading product, was, for practical purposes, a museum piece. Personal computers—the Apples, Ataris, Commodores, and IBM's Personal Computer—provided more computing power for the buck than was dreamed of in 1969.

Some argue that IBM's litigation strategy of throwing in battalions of lawyers and paralegal assistants prove that antitrust is not an effective weapon against a huge corporation, especially since no company has yet been successful in defeating IBM in private antitrust suits (although Telex got pretty close).

But the results in the federal government's case against AT&T prove that much of the blame for the incredible delays in *U.S. v. IBM* rests on the shoulders of Chief Judge Edelstein. The AT&T case began in 1974, five years after IBM, and was settled on 8 January 1982, the same day that Baxter gave up on IBM. Baxter got most of what he wanted out of AT&T. The government had presented its case in a fairly short and snappy trial that began 4 March 1981 and lasted four months. Thereafter, Judge Greene refused AT&T's request to dismiss the case entirely, and Bell began to present defense witnesses in September; this continued until a recess was called on 18 December. The trial was scheduled to begin again on 12 January 1982, and all of AT&T's evidence was to have been presented by 20 January!

The contrast between Judge Greene and Judge Edelstein was incredible. Judge Greene made the parties do their homework, do it fast and do it thoroughly. He did not allow delays. Judge Edelstein engaged in continuing catfights with IBM and even conducted the trial in ways not seen elsewhere. For example, hundreds of pages of testimony were written in advance. Rather than just accept these as evidence, Judge Edelstein would have them read into the record by court clerks while lawyers from both sides sat and listened (the judge being occupied elsewhere during the reading).

Did the case have any effect on the computer industry? While the government did not succeed in breaking up IBM or restructuring "competition" in data processing, the very existence of the lawsuit probably was a factor in the development and survival of a number of IBM's competitors. To the extent that IBM's practices before the case was brought may have been predatory, these practices were placed under the microscope of judicial and public scrutiny. During the entire 13 years, IBM always had hanging over it the spectre of an unfavorable decision. To what extent this caused Big Blue to stay its hand in competing with its rivals, both large and upstart, we shall probably never know. But common sense argues that the company would have been foolish to be aggressive in ways that might have brought it into more judicial or governmental disfavor. Since the dismissal of the government's case, there are indictions that IBM marketing has become more aggressive.

It may be that, when economic historians study the cases brought against IBM under the antitrust laws, particularly by the federal government, they may conclude that because these cases were brought, even though no plaintiff won at trial, the very existence of these cases provided a climate in which the computer industry could flourish during the 1970s and 1980s.

Notes

□ Parts of this article are abridged and updated from the following articles by the author:

"The Computer Industry and Antitrust," EDP Industry Report, Special Report April 1969, Copyright 1969 by International Data Corporation.

"United States v. IBM 1969–1973," 5 *Computer Law Service*, Section 7-1, Article 6, Copyright 1974 by Robert P. Bigelow.

□ The material on pages 184–188 discussing the period May 1975 to April 1978 are abridged from two articles by J. Thomas Franklin, Esq.:

"United States v. IBM—What the Case will Mean for the DP Industry—What Users Can Do," Computer Law and Tax Report, September 1975, Copyright 1975 by Roditti Reports Corp.

"United States v. IBM—An Interim Report," *ibid.*, October 1978, Copyright 1978 by Roditti Reports Corp.

□ The excerpt on pages 196–197 from *Lions of the Eighties* is reprinted by permission of Doubleday & Company. Copyright 1982 by Paul Hoffman.

□ Additional References

"IBM and the Courts: A Six Year Journal," International Data Corporation, March 1975.

Goulden, Joseph C., *The Benchwarmers*, Weybright and Talley, Inc., 1974, pp. 75–113.

Fisher, McGowan, and Greenwood, *Folded, Spindled and Mutilated: Economic Analysis and U.S. v. IBM*, MIT Press, 1983.

Franklin, J. Thomas, *U.S. v. IBM, An Interim Analysis*, Computer & Communications Industry Association, 1977; *Second Interim Analysis*, 1978.

□ While there have been countless newspaper and magazine articles on the case and its settlement, the following seem particularly useful:

"Bigness Under Attack," *Business Week*, November 11, 1972, p. 110.

Pantages, "Justice v. IBM: Still Many Questions," *Datamation*, March 1980, p. 74.

Gardner, "Waiting for the Judgment Day," *Datamation*, April 1980, p. 52.

Verity, "IBM Wins Again," *Datamation*, February 1982, p. 46.

In Quest of a Pangram

An English explorer's self-referent account of his hybrid machine for solving a challenging word puzzle.

Lee C.F. Sallows

The Pangram Problem

In February 1983, a Dutch newspaper, the *Nieuwe Rotterdamse Courant,* carried an astonishing translation of a rather tongue-in-cheek sentence of mine that had previously appeared in one of Douglas Hofstadter's *Scientific American* columns ("Metamagical Themas," January 1982). Both the translation and an article describing its genesis were by Rudy Kousbroek, a well-known writer and journalist in Holland. Here is the original sentence:

Only the fool would take trouble to verify that his sentence was composed of ten *a*'s, three *b*'s, four *c*'s, four *d*'s, forty-six *e*'s, sixteen *f*'s, four *g*'s, thirteen *h*'s, fifteen *i*'s, two *k*'s, nine *l*'s, four *m*'s, twenty-five *n*'s, twenty-four *o*'s, five *p*'s, sixteen *r*'s, forty-one *s*'s, thirty-seven *t*'s, ten *u*'s, eight *v*'s, eight *w*'s, four *x*'s, eleven *y*'s, twenty-seven commas, twenty-three apostrophes, seven hyphens and, last but not least, a single *!*

Complete verification is a tedious task; unsceptical readers may like to take my word for it that the numbers of letters and signs used in the sentence do indeed correspond with the listed totals. A text which inventories its own typography in this fashion is an example of what I call an *autogram*

LEE SALLOWS is an English electronics engineer employed at the Psychology Laboratory of the University of Nijmegen. Besides the design and construction of electronic instruments associated with psychological experiments, he does a good deal of translation work, mostly of scientific and technical papers. A self-confessed dilettante, his interests have included ham radio, psychoanalysis, classical guitar, recreational mathematics and linguistics, impossible figures, logical paradoxes, Sherlockian studies, runology, mountain walking, and writing. A further two-part article of his on a related topic in computational linguistics has subsequently appeared in ABACUS Fall 1986 and Winter 1987 (Volume 4, Numbers 1 and 2).

Reprinted from ABACUS, Volume 2, Number 3, Spring 1985.

(*autos* = self, *gramma* = letter). Strict definition is unnecessary, different conventions giving rise to variant forms; it is the use of cardinal number-words written out in full that is the essential feature. Below we shall be looking at some in which the self-enumeration restricts itself to the letters employed and ignores the punctuation.

Composing autograms can be an exacting task, to say the least. The process has points in common with playing a diabolically conceived game of patience. How does one begin? My approach is to decide first what the sentence is going to say and then make a flying guess at the number of occurrences of each sign. Writing out this provisional version, the real totals can be counted up and the initial guess updated into an improved estimate. The process is repeated, trial and error leading to successively closer approximations. This opening soon shades into the middle game. By now all of the putative totals ought to have been corrected to within two or three of the true sums. There are, say, 9 *f*'s in fact but only *seven* being claimed, and 27 real *t*'s where *twenty-nine* are declared. Switching *seven* with the *nine* in *twenty-nine* to produce *nine f*'s and *twenty-seven t*'s corrects both totals at a single stroke. Introducing further cautious changes among the number-words with a view to bringing off this sort of mutual cancellation of errors should eventually carry one through to the final phase.

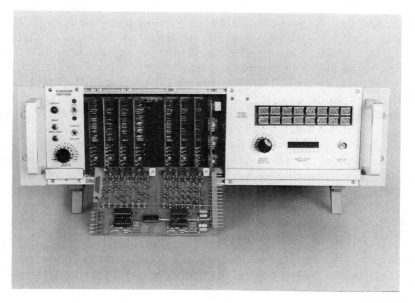

The automatic number-word selector board that transformed the original pangram machine into the Mark II version. On the left, 18 window-detector chips determine the number of *g*'s, *l*'s, *x*'s, and *y*'s. At right, 4 more integrated circuits and 24 transistors switch in the appropriate PROFILES on the resistor-bearing cards above.

The end game is reached when the number of discrepancies has been brought down to about four or less. The goal is in sight but, as in a maze, proximity is an unreliable guide. Suppose, for instance, a few days' painstaking labor have at last yielded a near-perfect specimen: only the *x*'s are wrong. Instead of the *five* claimed, in reality there are 6. Writing *six* in place of *five* will not merely invalidate the totals for *e, f, s, and v*, the *x* in *six* means that their number has now become 7. Yet replacing *six* with seven will only return the total to 6! What now?

Paradoxical situations of this kind are a commonplace of autogram construction. Interlocking feedback loops magnify tiny displacements into far-reaching upheavals; harmless truths cannot be stated without disconfirming themselves. Clearly, the only hope of dehydrating this Hydra and getting every snake-head to eat its own tail lies in doctoring the text accompanying the listed items. In looking at the above case, for example, only a fool will fail to spot instances where style has been compromised in deference to arithmetic. Short of a miracle, it is only the flexibility granted through choice of alternative forms of expression which would seem to offer any chance of escape from such a labyrinth of mirrors.

This is what made Kousbroek's translation of my sentence so stunning. Number-words excepted, his rendering not only adhered closely to the original in meaning, it was simultaneously an autogram in Dutch!

Or at least, so it appeared at first sight. Counting up, I was amused to find that three of the sums quoted in his sentence did not in fact tally with the real totals. So I wrote to the author pointing out these discrepancies. This resulted a month later in a second article in the same newspaper. Kousbroek wrote of his surprise and dismay on being caught out by the author of the original sentence, "specially come over from America, it seems, to put me right." The disparities I'd pointed to, however, were nothing new to him. A single flaw had been spotted in the supposedly finished translation on the very morning of submitting his manuscript. But a happy flash revealed a way to rectify the error in the nick of time. Later a more careful check revealed that this "brainwave" had in fact introduced even more errors elsewhere. He'd been awaiting "the dreaded letter with its merciless arithmetic" ever since. The account went on to tell of his titanic struggle in getting the translation straight. The new version was included; it is a spectacular achievement.

The tail concealed a subtle sting, however. At the end of his story Kousbroek threw out a new (letter-only) autogram of his own:

Dit pangram bevat vijf *a*'s, twee *b*'s, twee *c*'s, drie *d*'s, zesenveertig *e*'s, vijf *f*'s, vier *g*'s, twee *h*'s, vijftien *i*'s, vier *j*'s, een *k*, twee *l*'s, twee *m*'s, zeventien *n*'s, een *o*, twee *p*'s, een *q*, zeven *r*'s, vierentwintig *s*'s, zestien *t*'s, een *u*, elf *v*'s, acht *w*'s, een *x*, een *y* en zes *z*'s.

A finer specimen of logological elegance is scarcely conceivable. The sentence is written in flawless Dutch and couldn't possibly be expressed in a crisper or more natural form. In ordinary translation it says, "This pangram contains five *a*'s, two *b*'s, two *c*'s, . . . (etc.) . . . one *y*, and six *z*'s." [A *pangram*, it is necessary to explain, is simply a phrase or sentence containing every letter of the alphabet at least once (*pan* = all, *gramma* = letter). This article is about self-enumerating pangrams—pangrams which are simultaneously autograms. In such pangrams, some letters will occur only at the point where they themselves are listed (look at *k*, *o*, *q*, *u*, *x*, *y*).] Following this pangram came a devilish quip in my direction: "Lee Sallows will doubtless find little difficulty in producing a magic English translation of this sentence," wrote Kousbroek.

Needless to say, I didn't manage to find any errors in *this* sentence of his!

Autograms by Computer

Rudy's playful taunt came along at a time when I had already been looking into the possibility of computer-aided autogram construction. Anyone who has tried his hand at composition will know the drudgery of keeping careful track of letter totals. One small undetected slip in counting can later result in days of wasted work. At first I had envisaged no more than an aid to hand composition: a program that would count letters and provide continuous feedback on the results of keyboard-mediated surgery performed on a sentence displayed on screen. Later I began to wonder what would happen with a program that cycled through the list of number-words, checking each against its corresponding real total and making automatic replacements where necessary. Could autograms be evolved through a repetitive process of selection and mutation? Several such LISP programs were in fact written and tested; the results were not unpredictable. In every case processing would soon become trapped in an endless loop of repeated exchanges. Increasing refinements in the criteria to be satisfied before a number-word was replaced would win only temporary respite from these vicious circles.

What seemed to be needed was a program that could look ahead to examine the ramifications of replacing *nineteen* by *twenty*, say, before actually doing so. But how is such a program to evaluate or rank prospective substitutions? Goal-directed problem solving converges on a solution by using differences between intermediate results and the final objective so as to steer processing in the direction of minimizing them. The reflexive character of autograms frustrates this approach. As we have seen, proximity is a false index. "Near-perfect" solutions may be anything but near in terms of the number of changes needed to correct them, while a sentence with as many as eight discrepant totals might be perfected through replacing a single number-word. If hand-composition is obliged to rely on a mixture of guesswork, word-chopping, prayer, and luck, how can a more intelligent strategy be incorporated into a program?

I was pondering this impasse when Rudy Kousbroek's challenge presented itself, distracted my attention, and sent me off on a different tack.

The sheer hopelessness of the undertaking caught my imagination. But was it actually impossible? What a comeback if it could really be pulled off! The task was to complete a letter-only autogram beginning, "This pangram contains. . . ." A solution, were it discoverable, must in a sense already exist "out there" in the abstract realm of logological space. It was like seeking a number that has to satisfy certain predetermined mathematical conditions. And nobody—least of all Kousbroek—knew whether it existed or not. The thought of finding it was a tantalizing possibility. Reckless of long odds, I put aside programs and launched into a resolute attempt to discover it by hand-trial.

It was a foolhardy quest, a search for a needle in a haystack without even the reassurance of knowing that a needle had been concealed there in the first place. Two weeks' intermittent effort won only the consolation prize of a near-perfect solution: all totals correct save one; there were 21 *t*'s instead of the 29 claimed. With a small fudge, it could even be brought to a shaky sort of resolution:

t t t t t
  t
  t
  t
   this pangram contains five *a*'s, one *b,* two *c*'s, two *d*'s, twenty-seven *e*'s, six *f*'s, three *g*'s, five *h*'s, eleven *i*'s, one *j,* one *k,* two *l*'s, two *m*'s, twenty *n*'s, fourteen *o*'s, two *p*'s, one *q,* six *r*'s, twenty-eight *s*'s, twenty-nine *t*'s, three *u*'s, six *v*'s, ten *w*'s, four *x*'s, five *y*'s, and one *z.*

To the purist in me, that single imperfection was a hideous fracture in an otherwise flawless crystal. Luckily, however, a promising new idea now suggested itself. The totals in the near-solution must represent a pretty realistic approach to what they would be in the perfect solution, assuming it existed. Why not use it as the basis for a systematic *computer search* through neighboring combinations of number-words? Each of the near-solution totals could be seen as centered in a short range of consecutive possibilities within which the perfect total was likely to fall. The number of *f*'s, say, would probably turn out to lie somewhere between two and ten, a band of nine candidates clustered about "six." With these ranges defined, a program could be written to generate and test every combination of twenty-six number-words constructible by taking one from each. The test would consist in comparing these sets of potential totals with the computed letter frequencies they gave rise to, until an exact match was found. Or until all cases had been examined. Blind searching might succeed where cunning was defeated.

PROFILEs. It isn't actually necessary to deal with all twenty-six totals. In English there are just ten letters of the alphabet which never occur in any number-word between *zero* and *hundred,* the one too low and the other too high to appear in the pangram. These are *a, b, c, d, j, k, m, p,*

The SUMPROFILE

LABEL	e	f	g	h	i	l	n	o	r	s	t	u	v	w	x	y	NUMBER-WORD	LETTER
27	3	0	0	0	0	0	2	0	0	1	2	0	1	1	0	1	twenty-seven	E
6	0	0	0	0	1	0	0	0	0	1	0	0	0	0	1	0	six	F
3	2	0	0	1	0	0	0	0	1	0	1	0	0	0	0	0	three	G
5	1	1	0	0	1	0	0	0	0	0	0	0	1	0	0	0	five	H
11	3	0	0	0	0	1	1	0	0	0	0	0	1	0	0	0	eleven	I
2	0	0	0	0	0	0	0	1	0	0	1	0	0	1	0	0	two	L
20	1	0	0	0	0	0	1	0	0	0	2	0	0	1	0	1	twenty	N
14	2	1	0	0	0	0	1	1	1	0	1	1	0	0	0	0	fourteen	O
6	0	0	0	0	1	0	0	0	0	1	0	0	0	0	1	0	six	R
28	2	0	1	1	1	0	1	0	0	0	3	0	0	1	0	1	twenty-eight	S
29	2	0	0	0	1	0	3	0	0	0	2	0	0	1	0	1	twenty-nine	T
3	2	0	0	1	0	0	0	0	1	0	1	0	0	0	0	0	three	U
6	0	0	0	0	1	0	0	0	0	1	0	0	0	0	1	0	six	V
10	1	0	0	0	0	0	1	0	0	0	1	0	0	0	0	0	ten	W
4	0	1	0	0	0	0	0	1	1	0	0	1	0	0	0	0	four	X
5	1	1	0	0	1	0	0	0	0	0	0	0	1	0	0	0	five	Y
	7	2	2	2	4	1	10	11	2	24	7	1	2	5	1	1	INITIAL TEXT CONSTANTS	
	27	6	3	5	11	2	20	14	6	28	21	3	6	10	4	5	SUMPROFILE	

FIGURE 1. A stack of PROFILEs and initial text constants are added to produce a SUMPROFILE. The example shown is the hand-produced near-perfect pangram. All SUMPROFILE and label numbers coincIde except that for *T*.

q, and *z*. The totals for these letters can thus be determined from the initial text and filled in directly:

This pangram contains five *a*'s, one *b*, two *c*'s, two *d*'s, ? *e*'s, ? *f*'s, ? *g*'s, ? *h*'s, ? *i*'s, one *j*, one *k*, ? *l*'s, two *m*'s, ? *n*'s, ? *o*'s, two *p*'s, one *q*, ? *r*'s, ? *s*'s, ? *t*'s, ? *u*'s, ? *v*'s, ? *w*'s, ? *x*'s, ? *y*'s, and one *z*.

This leaves exactly sixteen critical totals. Counting up shows that there are already 7 *e*'s, 2 *f*'s, 2 *g*'s, 2 *h*'s, 4 *i*'s, 1 *l*, 10 *n*'s, 11 *o*'s, 2 *r*'s, 24 *s*'s, 7 *t*'s, 1 *u*, 2 *v*'s, 5 *w*'s, 1 *x*, and 1 *y:* sixteen constants which must be added to those letters occurring in the trial list of sixteen number-words.

Though straightforward in principle, the program I now set out to write carried its practical complications. Number-words lack the regularity of numerals (in whatever base notation), still less the harmony of the numbers both stand for. An obvious step was to replace number-words by PROFILEs: alphabetically ordered sixteen-element lists representing their letter content. The PROFILE for *twenty-seven*, for instance, would be:

```
e   f   g   h   i   l   n   o   r   s   t   u   v   w   x   y
(3  0   0   0   0   0   2   0   0   1   2   0   1   1   0   1)
```

The letters above the list are for guidance only, and form no part of the PROFILE itself. A special case was the PROFILE for *one* which provided for the disappearance of plural *s* ("one *x*, two *x*'s") by including -1 in the *s* position. PROFILES for all number-words up to *fifty* (anything higher than *forty* was unlikely ever to be needed) were stored in memory, and a label associated with each. These labels were chosen to coincide with the number represented. The label for the PROFILE of *twenty-seven*, for example, would be the decimal number 27.

Starting with the lowest, a simple algorithm could now generate successive combinations of labels (that is, numbers) drawn from the sixteen pre-defined ranges. We shall return to these in a moment. Each set of labels would be used to call up the associated set of PROFILES. These sixteen PROFILES would be added together element for element, and the resulting sums in turn added to the above-mentioned constants so as to form a SUMPROFILE; see Figure 1. The SUMPROFILE would thus contain the true letter frequencies for the presently activated sentence (the sixteen number-words represented by the current combination of labels plus residual text). All that remained was for the program to check whether the numbers in the SUMPROFILE coincided with the present set of PROFILE labels. If so, the candidate combination of number-words agreed with the real totals and the pangram had been found. If not, generate the next combination and try again. . . .

The simplicity of this design conveys no hint of the uncounted alternatives reconnoitered before reaching it. The "obvious" PROFILES were not quite so conspicuous as suggested, being in fact a later improvement over a previous look-up table. Weeks were spent in exploring a quite different approach which sought to exploit the mutual-cancelling technique formerly used in hand-composition. By the time the final version of the program had come into focus, half a dozen prototypes lay behind and several months had slipped by. In the meantime, cheerful enthusiasm had given way to single-minded intensity as the problem wormed its way under my skin. Neither was I working entirely alone. Word of the pangram puzzle had spread among colleagues, discussion sprang up, and contending design philosophies were urged. At one stage, complaint of "excessive CPU-time devoted to word games" came in from the University of Nijmegen Computing Centre, whose facilities had been shamelessly pressed into service. This was when rival programs were running simultaneously. It was bad enough to be in search of a Holy Grail that might not even exist; the thought of someone else finding it first added a sticky sense of urgency to the hunt.

The question of determining the exact ranges of number-words to be

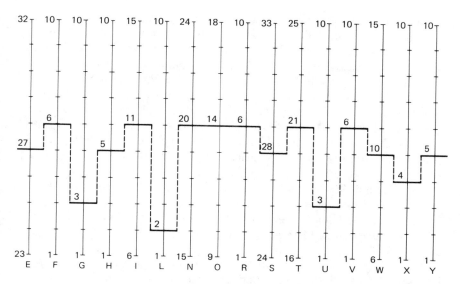

FIGURE 2. The range of frequency values to be considered for each letter that appears in number-words.

examined seemed to me an essentially trivial one, and I put it off until last. The important thing was to get the program running. For the time being it was enough to decide what the lowest combination was going to be, and to let the algorithm generate all possibilities up to, say, ten higher for each number-word. In terms of software it was convenient for ranges to be of equal length; ten might be unnecessarily high, but better the net be too large than that the fish should escape. Since the totals in the near-solution were to define the midpoint of these ranges, their lower limits would commence at about five less. "Fourteen *o*'s," for instance, implied a range running from nine up to eighteen (or perhaps ten up to nineteen). The values actually settled upon—on the basis of pencil-and-paper trials with near-autograms—can be seen in Figure 2. Ranges for each of the sixteen critical letters are represented as vertical scales with numbers (standing for number-words) indicating their starting and finishing totals. Within these ranges fall the hand-produced near-solution sums tracing out a histogram silhouette. In most cases these are, by definition, situated roughly in the middle of the range. For the low totals *l*, *g*, and *u*, however, this is impossible: in a pangram all letters must occur at least once; the range cannot extend below *one* (see Figure 2).

Combinatorial Explosion

At long last the program was finished and started. Roughly a million combinations had already been tested during the development period. The trouble with previous versions had been their hopelessly slow speed. Even the latest program could only test something like ten new combinations per second. This was still sluggish, but bearing in mind the hefty letter-crunching involved (16×16 additions in calculating the SUMPROFILE alone, for example), I thought it probably couldn't be greatly improved upon. Vaguely I wondered how long it would take before a solution popped up. Being a greedy consumer of valuable processor-time, the program ran at nights as a low-priority "batch-job" on the Computing Centre's VAX 11/780 machine. Every morning I would hasten to call up the job file, running my eye swiftly down the screen in search of "EUREKA!", which would precede a printed record of the magic combination of number-words. As day succeeded day without result, the question of how long it would be before all possibilities had been exhausted gradually assumed importance. It was a matter I had never given any serious attention. 10^7 cases had already been examined. Let's see, how many would there be altogether. . . ?

The calculation is an absurdly simple one and even now I blush to recall first seeing what the result implied. Programatically the ten totals in each of the sixteen ranges are cycled exactly like the 0–9 digits on the rotating number-discs of the familiar tape-counter or odometer. Advancing this software counter a single step results in the next combination of totals being clicked into position, ready for the pangram test. The all-zero state will correspond to the first or lowest set of number-words: the bottom row of scale numbers in Figure 2. Just as the mechanical counter begins at 0 and steps in turn through every number (that is, every possible digit sequence) up to the highest, so the program runs through all possible combinations up to that coinciding with the top row in Figure 2. In effect, we are systematically examining every single histogram that can be plotted. About halfway through the process, the example shown for the near-solution totals will come up for testing. How many such graphs can be drawn in Figure 2? The answer is clearly the same as that number displayed on our sixteen-digit odometer after stepping through all possible positions: a string of sixteen 9s (plus one for the zero-position) = 10^{16}. Is there a golden vein running through the ten-deep strata? A milky nipple crowning the Gaussian breast? At a speed of ten combinations per second, to find out is going to take $10^{16}/10$ seconds. A pocket calculator soon converts this to more intelligible units. There seemed to be something wrong with the one I was using. Every time I worked it out the answer was ridiculous: *31.7 million years!*

I was so unprepared for the blow contained in this revelation that initially I could hardly take it in. The whole object of turning to a computer in the first place had been to canvass huge numbers of combinations fast. Now that the truth had dawned, I began cursing my naivete in ever embarking on such a fool's errand. True, I was an electronics engineer, not a professional programmer. However, the more I contemplated the kind of speeds at which a realistic program would have to run, the more preposterous the whole computer venture appeared. Conceivably a somewhat faster program could be written. But even checking at a rate of one million combinations/second, it would take three hundred and seventeen years to run through the ten-deep range of possibilities!

Yet thoughts of millions of combinations per second put me in mind of *megahertz*. And megahertz brought my thoughts back to Electronics. This in turn prompted an idea, a fanciful notion, for the first few days no more than an idle phrase repeated in the head, a good title perhaps for a science-fiction story: *The Pangram Machine*.

Initially I didn't take the thought seriously. I was disconsolate after the embarrassing failure of the computer project, and the absurd expression "pangram machine" mocked hollowly at the back of consciousness. Yet suddenly the vague intuition began to crystallize; in a flash I saw how a central process in the program could be simulated electronically. Taking this mechanism as a starting point, I tried translating other aspects of the algorithm into hardware. It worked; it was easy. A few hours later, I was amazed and thrilled to find the broad outlines of an actual design already clear in my mind.

The Phoenix now emerging from the ashes of the Pangram Quest soared serenely to the sky, smoothly circled, swiftly swooped, and soon bore me off, a helpless prisoner in its relentless talons. For the next three months I would be pouring all my energy into the development and construction of a high-speed electronic Pangram Machine.

The Pangram Machine

How seriously should a word puzzle be taken? Though only the size of a smallish suitcase, the apparatus to emerge from three months' intense activity packed more than two thousand components onto thirteen specially designed printed circuit cards. More than a hundred of these were integrated circuits or "chips," each containing on the average something like fifty transistors. Foresight of this complexity might have dissuaded me from starting. In the event, the completed machine turned out to involve a good deal more electronics than originally planned. Readers uninterested in technical details may prefer to skim the following section.

At the heart of the device is the electronic equivalent of a continuously-stepped sixteen-digit odometer: a clock-driven cascade of sixteen Johnson-counters; see Figure 3 for all that follows. The clock is a simple 1-MHz square-wave generator producing a continuous train of 10^6 pulses every second. As mentioned above, however, even checking at this rate, ten-deep ranges would take 317 years to explore. A reduction was therefore demanded, the choice of new range-length being primarily determined by the availability of standard 8-output devices. Each counter is thus a circuit

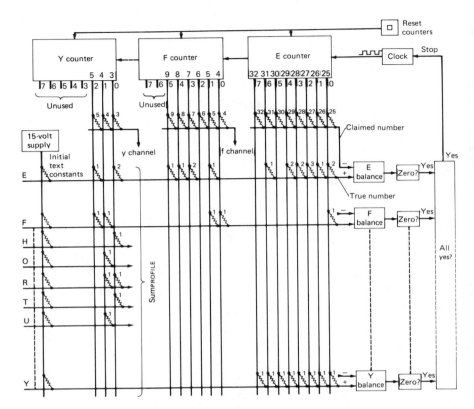

FIGURE 3. The design of the Pangram Machine.

having eight outputs, which become consecutively activated by successive pulses presented to its single input. Before the clock is started, a RESET button on the control panel (see photo, page 201) enables all counters to be initialized or "zeroed," meaning that all "0" outputs are made active. As the clock ticks, the activated output of the first counter in the chain changes from "0" to "1" to "2," etc., so that after seven clock pulses output "7" will be activated, whereupon the next pulse reactivates "0" and the process begins anew.

Coupling between counters is like that between odometer discs in that, after completing one cycle, it is arranged for a single pulse to be sent to the input of the following counter in the cascade. Eight cycles of the first are thus needed to step the second counter through one. In this way every new clock pulse results in activating a unique combination of sixteen output lines. After 8^{16} pulses, all combinations will have been run through and, unless halted, the entire process will begin again.

Even so, calculation shows that running time must still be measured in *years* unless some further limitations are introduced. In fact, the cycle-length of counters is individually presettable. With a preset cycle-length of 5 for instance, a counter's "0" line becomes reactivated on the sixth input pulse, while outputs "5," "6," and "7" remain unused. In this way, the range-length for different letters is individually adjustable, and a shorter total running time can be achieved (at the price of narrower ranges). Figure 3 shows that the y-counter's cycle-length has been reduced to 3, for example. Later we shall turn our attention to the actual set of ranges used.

Now just as in the computer program, the object of activating different combinations of output lines is to call up sets of PROFILES whose corresponding elements will be added together so as to form a SUMPROFILE (as discussed above; I leave the initial text constants temporarily out of account). Electronically the instantiation and addition of PROFILES can be achieved using either digital or analog techniques. The former is far preferable, but costly. The analog technique is less predictable in performance but, in this case at least, made attractive by its relative simplicity. Here, as elsewhere, financial limitations meant that design was influenced by what the junk-box had to offer. In the end, I was forced to use an analog approach; but since other parts of circuitry are digital (the counters, for instance), the overall design is really a hybrid.

Accordingly, the PROFILES "called up" by activated counter outputs take the form of resistor fan-outs feeding specific patterns or profiles of discrete current levels into sixteen common lines representing the SUMPROFILE. Every counter output is associated with a predetermined number-word (shown in counter boxes). An activated output is one transistor connected to a 15-volt supply and thus able to deliver current; nonactivated outputs are simply left unconnected (these are so-called open-collector outputs). The PROFILE of each number-word is implemented as a set of resistors connecting the counter output to appropriate SUMPROFILE lines. These are the horizontal lines $E, F, \ldots (H, \ldots O, \ldots R, \ldots T, U,) \ldots Y$ shown in the diagram. (Sixteen 0.5-ohm resistors, not shown but electrically important, connect each of these to ground or zero volts).

Current drawn from activated outputs thus divides into a number of resistor-adjusted streams and is distributed over the $E, F. \ldots Y$ lines of the SUMPROFILE so as to represent the contribution of each PROFILE-number. PROFILE summing is thereby achieved almost without doing anything: the current produced in each SUMPROFILE line (and hence the voltage over its 0.5-ohm resistor) is simply the aggregate of the subcurrents injected into it via the resistors in the presently activated set of PROFILES.

The number and value of the resistors used in each case depends entirely on the PROFILE being simulated. Choosing an arbitrary unit of current to represent one letter, double this value will stand for two, and so on. In fact, with the exception of *seventeen* which alone contains four e's, values in the PROFILES are always 0, 1, 2, or 3. Since 0 is indicated by no current = no connection, all PROFILES (excepting that for *seventeen*) can be implemented by resistor sets built up from just three discrete values of resistance: x ohms, $x/2$ ohms, and $x/3$ ohms, yielding current levels of 1, 2, and 3 units, respectively. (In reality $x = 3920$ ohms, a high value relative to the 0.5-ohm resistor over which the sum voltage falls; this is important for achieving summing linearity). A concrete example is shown for the y-counter's *three* and *four*. The small diagonal zigzags are the resistors. The numbers printed alongside represent not their resistance but the number of current units (15 volts/3920 ohms = 3.82 mA) they pass into the SUM-PROFILE line: *three* = 2 e's, 1 h, 1 r, 1 t; *four* = 1 f, 1 o, 1 r, 1 u.

So far so good: the current entering each + input of the boxes marked BALANCE is a measure of the number of e's, f's, etc., actually occurring in the present set of sixteen activated number-words; every microsecond a new set is switched in. But the SUMPROFILE is incomplete without the initial text constants—themselves comprising no more than a special PRO-FILE and thus representable as a set of fixed-bias currents. Hence a further array of sixteen resistors permanently connected from the 15-volt supply to each SUMPROFILE (see Figure 3).

Now in the program SUMPROFILE, totals (representing true letter frequencies) are compared with the labels of the PROFILEs (the numbers corresponding to the number-words) to check for pangramhood. These label-numbers are simulated by an extra resistor-determined current derived from each counter output (top rows of resistors). *E*-label currents are fed to the − input of the *E* BALANCE box, *F*-label currents to the − input of the *F* BALANCE box, and so on. Comparison of SUMPROFILE and label currents takes place in the BALANCE boxes; each box is a differential amplifer whose output voltage is a fixed multiple (the amplification factor) of the difference between its two input currents (or voltages, depending on how you look at it). In this way SUMPROFILE and label-numbers are weighed against each other in the BALANCE; only if they are equal will the output voltage be zero or close to zero volts. Of course, all sixteen pairs are weighed simultaneously.

The rest ought to be obvious. The "ZERO?" boxes are window-detectors: circuits signalling a logical 1 ("yes") if their input voltage lies within a predetermined voltage range or "window." The window in this case is a narrow one centered on zero volts ($+/-$ 50 mV). All window-detector outputs go to a sixteen-input AND-gate ("all yes?"). If sixteen zeros turn up together, the AND-gate will fire, stopping the clock, freezing the counters, and turning on an inessential but comforting EUREKA! lamp mounted on the control panel. The magic set of number-words sought will now be represented by the frozen combination of activated outputs. In order to signal which these are, counter positions are indicated (in binary code) in the form of sixteen groups of three light-emitting diodes (LEDs) visible through a red plexiglass front panel. Using a table to translate LED patterns into number-words, it will remain only to double-check the result by hand and, if it is correct, ring for the champagne.

Though all very well on paper, in reality the analog techniques used in the machine are messy. Circuit capacitance and amplifier settling times set a practical limit to speed of operation. When the clock ticks and switches in a new set of PROFILES, electronic havoc breaks loose as overshoots, oscillations, glitches, and gremlins conspire to drive window-detectors into palsied indecision. After a while, electrons begin to simmer down and circuits settle out into a new steady state. For this reason, rather than going straight to the STOP input of the clock as shown in Figure 3, the AND-gate output is actually sampled some 900 nanoseconds after clock pulse onset—that is, at the last moment of the clock cycle, only 100 nanoseconds before the next pulse arrives. This idea, among others, was due to Willie van Schaijk, without whose friendly and expert assistance the machine might never have left the ground. Using the (TTL) technology at my disposal, a clock frequency of 1 MHz is the highest I was able to achieve under these circumstances. Given more funds, it would probably not be difficult to improve on this by a factor of ten. Digital techniques bring their own problems; I am not convinced that a worthwhile gain in speed could be won for the large investment needed.

Although all sixteen counters have eight outputs each, it is impossible to exploit these unresistrictedly, since to examine all possible combinations at a clock rate of 1 MHz would still take $8^{16}/10^6$ seconds = 8.9 years. Range lengths were therefore tailored to each letter so as to retain a reasonable chance of finding the pangram while bringing the running time down to about one month. Flexibility was maintained by providing printed circuit cards with easily alterable solder-links allowing preadjustment of each counter's cycle length. Selection of the ranges to be used was a ticklish business, involving careful analysis of letter frequencies in number-words. Those finally settled upon can be seen in Figure 4 (numbers under RANGE stand for number-words).

Notice that e, having a high frequency and being therefore less predictable than other letters, receives the maximum range length of 8. On the other hand, y, occurring exactly once in every number-word from *twenty* upwards but in no others, can only appear 3, 4, or 5 times in the pangram *given the ranges for* e, n, s, *and* t. This is hardly a trivial insight: were y's range length increased to 4, ten days would be added to running time. As it is, to run through the combinations generated by the ranges in Figure 4 will take $(8 \times 6 \times 6 \times 6 \times 7 \times 4 \times 7 \times 6 \times 6 \times 7 \times 7 \times 6 \times 6 \times 7 \times 6 \times 3)/10^6$ seconds = 31.36 days. Anything longer would have been unendurable.

In the program, the PROFILE for *one* contained -1 in the s-position to cancel what would otherwise be an s too many in the initial s- contant. However, minus values are not resistor-representable in the machine. As seen in Figure 4, there are only three letters (l, u, x) in whose ranges *one* occurs. To deal with these cases, after reducing the initial s-constant by 3, an s is added to the PROFILES of number-words higher than *one* in their ranges. The range for l thus becomes: *one, two + s, three + s, four + s;*

The SUMPROFILE

LETTER	NEAR-SOLUTION TOTAL	RANGE	RANGE LENGTH	INITIAL CONSTANT
E	27	25–32	8	7
F	6	4–9	6	2
G	3	2–7	6	2
H	5	3–8	6	2
I	11	8–14	7	4
L	2	1–4	4	1
N	20	17–23	7	10
O	14	12–17	6	11
R	6	3–8	6	2
S	28	24–30	7	21
T	21	18–24	7	7
U	3	1–6	6	1
V	6	3–8	6	2
W	10	7–13	7	5
X	4	1–6	6	1
Y	5	3–5	3	1

FIGURE 4. Ranges of values of number-words as actually built into the Pangram Machine.

in other words, number-words above *one* bring their plural *s* with them. There is no reason why this couldn't be done for every number-word in every range (with corresponding reduction in the *s*-constant), but it would mean a lot of extra resistors.

Failure

After twelve weeks' concentrated effort, the machine drew near to completion. As a prototype, it had posed a host of technical problems to be faced and overcome. First there had been a pilot phase to investigate the feasibility of an analog implementation. How fast could the critical summing and balance circuitry perform? Despite normal pessimistic expectations, small-scale trials yielded promising results. The only way to discover whether the full-scale version would function satisfactorily was to build it. At length the long program of design and construction culminated on the day the machine stood ready for a crucial test: would it successfully identify and halt at a magic combination?

To find out, I introduced deliberate changes in the resistor-represented initial text constants; by feeding the machine with false data about letter-frequencies in the introductory text, I could trick it into halting at a prearranged pseudo-magic combination. Subtracting *o* and adding an *i* and *n* should cause it to stop at that combination of real totals represented in the previously discussed hand-produced solution: "twenty-one," the true number of *t*'s, then replacing "twenty-nine." Using the "manual clock" and "select counter" controls to preadvance the five highest or "most significant" counters in the odometer chain *(u, v, w, x, y)* to their appropriate totals (3, 6, 10, 4, 5), it would take only a few minutes for the faster-cycling counters to reach the remaining numbers in the magic combination. Starting the clock, I watched anxiously as the changing pattern of binary-coded LED displays reported the steady increment of counter positions.

Suddenly and soundlessly the counters locked, the EUREKA! lamp came on, and the correlation monitor confirmed sixteen hits in a row. This was it; the machine had passed the acid test. With the correct text constants loaded and a few other loose ends tied up, one week later all was ready for the launching of this singular rocket on its thirty-two day voyage into the unexplored regions of logological space.

Lift-off came on 3 October 1983, almost eight months following the publication of Rudy Kousbroek's audacious challenge. Cees Wegman, a spiritual godfather to the project who had watched sympathetically through the long months as I gracelessly declined from suave insouciance to crazed intensity, came along to perform the deed of honour. A bottle of wine was broached, and three of us sat with glasses raised as he ceremoniously clicked the starting switch to RUN (it was a fitting tableau for some quixotic latter-day Velasquez, I couldn't help musing).

The ensuing period found me hovering nervously over the machine. Among other things, there was the nagging worry of machine reliability; what guarantee was there of faultless operation over so long a period? The answer of course was *none*. All I could do was maintain sporadic surveillance with an oscilloscope, and halt the machine at three-day intervals to perform checks with the pseudo-magic combination. After a while the suspense became nerve-racking. Mornings were worst. On waking, the first thought in consciousness would be *has it halted?* It took nerves of iron to go patiently through the morning's ablutions before tensely descending to the living room where the machine was installed on my writing bureau. Opening the door with great deliberation, I would quickly go in and transfix the machine with a questioning gaze. And there would be the flickering LEDs as the counters slowly switched their way through the 2.71×10^{12} combinations. One million a second for 31.366 days. It was a torturing experience. The novelty of watching the machine soon wore off and the edge of expectation blunted, but a single second's distracted attention was accompanied by the thought that another million chances had already elapsed, so perhaps NOW??? . . . and my glance would be wrenched back to the twinkling array of lights. After months of frenzied activity in building the machine, this period of enforced waiting was a cruel contrast of frustrated inertia and protracted disappointment.

But it was highly conducive to thinking up means for shortening that time. Before long, I saw that by halting the machine at key points in its travel and limiting the cycle-length of certain counters through calculated intervals, redundant checks on predictably invalid blocks of combinations could be obviated. Temporarily truncating the t-counter's range to exclude *eighteen* and *nineteen,* for instance, meant that all values of t contained a y so that y could only occur four or five times. Testing cases for which $y = three$ could thus be skipped during such a phase. Using dodges of this kind, I was able to slice nearly ten days off the originally estimated running time.

Meanwhile the grains of sand—and of hope—were inexorably running out. Day succeeded day and week succeeded week with no sign of a EUREKA! By 25 October, twenty-two days after launching, the machine had checked out every (undisqualified) combination of number-words within its capacity without finding the magic pangram. Since oscilloscope monitoring and a subsequent test with the modified initial text constants showed the machine to be functioning properly, I was not in any serious doubt about this negative result.

The crushing truth was that there never had been a needle in the haystack; the Quest for the Pangram had failed.

Logological Space

Though a bitter disappointment, the failure of the quest was not yet an irreversible defeat. A remote chance lingered that the magic combination lay yet undetected just outside the ranges of number-words examined. More promisingly, alternative translations remained to be explored. At the top of the list was "this pangram comprises . . .", a rendering of the Dutch *bevat* on a par with "contains." This would only entail a new set of initial text constants.

The prospect of a further month in purgatory, however, was anything but inviting. Yet much had happened during the long weeks of waiting. In the range-limiting stratagem used to shorten the previous run had lain the seed of a powerful new development. Many hours' thought had been given to this, and already detailed preparations were in hand for a Mark II version of the machine incorporating extensive modifications.

Consider the number-words in the range for y: *three, four, five;* the letter y itself occurs in none of them. Put differently, whichever of y's

PROFILES may be activated, the actual number of y's can never be affected; in this sense y is an independent variable. Great advantage can be taken of this by adding new circuitry which *measures* the number of y's present in the currently activated combination and uses the result to switch in the appropriate y-PROFILE. In short, the y-counter can be replaced by an *automatic number-word selector*. And discarding the y-counter from the cascade will mean *dividing the running time by three* (see Figure 5).

The real power of this refinement emerges on seeing that the same trick can be worked for any letter not appearing in the number-words making up its own range. G and l are two such; provided *six* is dropped from its range, so is x. This then was the scheme to be realized in the blueprint for the new Mark II machine. With the g, l, x, y counters removed from the cascade, running time falls to only $(8 \times 6 \times 1 \times 6 \times 7 \times 1 \times 7 \times 6 \times 6 \times 7 \times 7 \times 6 \times 6 \times 7 \times 1 \times 1)/10^6$ seconds or *one hundred and*

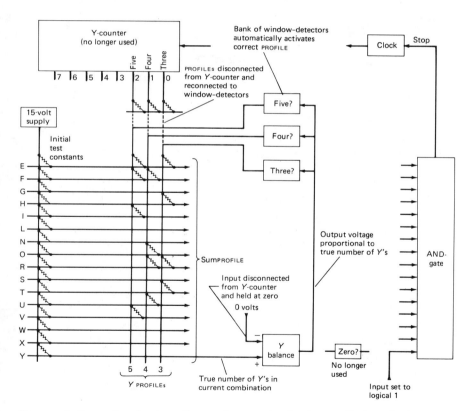

FIGURE 5. Example of automatic number-word selection applied to the letter y. A voltage proportional to the number of y's occurring in the present combination is classified by a bank of three window-detectors, one of whose outputs will activate the appropriate PROFILE.

five minutes! The perspective opened up by this dramatic improvement carried further implications in its wake.

With the ability to explore so quickly, means would be required for easy loading of different initial text constants. Though electrically trivial, a flexible resistance-selection method was difficult to implement in the machine as it stood. The final (and not altogether satisfactory) system chosen uses a set of four tiny switches for each channel. The latter work in binary fashion, so that a constant or "weight" of anything from 0 through 15 letters can be introduced. Incorporating this bank of 16 × 4 PRESET LETTER WEIGHTS switches on the front panel involved some major surgery to the machine.

Another benefit of ultra-fast logological space travel is the chance to prospect further afield; that is, to expand ranges. Even if all twelve remaining counters are allocated a range length of 8 (the maximum available in this machine), running time comes out to only $8^{12}/10^6$ seconds = 19.08 hours. In two cases, l and y, the ranges of auto-selected letters may themselves be increased, an expansion that has its uses with initial texts containing l's and y's; for instance, "This pangram employs. . . ." The g in *eight* and x in *six* make further extension impossible for g and x. In reality, impatience to get on dissuaded me from expanding range lengths until later so that running time was kept below two hours during initial explorations.

Besides serious mechanical alterations, the modifications sketched above called for a further printed circuit card carrying twenty-four new integrated circuits, the same number of transistors, and a few dozen associated components. The increased electrical drain meant in turn an extra D.C. power supply. Space was cramped, and the rise in internal heat dissipation threatened to upset the temperature-sensitive differential amplifiers. Notwithstanding these demands and difficulties, within a month the new souped-up Pangram Machine Mark II stood poised for its maiden flight.

Following a last-minute test with the modified initial text constants, now easy to enter via the front-panel switches, I started off with a recheck of "This pangram contains . . .". With running time down to under two hours, one could afford to be thorough. This time there was no wine, no ceremony, no Velasquez and, as anticipated, no result.

In the meantime I'd worked out the initial text constants for "This pangram *comprises* . . .", and as soon as the first run was over, I loaded these and set the machine searching again. Two hours later, the counter LEDs showed that the second run had been completed, and I was confronting another disappointment. That truly was a tragedy; it meant that no really perfect English translation of the Dutch pangram existed. It seemed to me an unwarranted injustice; and, brushing aside a tear, I marked it down as another of the things I mean to ask God about on Judgment Day.

Even so, many excellent alternative renderings remained to be tried.

These might not qualify as literal translations of *bevat* but would at least preserve the spirit of the original. "This pangram *comprises* . . ." was therefore followed in quick succession by "This pangram *consists of,*" "*is composed of,*" "*uses,*" "*employs,*" and "*has.*" Every one of them without success!

By now I was beginning to wonder just how long this might go on. Given a random introductory text of, say, twenty-five letters, what is the probability that an associated self-enumerating list exists? Short of examining all possible twenty-five-letter strings one at a time, I saw no way of answering the question. One in a hundred? One in a million? As it happens, the answer turns out to be something closer to one in ten.

On the second day of exploration I was sitting in front of the machine during its eighth run when suddenly the EUREKA!-lamp came on and my stomach turned a somersault. Rigid with excitement, I carefully decoded the LED displays into the set of number-words represented. A painstaking check completely verified the following perfect pangram:

This pangram lists four a's, one b, one c, two d's, twenty-nine e's, eight f's, three g's, five h's, eleven i's, one j, one k, three l's, two m's, twenty-two n's, fifteen o's, two p's, one q, seven r's, twenty-six s's, nineteen t's, four u's, five v's, nine w's, two x's, four y's, and one z.

I leave it to my readers to imagine the scenes of wild intemperance following upon this victory. Despite a hangover, next morning copies of the pangram were happily handed out among friends and colleagues who had patiently borne with me through the long months of pangrammania. Notable, if unsurprising, was that nobody felt disposed to examine the sentence for a discrepancy. Not unnaturally, I came in for a few kind words of congratulation, and some even looked at me with an unspoken "How does it feel to climb Everest?" on their lips. Like a dishrag, actually; I still hadn't recovered from the previous evening's celebrations.

The zenith of glory was yet to come. Returning home at lunchtime, I found a magnificent trophy awaiting. I had set the machine running once more, early in the morning, and it had halted again at a new solution. Changing "and" to "&" in the natural English rendering of Rudy Kousbroek's pangram, a last desperate bid for a perfect magic translation had finally met with success. The Quest for the Pangram had ended in triumph!

This pangram contains four a's, one b, two c's, one d, thirty e's, six f's, five g's, seven h's, eleven i's, one j, one k, two l's, two m's, eighteen n's, fifteen o's, two p's, one q, five r's, twenty-seven s's, eighteen t's, two u's, seven v's, eight w's, two x's, three y's, & one z.

Editor's Note

The sequel to Sallows pangram adventure can be found in his complete original article: ABACUS *Volume 2, Number 3, Spring 1985.*

220   Lee C.F. Sallows

References

Dewdney, A.K. "Computer Recreations." *Scientific American,* October 1984, pp. 18–22.

Hofstadter, Douglas R. "Metamagical Themas." *Scientific American,* January 1982, pp. 12–17.

Kousbroek, Rudy. "Welke Vraag Heeft Vierendertig Letters?" *Nieuwe Rotterdamse Courant,* Cultureel Supplement **640,** 11 February 1983, p. 3.

———. "Instructies Voor Het Demonteren Van Een Bom. *Nieuwe Rotterdamse Courant,* Cultereel Supplement **644,** 11 March 1983, p. 9.

———. *De Logologische Ruimte.* Amsterdam: Meulenhoff, 1984, pp. 135–53.

Slimmerick*

by Lee Sallows

"Here's a quirky quotation," said Quine,	30
"That preceeds a prediction of mine:	29
'If a limerick's good	16
Then its syllables could	21
Only add up to be thirty-nine' . . . ."	23
Quipped a self-referentialist (Me),	28
"Self-fulfilling is my prophecy:	26
If *this* limerick ends	18
As its author intends	18
Then its word count will reach twenty-three!"	36
Answered Quine, ". . .I'd been waiting for you,	32
On discovering *letters* too few:	26
For I'd already guessed	19
Your whole poem's expressed	23
In *three hundred and seventy-two!!*	27
	———
	372

* "Slimmerik" is Dutch for a "cunning one."

The first two lines of the poem carry an allusion to the contemporary philosopher W. V. Quine's famous rendering of Epimenides' paradox "This sentence is false":

    "Yields a falsehood when appended to its own quotation"
    yields a falsehood when appended to its own quotation.

Here the subject of the sentence—the phrase in quotes—*is* appended to its own quotation; the resulting sentence is, in fact, a quirky quotation preceding a prediction that the operation will yield a falsehood. Quine's object was to achieve self-reference while avoiding the expression "this sentence" which, it has been argued, cannot really refer to anything.

Microcomputing in the Soviet Union and Eastern Europe

In spite of transferred technology, these nations have nothing to equal what is working well in the West.

ROSS ALAN STAPLETON AND SEYMOUR GOODMAN

This is an overview of microcomputing in the CEMA (Council for Economic Mutual Assistance) nations, showing the effects of national similarities and differences, intra-CEMA cooperative efforts, and indigenous capabilities, as well as the influence of technology transfer from the West. CEMA includes the Soviet Union and the six East European Warsaw Pact nations: Bulgaria, Czechoslovakia, East Germany (GDR), Hungary, Poland, and Romania. (While Cuba, Mongolia, and Vietnam are also CEMA members, their contributions to microcomputing are negligible.)

Historical Background

Computing in the U.S.S.R., Czechoslovakia, East Germany, and Poland got off to respectable starts during the 1950s. The "East/West computer gap" began to open up in the mid-1950s, and became very substantial by the late 1960s. CEMA progress was not insignificant, and a steady flow of new computer models appeared. Though not especially innovative, these

ROSS ALAN STAPLETON is a Ph.D. student at the University of Arizona. He did his undergraduate work at the University of Michigan, majoring in computer science and Russian. His primary research interests are microcomputer and microprocessor architecture and technology transfer.

SEYMOUR GOODMAN is Professor of Management Information Systems and Policy at the University of Arizona. He received his education at Columbia University and Cal Tech, and has held positions at the University of Virginia, the University of Chicago, and Princeton. His primary research interests are international developments in computing and the design and implementation of information systems for trend and policy analysis.

This is an editor-shortened version of the original article that appeared in ABACUS, Volume 3, Number 1, Fall 1985.

Some Terminology

Bit Slicing	Bit slicing is a technique whereby a CPU is made up of a number of identical sections, connected in parallel; for instance, a 16-bit computer could be constructed with four 4-bit bit-slice chips. One benefit of bit slicing is that less complex chips may be used, the drawback being that more chips (and hence more circuitboard space for the CPU) are required. In the West, far more small computers are constructed on the basis of single-chip microprocessors than in the CEMA countries, where bit-slice chips are extensively used.
DIP (Dual In-Line Package)	This is the standard IC package, with two rows of pins. A number of other package types are used by the Soviets and in the West, including quad in-line packages (four rows of pins).
Soviet IC Classification Code	By various state and branch standards, Soviet integrated circuits are identified by a device code. The following is an example of the current classification for the K1804VS1 (said to be equivalent to the AMD 2901):

K = an integrated circuit for general (normal temperature range) use
18 = a microprocessor class
04 = the particular family
V = a complex arithmetic element
S = a processor element
1 = identification of this device, as distinguished from others matching the four previous classifers

Prior to the revamping of the IC code in the early 1980s, there was no "V" classification. Instead, the classification "IK" covered all of the types now under "V"; thus the K1804VS1 and K1804VU1 (a microinstruction interpreter) would have both been K1804IK, with different final identification digits. Through this system, most circuits can be identified in terms of their general functions by IC designation alone.

were not simply copies of Western machines. U.S. industry left the Soviets and East Europeans far behind, however, when it discovered a vast market for computer products across a broad spectrum of users. A number of American vendors had considerable experience with the production, servicing, and marketing of a range of electromechanical products intended for large user communities. The corresponding government ministries among the CEMA members were much more limited in their perceptions of application areas for computing, in their effective customer base, and in their technical capabilities.

During the 1960s, serious problems forced the CEMA countries to reevaluate their perceptions and practical efforts. These problems included lower productivity and growth rates, difficulties with the management of complex systems like transportation networks, and problems in keeping up with the West in military and space technologies. By 1969, decisions had been made to upgrade computer capabilities significantly as one means of coping with these problems. To accomplish this objective, CEMA followed a cautious strategy of risk avoidance. Part of this strategy was to duplicate and adopt Western systems.

Several U.S. mainframe and minicomputer designs have been duplicated in two major intra-CEMA programs. The better-known of these programs is the ES (*Yedinaya Sistema,* or Unified System) mainframe effort, begun in 1967 and now entering its third major phase. It is based on the IBM 360/370 family. Excepting a few Soviet large-scale scientific computers, the ES machines are now essentially the only mainframe production family in CEMA. The SM (*Sistema Malykh,* or Small System) program for small computers was undertaken in 1974, and was initially split between the duplication of Hewlett-Packard and DEC architectures. The overall degree of compatibility among the SM models is somewhat less than that in the ES family, and the SM machines do not dominate the CEMA small-computer scene as completely as the ES models dominate the mainframes.

The development of microcomputing in CEMA has lagged the industries of Western countries (here defined as the U.S., Western Europe, and Japan), partly because of qualitative and quantitative deficiencies in the microelectronics and computer-manufacturing industries, and partly because of a lack of good host socioeconomic environments. Both the level of component support and the perception of the role of microcomputing in the economy appear to be changing in a direction that favors the more extensive introduction of microcomputing throughout CEMA. There have been indications of late that the importance of microcomputers both as scientific workstations and educational tools has been recognized, and that microcomputer development is to be strongly emphasized in future economic planning. Steps aimed at alleviating deficiencies in the many facets of a complete microcomputer program have been either initiated or proposed. Among these are plans to increase the capability of the microelectronics industries, to establish microprocessor production capabilities in the more backward East European nations, to reorganize industry for automated mass production, to establish CEMA-wide hardware and software standards, and to increase the level of computer literacy.

Visible progress has been made in improving the component support for microcomputing, particularly in the production of microelectronic circuits. Prior to the 1980s, component support was either deficient or virtually absent outside of modest programs in the Soviet Union and East Germany. As a result of agreements made in the last few years at CEMA Sessions (essentially economic summit conferences), intra-CEMA programs covering the microelectronics component base have led to improvements in this area. These agreements, representing policy decisions at the highest levels among all of the member nations, have affected the direction of the computing industries, particularly those of the less advanced nations. A substantial microelectronics industry is maturing in Czechoslovakia, and the foundations for one have been laid in Hungary via Soviet licenses for two integrated-circuit production facilities.

These developments have effectively resulted in the creation of a number of standards across CEMA. Chief among these has been the adoption of the Intel microprocessor line, and a fair number of Intel devices have been duplicated by various CEMA countries. In addition to establishing microprocessor production capabilities in nearly all of the CEMA countries, the current trend has been to produce more general-purpose microprocessors of the type used in microcomputers; by contrast, past production had been largely of bit-slice chips for use in specialized applications, minicomputers, and industrial controllers.

A benefit of adopting a Western hardware architecture, in addition to the greatly reduced system development time, is the ability to profit from Western software. Indications are that compatibility with Western machines is being sought to capitalize on the strength of the Western software industries, for, with few exceptions, the CEMA nations themselves are weak in software capabilities.

With respect to CEMA national policies, the last major area of concern is the introduction of computing to the population. The spread of computer literacy and the high level of computer technical education in the West have yet to be mirrored in the East.

Technology transfer from the West in various forms has been a component of the growth of the CEMA computing industries. It is important to remember, however, that fundamental differences in Communist and Western societies make it impossible to transfer an unaltered microcomputing environment from West to East. The CEMA countries are having serious problems coming up with effective counterparts for what is working reasonably well in the West.

The Microprocessor/Microcomputer Inventory

Microprocessors

The first requirement for a microcomputer industry is the establishment of the underlying microprocessor and components base. By far the most extensive microprocessor industry in CEMA is that of the U.S.S.R., which currently produces more than a dozen types of single-chip and bit-slice devices. It should be noted here that the Soviets make little distinction between bit-slice and single-chip microprocessors. In the West, "micro-processor" usually refers only to single-chip devices.

The Soviets have built up a range of devices through two major development phases, corresponding roughly to the tenth (1976–80) and eleventh (1981–85) Five-Year Plans. The first phase was the creation of the K58X microprocessor families, ten distinct groups designated K580 to K589 (Table 1). These groups cover a broad spectrum of logic technologies and device types. Little has been seen of the K585, which may have never left the development stage. However, most of these devices have been available since about 1979, and references to their use have been encountered frequently enough to indicate large-scale production.

At least four of the families (the K580, K581, K584, and K589) have been identified as analogs of Western predecessors, and three of these are among the most widely used of the Soviet microprocessors. It is not always clear to what degree the Soviet chips are faithful reproductions, and we will use the term "analog" to denote what is probably a functional copy—a device with nearly identical functional components, whether or not the chip is laid out in exactly the same pattern, with exactly the same line widths, using identical manufacturing processes. For a microprocessor, this would mean that all the same functions are performed on the chip, the number and use of registers are identical, and the instruction logic is equivalent.

One microprocessor for which this information is known is the Soviet K580IK80, from the K580 family. The K580IK80 is virtually identical to the Intel 8080, and provides exactly the same pin functions. The K580IK80 is packaged in a 42-pin dual inline package, with two more pins than the

TABLE 1. Soviet microprocessors and bit-slice devices, K58X group

Family	Technology	Description
K580	n-MOS	8-bit general-purpose microprocessor (functionally equivalent to the Intel 8080)
K581	n-MOS	16-bit microprocessor (analogous to the Western Digital LSI-11/2)
K582	IIL	4-bit bit-slice device
K583	IIL	8-bit bit-slice device
K584	IIL	4-bit bit-slice device (analogous to the Texas Instruments SBPO400)
K585	STTL	unknown; either 2- or 4-bit slice
K586	n-MOS	16-bit general-purpose microprocessor
K587	CMOS	4-bit bit-slice device
K588	CMOS	16-bit bit-slice device
K589	STTL	2-bit bit-slice device (analogous to the Intel 3000)

IIL: ion-injection logic; STTL: Schottky TTL.

8080's 40-pin DIP; but two of the K580IK80's pins are unused (the 42-pin package may be more standard for the Soviets, and their devices also have narrower pin spacings). Similar functional comparisons may be made between other K580 and Intel 8080 support chips, leading to the conclusion that the K580 family, at least, is a functional duplicate of a Western predecessor. Information on other Soviet chips, including references in Soviet product descriptions citing U.S. patents, further supports the theory that those devices are fairly close duplications.

By the beginning of the second phase, the importance of the microprocessor seems to have been more fully appreciated by the Soviets, with a number of changes in nomenclature and approach indicating a more carefully thoughtout program. The code by which all Soviet microelectronic devices are classified was changed, adding a range of subclasses for microprocessor chips, all of which had been previously lumped under the heading of "general arithmetic devices." For the first time an ECL (emitter-coupled logic) bit-slice chip was introduced.

The second phase also developed the first single-chip microcomputer, with RAM, ROM, and I/O on the same chip as the processor. There is evidence that some of the K58X families were expanded at this time to single-chip versions. Table 2 lists the devices in the resulting K18XX group.

Whereas both the Soviet Union and East Germany have had a microprocessor production capability for a number of years, and produce a wide range of microelectronic components, only recently have the other CEMA countries started to produce microprocessors. Before 1982, they had to import microprocessors and supporting circuits from the U.S.S.R. or GDR. The East German U880 (a Zilog Z80 analog) and the Soviet K580 have been the basis for many East European microcomputers. Czechoslovakia began domestic production of the MH 3000, a 2-bit bit-slice chip which, like the Soviet K589, was based on the Intel 3000 family The real move toward broad microprocessor production in CEMA began with the introduction of 8-bit general-purpose chips based on the Intel 8080.

TABLE 2. Soviet microprocessors and bit-slice devices, K18XX group

Family	Technology	Description
K1800	ECL	4-bit bit-slice device (analogous to the Motorola MC 10800 family)
K1801	n-MOS	16-bit single-chip microcomputer
K1802	STTL	8-bit bit-slice device
K1803	unknown	unknown single-chip microcomputer
K1804	STTL	4-bit bit-slice device (analogous to the American Micro Devices AMD 2900 family)
K1810	unknown	said to be equivalent to the Intel 8086

ECL: emitter-coupled logic.

During 1981–82, at the 35th and 36th CEMA Sessions, agreements were made for the mutual development of microelectronic and microprocessor technology. Reportedly, one of the most important areas of discussion at the CEMA executive meeting in June 1984 was "microelectronics, microprocessor technology, and industrial robots." These agreements seem to be providing direction for the current microprocessor efforts in Eastern Europe.

Poland has begun production of its first microprocessor, the MCY 7880, reported to be equivalent to the Intel 8080. Two more microprocessors, the 4-bit MCY 7804 and the 8-bit MCY 7848, are planned for production in 1985.

The 7804 may be based on Intel's original 4004 microprocessor, and the 7848 is described as analogous to the Intel 8048 single-chip microcomputer. Despite the fact that a chip like the 4004 is nearly fifteen years old, and may only now be entering production in Poland, there are a number of points in its favor. It is a simple device within CEMA manufacturing capabilities, and there is a need for 4-bit general-purpose microprocessors in these economies. The 4004 is a well-documented member of what is now a full 4- to 16-bit line of Intel devices. Although this is a rather abnormal sequence of device development, it is not entirely unreasonable. CEMA possess the technology for the serial production of 8-bit microprocessors; and 16-bit general-purpose microprocessors are just beginning to be introduced. At the same time, there is a void at the low end of the microprocessor scale, and a need for something comparable to our Western precursors of the 8-bit general-purpose microprocessor families.

Czechoslovakia, following the introduction of two microprocessors already produced in the U.S.S.R., is expanding its line in much the same way as Poland. Currently in production are the MH 3000 and the MHB 8080, said to be equivalent to the Intel 8080. Plans for the production of "integrated circuits with properties equivalent . . . to the Intel 8048, 8035, and 8748" were set in motion in 1984. As in Poland, the expansion of the microprocessor industry in Czechoslovakia represents a broadening of the range of device types to fill in the holes in the fledgling industry.

Only one microprocessor is known to be in production in Hungary. The 8080PC, another analog to the Intel 8080, has been produced with some support chips, all with device numbers similar to the Intel counterparts. The recent establishment of two microelectronics plants in Hungary by the Soviets—with training of personnel carried out in the U.S.S.R., and a license to produce the Soviet K586 microprocessor—may herald improvements in the industry. At the same time, it is reported that Hungary is finding it hard to be a competitive microelectronics producer, and may try to fill the role of a semi-custom chip producer, being unable to compete in volume industries or to sustain itself solely on specialized chips.

The SM 600 series, duplicating the Motorola 6800 family, has been in production in Bulgaria since the late 1970s, possibly as early as 1975.

Romania does not seem to have an indigenous microprocessor production capability, though there are indications that the first pilot production of an indigenous device may have occurred late last year.

By far the strongest microprocessor industry outside of the U.S.S.R. is that of East Germany. Its showpiece device, the U880, is in wide use throughout CEMA. The U880 is a copy of the Zilog Z80 which, although descended from the Intel 8080, is not compatible with later Intel models. Previous developments include the U808, analogous to the Intel 8008. Planned, and evidently available in limited sample production, is an equivalent to the Zilog Z8000. The production of such a chip, a true 16-bit microprocessor, would be a major step up.

The microprocessors produced in the East European CEMA nations are shown in Table 3.

Peripheral chip support for the microprocessors is in many cases woefully inadequate. The Soviets and East Europeans have mastered the production of the processor itself, and the simplest of support chips, including the recent introduction of 64-kbit RAM chips, which became available in Hungary in 1984, in sample lots imported from the U.S.S.R. However, they have failed to produce important I/O interface chips, dedicated controllers, and complex support chips such as memory management units and co-processors.

A number of functions reduced in American machines to single chips will require entire boards in comparable Soviet microcomputers, since the needed LSI devices are not produced. A possible explanation is that in the quota-directed economy and Five-Year-Plan-oriented development environment, such secondary devices were not as seriously considered, given the limited capabilities of the Soviet microelectronics industry, and their functions were duplicated with a number of simpler chips. As a result,

TABLE 3. East European general-purpose microprocessors and bit-slice devices

Country	Family	Functional analog	Word size
Bulgaria	SM 601	Motorola 6800	8 bits
Czechoslovakia	MHB 8080A	Intel 8080A	8 bits
	MH 3002	Intel 3002	2-bit slice
	MHB 8035	Intel 8035	8 bits
	MHB 8048	Intel 8048	8 bits
Poland	MCY 7880A	Intel 8080A	8 bits
	MCY 7835	Intel 8035	8 bits
	MCY 7848	Intel 8048	8 bits
Hungary	8080A	Intel 8080A	8 bits
GDR	U808	Intel 8008	8 bits
	U880	Zilog Z80	8 bits
	U830	N/A	8-bit slice
	U8002	Zilog Z8002	16 bits

despite having introduced more than a dozen microprocessors, there is little component "glue" with which to build compact, efficient, modern microcomputer systems.

As a whole, the CEMA components industries are weak, and all are having trouble satisfying domestic needs.

East Germany is a major microprocessor exporter, and the U.S.S.R. is a large exporter of RAM chips. While Polish microprocessor production is insignificant, necessitating imports, there are plans to produce peripheral support chips to augment Soviet microprocessors. One of the features of the planned microcomputer "revolution," with its emphasis on CEMA-wide hardware standards, is national specialization in assigned areas of components production. This division of labor may not be without its drawbacks, however, as a number of cases of trade problems have surfaced. For example, Czechoslovakia has been unable to meet the demand for microelectronics exports, with up to half of the requests remaining unsatisfied, and Hungary is reported to have had problems obtaining parts due to rigid production quotas in other CEMA countries. Besides, most producers would prefer to sell to customers who pay in hard currencies.

Powerful 16- and 32-bit microprocessors are normally unavailable to the CEMA microcomputer system designer, although limited quantities have been obtained from the West in spite of export controls. Some general-purpose 16-bit chips are just becoming available, but not in large quantities. No references to 32-bit devices in any stages of development have been found. Table 4 represents a comprehensive overview of CEMA microprocessor developments, organized by year of first appearance, and juxtaposed with a number of important Western chips.

Microcomputers

Most Soviet microcomputers currently in extensive production fall into two major classes, both of which are intended for application in industry, and not for general-purpose or personal use. Although "personal computers" have been seen in recent years (most notably the "Agat" copy of the Apple II), these have not yet achieved large-scale serial production status.

The first class of Soviet microcomputers, the Elektronika S5, consists of small controllers and built-in microcomputer modules for process control and industrial automation. These machines are a series of micros ranging from early multi-board, bit-slice-based models to devices installable as controllers in single-board configurations. The family nomenclature describes three phases in development, as follows:

□ The Elektronika S5-01 and S5-02 are the earliest models. They are built with 8-bit bit-slice chips, with a total word size of 16 bits, arrayed on three boards. The base K536 chip family was introduced in 1975, and appears to have been the only LSI microprocessor available until the

East/West Microprocessor Time Line

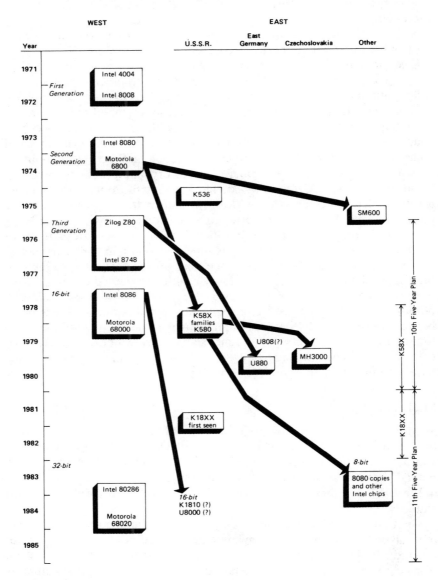

Table 4

Dates for CEMA microprocessors are a mixture of *introduction, announcement,* and *first application* dates; their actual "birth dates" may range over a year or more from the time indicated. In the case of the SM600, although references can be found as early as 1975, there are indications that effective production may have come several years later.

introduction of the K58X families in the late 1970s. These first-generation S5 micros are physically large, with more than 40K bytes of RAM, and are more capable of acting as stand-alone devices than the later models are. The S5-02 apparently differs from the S5-01 only in having a larger ROM.

☐ The Elektronika S5-11 and S5-12 are single-board versions of the earlier models. They have a much smaller RAM (a total of 128 bytes). This would permit only the execution of "canned" programs from ROM, and is characteristic of machines designed to be built into a process for a preprogrammed task.

☐ The Elektronika S5-21 is a single-board microcomputer based on the K586 single-chip microprocessor. The K586, described as a "special development," appears to represent the engineering of the bit-slice-based instruction set of the previous S5 machines into a single 16-bit microprocessor. It has been inaccurately described as a Soviet copy of the Intel 8086—which would have been a remarkable achievement inasmuch as the K586 was first seen in the late seventies, at roughly the same time the 8086 became available in the West. Although a 16-bit microprocessor, the K586 is limited in its address space, and has a clock speed less than half that of the 8086. The S5-41, very recently encountered in the Soviet literature, is described as a single-board microcomputer with a much higher throughput rate than the S5-21. No information on its processor base is known.

The second class of Soviet micros is that of stand-alone devices, intended either as general-purpose controllers or as small minicomputers. The Elektronika 60 family, with several models based on a single LSI-11 analog, is the prime example, and has been the most widely used of Soviet microcomputers. The Elektronika 60 has the same instruction set as the PDP-11-like SM-3 and -4, and as such has access to a large body of software. As with the S5s, these are 16-bit microcomputers, suited to industrial applications, but used also in research institutes. Unlike the S5s, designed to be tied to a single task or user, the Elektronikas are typically configured for multiple users, supporting a number of peripherals, and allowing the use of a front-end processor (the Elektronika MT-70). This characterizes a fairly powerful micro incorporating many minicomputer features.

The Elektronika N Ts* microcomputers, though designed with much the same instruction set as the Elektronika 60, appear to be used in built-in applications. The descriptions of these devices suggest SBC (single-board computer) configurations, with a minimum of components. All are based on CMOS bit-slice chips, configured for a 16-bit word. CMOS technology, with its low power requirements and resistance to electrical noise, would enable the use of the N Ts family in a wide range of applications, both in the factory and in the field.

---

*Ts is one letter in the Russian alphabet.

As part of the second phase of the SM program, several new Soviet micros have entered production. Of these, two are particularly significant: the SM-1300 and the SM-1800. The SM-1300 is based on K589 bit-slice circuits, with a 16-bit word. The SM-1800 is based on the K580. While one of its possible configurations is as an encased, desktop microcomputer, the SM-1800 is designed for a rather large (280 × 490 × 800 millimeter) frame, with considerable expandability through peripheral boards. Its intended application is more along the lines of digital control of experiments and processes, rather than to support an interactive human user.

There have been some limited nonindustrial applications of microcomputers in the form of small machines designed for business data processing, or "keyboard computers" that are mainly programmable calculators. The low-end "Iskra" models are based on the K580, and used for simple numeric and text processing. Some desktop models in the Elektronika series also seem to be used for the same sort of data processing. These machines are small, do not share a common instruction set, and are less powerful than the three Elektronika families described above. What there is of computerized office automation in the U.S.S.R. seems to be implemented with high-end machines such as the Iskra-226 micro/mini-computer. The Iskra-226, which is said to be compatible with the Wang 2200, weighs up to 166 kilograms, costs 30,000 rubles (over $40,000 at the official rate of exchange), and is designed around a single CRT, though it will apparently multi-task up to four jobs.

Signs of major developments in applications outside of the industrial sector came with the high-level announcements that the Soviet Union was adopting two Western microcomputers, the Apple II and the IBM-PC, as models for state-standard educational and scientific/technical personal computers, respectively. The few machines referred to as being "personal computers" up to now have been single-user workstations; for example, a microcomputer-based CAD (computer-aided design) system for engineering. The Apple II has been functionally duplicated in the "Agat" system, which was exhibited in 1983. The IBM-PC-compatible microcomputer has not reached production, but at least two pilot/prototype systems have been encountered.

The first of these is the joint Hungarian/Soviet "Janus." It is a dual-microprocessor micro, using a Z80 (possibly the East German U880), and a 16-bit board. One of the available 16-bit boards (at least three different types have been seen) uses an 8088, which is undoubtedly a Western import. The international sharing of the effort involves the delivery of Soviet circuitboards to the Hungarians for assembly and testing. It is not clear how many of the components are supplied by the Hungarians, though they could also be the importers of the required Western parts.

The second machine is a joint Soviet/East German effort designated the MMS-16 (Microcomputer Modular System). It is reportedly a product of a six-corporation East German consortium (including Robotron, the primary computer manufacturer in the GDR), and makes use of the Soviet "K1810 VM 86" CPU. It is believed that the Soviets are trying to bring an Intel 8086 to production, and the K1810 designation and description fits the 8086. This might reflect either the use of a prototype Soviet chip, or the temporary use of Western chips. A prototype of the MMS-16 was first exhibited in East Germany in 1984.

Undertaking serious production of a few standard microcomputer models is a new development for the Soviet industry. Production volumes of all machines seen thus far are low compared to Western production, and it may be that no microcomputer is mass-produced at this time.

The machines produced in the GDR are intended to be incorporated into larger systems, and are called modular, probably indicating that they are standard microcomputers with a simple base configuration expandable with system peripherals. Support for these machines also seems to be relatively good. East German microcomputers are based on indigenous microprocessors that have been available since 1978. Since the start of the 1980s, 40 to 50 thousand microcomputers of all types have been produced.

The first domestic microcomputer was the K1510, produced by the Robotron Combine; the Mikroelektronik Combine supplies microprocessors and other components. The K1510 was based on the GDR's first indigenous microprocessor, the U808, an analog of the Intel 8008. The K1510 should now be undergoing a phaseout. Its successor, the K1520, is based on the U880, the copy of the Z80. The K1520 is in wide use and fairly well supported.

The GDR K1600 series (with configurations designated 1610, 1620, and 1630, the last-named being an OEM microcomputer complex) is based on the U830, an 8-bit bit-slice chip designed with a 16-bit word.

Each of the three GDR series has one or more SM designations: SM-1624 (SM-50/10-1) for the K1510, SM-1626 (SM-50/40-2) for the K1520, and SM-50/50-2 for the K1600.

In 1984 the first two East German personal computers were exhibited at the Leipzig Spring Fair: the Robotron Z9001 and the Mikroelektronik HC-900. Both are based on the U880, and, while many of the U880-based machines in CEMA use CP/M as an operating system, their manufacturers claimed the operating systems of these two machines to be their own independent developments. The new microcomputers are intended for applications in education, and for personal computing. However, in a section entitled "Not for Hobbyists," an East German review of the Leipzig Fair noted that these computers would be expensive and available only to larger organizations. The likelihood of their being bought by hobbyists or individuals was considered very slim. First-year production plans for the Z9001 were for up to 1,000 units, and there are plans to introduce the same model into the schools.

Microcomputer production by the other CEMA countries is small, con-

TABLE 5. Some major CEMA microcomputers

Microcomputers, by country of manufacture	Word size (in bits)	CPU	RAM, other memory (bytes)	Year first encountered
USSR				
Elektronika 60	16	K581	56K (8K I/O space)	1979
Elektronika S5-01	16	K536	up to 12K (20K ROM)	1975
Elektronika S5-11	16	K536	256 bytes (2K ROM)	1976
Elektronika S5-21	16	K586	512 bytes (4K ROM)	1980
Elektronika S5-41	16	unknown	2–8K RAM or EPROM	1983
Elektronika N Ts-03	16	K587	32–256*	1980
Elektronika N Ts-04	16	K587	32–256*	1982
Elektronika N Ts-80	16	K584	56K (4K ROM)	1980
Elektronika N Ts-80-20	16	K1801	56K (8K ROM)	1983
Elektronika DZ-28†	(one of a number of desktop machines of various design)			
Iskra 250‡	16	K1810VM86	64–256K	1984?
SM-1800	8	K580	64K	1982
SM-1300	16	K589	64–256K	1982
Agat	8	unknown	32–128K (16K ROM)	1983
Janus (with Hungary)	8/16	U 880/various	64K/64K–1M	1984
MMS-16 (with East Germany)	16	K1810	unknown	1983
East Germany				
K1510	8	U808	16K (RAM and ROM)	1978
K1520	8	U880	64K–128K	1978
K1600	16	U830	up to 256K	1981
Z9001	8	U880	16K–64K	1984
HC-900	8	U880	32K–8M§	1984
Hungary				
MO8X	8	Z80-type	64K (6–12K EPROM)	1982
Aircomp-32	8	Z80-type	32K	1983
Homelab II	8	Z80-type	17K (10K EPROM)	1982
Proper 16	8	Intel 8088	32K (48K ROM)	1983
Poland				
Mera 60	(domestically assembled Elektronika 60)			1979
Meritum 1	8	Z80-type	16K (14K ROM)	1983
Czechoslovakia				
SM-50/40-1	8	8080-type	up to 64K	1981
Bulgaria				
IMKO-2 (Pravets-82)	8	unknown	no more than 64K	1980
Romania				
Felix M118	8	K580	16K	1982
Felix Cub	8	K580	64K	1983

*Data on memory sizes for the N Ts machines is often contradictory, with a wide range as indicated. Upper values probably represent address space (64K 16-bit words), while the actual implementations probably range from 8K to 64K bytes of RAM or ROM.

†The DZ-28 may actually be the D3-28, the Cyrillic Z being nearly indistinguishable from 3.

‡This is said to be a Soviet copy of the IBM-PC.

§The HC-900 is said to be able to address up to 8 megabytes made up of 64K modules, probably using banking. No such use has been yet seen.

sisting of a few machines based on components from the U.S.S.R. or East Germany. The one exception, Hungary, stands in sharp contrast to the rest of CEMA in its economic incentives for small business and entrepreneurial activities. According to one source, over eighty microcomputer and minicomputer types are being produced in Hungary, though the total production is a scant 5,100 units. This represents the output of at least two dozen firms, ranging from large corporations of several thousand employees to "firms" composed of a few designers, producing very few machines. One of the more interesting microcomputers in Hungary, the Homelab, was originally designed and built by two brothers—both students—who founded a two-man private company. Homelab III, the latest version, is now in production. However, in the Hungarian microcomputer industry, a significant producer may be one that can deliver a hundred units per year. The small scale of the industry is dramatically revealed by the figures for microcomputer imports from the West. In 1984 there were over 4,000 Commodore 64s in Hungary, more than six times the number of any indigenous model or socialist import.

The entrepreneurial freedom enjoyed by Hungarian firms is not without its price. These are small firms, most of them producing perhaps a dozen machines a year, and probably unable to provide much in the way of user support. Also, the Hungarian industry will most probably undergo some kind of shakeout, similar to the one occurring in the West, as standards emerge and less popular machines are squeezed out of the market. Still, at the present time, Hungary is in a good position to profit from its access to the West, and from the flexibility of its economy. Hungary is in some respects the CEMA scavenger, and an incredible array of microcomputers from almost everywhere have been seen.

An interesting note by a Hungarian source, illustrating one of the many quirks in the domestic industry, relates to a state regulation that permits no more than 8% of a microcomputer's components to be Western imports. A number of microcomputers have been produced based on rather contemporary U.S. chips like the Motorola 68000 and the Intel 8088. The source indicates that some enterprises beef up their machines with extraneous domestic components, simply to permit the use of more Western chips within the 8% limit.

Table 5 presents a number of the most important CEMA microcomputers. It should not be regarded as a complete list, but most of the major machines in general use have been included.

The Host Environments

There is no general, public microcomputer-user community in the Soviet Union. The vast majority of computers are used to complement or substitute for larger machines in the support of industrial processes and technical data processing. Peripherals are not intended for personal computing use. The planned standard microcomputers, the Agat and the IBM-PC-compatible, have yet to be seen as anything but prototypes or early-production models. The Agat may only be available in the Soviet Union as a leased unit; and estimates ranging from $3,000 to $17,000 have been given for the price of the system, making it an unattractive home or export item, even for CEMA customers.

The other East Europeans seem more supportive of individual and business uses than the Soviets are. Most of the East German microcomputers appear to be used in business data processing systems. Hungary is a particularly ripe environment for business microcomputing, as its economy supports the formation of small (including privately-owned) firms, for which the microcomputer is the only affordable form of computing.

Czechoslovakia, which does not have a substantial general-purpose microprocessor/microcomputer development systems, based on both its MHB 8080 and MH 3000 systems. Czechoslovakia seems to have limited most of its microcomputing to industrial applications.

Bulgaria's microcomputer industry and user community is small.

Romania produces 8080-based microcomputers, despite a lack of indigenous microprocessor production. The Felix micros are all small, more-or-less general-purpose machines, and are made with imported Soviet K580s.

Despite a fairly commendable start in the 1950s, the Polish computer industry has fallen on very hard times during the last decade. It has no effective microprocessor base—with production just recently under way on its own 8080 analog—and has managed only a small number of microcomputers.

Peripherals

At the system level, a severe lack of important peripherals characterizes all of the CEMA industries. Television receivers (usually black-and-white) are almost always used as displays. Screen width is probably restricted to forty columns, making text processing on microcomputers inconvenient and laborious.

Winchester hard disks are unavailable for microcomputer systems. Both 8" and 5.25" floppy-disk drives are in production, although still not widely available. As with displays, the vast majority of stand-alone microcomputers are being used without advanced mass-storage peripherals. Cassette tape recorders are widely used, and those microcomputers in industry are often equipped with paper tape I/O devices.

Printers, plotters, and other hardcopy devices are among the most neglected components although several thousand suitable dot matrix printers were planned for production last year in Hungary.

Networks

So far, we have seen no references to modems for microcomputer tele-communications, nor to access to computer networks of the kind that have become popular in the West. It can be assumed that there has been little use of microcomputers in this capacity. One reason is the generally poor condition of the telephone facilities in the CEMA countries. Estimates indicate line qualities about two orders of magnitude worse than U.S. lines; error rates of 2 bits per hundred were reported in Czechoslovakia's switched phone system.

A final, more deeply rooted problem is that the political structures of the CEMA countries are not hospitable to network communications. The hierarchical Soviet socioeconomic structure, in particular, is fragmented into all manner of intentionally uncommunicative fiefdoms at the middle and lower levels where information is closely controlled. Resources under one organization are unlikely to be made available to others except by direct edict. Even if the hardware were available, it is unlikely that any serious networking at the microcomputing level would be instituted. Attempts at large-scale institutional networks, including systems in the Academies of Science and a nationwide system of collective-use computer centers in the U.S.S.R., have not been very impressive or successful. So it is probable that microcomputer networking, which has received no support, will continue to be neglected in most of the CEMA countries—Hungary being the most likely exception.

Maintenance

No less important than machine production is the provision of a sufficient level of maintenance to keep the machines in operation. The customer-service sectors in most of the centrally planned economies are notoriously poor and fragmented. This is particularly true of the U.S.S.R.

It is likely that many CEMA microcomputer users are in similar positions: equipment is supposed to be available, but is not necessarily obtainable or supported beyond initial installation.

Because of the lack of telecommunications facilities, the user communities are badly fragmented, and there appears to be little opportunity for user interaction outside of a few professional and semiprofessional conferences and publications. Again, Hungary is an exception, with an active community of computer hobbyists and at least one good micro-computing journal. *Mikroszamitogep Magazin* is published under the auspices of the Neumann Janos Society (John von Neumann was a Hungarian émigré), and is comparable to a journal like *Byte* or any of the American magazines dedicated to particular user groups.

Prospects for the Assimilation of Microcomputing in CEMA Countries

The greatest difference between the microcomputing programs of East and West is in the quality and scale of their technical accomplishments. The CEMA countries are roughly five to fifteen years behind in all the necessary elements. The East European industries are only now introducing respectable quantities of the kind of microprocessors that were widely available in the West a decade ago. They do not seem capable of producing anywhere near the number of microprocessors, support chips, and peripherals required to make microcomputers available to their broad general economies, much less the general populace. For example, Mikroelektronik, the GDR's primary microprocessor producer and a major manufacturer for all of CEMA, was making an annual total of 135,000 8-bit units (representing three different models) as of 1983. This is in sharp contrast to that year's U.S. production of 15,000,000 8-bit 65XX microprocessors alone.

Given the advanced state of the Western microcomputing industries and user communities, it is to be expected that the Soviets and East Europeans would like to adopt some of the features that have worked well. Using the Western hardware base makes sense for several reasons, and would be a continuation of the general policies behind the ES and SM programs. This is probably the only way to prevent the microcomputing programs falling behind even more rapidly. Such a policy provides important software and user-experience advantages, and copying the hardware is the least troublesome strategy in political and social terms.

The call for a standard of two personal computers—the Agat (Apple II) for education, and the IBM-PC-compatible for scientific and technical use—represents a calculated attempt to correct major faults in the CEMA microcomputing effort. The architectures of these machines are well tested by a user community that is far larger, more aggressive, and more sophisticated than the user communities in CEMA. Problems have been ironed out over years of widespread use, and the Western marketing process has filtered out less competitive and less well supported systems. The choice of proven Western hardware models allows the CEMA producers to take substantial design shortcuts, and avoids the risk of failing with new architectures. Both the Apple and IBM-PC lines are strongly supported in the West, permitting Soviet designers and engineers to choose from expanding families of compatible boards, peripherals, and upgrades.

Just as important as the hardware benefits are the advantages of access to a large, mature, and expanding body of Western software. As with hardware, Western users have provided extensive software testing, product debugging, and market research which the CEMA program planners could not possibly have gotten from their own user communities. The programming languages available for CEMA micros are nearly all Western imports, as are the operating systems for most of the 8-bit machines. A few scattered references to indigenous software developments indicate that some work has been done, but it is clear that Western systems are imported to save time and effort, and to compensate for serious short-comings in the CEMA software industries. There is evidence that Western software packages such as WordStar and Visicalc may be in use along with the CP/M operating system on the CEMA Z80-type machines. There is little or no Eastern or Western barrier to the flow of commercial microcomputer software into the East.

In the areas of policy and host environments, it remains to be seen to what extent the CEMA nations will absorb Western concepts of the use of microcomputers and of the structure of of the industry. Major problems exist in the areas of hardware, telecommunications, and the simple diffusion of computer literacy throughout society. One reason microcomputing in CEMA will not soon become a threat to government control of the form and content of communications is the sheer lack of communications facilities, both in the general economies and in the personal lives of the citizenry. Likewise, the supporting industries required by microcomputing are either weak or completely absent. In particular, the software, service, and educational sectors are both underdeveloped and malformed compared to what exists in the West; even allowing for differences in economic practice, these deficiencies are clearly severe handicaps.

Another major East/West difference concerns the distribution of the technology across society. Whereas in the West, microcomputing has been widely applied in industry, business, education, and the home, the CEMA countries have placed microcomputing only in large industrial and research facilities. There is some small-business and educational use, but almost no personal or small-organizational use. Whether this is due to a severe shortage of the machines, or a fundamental philosophy of the role of microcomputing in the economy, the end result is that computing has yet to reach the general public, and the microcomputer is not pervasively applicable and available. Computer literacy is far below that of the West. Again, the reasons for this go to the root differences between the Western and CEMA socioeconomic systems.

Some problems are starkly political. It has been suggested that microcomputing, especially if pervasively used, would promote undesired levels of interpersonal communication, with each micro becoming a high-powered potential printing press for *Samizdat* and other illegal publications [see the REPORT FROM EUROPE in ABACUS, Winter 1985]. Western views of the impact of microcomputing in the East have stressed the idea that the Soviet leadership will be forced to impose stringent controls to suppress the use of micros by dissident elements. Soviet control of photocopy machines is cited as a precedent; there may be similar problems now with videocassette recorders. Clearly, microcomputers have far greater potential.

Along these lines, it is interesting to note that one of the current catch-phrases in the Soviet literature is "the collective use of personal computers," a rather paradoxical term. The term "collective" implies that microcomputers are to be shared by groups of users, possibly under supervision. An individual's access might be limited to training and closely controlled problem solving.

One thing is clear: the CEMA countries, and especially the U.S.S.R., will have to contend seriously with the problems and opportunities presented by microcomputers and related technologies, such as robotics. The impact of these technologies in the West has already been significant enough that CEMA must absorb these technologies on a large scale if they are to be economically, militarily, and ideologically competitive. The last point, ideology, is particularly important, as one of the selling points of Marxism/Leninism is the idea that it is historically destined to be scientifically and technologically more progressive than capitalism or liberal socialism.

References

This article is based on the analysis of several hundred sources. A fairly extensive bibliography of useful material may be obtained by writing to the authors at the University of Arizona, MIS Department, Tucson, AZ 85721. Here are selected additional readings:

Davis, N.C., and Goodman, S.E. "The Soviet Bloc's Unified System of Computers." *ACM Computing Surveys* **10** (1978): 93–122.

Goodman, S.E. "Software in the Soviet Union: Progress and Problems." *Advances in Computers* **18** (1979): 231–87.

Goodman, S.E. "U.S. Computer Export Control Policies: Value Conflicts and Policy Choices." *Communications of the ACM* **25** (1982): 613–24.

Goodman, S.E. "Socialist Technological Integration: The Case of the East European Computer Industries." *The Information Society* **3**, 1 (1984): 39–90.

Goodman, S.E. "Technology Transfer and the Development of the Soviet Computer Industry." Draft report prepared for the Center for Strategic and International Studies, Georgetown University, Washington, DC, May 21, 1984.

Goodman, S.E.; McHenry, W.K.; and Stapleton, R. A. "General-Purpose Computer Systems in the Warsaw Pact Countries." *Signal* **39**, 4 (1984): 97–101.

Chess Computers

A critical descriptive analysis of the currently available commercial chess computers.

Danny Kopec

During the past few years, computer professionals and laypeople alike have often asked me: "How well do chess computers play? Can you beat them?"

The answer to the first question is entirely relative—it depends on what you mean by well. The United States Chess Federation (U.S.C.F.) rating scale is divided into eight categories called *classes,* spanning 200 points each (see Table 1). The best commercial chess computers are rated in the 1900s, putting them high in Class A—below the Experts but above good club players, who might be rated around 1700 (Class B), and in with the top high-school-team players. The top-rated chess program is the former World Champion BELLE (authored by Ken Thompson and Joe Condon of Bell Laboratories), which was the first program to receive a Master rating (2203) at the last World Computer Championship in New York City in October 1983. BELLE has, on occasion, beaten human masters in serious tournament play (at the international level, human chess is played at a rate of 40 moves in 2½ hours, while in national tournaments the rate of play is slightly faster, perhaps 40 moves in 2 hours or 30 moves in 1½ hours).

The answer to the second question is yes. Being rated 2410 by the World

DANNY KOPEC, a native New Yorker, received a Ph.D. in machine intelligence in 1983 from the University of Edinburgh, after doing research in computer chess with Professor Donald Michie from 1976. He is presently teaching artificial intelligence and programming languages at The University of Maine at Orono. In addition to ranking amongst the top 50 players in the U.S., Dr. Kopec's chess honors include winning the Scottish Championship 1980–1, and achieving a second-place tie for the 1984 Canadian Championship. In December 1984 he completed the requirements for the title of International Master while finishing second in the First Labate's Chess Centre International in Los Angeles.

This is an editor-shortened version of the original article that appeared in ABACUS, Volume 2, Number 4, Summer 1985.

Glossary

Tactical play	The opposite of strategic play. This style is typified by direct threats and forcing sequences of moves such as exchanges, checks, or sacrifices.
Quiescent position	A position in which there are no forcing exchange sequences or checks. A quiet position.
Underpromotion	Promoting a pawn to a piece other than a queen.
Book line	A sequence of opening moves which can be looked up in a book.
Ply	A half-move; for example, **white's** first move in a game, such as 1 e4.
Positional play	Synonymous with strategic play, this is the style of play in which maneuvering the pieces to better squares is the goal.
Mate-finder	A component of a computer-chess program which is devoted exclusively to finding a forced checkmate.
Square of the pawn	A way of facilitating the computation of whether a defending king can interfere with a pawn's race to promotion by constructing a square. A **white** pawn on c5 would define a square whose corners are the squares c5, g5, g8, and c8. If the **black** king can step into the square of the pawn, he can "catch" it.
Swiss system	A method of determining tournament pairings which employs ratings to order and match players with similar scores.
Full-width search	Synonymous with exhaustive search, this term means that the game tree is searched to a fixed depth along every branch.
Selective search	A search of the game tree to a fixed depth, which eliminates certain branches based upon some information.
Algebraic notation	A widely employed chess notation which labels the board from **white's** point of view, with files *a* to *h* and ranks 1 to 8.
Descriptive notation	Synonymous with English notation, this notation employs piece names and their file names, e.g. N-N5, to describe chess moves. (For a more detailed discussion of chess notation, see ABACUS, Winter 1985, page 75.)
Threefold repetition	When the same board position occurs three times in a game with the same player to move, that player may claim a draw.
50-move rule	If 50 moves pass during which there are no pawn moves or captures, a draw may be claimed by either side.
Infinite level	A feature of programs that allows them to "think" until stopped.

Chess Federation (the Federation International des Echecs or F.I.D.E.), I should be able to beat any current computer chess program in a slow tournament game. David Levy, the well-known chess/computer-chess author and out-of-practice International Master, has made a reputation for challenging computer chess programs. In April 1984, he defeated the current World Computer Chess Champion, CRAY BLITZ (rated around 2150, and authored by Robert Hyatt and Albert Gower of the University of Southern Mississippi along with Harry Nelson of Cray Research), winning 4 to 0 in a challenge match [see ABACUS, Winter 1985, pages 72–77]. However, this is probably the last decade when human masters will be able to feel comfortable playing against the best computer programs. The crucial change will come when programs surpass the 2300 rating threshold, 2300 being the level where truly strong play at an international calibre is said to begin.

Yet there is one form of chess where the best computer chess programs can occasionally defeat the best human players (even Grandmasters), and that is in speed chess. In this form of chess the players are allowed only five minutes for the entire game. Chess computers play five-minute chess by averaging five seconds per move; hence, if the game goes beyond sixty moves they lose on time. Here depth and speed of search evidently more than compensate for the computer's deficits in chess knowledge. This is not the case in slow tournament chess, where planning and structural themes employing knowledge, calculation, and pattern-based play reign supreme. In ordinary tournament play a top-flight Master player can usually capitalize on a structural defect in an opponent's position by weaving through tactical† complications, and avoiding blunders to the point where a quiescent position is reached. (Throughout this article, a dagger [†] indicates an expression that can be found in the glossary on the left.) Such a position is the manifestation of a good plan, and the ensuing tactical skirmishes are often episodic parts of a grand strategy. In this way, human Masters (rated over 2300) have been able to maintain their superiority over even the best computer chess programs running on supercomputers.

Nonetheless, researchers in computer chess remain optimistic about what the future holds. At the 1984 ACM Annual Conference Session on Computer Chess, Monroe Newborn, president of the International Computer Chess Association, predicted that there would be a Grandmaster-level program within the next three years. Although progress has been steady through the 1970s to the present near-master level of BELLE and CRAY BLITZ, I consider this prediction rather optimistic. The next 200 rating points of strength will be most difficult to achieve; and even when they are achieved (whether through an increased depth of search or more chess knowledge), there will still be one more class to go before the Grandmaster level is attained. In this article, we will not survey the research programs running on large mainframes, but rather the stand-alone chess computers sold commercially, and the commercial chess programs marketed for personal computers.

Chess Ratings

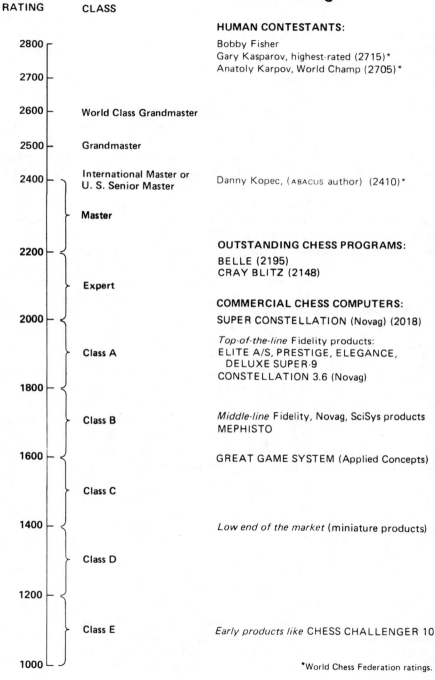

RATING   CLASS

HUMAN CONTESTANTS:

2800
Bobby Fisher
Gary Kasparov, highest-rated (2715)*
2700
Anatoly Karpov, World Champ (2705)*

2600   World Class Grandmaster

2500   Grandmaster

2400   International Master or
       U. S. Senior Master   Danny Kopec, (ABACUS author) (2410)*

       Master

2200
                                    OUTSTANDING CHESS PROGRAMS:
                                    BELLE (2195)
                                    CRAY BLITZ (2148)

       Expert
                                    COMMERCIAL CHESS COMPUTERS:
2000   SUPER CONSTELLATION (Novag) (2018)

                                    Top-of-the-line Fidelity products:
       Class A   ELITE A/S, PRESTIGE, ELEGANCE,
                                       DELUXE SUPER-9
                                    CONSTELLATION 3.6 (Novag)
1800

       Class B   *Middle-line* Fidelity, Novag, SciSys products
                                    MEPHISTO

1600   GREAT GAME SYSTEM (Applied Concepts)

       Class C

1400   *Low end of the market* (miniature products)

       Class D

1200

       Class E   *Early products like* CHESS CHALLENGER 10

1000
                                    *World Chess Federation ratings.

A Short History

Since the first chess computers were developed and marketed about eight years ago, the industry has undergone several important developments to meet consumer demands and to try to get ahead of the competition. The early products, such as CHESS CHALLENGER I, COMPUCHESS, and BORIS, played very poorly, and had extremely awkward input facilities. Standard chess rules including castling, *en passant,* and under-promotion[†] abilities were not available. Manufacturing quality control was also very bad, but buyers were generally eager enough to overlook this. Despite high prices and poor service, there were customers. But only one of the original companies has retained a strong role in the industry since its beginning: Fidelity Electronics (now called Fidelity International), the manufacturer of the CHESS CHALLENGER series. Early products such as Fidelity's CHESS CHALLENGER 10 (successor to the CHESS CHALLENGER 1) and Applied Concepts' BORIS, costing $250 to $300 and highly publicized, actually played little better than 1100 chess.

The market really boomed at last in 1979, when Fidelity introduced the CHESS CHALLENGER 7 for under $120. This was Fidelity's most successful product ever, with a total of 600,000 sold. Around 1980 a number of competitors appeared on the market, often making exaggerated and even false claims of master-level products. The strongest product at the time was SARGON 2.5, programmed by Kathe and Dan Spracklen and designed by Applied Concepts with the help of Chafitz Inc. This software product was available for the Apple 2 and TRS-80 computers, and played roughly 1650 chess. SARGON 2.5 developed into two distinct, stand-alone chess computers: the Modular Game System (from Applied Concepts) and the Auto Response Board (manufactured by AVE Microsystems). Both played at a 1500 rating, some 300–400 points better than their predecessors.

The concept of modularity, meaning that a consumer can buy the main product and then continually upgrade it by adding improved and inexpensive modules, has never lived up to its promise. The upgrade modules have been slow to get into production, are not cheap ($100–150), and have not produced convincingly stronger play. Such modules as the

◁———————————————————————————

TABLE 1. The U.S.C.F. rating system and current positions of chess computers on it. Classes on the United States Federation rating scale are represented in terms of 200-point-spans such as 1600–1799 (Class B), 1800–1999 (Class A), 2000–2199 (Expert), and 2200–2399 (Master). International Masters normally obtain ratings of around 2400, Grandmasters near 2500, and super Grandmasters (the world's top 20) around 2600. The World Champion, Anatoly Karpov, is rated 2705—and his challenger Gary Kasparov is rated highest at 2715—on the World Chess Federation scale (which gives a somewhat lower rating for a player than the U.S.C.F. scale).

CAPABLANCA (for endings) and STEINITZ (the more recent and essentially complete game cartridge), while appealing in principle, could cost over $1000 in total (even in 1984), and guaranteed no better play than a present-day $200 product. Other companies such as SciSys, Novag, and Conchess have also delved into modularity without notable success. At present, the more popular and successful cartridges are those for improved and extensive opening play (some, for example, nearly comprising the complete five volumes of the *Encyclopedia of Chess Openings*). Also quite popular are printer or clock attachments for recording play.

In 1980, although Fidelity had about 90% of the U.S. market and about 30% of the remaining worldwide market, no one was doing much to improve the quality of play. Instead, gimmicks like the VOICE CHALLENGER, which could announce the moves played, were introduced. There was little progress between 1980 and early 1982 in terms of playing strength. But in late 1982, with the appearance of such products as Fidelity's ELITE, SciSys's MARK V, and Hegener and Glaser's MEPHISTO II, there was a quantum leap of some 100 to 200 rating points, reaching the vicinity of the Class A (1800) level.

A major factor which determined Fidelity's continued success was the hiring of the Spracklens (a husband-and-wife team) as their programmers. Since that time, their products have been continuous leaders in terms of strength, playing features, and economical pricing. Although Fidelity has yet to produce a machine officially rated over 2000, it has maintained a leadership position in a fast-changing and demanding industry across the top, middle, and low end of the market line. So while several competitors fell by the wayside, including Conchess and Applied Concepts, Fidelity was almost without competition in America from 1980 (its best year, with a wholesale turnover of some $40 million worldwide) until late 1983. In 1983 Fidelity had about 50% of the market outside the U.S., and in 1984 maintained about 75% of the U.S. market.

Main Products of the Past Two Years

While the original article in the Summer 1985 issue dealt in detail with the main products of the past two years and presented a large comparative tabulation, this editor-cut version only takes up those at the top and bottom of the line.

Current Top-of-the-Line Products

The two top-of-the-line chess computers available (as of March 1985) in terms of playing strength, features, and price are Fidelity's ELITE A/S—hereafter referred to as ELITE—and Novag's SUPER CONSTELLATION, listing at $600 and $400 respectively.

The SUPER CONSTELLATION, a product which made its appearance on the commercial microcomputer market in the fall of 1984, recently became the first microcomputer program rated "Expert" (2018). This rating was established via forty games against humans organized by the newly-established U.S.C.F. Computer Rating Agency. Its rating puts SUPER CONSTELLATION among the top 11% of U.S. chess players. The rating of the most recent version of ELITE (A/S-C, which is 4.0 MHz over A/S-B's 3.0 MHz) is estimated to be just over 2000 as well. A comparison of these two programs across a number of features appears in the panel on page 251.

One of SUPER CONSTELLATION's special features is that it can checkmate with bishop and knight, playing at five seconds per move—something beyond the capability of many strong human players below the master level, even at tournament time controls. In general, SUPER CONSTELLATION knows more about the end game than other programs, including important pieces of information such as the "square of the pawn,"† the idea that rooks belong behind passed pawns, etc. Its middle-game play is enhanced by about 160 instructions devoted to chess knowledge and standard positional or tactical themes. About 75% of these instructions encourage active play for particular types of positions, while the remaining 25% attempt to prevent errors.

Fidelity's ELITE comes with a 55-page owner's manual which describes its numerous possible modes of operation and playing features. There are 39 squares, with special functions including the setting of eight levels for average response time, different types of search, mate-solving, and voice controls, among others. The ELITE has an "experimental chess" mode whereby the type of search it is to employ—iterative or noniterative—can be specified and viewed. In the iterative mode, the program first decides on the type of position it is in (tactical or positional) and what specific routines it must use (such as special-purpose subroutines for pawn endings). An ordered move list is determined according to material and positional scores for every move at every ply depth. The search continues until a predetermined depth has been reached. The noniterative (depth-first type) search will analyze each of the moves from the initial position to a set depth after these moves have been sorted by the positional analysis. It is easy to see how the ELITE can be a useful experimental computer-chess tool.

The Third World Microcomputer Chess Championship (a seven-round, Swiss System† event held in Budapest, Hungary, 13–19 October 1983) was won by the ELITE, with a score of 6 points out of a possible 7. There were eighteen entrants from eight countries, with six commercial companies represented by fourteen of the eighteen entries. This was the third time in as many World Microcomputer Chess Championships that a Fidelity product won, and the undefeated ELITE distinguished itself with a very large, specially prepared opening book, characteristically solid and cautious play based on material gain, and some luck against Novag's

FIDELITY-X versus NOVAG-X

The following game was the third-round showdown between FIDELITY-X (a prototype of the ELEGANCE just prior to its release) and NOVAG-X (a prototype of the SUPER CONSTELLATION just prior to its release last fall) at the Canadian Computer Chess Invitational Championship (CCCIC) 1984, which took place 27-29 July 1984 at McGill University's School of Computer Science. FIDELITY-X won the tournament with a 5–0 score, while NOVAG-X scored 3–2 for third place in a field of three academic and three commercial entries.

Here you find all one could ask for from a game of chess, including some very interesting opening play by FIDELITY-X **(black)**, middlegame complications in which NOVAG-X misses a chance to mate in 7 ply by sacrificing a rook, and finally a protracted end game. The main features of the play illustrate very well the strengths and weaknesses of present-day chess computers, particularly the need for a more pattern-based approach and the importance of knowledge and goals in the end game. The annotations appeared in the September 1984 issue of the *ICCA Journal,* and later in Volume #70 of *En Passant,* the Canadian chess publication.

White: NOVAG-X
Black: FIDELITY-X
Queen's Gambit Accepted

1	d4	d5
2	c4	dxc4
3	Nf3	Nf6
4	e3	e6
5	Bxc4	c5
6	0—0	a6
7	Qe2	b5
8	Bb3	Bb7
9	Rd1	Nbd7
10	Nc3	Qb8

Up to here and **white's** next move, the play is in both programs' books.

In fact, the game SCHACH 2.7. vs. FIDELITY-X (WCCC, New York, 1983) reached this position when **white** played **11 d5** and the game continued: **11** . . . exd5 **12** Nxd5 c4 **13** Nxf6+ Nxf6 **14** Bc2 Bc5 where **black** is not worse. For a full annotation of that game, see *Computer Chess Digest Annual* 1984, pages 68–9.

Around 1930, in the heyday of Alekhine, this opening was a very popular choice for **black.** It is solid and reliable if **black** plays carefully.

11	a3	Bd6
12	h3	0—0
13	Bc2	b4!?

—a double-edged move whereby **black** truly tries to wrestle the initiative by depriving the WN of its control of d5 and e4, at the expense of relinquishing the a4 and c4 squares to **white** and giving him a half-open a-file. I would prefer . . . Re8 or . . . Rd8.

14	axb4	cxb4
15	Nb1	

—the best square in order to redevelop from d2 to c4 or support the advance e4.

15	. . . .	Bxf3?!

A surprising move, in that it trades off **black's** best piece. Still recommended is . . . e5 or . . . Re8.

16	Qxf3	Rc8
17	Bd3	a5

At this point NOVAG-X tried to play **17** . . . e5, and it was discovered that up to this move in the game, it did not think that there was a BR on a8. This move probably had not affected any of its moves so far, and thus they were "replayed" to this position but with a BR on a8. In the meantime, Sidney Samole adjusted FIDELITY-X's internal time-clock to account for this time out. This played an important role later in the game.

18	Nd2	a4
19	Nc4	e5!?

I would have preferred . . . Bc7, pre-

To be continued

Continued

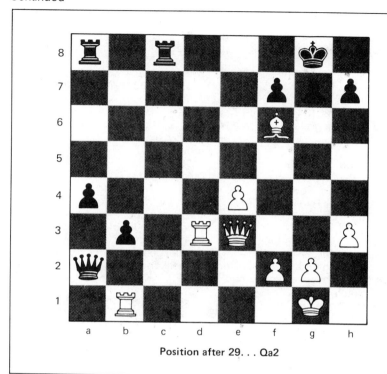

Position after 29 . . . Qa2

serving the bishop and preparing . . . e5. The text is very provocative.

20	Nxd6	Qxd6
21	dxe5	Qxe5
22	Bd2	Rab8

An unusual position in that **black** is still better, despite having given up his bishops cheaply. If **23 Rxa4**, then **23** . . . Nc5 **24** Ra5 Qxb2 is very good for **black**.

| 23 | e4 | Qxb2 |
| 24 | Bf4 | Ra8 |

Black could now transpose into a comfortably winning end game with **24** . . . Ne5; e.g., **25** Bxe5 Qxe5 **26** Rxa4 b3, etc.

25	Qe3	Nc5
26	Rab1	Qa3
27	Be5	

—a critical position, with the BQ displayed offside. **White's** bishops offer good attacking chances in any case, but **black's** best defense is probably **27** . . . Nfd7.

| 27 | . . . . | Nxd3 |
| 28 | Rxd3 | b3? |

Here the regroupment of the BQ (even at the expense of a good connected passed pawn) is absolutely essential; i.e., **28** . . . Qa2 **29** Rxb4 Qe6, etc.

| 29 | Bxf6 | Qa2 [see diagram] |
| 30 | Rbd1 | |

Suddenly **white** has a win but misses it. After **30** Qg5, **white** soon forces mate. [see note on p. 258.]

| 30 | . . . . | Qa3 |

—The only defense. If **30** . . . . gxf6, **31** Qh6 wins.

| 31 | Qg5 | Qf8 |
| 32 | Qh6 | |

To be continued

Continued

Fancy, but not effective. Better and more consistent was **32** Rg3 g6 **33** Bd4 when **white** should win.

32	. . . .	Rc6
33	Rg3	g6
34	Qxf8 +	

Now **white** should definitely not exchange queens (**34** Qf4), as his chances of mating **black** are greatly diminished.

34	. . . .	Rxf8
35	Bg5	Re8
36	Re3	b2
37	Red3	Rb6
38	Rb1	Rxe4
39	Rd8 +	Kg7
40	Be3	

Neither side has played best for the past few moves. Now, however, FIDELITY-X, which had 10 minutes for its last three moves to time control, has 3½ minutes left on its real clock to make its 40th move. This tight time situation was probably a result of an error in the internal schedule, which Mr. Samole had reset earlier when NOVAG-X discovered that it had no **black** rook on a8.

The suffering and expressions of the two Samole brothers before FIDELITY-X, finally made its 40th move—with just 30 seconds left—were no less than those of a chess player in a tough game. This scenario and the position where NOVAG-X missed a forced mate were worth paying to see.

40	. . . .	Rb3
41	Bd4 +	f6
42	f3	Re2
43	Rd5	Rc2
44	Kh2	a3
45	Ra5	Rc1
46	Rxa3	Rxa3
47	Rxb2	Rc6
48	Kg3	Ra4
49	Be3	h5

—a worthwhile space-gaining pawn advance. However, **black's** subsequent locking of the K-side pawns is a bad idea.

50	Rd2	Rac4
51	Rd8	h4 +
52	Kf2	Rc2 +

53	Bd2	Kf7
54	Ke3	Ra2

Better would be **54** . . . . Rb2, followed by **55** . . . Ke7 and **56** . . . Rd6, whereby **black** wins quickly.

55	Kd3	Rcc2
56	Ke3	Ke6
57	Bd4	g5

57 . . . .Ra6 and . . .Rd6 still wins quickly by forcing the exchange of rooks.

58	Rd3	f5
59	Rd4	Ke5
60	Rd3	f4 +

Now, by the rules of the tournament, the game could have been adjudicated (a win for **black**). However, Fidelity sportingly agreed to play on to the next control at move 80 to try to demonstrate the win.

61	Ke2	Ke6
62	Rd8	Rab2
63	Kd1	Ke5
64	Rd3	Kf5
65	Bc3	Ra2

Here **65** . . . Rxc3 and **66** . . . Rxg2 wins easily.

66	Bd2	ke6
67	Rd8	Rcb2
68	Ke1	Ra1 +
69	Ke2	Ra6
70	Kd1	Rc6
71	Re8 +	Kf6
72	Rd8	Rcc2
73	Rd6 +	Ke7
74	Rd5	Ke6
75	Rd8	Ra2
76	Ke2	Kf5
77	Kd1	Kf6
78	Rd7	Ke6
79	Rd8	Rcb2
80	Ke1	Ke7

Although FIDELITY-X, has not demonstrated any progress during the last 20 moves, the game was now adjudicated as a win for **black**. The winning plan after **81** Rd5 starts with . . . Ra6 followed by . . . Rd6, and **black** can make steady inroads while offering the trade of rooks. **White** eventually runs into *Zugzwang*. Ironically, NOVAG-X as **black** is able to find the plan (**81** . . . Ra6) but goes astray later.

NOVAG-X and SUPER CONSTELLATION, both of which had winning positions against it but "overlooked" three-fold repetitions. The Fourth World Microcomputer Chess Championship was held in Glasgow, Scotland in September 1984, and ended in a four-way tie among FIDELITY-X, MEPHISTO-X, PRINCHESS-X (Sweden), and PSION (England), each with 5 points out of a possible 7 points, in a field of nineteen competitors. A number of commercial participants entered more than one product; Novag did not participate.

Which is the stronger, ELITE or SUPER CONSTELLATION? Dan Spracklen recently told me that in a twenty-game match between an experimental ELITE and an off-the-shelf SUPER CONSTELLATION, played with tournament time controls (40 moves in 2 hours) in his laboratory, with each playing 10 whites and 10 blacks, and no opening library, ELITE obtained a score of +6 (11 wins, 5 losses, and 4 draws). It is important to bear in mind that a computer chess program's success against another program does

Features of the *SUPER CONSTELLATION* and *ELITE*

● Appearance. The SUPER CONSTELLATION is very similar to the CONSTELLATION in terms of unit size (12" × 9¾") and has a neat, modern look. However, the ELITE, with its inlaid wooden sensory board and wooden pieces, is beautiful, and provides an elegant piece of furniture in any home.

● Peripherals. ELITE has a built-in clock, while for both there is an optional printer. A Novag chess clock is available for $90. Such an addition may appeal to the serious chess student or those who enjoy speed chess.

● Opening book. The SUPER CONSTELLATION has an opening book of 21,700 moves, about one-fifth of the lines appearing in boldface type in ECO. These lines include some variations 22 moves deep; but in order to meet the special needs of strong players, there is also a built-in option of "customizing" its opening book with up to 1200 additional moves, with variations up to 35 moves long and ordered by priority according to

user's tastes. In contrast, ELITE has a modest opening book which can be supplemented with the cartridges mentioned earlier, each offering between 5,000 and 20,000 additional opening moves.

● Playing Facilities. If hopelessly lost (ELITE with mate impending, SUPER CONSTELLATION in materially hopeless situations as well), both programs are capable of resigning. Both can also recognize and announce all forms of draws, including threefold repetition†, the 50-move rule†, and stalemate. Both also offer a takeback feature for the entire game. Both provide eight preset playing levels ranging from speed chess to infinite. Finally, both programs are capable of displaying the depth of search for a move; this averages 5—6 ply in the middle game at tournament levels, and 10 or more ply in the end game. At infinite levels†, the SUPER CONSTELLATION's 4-LED binary system can display a search depth of up to 15 ply, while ELITE can go beyond 20 ply.

not give an accurate prediction of its success against humans. Only more serious tournament tests can tell us which is stronger; but SUPER CON-STELLATION'S results have been particularly impressive, leading to its 2018 "Expert" rating.

Two other top-of-the-line products deserve mention, not for their strength of play—which is rather average—but for their other features. Milton Bradley's GRANDMASTER (a misnomer) lists at $500, and employs magnets under the board (a technique designed by David Levy) which enable the pieces to appear to move by themselves. Novag's ROBOT AD-VERSARY (with an 18½″ × 18½″ unit, 10″ board, 2¼″ king, listing at $1600!) has a unique mechanical arm which executes all the machine's moves. It has other standard features, including a modular capability, but offers no great strength of play.

Miniature Products: The Low End of the Line

The first miniature-sized, truly portable, strong chess computer to appear on the market was the MEPHISTO from Hegener and Glaser, West Germany. At the time of its appearance (1983), there was much excitement about this product due to its size, strength, and humanlike style of play. Despite a departure from the standard brute-force approach (in that emphasis is on more exact evaluation of chess positions rather than deeper search) and although it ran on a much slower microprocessor (68000 at less than 1 MHz), programmers E. Henne and T. Nitsche produced a machine which was, as Irazoqui stated in the *Computer Chess Digest* 1983, "the second-strongest chess computer available and in many instances as fun to play with as PRESTIGE (then the best Fidelity product)." Its rating was established by Irazoqui at 1820, and in his opinion it was "more active and interesting" than ELITE (then Fidelity's second-best product). MEPHISTO had a slower clock-speed and shorter depth of search (in the middle game, 4 ply rather than 5 ply with a full-width search†; 8 ply as compared with ELITE'S or PRESTIGE'S 10 ply in a selective search†)—which explained why its tactical play was somewhat weaker than that of competitor products. In the end game, MEPHISTO'S search fell 2–3 ply short of PRESTIGE'S maximum depth of 9–10 ply. This, coupled with the inability to centralize its king when necessary, was responsible for ME-PHISTO'S considerably weaker end-game play (estimated at 1400). In the end game, the king is usually expected to play a more active role, and this is often achieved by bringing him to the center. Nonetheless, in 1983, with an optional auto-response board for $100, MEPHISTO and its $270 successor, MEPHISTO II, seemed very appealing and interesting products to buy.

In late 1983, Hegener and Glaser released MEPHISTO III, which, in the words of Irazoqui, was "positionally more refined . . . tactically faster

and more coherent . . . a better endgame player" than MEPHISTO II. Irazoqui continued: "But being much more selective (it looks ahead typically
one or two ply full-width and 8 to 20 ply selectively), it has a definite
tendency to overlook a tactical stroke and lose immediately, even after
achieving a winning position. . . . " Hence, MEPHISTO III was by no means
a definite improvement over MEPHISTO II, and thus could only be deemed
a major disappointment.

During the past year, there has been an increased interest in miniature
products. The Hong Kong-based company SciSys has produced TRAVEL
MATE (which lists at $35), the cheapest available chess computer (it can
neither set up or verify positions), and EXPLORER ($70). Another manu-
facturer that specializes in portable units is Hanimex (Northbrook, IL).
Its COMPUTACHESS II (with carrying case) and III list at $50 and $80, respectively, and are particularly suitable for the novice.

The miniaturized units tend to use pegboards, operate on batteries, and
have limited playing features. In the past year, Fidelity and Novag have
also started to show a greater interest in the area of products priced under
$100. Novag has introduced the MICRO III (listed at $60), which comes
with a pegboard, has seven levels of play, provides a 2-ply take-back, and
runs on batteries or adaptors; Novag also released the PRESTO ($90), which
has modular capability and is particularly suitable for newcomers to the
game. Fidelity has the MINI-SENSORY CHALLENGER ($60), which was one
of the first peg travel sets. It can't take back, has four levels, and has
optional cartridges for Advanced Play, Great Games, and Book Openings.
The top-of-the-line pegboard unit is Applied Concepts' PRODIGY ($150)
with a built-in clock, 6-ply take-back facility, and nine levels of play. In
a few years, with further micro-miniaturization, I suspect that top mini-
units will be as strong as today's CONSTELLATION and DELUXE SUPER 9
(Class A).

The *1984 Chess Life Computer Buying Guide,* reproduced as Table 2
in the original of this article in the Summer 1985 issue of ABACUS, gives
complete information on the products discussed here and a few more besides while the best are classified in Table 4 of the same ABACUS issue.
Table 4 is likewise taken from Gertler's excellent November 1984 *Chess
Life* article, "So You Want To Buy a Chess Computer."

Software Products for Personal Computers

Although chess-playing programs for personal computers have existed for
some years, only recently has there seemed to be much interest in their
quality, number, and strength. Hayden Software has suddenly initiated
energetic marketing of SARGON III, another product of the Spracklens,
which has versions compatible with various personal computers and performs at 1815 (U.S.C.F. rating). Additional disk space allows for a massive

opening library, typically ranging up to 15 moves in depth, and with a total of 68,000 positions. Game scores are easily recordable on disk, and most of the standard features of stand-alone machines such as take-back, move suggestions, and various levels of play are available. It is competitive with stand-alone products such as the SUPER 9, and, like most chess computers, it plays well tactically, and not well positionally. Besides its $50 cost, SARGON's most appealing feature is its compatibility with Apple (II, II +, IIe and IIc, and MacIntosh), IBM (PC, PC-XT, and Compaq), and Commodore 64 computers.

David Levy and his colleagues at Intelligent Software in London have produced INTELLIGENT CHESS, which runs on the IBM-PC, has excellent interface facilities and color graphics, and plays the openings well. However, its search would have to be deepened for it to attain a reasonable quality of middle-game play.

Other computer chess researchers, notably Larry Atkin and David Slate of the long-dominant Northwestern University program, and Bruce Wright of Duke University's former leader DUCHESS, have recently turned to producing software for PCs. Atkin and Slate produced Odesta's CHESS 7.0, which is a takeoff from their MORPHY, STEINITZ, and other GREAT GAME MACHINE modules. It plays about 1700-level chess, and is compatible with the Apple II or IIc and the IBM-PC. Wright has released CHESSWRIGHT, which has many nice features, including accepting and responding to input in either algebraic† or descriptive† notation, seven levels of play, and the ability to save and restore games on disk. It also has an extensive opening book; it can be used to set up problems, and has a digital chess clock among many other facilities, although its strength in terms of rating is still undetermined.

In short, the software products for personal computers offer many nifty user interface and set-up facilities. For under $50, it is possible to purchase disks with additional opening libraries and stored games. The fact that personal-computer programs are not yet quite up to the standards of stand-alone chess computers is primarily due to the higher performance of the 6502 microprocessor (commonly used in the stand-alone chess computers),

--▷

The photos that follow provide just a hint of the diversity of different chess computers. Among the products offered by Fidelity International are: the top-line ELITE A/S, of which a preliminary version won the 1983 World Microcomputer Chess Championship in Budapest (A); the ELEGANCE, a prototype of which won the Canadian Computer Chess Invitational Championship 1984 (B); and the new EXCELLENCE, which was designed as an outstanding modestly-priced model (D). The AMBASSADOR was a midrange unit marketed by Conchess (C); the SciSys CHESS CHAMPION Mark V is an inexpensive portable unit (E). The SUPER CONSTELLATION, Novag's strongest product, was the first Expert-rated microcomputer (F). [Pictures A, B, E, and F courtesy of the U.S. Chess Federation.]

A

D

B

C

E

F

compared to the 68000 and 8088 microprocessors used in the Apple and
IBM personal computers, respectively.

Future Prospects

Professor Donald Michie has some very interesting things to say about
future prospects in an interview conducted by H.J. van den Herik, ''Computer Chess Today and Tomorrow,'' which appears in the *Computer Chess*

CONSTELLATION-X versus Jerry Simon

The following game is historic because it is the first in which a microcomputer chess program beat a
rated master under tournament conditions. (Notes are based on Scott
McDonald's comments in the *Computer Chess Digest* 1984, page 25.)

U.S. Open, August 1983, Round 1.
White: CONSTELLATION-X. **Black:** Jerry Simon (2207). English Opening.

	W	B		W	B
1	c4	e5	29	Re8 +	Kg7
2	Nc3	Nc6	30	d5 +	Kh6
3	Nf3	Nf6	31	dxc6	Qh2 +
4	g3	d6 (a)	32	Kf1	Rxg3
5	Bg2	Be6	33	Be3! (k)	Qh1 +
6	d3	Be7	34	Ke2	Qh5 +
7	0–0	Qc8	35	Kd3	bc
8	Qb3 (b)	0–0	36	Qf6 +	Qg6
9	Nd5! (c)	Bd8	37	Qh4 +	Kg7
10	Bg5	Rb8	38	Qd8	Kh6
11	Nxf6 +	gxf6	39	Qxc7 (l)	d5
12	Bh6	Re8	40	Qxa7	dxc4 +
13	Qc3	Bh3	41	Kxc4	Rg2
14	Rac1	Bxg2	42	Qd4	Rc2 +
15	Kxg2	Qg4 ?! (d)	43	Kb3	c5
16	Bd2	f5	44	Qd5	Rh2
17	h3	Qh5	45	Qxc5	Rh3
18	e3	Re6 (e)	46	Kc2	Rh2 +
19	d4 (f)	e4?	47	Bd2	Qg2
20	Ng1	Rg6	48	Qf8 +	Kh5
21	f3!	Bh4	49	Qxf7 +	Kh4
22	Ne2	Bg5	50	Qe7 +	Kh5
23	Nf4! (g)	Bxf4	51	Qxh7 +	Kg4
24	exf4	Re8	52	Qg7 +	Kf3
25	fe	Rxe4 (h)	53	Qc3 +	Kf2
26	Rce1	Re2 + (i)	54	Qe3 +	Kf1
27	Rf2	Rxf2 +	55	Qe1	Mate
28	Kxf2	Qxh3 (j)			

Notes

(a) A solid but passive move which took the computer out of its book. Usual moves are **4 . . .Bb4** and **4 . . .d5**.

(b) CONSTELLATION prevents **black's** planned bishop trade with **8 . . .Bh3**.

(c) A useful centralization. If **black** plays Bxd5, **white** has play on the half-open c-file after cxd5. With this and its next move, CONSTELLATION-X demonstrates some understanding of pawn structure play.

(d) More sound was **15 . . . f5** here.

(e) Better was **18 . . .Bf6**.

(f) CONSTELLATION-X completes its planned break, although with **19 . . .ed 20 ed Re4 black** would have some play.

(g) The N must be removed, when **black** will soon suffer from his weaknesses on the dark squares.

(h) **Black** tries to press the attack.

(i) Better was **26 . . .Rh6**.

(j) **Black** has played an intuitive piece sacrifice based upon the exposed position of the WK; but now, since deep and precise calculation are the order of the day, CONSTELLATION-X must be winning.

(k) The only move (since **33 Qxg3 Qxq3 34 cxb7** allows Qf3 + where **black** wins), and now the WK escapes.

(l) **White** now has an easily won game.

Digest 1984. Although Michie discusses computer chess in general, a number of his points are relevant to the future role of commercial chess computers in particular. His basic position is that computers will continue to pervade every facet of chess as long as Grandmasters and the professionals who make a living from the game allow them to do so. Indeed, I doubt that the chess elite could do anything to alter this trend, even if that were their intention. Human chess has already benefitted a great deal from computer chess in terms of analysis, opening and end-game theory, and understanding. Chess computers can already serve as excellent learning tools for the human novice or intermediate player.

By 1990, Michie foresees that we may well have a World Chess Champion of machine origin, and if we don't, then cooperation with computers could bring the level of World Championship caliber chess by humans over the 3000 rating mark! Hence, Michie perceives that computer chess may best serve as a ''support-vehicle'' for human chess masters, and therein lies the principal challenge to computer science and artificial intelligence. In my opinion, this forecast is a bit optimistic. Even if we do have a World Chess Champion of machine origin in 1990, I very much doubt that it will be through artificial intelligence techniques such as an attempt to decode the chess knowledge in a Grandmaster's head! Research trends and developments during the past ten years do not support Michie's forecast.

Michie suggests that there may even be a new class of tournament comprised solely of human/machine combinations, which he calls ''man-machine consultation chess.'' In the event that machines become too strong for humans, there would be restrictions or rations on the amount of resources (such as CPU time) allotted to each competitor, much as in the case of car or motorcycle racing. The point is that there would still be interest in human competitive chess, and interest in computer chess would turn from considerations of strength of play to the evaluation of programs as possible learning tools for humans.

Postscript

A final note about the outcome of FIDELITY-X versus NOVAG-X (page 248): While this article was in production, Kittinger reported to me that the SUPER CONSTELLATION now finds **30** Qg5 after 6 minutes of think time. It had apparently searched one ply short of being able to find the mating sequence.

Acknowledgments

The author wishes to thank Dan and Kathe Spracklen, Dave Kittinger, Mr. Jean Leduc of CERVO-2000, and Enrique Irazoqui for providing useful information. The U.S. Chess Federation welcomes any enquiries regarding commercial chess computers; their address is 186 Route 9W, New Windsor, NY 12550.

References

Gertler, David. "So You Want to Buy a Chess Computer." *Chess Life* **39**, 11(1984):28–30.

Irazoqui, Enrique, ed. *Computer Chess Digest Annual*, Vols. 1 and 2. New York, 1983, 1984.

Kopec, Danny. "The Canadian Computer Chess Invitational Championship (CCCIC) 1984." *ICCA Journal* **7**, 3(1984):155–63.

Levy, David. "Chess Master versus Computer." *ICCA Journal* **7**, 2(1984):106–17.

Welsh, David E. "Super Constellation: It's Time for Skeptics to Take a Second Look at Chess Computers." *Chess Life* **39**, 11(1984):26–7, 82.

Departments

In keeping with its *Scientific American* model, ABACUS includes several departments that appear in every issue and all of which are represented in the following samples. In most cases, they are written by the department editors, although sometimes, as in the case of the Computers and the Citizen sample, they are not.

Each department editor has his or her own purpose. For example, the Book Reviews are not limited to newly published books, but often take up the few classics of computing, attempting to suggest a short list of books for a personal professional computing library. The Problems and Puzzles editor tries to challenge and entertain his readers and get feedback from them. The Computer Press column, suggested by A.J. Liebling's articles on The Wayward Press in *The New Yorker,* is intended to provide constructive but entertaining criticism of this part of the computing milieu.

Book Reviews

Books for Every Professional

Developing a short list of books for a personal computer science library.

Eric A. Weiss

My ABACUS reviews will develop a short list of those basic and fundamental books that should be in the personal collections of serious computing professionals. I will review some of the best books on computing, those few of the thousands published that are recognized as being better than any others. The evidence of this recognition is the book's market domination of its niche, the book's longevity (often in successful and successive editions), and the frequency with which it is referenced by readers and writers. In most cases the superiority has been achieved against many competitors, although some books excel in their categories simply because they are alone in them.

In identifying books of the high quality needed for the ideal computing office library I will consider both the new and the old. I will not review obscure books, and I will only comment on bad books to contrast them with the best.

Ideally, personal collections should contain those few volumes that computing professionals find so important and so useful that they must have their own copies—at least in their offices if not on their desks. Usually the collection is started with one's first computer book plus a few retained college textbooks. As time passes and the professional's career develops, specialized books are added and obsolete texts are discarded. Occasionally

Eric A. Weiss is a free-lance writer and editor. He received his degree in electrical engineering from Lehigh University and for almost four decades guided the Sun Company in computer use. At the same time, he wrote or edited seven computing textbooks and participated in the publication programs of several technical societies. He was the first chairman of the ACM Publication Board, and is now Associate Editor of *Computing Reviews,* Biographies Editor of the AFIPS *Annuals of the History of Computing,* and Chairman of the Editorial Board of the *Ralston Encyclopedia of Computer Science and Engineering, Third Edition.*

Reprinted from ABACUS, Volume 1, Number 1, Fall 1983.

a new basic reference will replace an old one. Such a professional library represents many things: one's present interests and some past interests, one's individual willingness and need to use and own books, and one's judgment as to which books are useful. Thus, the collection is very personal, and a glance at the books in it will reveal much about the owner.

The ideal professional library that my reviews will develop will, of course, reflect my own interests and personality, in spite of my efforts to conceal them; but since my reviews will be comparative—that is, in making each selection I will describe several books while justifying my choice—readers may apply their own prejudices and make their own selections.

INTERRUPT

Andrea Frankel, in a letter to the *WholeEarth-Review* (July 1985), comments on the amusing bulletin board convention of inserting "SMILEYs"—combinations of characters that, turned 90°, look like smiling faces. A SMILEY is placed at the end of a comment "which, if said in person, would need to be softened by a smile." Indeed, absent visual contact, it is often difficult to determine whether something expressed via the printed word is meant as a joke or not, whether the originator of an electronic message "is good-naturedly mouthing off or mounting a serious attack."

Five individual SMILEYs are described in the letter:

: -)   a standard smile

; -)   a winking smile

B -)   a smile by an eyeglasses wearer

8 -)   a smile by a granny-glasses wearer

: @)   a smile by someone with a fat nose

The presence or absence of a SMILEY can be an important piece of electronic "body language" data, as witness the comment: "That person should be sentenced to a year of real-time programming in COBOL! : -)"

The Fifth Generation: Banzai or Pie-in-the-Sky?

A suggested U.S. response, with advice on the best Artificial Intelligence books.

Eric A. Weiss

Glendower: I can call spirits from the vasty deep.
Hotspur: Why, so can I, or so can any man;
  But will they come when you do call for them?

—*King Henry IV, Part I, III.i.*

The Fifth Generation: Artificial Intelligence and Japan's Computer Challenge to the World, by Edward A. Feigenbaum and Pamela McCorduck (Addison-Wesley, Reading, MA, 1983).

This book is a warning, a clarion call to action, and the most recent example of an overenthusiastic promotional piece for Artificial Intelligence (hereafter often called AI). It describes Japan's extremely public and explicit plan to dominate world computing within the next decade and a half, evaluating it in the light of Japan's capabilities and recent record. It concludes that the threat is real and significant, for, the book says, even if Japan cannot achieve everything proposed, on schedule, by concentrating on AI Japan will move far ahead of the U.S. The book calls for strong and immediate action so that the U.S. can keep its lead in AI. Throughout, the authors expound the present and future wonders of AI, sometimes (as is traditional in that discipline) confusing what will be or may be with what is.

In this column I will review the book and give my own evaluation of the threat and what the authors say we should do about it. Because Artificial Intelligence is the key aspect of the hardware and software of the Japanese Fifth Generation, I will review the state of Artificial Intelligence today, and recommend a few basic AI books for the reader's personal library. Finally, I will make my own suggestion of an appropriate U.S. response to the Japanese challenge.

Reprinted from ABACUS, Volume 1, Number 2, Winter 1984.

The Fifth Generation: The Book

The book opens by saying that "Japanese planners view the computer industry as vital to their nation's economic future and have audaciously made it a national goal to become number one in this industry by the latter half of the 1990s." They will avoid a head-on confrontation now with the American firms that dominate today's marketplace; instead, they will move rapidly to build major strength in an area of computing that will have great economic potential in the 1990s but is now being overlooked by "the shortsighted and complacent Americans." That area is knowledge engineering, the current hot button in Artificial Intelligence. "They [the Japanese] aim not only to dominate the traditional forms of the computer industry but to establish a 'knowledge industry' in which knowledge itself will be a salable commodity like food and oil."

To succeed, the project must produce within ten years the computer hardware and software for knowledge engineering in a wide range of applications—including expert systems, natural language understanding by machine, and robotics. The hardware will be specifically designed for AI applications. The systems will support very large knowledge bases, allow very fast associative retrievals, perform logical inference operations at the current speed of arithmetic operations, and use parallelism in program structure and hardware; and they will be easy to use because much of the input and output will be in the form of images and natural speech. The plan requires the creation of essential subsystems for problem-solving and inference, human/machine interaction, and a special kind of knowledge base.

At this point, an explanation is needed of some common words used by the authors and Artificial Intelligence practitioners in a special way. "Knowledge" means what ordinary computer people would call "data" or "information" combined with the rules or procedures for its use. "Knowledge" is distinguished from ordinary data and rules by the unfixed form and organizational structure of the data and the uniqueness of the procedures used. "Problem-solving and inference" has the operational meaning that when an unknown problem is given, the computer system will automatically draw meaningful, novel, and correct conclusions using stored inferences, rules, procedures, and data.

The Japanese plan is not secret. The multi-author proceedings of the 1981 Tokyo kick-off conference have been published in English as *Fifth Generation Computer Systems* (edited by T. Moto-oka). The Feigenbaum/ McCorduck book and the proceedings are in agreement, the book being somewhat more popularized and hortatory and the proceedings more technical and detailed. While the proceedings give specific goals, the plans for getting to them are far more vague than U.S. project approvers would require. A blind and overweening confidence that worthy or essential goals can be reached without knowing the sequence of detailed and achievable steps is said to be an integral part of the Japanese culture. This characteristic may be considered praiseworthy for showing confidence that the creative genius of the researchers will find novel solutions to both the obvious and the unexpected problems, or can equally well be seen as blameworthy for depending on national willpower to reach impossible ends.

Both the popular and the technical U.S. press have reported on the project. *Time,* in its Japanese issue of 1 August, devoted a page and a picture to the youthful team which will make dumb machines act as if they had human intelligence, producing among other prodigies:

□ a speech-actuated typewriter with a 10,000-word vocabulary;
□ an optical scanner that can read written Japanese characters;
□ an automatic translator that can translate Japanese text into other languages with 90% accuracy.

The last half of the book considers foreign responses to the threat and proposes some alternatives for America, as follows:

□ Muddle through.
□ Form domestic industrial consortiums to meet the challenge.
□ Form a major joint venture with the Japanese.
□ Forget about hardware and focus on software.
□ Form a national laboratory to promote knowledge technology.
□ Prepare to become the first great agrarian postindustrial society.

The authors' favorite option is a national laboratory, the National Center for Knowledge Technology, "a cooperative effort . . . to ensure well-educated researchers, fruitful research, and an end to the frittering away of resources in short-term get-rich schemes that benefit the very few." Although funded at first by the government, it would not be a government agency. Although partially funded by the military, it would be free of military control. The staff would not be civil servants but temporary loaners from industry and academia.

The style of the book is almost entirely McCorduck's, very much like her earlier gossipy explanation of and paean to AI, *Machines Who Think.* It is a very clear, easy-to-read, anecdotal, modern popular magazine-style volume, full of names, trivia, quotations, and gossipy stories. Feigenbaum's thoughts are obviously here, sometimes directly quoted, often embedded in the fast-flowing text; but his own writing style is seldom visible. Most AI concepts are well and clearly stated, some are overpopularized, and only a few remain mysteriously shrouded in pedantic phraseology. The book got wide acceptance by several specialized book clubs before publication, and made it to the business shelves of the chain bookstores rather than to the computer book racks.

Both the book and the project will be vigorously promoted, will become well-known, will stimulate a lot of public and private discussion and some thought. Computer professionals who must keep up with current public developments (or at least give that appearance) should have the book visible in their offices, and should have an opinion about it and the project.

The Fifth Generation: The Project

Now I will take up the project itself. The book lists all the reasons why the project might fail:

- ☐ It is too risky and futuristic for private Japanese firms.
- ☐ It requires scheduled technical breakthroughs.
- ☐ It faces major challenges.
- ☐ It departs seriously from traditional Japanese practice in its emphasis on youth, and in depending on innovation rather than evolution.
- ☐ It faces resentment and hostility from older Japanese leaders.
- ☐ The Japanese lack too many assets: experience in AI, software expertise, trained computer scientists, equipment, theory, understanding.

The book rests its faith in success on:

- ☐ the vision of project leaders;
- ☐ the hope, enthusiasm, devotion, and hard work of youth;
- ☐ the promising path chosen;
- ☐ the rich Japanese engineering talent;
- ☐ the importance of the goal to Japan;
- ☐ the national will and self-esteem.

In July, *Datamation* reported how several computer specialists replied to the question, "Can They Do It?" The more outspoken used such terms as "sold a bill of goods," "blue sky," "pie in the sky," "media event," "wish list," and "not a challenge." The more cautious said "ambitious," "new ideas," "new thinking," "maybe so," "may move faster than the U.S.," "a catalyst," and "a threat." All agreed that while the project will not achieve all its goals it would accomplish something. All agreed that the U.S. was not doing enough to protect its industry's position, and suggested various low-profile steps. All agreed that the announcement had not influenced what they were doing.

My own conclusion is that the *Datamation* critics are right. The project will not reach all its goals on time; some things will be accomplished, some of the original goals will be reworded and reinterpreted, some face will be lost; perhaps there will be some suicides, both real and figurative.

The U.S. Reaction

The general U.S. reaction will be that of the *Datamation* experts—the project is interesting but not threatening, and not worth imitating. Some parts of the computing industry, commercial, academic, and military, will try to use the threat of the project to frighten Congress or the DoD into half-hearted action to counter the Japanese, just as the DoD and their contractors have long and effectively used the Russian threat. The results will be a lot of talk, some arm-waving, some cooperative research, some special-interest legislation, some fiddling with antitrust and patent rules, some fruitless national planning, and some off-and-on funding of well-loved computing projects. The response favored by the authors, the National Center for Knowledge Technology, contradicts U.S. culture as much as the Fifth Generation Project contradicts Japanese culture. Like the project itself, it is pie-in-the-sky.

Altogether, the U.S. will respond with a twitch and a yawn. This is unfortunate, for there is a better response which I will suggest at the end of this column.

Artificial Intelligence

The leaders of the field describe Artificial Intelligence as the effort to make machines that can reason and perceive. Such an effort started in the 1950s with Alan M. Turing's specificication of an operational test of whether a computer could think, Claude E. Shannon's discussion of a how to program a computer to play chess, Norbert Wiener's and John von Neumann's speculations about man/machine identities, and Ed Berkeley's unfortunately titled but widely read introduction to the wonderful world of computing, *Giant Brains or Machines that Think.* This period of beginnings coincides with the hopeful youth of today's old heads in computing.

If Artificial Intelligence is defined in a broader and more commonsense way as the machine imitation of any kind of human intelligence, its roots can be seen to go back to the ancient myths and legends about machines that acted as if they were people, or statues that, like Pygmalion's Galatea or the Golem of Prague, were given sentient life. But except for these stories and a few isolated cases, it was not until the latter part of the Industrial Revolution that mechanical devices were generally substituted for human actions, actions that when done by people clearly required some kind of understanding, thought, and intelligence. These devices first appeared as automatic water-level and engine-speed controllers, then as temperature regulators; and finally, in the first half of this century, there emerged moderately sophisticated but extremely successful inanimate controllers of steady-state activity and continuous chemical fluid processes, automatic helmsmen of steamships, and aircraft autopilots.

The chief ingenuity of these early controllers lay in the devices which linked the sensing means (level, flow, heading), with the actuators (valves, rudders, elevators). At first the automatic linking devices had to be cobbled together out of rods, levers, gears, and pneumatic and hydraulic pushers, and later out of vacuum tube electronic circuits and small electric motors. The cobbling was done by inventors, technicians, and engineers, and before World War II the work generally attracted only sporadic attention from scientists, mathematicians, and theoreticians.

Before its birth, while it was in gestation, the digital computer was recognized as a linking means so powerful, flexible, and capable as to push the whole concept of automatic control into a new world, a world in which it might rival the human brain itself. Alan M. Turing first wrote on the subject before the ENIAC had appeared. Later, in his 1950 seminal piece, "Can computers think?," he proposed the Turing test offering a standard by which one might decide whether or not a machine was sufficiently capable of imitating a human to be considered "thinking."

The Great Thinkers of the early days of computing considered the subject of Artificial Intelligence worth their attention. Norbert Wiener was convinced that there was a direct correspondence between the computer and the human brain. He inspired several generations of his MIT admirers to study one of the pair to get insights into the other. As more knowledgeable physiologists were drawn into the study, the misguided assurance of the mathematicians and the electrical engineers was damped down, although an important school of Artificial Intelligence, to which philosophers and newspaper writers are now attracted, still works the machine/human correspondence mother lode.

In those early days, before 1960, Artificial Intelligence was an exciting field. Huge, challenging problems of language translation, game-playing, medical diagnosis, and mathematical theorem-proving were attacked by devoted young people with hope, enthusiasm, devotion, and hard work, but with limited equipment, inadequate theory, and a lack of understanding. Early dramatic successes were first followed by overoptimistic predictions, and then by blocks, dead ends, and apparently limitless multiplication and inflation of the problems, which stopped further advances. Full of confidence, the explorers had climbed the eastern foothills of the Rockies certain that they would see the Pacific just beyond, but instead they faced the Sierra Nevadas.

Although a lot of effort was wasted and many will-o'-the-wisps were pursued into swamps, a great deal was accomplished. Important techniques were devised and eventually perfected for use in more mundane tasks. The future teachers, leaders, and thinkers of computer science were educated, and trained, and had some of their rough edges chipped off and their arrogance dampened.

In this period three curious and unique circumstances seemed to be characteristic of Artificial Intelligence.

First, any area in which success was achieved would split off from AI, establish its own culture, create its own societies, publications, and academic departments, and finally deny any connection with AI. Control engineers, whose two centuries of practice and theory contributed to the beginning of the field, never speak of their work as being part of AI, and often consider AI to be the domain of artsy-craftsy dilettantes. Robotics, which owes much to the theoretical and practical work of AI, is today so separate and so large that the major AI encyclopedia reviewed below, *The Handbook of Artificial Intelligence,* could not find room for the subject. (*Robotics: Applications and Social Implications,* by Robert V. Ayers and Steven M. Miller, is a good current reference.) Although game-playing, especially chess, was a wholly respectable AI endeavor in 1955, it is no longer a suitable subject for government-supported work, so the automatic chess players, who have now started to achieve the success that was predicted for them when AI was new, practice, improve, and publish on their own. (A multi-authored collection of papers gives the current chess situation: *Chess Skill in Man and Machine,* edited by Peter W. Frey.) Some other areas have become so successful and so common that their origins in Artificial Intelligence are forgotten, like the recognition of printed characters, image scanning and enhancement, primitive speech recognition, and AI's greatest contribution to the computer professional's tool kit, John McCarthy's list processing language (Lisp) and its clones.

Second, AI enthusiasts always seemed to promise too much, too soon, and with too much publicity. The name "Artificial Intelligence" in itself stimulates interest, especially among those ethical humanists who fear AI as a direct attack on the prestige, integrity, and humanity of the race. The aim of Artificial Intelligence, to reproduce human behavior with a machine, is more easily understood than most of the goals of computing, and often the early accomplishments of AI in a new line of exploration were astonishing and dramatic. All this seemed to lead those practitioners who were interviewed by the press to say too much, and to be careless about the distinction between what actually was and what they hoped would be, or at least to encourage the press in such carelessness. The consequence was an early excess of expectations in both the academic and commercial worlds.

But as the problems of advancing beyond the first stages proved difficult and expensive, and neither mermaids nor mermen popped out, most commercial AI efforts were cut off. Only the military—with its deep interest in secret magic and its hope of replacing the human race in one way or another—and the federal medical research sponsors—with their deep interest in curiosities, both artificial and human, and their hope of replacing doctors—have faithfully continued their support of AI throughout the last twenty years.

Third, the discipline never spread as widely in the academic community as the other parts of computing. Although the subject was taught at many places, until recently it was maintained in substantial health at only three major colleges and a scattering of lesser ones. The original centers at MIT (where Wiener worked) and Carnegie-Mellon (where Newell and Simon predicted great things) were joined by Stanford when John McCarthy carried Lisp to the West from MIT. In the AI world, Stanford Research Institute (now called SRI International for promotional purposes) must be considered as part of a general Stanford complex, for the personalities involved are comingled and frequently interchanged.

Just in the last few years this localization has been changing as AI accomplishments have become more evident, and the field is again promising. Other colleges have joined up, entrepreneurial professors have started several garage-based AI firms, and some minor computer vendors have named AI departments. (It is a significant circumstance, noted by Japanese objectors to the Fifth Generation Project, that IBM has not.) A few employers have advertised for AI specialists.

Artificial Intelligence has still another unique distinction. Alone among all the parts of computing, it has generated several severe critics, resulting in four books which were well-known when they were published. The first, Mortimer Taube's *Computers and Common Sense* (1961), implied fraud; the second, the National Academy of Sciences' *Language and Machines: Computers in Translation and Linguistics* (1966), condemned as useless and fruitless the research on mechanical translation as it was then being done; the third, Hubert Dreyfus's *What Computers Can't Do* (1972), presumed to set practical limits to what AI *could* do; and the fourth, Joseph Weizenbaum's *Computer Power and Human Reason* (1976), argued for moral and philosophical limits and restraints on computer and AI development and use. Each caused a flurry, and damped some of the wilder AI excesses, but only Weizenbaum is still well-known, perhaps because it appeals to humanists. The NAS report (by a blue-ribbon committee chaired by J.R. Pierce) hurt the most but, like the others, did not put any permanent spokes in the AI wheels.

AI Schools

Dispassionate observers can identify at least four different schools of AI, each with its own leaders and philosophy. All are attempting to cause the machine to do something that humans can do—fill the tank, fly the airplane, play chess, translate languages, hear, speak, read, see, interpret oil-well logs, give advice, act like an expert—but each school goes at it a little differently.

The first, the oldest school, is never called Artificial Intelligence. The members are pragmatists, engineers, technicians. They merely require results. They go at the task any way they can, and they judge their success by how well the task is accomplished, whether the result is used, whether it pays. They are unconcerned with how the job is done, what theory is applied, or what principles are established. The practitioners of this school are hidden in industry or disguised as members of academic disciplines which deny any AI connection.

This first school blends into a second, which, while also pragmatic, seeks more than mere accomplishment. It seeks insight and understanding, in the form of basic mathematical principles and theories that will extend and generalize the accomplishments and in addition will bring intellectual credibility and academic acceptance to the research and the researchers. This can be said to be the MIT school, which traces its roots to Claude Shannon and his Information Theory.

A third school, dating back to 1950 and Norbert Wiener, requires not only that the task be accomplished but also that it be done the way humans do it. This third school is even more concerned with theories and basic general principles than the second. These theories and principles are to link human tasks with their mechanization. Herbert A. Simon, computing's only Nobel laureate, is the intellectual leader of this group, which has its academic base in Carnegie-Mellon University. Members of this third school continue the search for the link between mind and machine that Wiener taught. They judge any success only in part by how well the task is accomplished, because they also require that there be some clear relationship between how machines do it and how humans do it. Thus this school attracts philosophers, physiologists, neurologists, psychologists, and theoreticians who hope to understand human behavior, human performance, and human functioning better.

A fourth, more recent school treats AI as a branch of applied logic. This is the school led by Nilsson and Feigenbaum that is centered at Stanford University and Stanford Research Institute. I summarize the philosophy of this school below in my review of Nilsson's text.

The second, third, and fourth schools of Artificial Intelligence are inclined to exclude from the field of AI all accomplishments of human performance, no matter how successful, which do not satisfy their own particular criteria. The second school, MIT-based, has a strong connection to mathematics, and is quick to label as trivial or uninteresting those solutions which are based on brute force rather than brilliance, or which are well-known or common. The third one, Carnegie-Mellon-based, considers that the name AI applies only to systems that exhibit some parallel with human performance or thought, or that reveal new insights into human behavior and thought. The fourth school, Stanford-based, rates as real AI only systems that incorporate or relate to symbolic logic. The most doctrinaire members of these last three schools consider that an Artificial Intelligence system must demonstrate or be based on AI principles (whether long-accepted or new ones).

As a consequence of all these restrictions, many early engineering accomplishments of the mechanical duplication of simple human performance are too obvious and well-known, too trivial, to be seriously considered by any part of the AI community as exhibiting intelligence. Several more recent electronic duplications of more complex human behavior, which do not meet the criteria of any of the important AI schools, are no longer considered to be part of AI—for example, autopilots, chess-playing machines, robots, automatic bank tellers, product-code readers, word-processing grammatic and spelling critics—in spite of the fact that some of these machines do what they do surprisingly well.

AI practitioners recognize the consequences of this situation which they have created for themselves but they blame it on their critics, saying that "once some mental function is programmed, people soon cease to consider it as an essential ingredient of 'real thinking.' " It results in the often-quoted rueful definition, "AI is whatever hasn't been done yet."

In this dispassionate distinction and description of these four schools of AI, I have simplified many complexities, overlooked much detail, and ignored exceptions. I have not been surgically precise, but the broad general picture is sufficiently correct to give the computing generalist a useful conceptual framework within which to consider AI today.

Artificial Intelligence Shelf References

Today's best AI books describe AI and where it is today. There are two encyclopedic treatments, two major advanced texts, one recent elementary text, and several excellent collections of papers. In addition there are a few popularizations, several minor general textbooks, many texts devoted to narrow parts of the field or to authors' hobbyhorses, and a steady flow of proceedings and publish-or-perish papers. Commercial publishers have rediscovered AI, and a flood of new books is expected in the next two years; but just now, the computer generalist need only consider five dominant books as candidates for his or her library.

The Three-Volume Handbook

The Handbook of Artificial Intelligence, Avron Barr, Paul R. Cohen, & Edward A. Feigenbaum, editors (William Kaufmann, Los Altos, 1981, 1982).

Although high-priced ($95.00 for a set of three volumes), this is the first choice as the non-specialist's shelf reference on Artificial Intelligence. The list of almost 200 editors, contributors, and reviewers is a directory of major AI figures. The 200 short, clear, well-written, jargon-free articles cover all the important ideas, present general overviews of the scientific issues, and give detailed descriptions and discussions of both AI techniques and exemplary AI computer systems. The writing and editing process have produced a remarkably uniform style and approach.

The editors define Artificial Intelligence as "the part of computer science concerned with designing intelligent computer systems, that is, systems that exhibit the characteristics we associate with intelligence in human behavior—understanding language, learning, reasoning, solving problems, and so on." The editors sidestep the point that philosophers and humanists consider to be important, which is: if a machine carries out the activities that *indicate* intelligence in humans, does this mean that the machine may be said to *know* or *understand* anything? They avoid the issue by identifying certain machine behavior as intelligent without saying that the machine itself is intelligent.

The volumes deal with Artificial Intelligence both in terms of its key concepts and its significant parts, both abstractly and in the context of actual applications. The concepts are: search, divide-and-conquer, semantic nets, means/ends analysis, hierarchical planning, augmented transition nets, procedural knowledge, blackboard architecture, scripts and frames, goal-directed and data-driven processing, and learning. The significant parts of AI are named by the section titles: Search; Knowledge Representation; Understanding Natural Language; Understanding Spoken Language; Programming Languages for AI Research; Applications in Science, Medicine, and Education; Automatic Programming; Models of Cognition; Automatic Deduction; Vision; Learning and Inductive Inference; Planning and Problem Solving.

Each chapter starts with an overview article which includes critical discussions. All three volumes are indexed together and cross-referenced.

The Two-Volume Perspective

Artificial Intelligence: An MIT Perspective, Patrick H. Winston and Richard H. Brown, editors (MIT Press, Cambridge, 1979).

These two volumes are collections of previously published MIT papers selected to introduce advanced topics and to characterize the MIT point of view. The editors consider AI to be "the study of intelligence using the ideas and methods of computation," but they decline to define intelligence. The editors furnish excellent introductions to each section and single-paragraph summaries of each paper. This editorial material alone will give the reader an excellent overall view of where AI is, what it has accomplished, and where it is heading, at least as seen from the perspective of MIT. Although varied in style and quality, the papers are authoritative and comprehensible because the quality of their writing is superior to the average academic standard (probably what the editors mean in saying "our choices were often dictated by nontechnical factors"). Each paper has extensive but not exhausting references, and one index covers both volumes. These two volumes are a lower-priced but more limited shelf reference alternate to the *Handbook.*

While both the *Handbook* and the *Perspective* cover much of the same ground, the *Handbook* is more detailed and more comprehensive. It omits only computer design, while the *Perspective* omits search, programming languages, and many applications—in particular, those outside the MIT perspective. Both sets assume readers who are skilled in computing without being AI specialists, but the papers in the *Perspective* have a more academic flavor than the encyclopedia-like tutorial articles of the *Handbook*.

Textbooks

If the computing generalist wants a textbook in addition to a shelf reference, there are three choices. Two are classics, one from the east coast and one from the west, while the third is a recent, more elementary book from the middle of the country. Both authors of the classics are AI leaders, both are master teachers, but they take different philosophical attitudes toward AI. The third author is an excellent teacher with a more inclusive AI philosophy.

Artificial Intelligence East

The older book (but more recently revised into a new edition) is *Artificial Intelligence,* by Patrick H. Winston (Addison-Wesley, Reading, MA, second edition 1983).

The 1977 first edition became the AI teaching standard. The second edition is a total revision of the first, reflecting the changes in the field, the solid results that have accumulated, and the increased maturity of both the field and the author. The focus is more on principles and less on case studies; the material on Lisp has been taken out and put into a new book (coauthored by B.K.P. Horn); old material has been revised or rewritten, or replaced by new material; chapters on logic and learning have been added, and there are more problems.

The author's philosophy, which might be said to be the MIT position, is that Artificial Intelligence is a branch of computation, and he is going to teach how it is done, how to build the artifacts associated with AI research and practice. Nils J. Nilsson, the author of the competing classic textbook, called the first edition an "easy-to-read and elementary treatment of AI ideas . . . containing an excellent introduction to AI programming methods." The chapter titles are: The Intelligent Computer, Description Matching and Goal Reduction, Exploiting Natural Constraints, Exploring Alternatives, Control Metaphors, Problem Solving Paradigms, Logic and Theorem Proving, Representing Commonsense Knowledge, Language Understanding, Image Understanding, Learning Class Distinctions from Samples, and Learning Rules from Experience. There is a 19-page bibliography. One can get a grip on the field by reading through the book, or become a beginning practitioner by studying it together with *LISP* by Patrick H. Winston and Berthold K.P. Horn (Addison-Wesley, 1981).

Artificial Intelligence West

Nilsson takes a more abstract approach in *Principles of Artificial Intelligence* (Tioga Pub. Co., Palo Alto, 1980).

He writes as clearly and teaches as well as Winston; but this book, as Winston says of it, presents AI as a kind of applied logic. This philosophy is strong at both Stanfords, the Institute and the University, and has had an obvious influence on both Fifth Generations, the book and the project. Nilsson particularly stresses generalized production systems and the predicate calculus, which he believes underlies the important present and future AI applications. His concern is with the kinds of data structures used, the types of operations performed on them, and the properties of control strategies used. The author teaches principles which he explains abstractly rather than by discussing them in the context of specific applications, although he includes some illustrations in the form of small examples.

The Prologue, an excellent overview, lists AI applications and makes brief descriptive, biographical, and historical remarks about each. Those listed are Natural Language Processing, Intelligent Retrieval from Databases, Expert Consulting Systems, Theorem Proving, Robotics, Automatic Programming Combinatorial and Scheduling Problems, and Perception Problems. A final section, "Prospectus," attempts a perspective on the entire AI enterprise to point out problem areas where future research is needed: novel AI system architectures, knowledge acquisition and learning, and the adequacy of AI processes and representational formalisms for dealing with knowledge, goals, beliefs, plans, and self-reference. Each chapter ends with exercises. The 35-page bibliography applies not only to the abstractions of the text, but to the whole AI field.

Nilsson would be the choice of a person who wanted to move from the broad generalities of the encyclopedias and the computational practicalities of Winston into the deeper abstractions of AI production systems. The reader wanting to avoid complete dependence on any one point of view would do well to supplement this text with *Readings in Artificial Intelligence,* Bonnie Lynn Webber and Nils J. Nilsson, editors (Tioga Pub. Co., Palo Alto, 1981). It contains 31 previously published original papers on AI theory and experiment, considered by the editors to be representative of the best thinking and research. The papers are grouped into 5 chapters: Search and Search Representations, Deduction, Problem-Solving and Planning, Expert Systems and AI Applications, and Advanced Topics.

The papers are photo-reproduced in their original form; each chapter starts with a one-page introduction, and a single subject index is provided.

Artificial Intelligence Central

Artificial Intelligence, by Elaine Rich (McGraw-Hill, New York, 1983).

This is a survey text which provides a readable introduction to the problems and techniques of AI. The author defines AI as "the study of how to make computers do things at which, at the moment, people are better." She also sees the ultimate goal of AI to be the construction of programs that solve hard problems. Her first chapter is an excellent overview of the whole field.

The author is a good writer and a good teacher. She surveys and clearly explains—in detail, with examples, and without pomposity—all the major techniques of artificial intelligence. She concludes that the important interacting aspects of every AI program are a knowledge-representation framework and problem-solving and inference methods. While the author index reveals a slight orientation toward Carnegie-Mellon, the book itself is not dominated by any of the several schools distinguished above. Indeed, this would be the text of choice for the most general and specific coverage of the field at an undergraduate or lower-division graduate level.

U.S. Response

On the basis of all this perspective, let me return to the Fifth Generation Project itself and suggest that the U.S. response should be thoughtful, considered, not guided by panic or fear, but based on principles this nation has found fruitful:

□ build on experience;
□ do what you do best;
□ encourage enthusiasm.

What has been our experience with foreign science and technology? We know that new scientific knowledge gives the greatest benefit to those nations which are most ready to exploit and use it, and this ready group may not include the originating nation. Although rocketry and space technology originated in Germany during World War II, they were ultimately most beneficial not to Germany but to the U.S. and Russia. Both victors commandeered German equipment and documents and kidnapped as many Nazi scientists as they could, and, unlike Germany, both were ready, willing, and able to use the transferred technology. German and Japanese automobile manufacturing genius used American technology to benefit

American drivers by allowing them to drive well-built automobiles. All three nations gained immensely; but, since U.S. drivers are rich and many, the U.S. got the biggest total advantage. The Japanese technological developments in shipbuilding at last got the U.S. out of a profitless and dying industry. Now the Japanese are performing the same service in the case of steel. By buying Japanese electronic products, the U.S. was able to shake off its devotion to the hot and outmoded vacuum tube, and American consumers got low-priced and reliable home entertainment equipment. Some U.S. industries wept and cried, suffered and died; some learned and lived. But American consumers and taxpayers benefited from better products, lower prices, and reduced government subsidies for industries that couldn't make it in the world market.

From this experience, the U.S. should look forward to reaping the benefits from whatever the Japanese Fifth Generation Project develops—and, just because we are bigger, richer, and stronger, benefiting more from these improvements than the originating nation. Indeed, the U.S. can learn from the Japanese to beg, buy, and borrow foreign technological developments and exploit them.

Closely allied with the principle of building on experience is the commonsense adage, "Do what you do best." We do not compete with the Japanese very well, but we do best in helping them. It was American money, American human aid and guidance that rebuilt Japan from its devastated end-of-the-war state to its present condition as an economic giant, changing it from a feudal, backward, fascist nation to the democratic state it is today.

So what does the U.S. do best? It is best at helping others, especially Japan, and at giving money away. Here the Department of Defense leads all the rest. Thus, the indicated course for the U.S. (on the basis of experience and a knowledge of what we do best) is to help the Japanese Fifth Generation Project in every way we can: by supplying grants of money; by loaning college professors; by buying and copying its products, exploiting its scientific and technological developments and breakthroughs as fast as they appear; and by ignoring or clucking sympathetically over any failures or missed schedules.

Finally, the basic rule of managing every human endeavor—but especially the creative work of artists, inventors, and scientists—is to encourage enthusiasm. One should never say "no" to innovators, never raise objections, never be negative, always be positive. Say "Go, go, go!" This the U.S. should do with the young, lively, enthusiastic Japanese. Encourage them. Cheer them on. Give them aid, encouragement, money, our leaders in AI. We can live in the certainty that whatever the Japanese develop we will buy or steal and use.

Young military people may murmur against this stance on the grounds that military developments must be home-grown and that the development of technology which might be used in weapons should be guided by the military. This assertion is borne out neither by history nor by the present public attitude of the DoD. In the last war that the U.S. won decisively, all the quick-firing Naval anti-aircraft guns were of Swiss and Swedish design; our mines, torpedoes, underwater echo-ranging equipment, hand grenades, mortars, and microwave radar had British origins, while our Great Atom Bomb was developed using Italian and German scientific breakthroughs, Belgian-owned African uranium, and Norwegian heavy water. (Of course, the Garand rifle, the jeep, the walkie-talkie, and C rations were purely U.S. contributions, later copied by other nations.)

Today, as in the past, many nations buy their weapons from others, choosing the best that a competitive free market offers. The advantages of letting another nation develop your military hardware are frequently and forcefully explained to other countries by the DoD and its industrial toadies, but these logical arguments as to why Germany or Japan or Argentina should buy U.S. weapons instead of developing their own are never put in their equally logical vice-versa form. So much for the chauvinistic argument that the military must control the development of the technology on which weapons depend.

Thus, the logical attitude for the U.S. to take toward the Japanese Fifth Generation Project is to support it and encourage it in every way. The more searchers there are for the Holy Grail, the more likely it is that some tin-plated cups will be discovered. In science and technology every useful and worthwhile discovery works to the benefit and harm of all mankind; but because the U.S. is big and rich and strong and ready to use and apply new discoveries, it can capture and exploit such developments to the most advantage, whenever and wherever they occur. "Them 'as got, gits!"

The danger is not that the Japanese will succeed—for their successes will result in U.S. benefits—but that somehow we will not make prompt use of whatever they accomplish. We might manage this neglect if we overdo our national inclination to fight them and compete with them, and consequently establish too strong and compelling a U.S. Fifth (or Sixth) Generation Project. Such a strong project might institutionalize so powerful a Not-Invented-Here decision-making process that we would systematically ignore the good things the Japanese will provide because our own stuff is so superior, or, more likely, because our own project is just about to provide a monumental red-white-and-blue breakthrough.

A related but more serious danger lies in the possibility that our military people will get their thumbs into the American AI efforts and make secret whatever they don't gum up. This could put any AI successes on the same path to disaster that the AEC provided for nuclear power, that the National Security Agency is pressing on encryption, and that the Commerce and State Departments are working up to control technology transfer. Even the best ideas can be killed, hurt, or at least delayed if hedged around with bureaucrats and secrecy limitations.

So what is the prescription for bigger, faster computers, and for the

Fifth Generation? We should press vigorously forward on all fronts in the unplanned and uncoordinated fashion that we all understand. We should let a thousand flowers bloom. We should encourage everyone, men, women, children, U.S., Japan, England, France. We should hand out money. We should transport experts. We should jump up and down. We should be ready to grab anybody's invention, even our own, and use it. We should be ready to seize winners and dump losers, even our own. We should look big, fearless, happy, and greedy, and not tiny, frightened, worried, and dumb.

While the Japanese may only be calling spirits from the vasty deep, there is a caveat. Be careful of sure things, for every American has heard this parental cautionary tale: "Someday you will meet a glib, well-dressed, assured, and plausible young man. He will bet you that he can make the Jack of Diamonds jump out of his deck of cards and spit in your eye. But do not bet, for if you do you will lose your money and end up with a wet eye!"

The conclusion is: don't bet on the Japanese, don't bet against them, don't fear them. Push forward with confidence that the U.S. will muddle through—if it can keep its government from making magnificent plans for everyone.

Books Reviewed

The Fifth Generation: Artificial Intelligence and Japan's Computer Challenge to the World, by Edward A. Feigenbaum and Pamela McCorduck, Addison-Wesley, Reading, MA, 1983, 275 pages, $15.55 (ISBN 0-201-11519-0).

The Handbook of Artificial Intelligence, Avron Barr, Paul R. Cohen, & Edward A. Feigenbaum, editors; William Kaufmann, Los Altos, 1981, 1982; Vol. I: 409 pages, $30.00 (ISBN 0-86576-005-5); Vol. II: 428 pages, $35.00 (ISBN 0-86576-006-3); Vol. III: 639 pages, $45.00 (ISBN 0-86576-007-1); 3 volumes, $95.00 (ISBN 0-86576-004-7).

Artificial Intelligence: An MIT Perspective; Patrick H. Winston and Richard H. Brown, editors; MIT Press, Cambridge, MA, 1979; Vol. I: 492 pages, paper, $12.50 (ISBN 0-262-73058-8); Vol. II: 486 pages, paper, $12.50 (ISBN 0-262-73059-6).

Artificial Intelligence, Second Edition, by Patrick H. Winston, Addison-Wesley, Reading, MA, 1983, 480 pages, $29.95 (ISBN 0-201-08259-4).

Principles of Artificial Intelligence, by Nils J. Nilsson, Tioga Pub. Co., Palo Alto, 1980, 476 pages, $30.00 (ISBN 0-935382-01).

Readings in Artificial Intelligence, Bonnie Lynn Webber and Nils J. Nilsson, editors, Tioga Pub. Co., Palo Alto, 1981, 547 pages, paper, $25.00 (ISBN 0-935382-03-8).

Artificial Intelligence, by Elaine Rich, McGraw-Hill, New York, 1983, 436 pages, $26.95 (ISBN 0-07-052261-8).

Books Mentioned

Fifth Generation Computer Systems, T. Moto-oka, editor; Elsevier North-Holland, Amsterdam, 1982, 287 pages, $49.00 (ISBN 0-444-86440-7).

Machines Who Think, by Pamela McCorduck, W.H. Freeman, San Francisco, 1979, 375 pages, paper, $9.95 (ISBN 0-7167-1135-4).

Giant Brains or Machines that Think, by Edmund C. Berkeley, John Wiley, New York, 1949, out of print.

Robotics: Applications and Social Implications, by Robert V. Ayers and Steven M. Miller, Ballinger Publishing Co., Cambridge, MA, 1983, 368 pages, $32.50 (ISBN 0-88410-891-0).

Chess Skill in Man and Machine, Second Edition, Peter W. Frey, editor; Springer-Verlag, New York, 1983, 329 pages, $28.00 (ISBN 0-387-90790-4).

Computers and Common Sense: The Myth of Thinking Machines, by Mortimer Taube, Columbia University Press, New York, 1961, 136 pages, $20.00 (ISBN 0-231-02516-5).

Language and Machines: Computers in Translation and Linguistics, Automatic Language Processing Advisory Committee, Division of Behavioral Sciences, National Academy of Sciences, National Research Council, Washington, DC, 1966, 124 pages, paper, free (out of print).

What Computers Can't Do: A Critique of Artificial Reason, by Hubert L. Dreyfus, Harper & Row, New York, 1972, 259 pages, paper, $6.95 (ISBN 0-06-090613-8).

Computer Power and Human Reason: From Judgment to Calculation, by Joseph Weizenbaum, W.H. Freeman, San Francisco, 1976, 300 pages, paper, $10.95 (ISBN 0-7167-0463-3).

LISP, by Patrick H. Winston and Berthold K.P. Horn, Addison-Wesley, Reading, MA, 1981, 430 pages, paper, $18.95 (ISBN 0-201-08329-9).

LETTER TO THE EDITOR

More on the Fifth Generation

I read Feigenbaum's and McCorduck's *Fifth Generation* with considerable exasperation, and I found Eric Weiss's review in the Winter, 1984 issue of ABACUS a wonderful antidote. His recommendations for a sensible response to the fifth-generation scare are excellent, but I doubt that they will be taken as seriously as the scare itself.

AI people denigrate excellent computer hardware and software because they don't do all the things that humans do, or because their way of doing things is different from ours. Computers have been better than humans— at some things—ever since the first relay machines were built, and the number of things at which they are better, and how much better they are, increase continually. Is it really sensible that computers should evolve into golems? Computers should imitate human behavior only if that's the best way to get the job done, and most often it isn't. And, why should computers be used to do things that they don't do very well at the moment? In exasperation I've said that artificial intelligence is real stupidity, and I can't say I regret making the remark.

A different and, I believe, a more sensible view of what the Japanese (and the world) are really up to is presented in a book *Information Technology and Civilization,* by Hiroshi Inose and myself (W.H. Freeman and Company, 1984). The senior author is Professor of Electronic Engineering at the University of Tokyo, past president of the Japanese Information Processing Society, vice-president of the Institute of Electronics and Communication Engineers of Japan and is a member of several Japanese government advisory councils, including councils advising MITI. His own research on digital switching, traffic-control and information systems is outstanding. I warn the reader, however, not to look for an explicit discussion of the Japanese "fifth generation" program, for it isn't mentioned in our book.

John R. Pierce
Professor Emeritus at the Center for Computer Research in Music and
*   Acoustics at Stanford*
Former Executive Director for Communications Research at Bell Telephone Laboratories
Former Professor of Electrical Engineering at the California Institute of
*   Technology*

Reprinted from ABACUS, Volume 1, Number 4, Summer 1984.

INTERRUPT

The special issue of the *Annals of the History of Computing* on Fortran's twenty-fifth anniversary (January 1984) contains some one-liners regarding that language:

"Fortran—'the infantile disorder'—is hopelessly inadequate for whatever computer application you have in mind today . . . too clumsy, too risky and too expensive." [Edsger Dijkstra]
"God is Real (unless otherwise declared in an explicit type statement or in an implicit declaration)." [B. Graham]
"Fortran is a language to avoid—unless you want some answers." [Anonymous]

The debate goes on, but we are solidly with Tony Hoare in his comment: "I don't know what the language of the year 2000 will look like, but I know it will be called Fortran."

In the Art of Programming, Knuth Is First; There Is No Second

The best-known books—and one less well known—by the foremost American computer scientist.

Eric A. Weiss

Each established discipline seems to have a single representative book: a book that most professionals have studied, and that every professional is aware of even if not really familiar with it. It is always an old book, with roots in the discipline's beginnings. It always deals with the basics. It is always clearly written by a recognized master. It is not necessarily comprehensive. In a diverse field it may apply only to part of the discipline; but it comes to represent the discipline's common ground, the part that all practitioners must know about if they are to be respected by their peers.

In mathematics the book is Euclid. In law it is Blackstone. For a writer it is Strunk and White. For decades, when engineering was satisfied to be a practical art without aspirations to becoming a mathematical science, the book was French's *Engineering Drawing*. Every publisher hopes to have such a book on its list, for it sells itself in enormous quantities throughout its long life.

The Art of Computer Programming

In computer science, this basic classic is Stanford professor Donald E. Knuth's great work *The Art of Computer Programming*. As explained in the panel on page 286, Knuth plans a set of seven volumes, of which he has done three so far. The first volume came out in 1968, the second in 1969, and the third in 1973. The most recent revision, in 1981, was of the second volume. *The Art* has been translated into several languages, including Chinese and Russian. Almost 300,000 copies have been sold, about half of this number being sales of the first volume. A convincing measure of its domination of the market is that no publisher will suggest that any

Reprinted from ABACUS, Volume 1, Number 3, Spring 1984.

title "competes with Knuth." Publishers will nominate books that are newer, simpler, lower-priced, easier to teach from, deeper in narrower areas, but none that are equal to Knuth as a reference book in all the areas he covers.

Knuth is completely authoritative. His subjects lie at the intersection of the worlds of abstract mathematics and practical computer use, and he recognizes both worlds. The minimum requirements of the reader are that he or she should be acquainted with computing to the extent of some elementary computer jargon and a little programming experience, having written, as the author says, "at least, say, four programs for at least one computer. . . . " While this kind of reader will find the books useful, to appreciate fully the significance and depth of everything in Knuth requires considerably more mathematical and computer experience and understanding.

Knuth's style is appealing and easily readable. Indeed, his style can create the impression that his subjects are simple when they are not. Although never obscure or confusing, he is frequently terse, and often omits or skips lightly over intervening steps in his reasoning process. This makes the books appeal to the mature reader whose computing background goes beyond the minimum Knuth suggests, but makes them hard going for novices. Thus, for average students, Knuth can only be used successfully as a teaching text when supported with carefully prepared supplementary lectures and carefully selected references.

The great strengths of these books are their authoritativeness, their broad coverage, and their terse clarity. They apply to the abstract mathematician with practical computing needs and to the computer user who needs the contribution of abstract mathematics, and they appeal to both. They say important things to a wide range of skill and interest levels. They are needed by the advanced or top-grade student and the experienced practitioner. For a decade after their first appearance they could be used confidently as a screen to test unfamiliar subjects. Even today, there are only a few exceptions to the rule that a subject not mentioned in Knuth is either very narrow and specialized or faddishly new. It is for all these reasons that the three volumes of *The Art of Computer Programming* deserve a permanent place on the reference shelf of the computer professional.

General Analysis

The broad areas that the books cover are identified both by the volume titles and by the publisher's classifications.

Volume 1:
   Fundamental Algorithms.
   Classification: Data Structures.

Volume 2:
   Seminumerical Algorithms.
   Classification: Analysis of Algorithms.

Volume 3:
   Sorting and Searching.
   Classification: Information Organization and Retrieval.

Knuth considers that his subject is "the theory of the properties of particular computer algorithms." More briefly, he also calls it "the analysis of algorithms," and sets this apart from numerical analysis by using the directly distinguishing phrase "nonnumerical analysis." But since he deals only with particular computer algorithms, he does not cover everything now contained under the giant tent of "the analysis of all algorithms." He teaches programming from a mathematical point of view—in terms of algorithms, a notion which he says in the first sentence of the first volume "is basic to all of computer programming."

Knuth describes and demonstrates practical techniques for use in sorting, searching, translating languages, theorem proving, simulation, solving mathematical problems in higher algebra and combinatorial analysis, and developing "software." (In his first preface [1967], he felt impelled to define "software" as "programs to facilitate the writing of other programs," meaning compilers and other programming tools.) His approach is to collect basic techniques from the literature, test them himself, coordinate and classify those that work, add his own inventions and variations, and then coordinate all this into a theory. He illustrates the techniques with applications to the design of programs. Although his intention was to bring the reader up to the frontiers of knowledge, even in his earliest volumes he admitted to providing algorithms that for the most part had been in use for several years.

His judgment in the selection of topics for his first volume ("Basic Concepts" and "Information Structures")) was so good that he was able to revise it five years later without perturbing the page numbering. This was not the case with the second volume ("Random Numbers" and "Arithmetic"), where the developments in computer science during the passage of twelve years required him to change almost 45% of the book.

Volume 1: Fundamental Algorithms, Second Edition

The first volume is made up of two parts, "Basic Concepts" and "Information Structures." The author calls these parts chapters but recognizes that this is a misnomer; his numbered sections are what would ordinarily be called chapters. I will go through the first monster chapter in detail because it is characteristic of the whole work in tone, structure, and approach.

It starts by defining *algorithm*, first with a short historical account of the word, and then by example, with a demonstration of Euclid's algorithm using the style in which all further algorithms will be presented. Finally the algorithm is displayed as a flow chart. Knuth introduces the notation of the left-pointing arrow as the replacement, assignment, or substitution operation, and the " = " sign to denote a condition which can be tested. By page 3, he finds it necessary to use his first unique piece of notation, a thick line "▌", the symbol mathematicians often use for the end of a proof, to indicate the end of an algorithm. Now he performs this algorithm for a specific case, and finally lists the five important features of any algorithm. He touches on why recipes are not algorithms; and from this, in a few sentences, he leads the reader through a simple analysis of an algorithm, briefly relates the concept of "algorithm" to mathematical set theory by using sets to define a computational method, and finally formulates the concept of "effectiveness" in the Markovian sense.

He has now completed his definition of *algorithm*. He gives nine exercises, each rated (as are all his exercises) in terms of difficulty on a scale of 0 to 50. In this same graceful, terse but didactic way, he rapidly goes through his list of the mathematical techniques and subjects that his readers should know about if they are to understand the rest of his work. This short list is not insignificant; it constitutes the guts of the chapter, and can take up a third to a half of a one-semester course.

This is what Knuth covers in 100 pages: mathematical induction; numbers, powers, and logarithms; sums and products; integer functions and elementary number theory; permutations and factorials; binomial coefficients; harmonic numbers; Fibonacci numbers; generating functions; analysis of an algorithm; and asymptotic representations.

In the middle of the chapter he comes to MIX, an imaginary pedogogical computer. He says that MIX represents the hardest decision he had to make while preparing the books. His problem must be faced by every author of a serious book about computing: What formal, precise language should be used to present and give specific examples of the techniques discussed? Should one use a high-level langugage, the machine language of a specific computer, or a pseudo-language developed especially for the purpose? He gives the reasons that convinced him that it had to be a machine-oriented language, and avoids the dilemma of which machine language to choose by designing his own "ideal" mythical computer; this has very simple rules of operation but is also very much like nearly every computer then (and now) in wide use. He introduces MIX, the machine and its language, and throughout the rest of the work he illustrates his algorithms with MIX programs. The endpapers of each volume display the tables of MIX and MIXAL (Mix Assembly Language) codes.

No other major author has adopted MIX, although Knuth published the descriptive pages separately as a small paperback. Pascal is the current choice of writers dealing with Knuth's subjects.

How It Started

These books have made their author rich, honored, and famous. In 1971 Donald Knuth was the first recipient of the Grace Murray Hopper award for young computer scientists; in 1974 he received ACM's Turing Award; in 1975 he was elected to the National Academy of Science; in 1979, at the age of 41, he accepted the National Medal of Science from the hand of the President of the United States; and in 1981 he was elected to the National Academy of Engineering. Knuth is not only famous but also articulate, friendly, charming, and accessible. He has not been shy in talking and writing about his work in public and in prefaces, so we have more information about how these books came to be written—and about the current status of the complete work—than we do for any other computing books.

It all started early in 1962 when Addison-Wesley invited Knuth, then a second-year graduate student at Cal Tech, to put what he knew about writing compilers into a book. In one day he sketched out twelve chapter titles, but only started to work seriously on the book a year later, after getting his Ph.D. His efforts to understand, check, and explain what he found in the extensive but unreliable computing literature of the time got him more and more interested and involved. By June 1965 he had finished his first draft—3000 handwritten pages—and in October he sent his publisher the typescript of Chapter 1. (This is how Knuth writes: a longhand first draft which is then tapped out with his own fingers into a typescript.) On the basis of this sample chapter, which is said to have been pretty much the same as the final version, the publisher estimated that Knuth was working up a 2000-page book. After further discussion and consultation the twelve chapters were readjusted, and the whole work was laid out to cover everything then known about programming, in seven volumes as follows:

1: Fundamental Algorithms
   1. Basic Concepts
   2. Information Structures

2: Seminumerical Algorithms
   3. Random Numbers
   4. Arithmetic

3: Sorting and Searching
   5. Sorting Techniques
   6. Searching Techniques

4: Combinatorial Algorithms
   7. Combinatorial Searching
   8. Recursion

5: Syntactic Algorithms
   9. Lexical Scanning
   10. Parsing Techniques

6: Theory of Languages
   11. Mathematical Linguistics

7: Compilers
   12. Programming Language Translation

After Volume I was finished, Knuth started working day and night on Volume 2. The excitement and the effort brought on a serious attack of ulcers in the summer of 1967 (or, as he says, "on what is now page 333 of Volume Two"), causing him to change his whole life-style so that he could carefully control his time and limit his commitments.

When Volume I was published, it was recognized as a work of genius, and an enormously valuable contribution to theoretical and practical computer science. Several early reviewers also commented on the audacity of the original proposal, and at least one of them said that what Knuth had set out to do was impossible.

Volume 2 was published in 1969, and Volume 3 in 1973. A revised edition of Volume 1 came out in 1973, and a revision of Volume 2 in

continued

Continued

1981. Thus we now have only the first six big chapters of a projected twelve-chapter work.

Distractions from writing **The Art of Computer Programming,** the completion of which Knuth still considers to be his lifework, resulted first in an inconsequential little paperback novel, **Surreal Numbers,** which is reviewed in the panel on page 288. A more serious interruption occurred when the author got into typographical research. In the spring of 1977 Knuth became seriously interested in computer-assisted typesetting, and thought he would turn for a just a year from **The Art of Computer Programming** to do a book on the subject. The one year stretched into five, and resulted in *Computers and Typesetting, Volume 1: TEX,* and *The TEXbook,* both for 1984 publication, and both impossible to cite accurately because Knuth insists that TEX can only be written properly by dropping the E a half-space—T$_E$X—easy for him to do but difficult for ordinary typesetters.

At the moment, **The Art** is on Knuth's back burner. No new editions are being prepared. He files current literature to be read later. He reports that Volume 4 has expanded so much that it may have to come out as Volumes 4A and 4B. For the next two years, he plans to complete the series of three books entitled *Computers and Typesetting,* summarizing what he has learned about typography, after which he will do a year of house-husbanding during his wife's sabbatical; and then, at last, he will return to writing Volume 4A.

The world waits.

Having laid out the basic mathematics that will be needed, and with his computer language in hand, Knuth turns to a few fundamental programming techniques, subroutines, coroutines, interpretive routines, machine simulation, input and output, and elementary buffering, ending the chapter with a thorough history and an annotated selective bibliography of these techniques.

The second half of the book, Chapter 2, is entirely concerned with what Knuth calls *information structures,* which today are usually called *data structures.* He summarizes their static and dynamic properties, their representation, and storage allocation. He gives algorithms for doing everything with these structures and their contents. He works out both long and short examples which introduce the reader to the subjects of topological sorting, polynomial arithmetic, discrete system simulation, operations on sparse matrices, algebraic formula manipulation, and the creation of compilers and operating systems. The chapter ends with another brief but excellent history and bibliography.

There are so many exercises in both chapters, and the answers given are so complete, that the "Answers to Exercises" section at the end of the book takes up 130 pages!

The author makes a wry comment on page 463—at the end of the text—using a Sherlock Holmes quotation from *The Valley of Fear:* "You will,

Mathematics On the Beach

Knuth's **Surreal Numbers,** a paperback novelette, entirely cast as a dialogue, is intended to emphasize the nature of creative mathematical explorations; to provide material which would help to overcome the lack of training for mathematical research work in our present educational system; to show how mathematics can be taken out of the classroom and into life; to urge the readers to try exploring abstract mathematical research by presenting a detailed case study based on John Horton Conway's recent approach to numbers, which he told Knuth about at lunch in 1972. The author's primary aim is not to teach Conway's theory, but to teach how one might go about developing such a theory.

Two characters, Alice and Bill, living in isolation on the edge of the Indian Ocean, discover a stone engraved with a truncated Hebrew manuscript giving Conway's basic rules for his "extraordinal" numbers. From this, the two ex-students explore and gradually build up Conway's number system.

The book is intended for college mathematics students at the sophomore or junior level. The author says that within a traditional mathematics curriculum it can probably be used best either (a) as supplementary reading material for an "introduction to abstract mathematics" course or a mathematical logic course: or (b) as the principal text in an undergraduate seminar intended to develop the students' abilities for doing independent work. Martin Gardner said of it: "I believe it is the only time a major mathematical discovery has been published first in a work of fiction."

Although the author may have had fun writing the book (in a single week of his sabbatical in Oslo), and while some devoted students may be willing to labor through it, it is not an entertaining novelette, not a well-written piece of fiction, nor is it as good a teaching mechanism as Knuth's straightforward tutorial writing as exemplified in **The Art of Computer Programming.** The cutesy concept of lovers living on the beach is distracting rather than entertaining. It is frivolous and gets in the way of Knuth's recitation of how mathematical searching and reasoning proceeds. The book is entirely dominated by the reasoning process, by the steps of logic taken, and by the mathematics. Consequently all claim to being a novelette, even at the level of *Flatland,* is lost.

The book is a failed experiment. It falls between the two stools of entertaining literature about mathematics and solid instruction in mathematics of the kind we have learned to expect of the author. It is unfortunate that Knuth, a man of infinite resource and a giant of present-day computer science, should have been allowed by his publisher to release such an ambitious piece of work in such a flawed and distressing form. The ability to write a novelette and the ability to cast mathematical work in a fictional form are very rare, as is the ability to judge clearly one's own writing.

I am sure, agree with me that if page 534 finds us only in the second chapter, the length of the first one must have been really intolerable."

Volume 2: Seminumerical Algorithms, Second Edition

Knuth has made the 1981 second edition of Volume 2 the test case for the new computer typesetting system he has been developing. (As noted in the panel on page 286, this diversion of his interest to questions of typography has to a large extent been responsible for the regrettable delay in the production of the remaining chapters of *The Art*.) The author feels so confident about this method of composition and checking, and is so anxious to root out errors in the text, that he offers a $2 reward to the first finder of each technical, typographical, or historical error. I found none.

Like all the volumes in the set, this one contains only two monster chapters, "Random Numbers" and "Arithmetic." *Seminumerical* in the title means that, while the algorithms concern numbers, they lie on the borderline between numeric and symbolic calculation. The author considers that the beauty of the algorithms will not be appreciated unless the beholder recognizes their relationship to the internal operations of a computer in terms of machine language. This is a further justification of MIX. The study of seminumerical algorithms is within the working domain of both system programmers and numerical analysts, and thus lies at the interface of applied mathematics and computer science. Knuth believes that every theorem of elementary number theory is in this chapter somewhere, most likely in the context of an algorithm.

Chapter 3, "Random Numbers," studies methods of generating random sequences, investigates statistical tests for randomness, and illustrates how random numbers are used in practice by teaching how uniform ones can be transformed into other types of random quantities, and ends with a section discussing randomness itself.

Chapter 4, "Arithmetic," discusses different systems of number representation and conversions between them; and treats of arithmetic on floating point numbers, high-precision integers, rational fractions, polynomials, and power series, including the questions of factoring and finding greatest common divisors.

Although these two chapters go further and deeper into mathematics and computer science than the first two chapters, Knuth maintains the same graceful style. His clear but often quick and sometimes superficial explanations are interspersed with formal mathematical statements. The rated-for-difficulty exercises are as numerous, and the answers as complete, as in Volume 1; but now the history and bibliography are not set out separately but are woven into the text, close to the applicable algorithms.

Volume 3: Sorting and Searching

This volume is titled with the names of its two chapters. It can be thought of as an extension of Chapter 2, the Information Structures chapter of the first volume, since it goes more deeply into the concept of linearly-ordered data and gives more applicable techniques. The subject might have been limited to sorting routines or data retrieval, but Knuth uses this practical part of the subject as the framework for discussing many general computing issues, issues which he first lists in the preface and then brings up in the text:

☐ How are algorithms discovered and improved?
☐ How can the efficiency of algorithms be analyzed?
☐ How can the better algorithm be chosen?
☐ What is meant by "best possible" algorithm?
☐ How does computing theory interact with practical computing?
☐ How can external memories be used efficiently?

Knuth believes that "virtually every important aspect of programming arises somewhere in the context of sorting or searching!"

Omissions

When the volumes first appeared, they almost managed to achieve the author's intent of including everything known about his selected parts of the art of computer programming. With the passage of time, the field has grown beyond the books; and some areas important today are not mentioned, or at least not well covered. For example, what is known about lists, string manipulation, and symbol handling now exceeds what little Knuth says about them. Knuth largely confines his treatment of files to the contents of immediately accessible memory, and the appropriate structures and techniques for files stored outside the main memory are hardly mentioned. The current devotion of the computer science community to structured programming is not recognized by Knuth; his algorithms and MIX itself are out of tune with this programming philosophy. Indeed, it is the need for structured programming that requires modern computer science teaching to use high-level languages, and to steer away from the flowcharts that Knuth suggests.

Having mentioned these omissions, which bear more on the use of Knuth as a text than as a reference, I must say again that there is nothing wrong with the books. They are simply no longer as complete a coverage of the growing field of programming as they once were; and in the areas associated with auxiliary storage and structured programming they are not up to date.

Conclusion

As explained in the panel on page 287, Knuth has written less than half of all the material he had planned for the complete *Art of Computer Programming*. But even the existing unfinished version, six chapters in three volumes, gives a coverage of both the mathematical and basic practical aspects of the art of programming that can be found in no other book or coordinated set of books—a coverage that is remarkable for its depth, correctness, clarity of presentation, and conciseness.

Books Reviewed

The Art of Computer Programming, Volume I: Fundamental Algorithms, Second Edition, by Donald E. Knuth, Addison-Wesley, Reading, MA, 1973, 634 pages, $32.95 (ISBN 0-201-03809-9).

The Art of Computer Programming, Volume II: Seminumerical Algorithms, Second Edition, by Donald E. Knuth, Addison-Wesley, Reading, MA, 1981, 700 pages, $32.95 (ISBN 0-201-03822-6).

The Art of Computer Programming, Volume III: Sorting and Searching, by Donald E. Knuth, Addison-Wesley, Reading, MA, 1973, 722 pages, $32.95 (ISBN 0-201-03803-X).

Surreal Numbers: How Two Ex-Students Turned On to Pure Mathematics and Found Total Happiness, by Donald E. Knuth, Addison-Wesley, Reading, MA, 1974, 119 pages, paper, $3.95 (ISBN 0-201-03812-9).

Books Mentioned

Mix, by Donald E. Knuth, Addison-Wesley, Reading, MA, 1970, 48 pages, paper, $5.50 (ISBN 0-201-03808-0).

Computers and Typesetting, Volume 1: T_EX, by Donald E. Knuth, Addison-Wesley, Reading, MA, 1984 (tentative), 750 pages, price not yet established (ISBN 0-201-13447-0).

The $T_EX$book, by Donald E. Knuth, Addison-Wesley, Reading, MA, 1984, 288 pages, $14.95 (ISBN 0-201-13448-9).

The Permanent Software Crisis
Recommended classics for those in the ever-sticky software engineering tar pit.

ERIC A. WEISS

The Start

Computer pioneers tell us that at the turn-on of the first computer, before the first program had even started to run, before the Great Machine came alive, while it sat there silently staring back at its anxious creators, the question of whether the First Program was correct came up, followed almost immediately by the question of whether anybody can write a correct program and be certain it is correct. A few minutes later, while these two questions were being explored experimentally by the designers and builders, with their hands and test probes deep in the machine's electronic entrails, emotional doubts about the competency of overpaid programmers were vigorously articulated. For all practical purposes, the three questions that swirled around in the first few minutes of life of the first computer remain unanswered to this day. They are:

- □ Is this program correct?
- □ How can correct programs be written?
- □ Why does programming cost so much?

The Status

These open questions are the basis of the software crisis that is repeatedly discovered and proclaimed anew. The discoverers confidently forecast that the crisis, if not cured, will cause total disaster for the computing industry. The crisis has continued for decades—not only unabated, but in an augmented and increasingly extended form. While there have been an uncounted myriad of often-repeated local software disasters, the pre-

Reprinted from ABACUS, Volume 3, Number 1, Fall 1985.

dicted global total disaster affecting all of computing has never happened. On the contrary, more and more and larger and larger complex software systems of unproven correctness and excessive cost have been created, delivered late, and put into use as the indispensible underpinning of more and more of our computer-dependent civilization. But this obvious contradiction has caused no diminution in the universal doom-crying; if anything, it has increased it. Today, as in the past, the software crisis is a continuing, growing, spreading, and well-known phenomenon.

The flavor of current opinion can be tasted in the introductory paragraphs from recent software articles displayed in the panel on the next page. Opinion ranges from the breathless but belated discovery of the crisis just this summer to sophisticated acceptance of its permanence. Authors of software books seem to feel obliged to include almost identical crisis-crying paragraphs in their early pages.

As the quotations show, the crisis is known to have three components, the relative quantities of which are varied from time to time and from weeper to weeper. These components, usually stated as complaints, are: software costs are too high; software is always unsatisfactory; and software is never delivered on time. Since these are the complaints made about every desirable human product from children to automobiles, the mystery is why, in this case, they have resulted in the repeatedly identified software crisis. At the end of this article I will suggest some explanations.

Blame

A growing permanent crisis must be blamed on somebody, and the natural scapegoat candidates are the incompetent and overpaid programmers. This identification of the guilty parties also dates back to the days of the earliest computers, and has resulted in a permanent hopeful conviction that the need for programmers is a temporary misfortune that will soon vanish, drying up the demand for new programmers and leaving those skilled in the arcane art without employment—a just fate for a needlessly arrogant tribe! The popularity of the no-more-programmers-will-be-needed belief rises and falls as messiahs bearing the latest true-light programming substitute in hardware, software, or system come and go. The hopeful feeling is always strongest among nonprogrammers, especially those who either have to manage programmers or pay for their products.

Action

If widespread energetic activity and overwhelming quantities of published material, courses, seminars, and speeches were effective, the software crisis would long ago have ended, for every computing society, periodical,

Recent Statements about the Software Crisis

"The software world has run head-long into the Software Crisis—Ambitious software projects are hard to manage, too expensive, of mediocre quality, and hard to schedule reliably. Moreover, all too often, software delivers a solution that doesn't meet the customers' needs."
—"Software: ICs" by Lamar Ledbetter and Brad Cox, *Byte*, June 1985, pages 307–315.

"Everyone agrees that software is expensive. But software costs continue to rise."
—"Software Cost and Productivity Improvements: An Analogical View" by Barry G. Silverman, *Computer*, May 1985, pages 86–96.

"The quest for automatic programming in the hope that programmers' productivity could improve dates back to the early days of computer science reseach . . . . Today the productivity problem has reached crisis proportions. The need for software and software engineers is growing exponentially, but productivity is only rising at a rate of about five percent a year."
—"Toward Automating the Software Development Cycle" by Karen A. Frenkel, *Communications of the ACM*, Vol. 28, No. 6 (June 1985), pages 578–590.

"Some of the most serious problems of software development were identified years ago but continue to resist practical solutions."
—"The Operational versus the Conventional Approach to Software Development" by Pamela Zave, *Communications of the ACM*, Vol. 27, No. 2 (February 1984), pages 104–118.

"A review of current literature would lead one to believe that the 'software crisis' is a recent development. Such is not the case. There has always been a software crisis.
—"Accommodating Uncertainty in Software Design" by Richard V. Giddings, *Communications of the ACM*, Vol. 27, No. 5 (May 1984), pages 428–434.

and conference repeatedly addresses the subject; literally hundreds of experts have proposed solutions; dozens of technical groups have been established specifically to attack the problem; and library and bookstore shelves are crammed with volumes giving analysis, advice, direction, and guaranteed solutions. As with most popular crises, a seething, profitable industry of associations, inventors, promotors, writers, talkers, publishers, teachers, enthusiasts, charlatans, true-believers, book-reviewers, and companies has been spawned. Indeed, while the crisis itself does not seem to harm the computing business, it is likely that its sudden solution and the end of the specialized crisis industry it supports would cause substantial financial harm.

Although much of the activity has amounted to crass exploitation of the fears of the crisis, and much has been fruitless duplication of obvious cliché advice, some real progress has been made. Many good things relating to programming and software have been discovered, rediscovered, promoted, and generally accepted. The best of today's software is better than the best of a decade ago. Many people have contributed to the major advances in the creation, discovery, and establishment of software principles, and many books have been written, but only a few books are classics. I will sketch the accepted and influential accomplishments, refer to the associated books, and finally make some recommendations.

Structured Programming

The dicta that a program should be written in a systematic and orderly fashion; should be comprehensible and coherent; should have a simple, straightforward, and transparent structure and not look like a bowl of spaghetti; should be made up of unified blocks or modules of manageable size; should use GOTOS as little as possible; and should not modify itself— these are now accepted principles. Writing programs according to such principles is popularly termed "structured programming."

From the earliest days, the best writers and teachers pressed for programming simplicity and coherence. In the early 1960s, Böhm and Jacopini published a mathematical proof that programming required only three kinds of control constructs and consequently that simplicity was always possible; at about the same time, several influential leaders of the computing community took strong stands in support of simplicity. The history of who did what when is given in Edward N. Yourdon's commentary in his collection of papers, *Classics in Software Engineering;* but it is generally accepted that the major figure in the creation, endorsement, and vigorous promotion of the principle and its brilliant extension to include almost all of what is now called "structured programming" was Edsger W. Dijkstra. Academic thinkers and writers—chiefly Hoare, Knuth, Naur, and Wirth— gave further support and paved the way for academic acceptance. In the 1970s, Yourdon's flood of seminars and instructional books spawned dozens of imitators, and made the practice accepted wisdom for commercial programmers. This very acceptance, adoption, and promotion of "structured programming" by IBM and other common folk has made at least one of its inventors and most influential early supporters stop using the phrase—a futile and sulky gesture, unworthy of a great man.

Niklaus Wirth, who says "programming is a constructive art" directed not at machines but at humans (but who also considers it to be an academic discipline in its own right), has continued to preach and teach the gospel of simplicity and clear straight principles. His books, *Systematic Programming: An Introduction* and *Algorithms + Data Structures = Programs,* have been more influential than you might guess from their brevity, but his greatest influence has been through the structured languages he has devised, Pascal and Modula. (Pascal is discussed by Henry Ledgard in his article, "Is Pascal Too Large?," in ABACUS, Volume 3, Number 1, Fall 1985.)

Programming Psychology

In 1971, *The Psychology of Computer Programming* by Gerald M. Weinberg introduced the novel idea that programming was not just a matter of hardware and software, but was a human activity that could be understood in terms of psychology, and indeed, that a unique psychology of computer programming existed which deserved study. The book is a landmark, and remains the best overall treatment of the subject. (Its novelty may be seen from the fact that the manuscript was rejected by Weinberg's regular publisher, for whom he had done several excellent early computing textbooks.)

Weinberg discusses programming as human performance, as a social activity, as an individual activity, and finally he cites programming tools and principles, most of which point toward the practices of structured programming. The power of the book is not in any detailed advice, admonitions, recommendations, or programming pearls, but in its teaching that all programming behavior, including one's own, should be observed, considered, taken account of, and sometimes adjusted. A reviewer commented, "One comes away with the feeling of having spent a pleasant but somewhat 'wasted' afternoon of reading, and, as the old joke goes, 'it ain't till you try to turn your head that you realize how sharp the razor was.' "

Software Engineering

It was at first believed that programming required the special skills and logical thought processes peculiar to mathematicians; that is, it was thought to be a trivial electrical engineering problem that mathematicians would soon dispose of. After the mathematicians had their first go at it, many people took the view that programming was an arcane and mysterious art; then a craft which could only be learned by apprenticeship; then a combination of all three; but the feeling has continued among an increasing number of mathematicians that programming needs the contributions that their discipline can offer.

As soon as practical programs were needed that were too large to be written by an unaided single genius and it became necessary to create software by using teams of cooperating programmers, the similarity of the task to project engineering became evident. This led to the now universally accepted concept of software engineering. Yourdon's recitation of its early development in his *Classics* mentions the writers who suggested this analogy, but the classic book is *The Mythical Man-Month: Essays in Software Engineering,* by Frederic P. Brooks, Jr. In it, Brooks recorded in 1975 what he had learned as project manager for the IBM System/360 and its operating system, OS/360, in a collection of interrelated thought-provoking didactic essays. His central argument is that large programming projects suffer management problems different in kind from small projects, due to the division of labor; their products should be subjected to formal review and testing, and they should be documented.

While all this now seems obvious, the concept and the prescriptions were novel in 1975, and seem to be rediscovered as each new organization, new manager, and new programmer create the disastrous "second system" that Brooks warns is "the most dangerous system a man ever designs," and make the perilous transition from small to large projects. His most important repeatedly discovered point is, in his own words: "Conceptual integrity is *the* most important consideration in system design. It is better to have a system omit certain anomalous features and improvements, but to reflect one set of design ideas than to have one that contains many good but independent and uncoordinated ideas." Brooks is literate, succinct, to the point, and unburdened with specific solutions.

Proof of Correctness

The long-lived idea that programming needs mathematical discipline has developed to the point where some contend that it is a branch of mathematics. (The millenium will have arrived when it becomes understood that mathematics is a branch of computing!) The necessary and desirable interconnection is endorsed by some mathematicians and rejected by others. The endorsers recognize that computing is a lively, growing, and important part of the new world, and that it offers endless problems which can readily be translated into mathematical form. The rejecters, chiefly the older and more traditional academicians, fear the consequences of the intrusion of a commercial machine and its accouterments into the holy precincts of mathematics. The rejecters are a monotonically diminishing group which it will soon be possible to prove does not exist and is not worth further mention, but the endorsers are influential leaders both in mathematics and in the theoretical aspects of academic computing science. Good or bad, like it or not, there are conceptual, personal, and practical links between programming and mathematics.

In the same 1965 landmark paper in which Dijkstra laid out—in a few short pages—the entire gospel of structured programming, he said, "The programmer's situation is closely analogous to that of a pure mathematician who develops a theory and proves results." This concept, that programming is a branch of mathematics and should be done as one does mathematics, has led Dijkstra and others to propose that just as mathematical correctness can be abstractly proven for mathematical theories, statements, and results, the same can be done for programs. Dijkstra's *A Discipline of Programming* tells how this can be done; and in *The Science of Programming,* David Gries makes Dijkstra's teachings understandable to college professors and their students.

Other computer-friendly mathematicians have developed their own methods of proving and verifying the correctness and completeness of programs, notably Floyd's inductive assertions, Hoare's axiomatic method, and Scott's fixed-point induction. Each of them is supported by his own popularizers. In *Structured Programming: Theory and Practice,* Linger, Mills, and Witt, like the mathematicians, teach that the central theme of systematic methods of program analysis and synthesis (that is, structured programming) is logical proof of mathematical correctness. They try to bring this message to practicing programming professionals in industry and government; but for academics, Dijkstra and Gries are the accepted texts.

Each of these writers gives examples of proving the correctness of small programs, and they all admit that as yet, methods of mathematical proof cannot be applied to the important real-life programs having hundreds or thousands or millions of lines of code. Being mathematicians, they take up the issue by resorting to mathematical induction, suggesting that what can be stated with assurance about one member of the set can ultimately, by extension, be proven applicable to all members of the set, even if the set is infinitely large. In other words, it seems to them at least plausible and at most certain that what can be done in the small, on small programs, can ultimately be done in the large, on the largest of programs. They encourage their colleagues, disciples, and graduate students to press in this direction, and many do.

Some professors who want computer science to be a respectable discipline, with content as intellectually challenging as mathematics, do research and give courses in the largely mathematical and logical subjects of proving and verifying programs, and are less enthusiastic about the more mundane aspects of software engineering. They accept as important but somewhat craft-like the analysis, design, and coding disciplines implied by the term "structured," but are usually indifferent and sometimes antagonistic to college courses about the aspects of software engineering that have to do with methods, procedures, organization, and economics; that is, that have to do with the management of people and resources rather than the management of symbols.

Classification

Thus, there are intellectual or philosophical divisions among those who do, those who teach, those who research, those who invent, and those who write about programming. I think of the major divisions as being arranged in a line placing far to the left those who, like Dijkstra today and Donald E. Knuth in the past, deem programming to be mathematics, or as David Gries says, a science, "work which depends on the knowledge and conscious application of principles." Far to the right I put those fur-

Knuth, Past and Present

Although Donald E. Knuth's classic books (reviewed in my Spring 1984 column) are titled **The Art of Computer Programming,** they are actually mathematics texts, and might better have been titled, as the author once intended, *The Analysis of Algorithms.* Knuth then considered programming to be, if not a branch, at least a twig of mathematics.

Recently he has been stressing the notion of *style* in programming; and in an interview in the May 1985 issue of *Computer Language* (an issue which has a parallel interview with Niklaus Wirth), he takes the position that "good programming is. . .an inherently creative act" and "the best way to program. . .is really to concentrate on explaining to a *person* what the computer is supposed to do rather than explaining to a *machine* what it's supposed to do. That's my new hobbyhorse, to say that people should think about the communication of the program while writing it."

Thus, I would position the old Knuth on the left of my line and the new Knuth to the right.

thest from the mathematicians, those who see programming as being a craft or an art, again defined by Gries as "requiring merely knowledge of traditional rules and skill acquired by habit." I neglect the eccentric splinter group of those who consider programming to be a racket, and spot to the right those who, like Knuth today, see it as chiefly communications. (An explanation of how Knuth's past and present views differ is given in the box on this page.) Followers of Naur and Hoare I put to the left.

I lump the bulk of those concerned with programming in the center with Wirth, Brooks, Weinberg, Kernighan and Plauger. They treat programming as a branch of engineering—that is, software engineering. Engineering as currently practiced is a blend of craft and science, applying principles where they are available but falling back on traditional rules and habitual skills wherever scientific principles are not available. The engineer's slogan is always, "Get the job done with what you have. We can't wait for perfection."

Recommendations

My recommendations of classic software books for the computing professional depend upon these classifications; what the professional thinks programming *is* determines which book I recommend. What you think is what you need to read.

If you consider programming to be a racket, or an arcane and mysterious art, or a craft that can be learned only by apprenticeship, no book can help you, so I recommend none.

If you consider programming to be a human endeavor strongly influenced by psychological interactions, you should have Weinberg at hand.

If you consider programming to be a branch of mathematics, you should have Gries. If you find Gries too easy, try Dijkstra himself. Hoare and Linger, Mills, and Witt propose mathematical alternates and variations. The recent book by Loeckx purports to describe the classic verification methods without demanding too much of the reader in terms of formal logic and semantics.

If you consider programming to be a kind of engineering, you should certainly have Brooks at hand. (Although he calls programming a craft, he actually treats it as if it is engineering.) Wirth can be recommended for those who want their software reference to have a more academic flavor. Yourdon's *Classics* provides such a splendid history and overview of software engineering as to be recommended in its own right. I agree with Yourdon that the paper in his collection by Barry Boehm, "Software Engineering," "is probably the best overall summary of the software field that I have yet seen published." You may want to supplement these with Kernighan and Plauger and the two Aron volumes, and dip into the books recommended for the mathematically minded to see how the development of principles derived from mathematics is going.

Reprise

After this description of the software crisis, discussion of some books, and recommendation of classics, we are left with two general questions: *Why is there a software crisis?* and *What is its probable future?*

Why Is There a Software Crisis?

Some insight into the mystery can be gained by considering why there is no continuing permanent hardware crisis. In the early 1950s, there were serious questions about the hardware. Were all the components of each new computer correctly wired together? Would these complex devices operate for any length of time without faults? How could reliable results be obtained in spite of the flaws and faults?

Indeed, early computer hardware often failed. The evidence of this hardware unreliability lies in the memories of those who were there, and is documented in the preoccupation with hardware failure of contemporary publications. The first glossaries defined a variety of reruns (*rerun, reset, restore, rollbakc,*), and checks (*built-in, duplication, mathematical, redundant*) that were commonly used to test for intermittent circuit glitches. Early computer runs were often repeated to prove that the machine could get the same result twice. Early computer designs included dual or even triple processors which would do identical tasks and compare results. Papers were published and discussions held on variations of the techniques of building reliable computers out of unreliable parts.

Maturity in the hardware design and construction changed all this, as it became clear that a computer was a more critical thing to design and build than a TV set and required more reliable parts and assembly techniques. The biggest change came about, first, when the immortal transistor replaced the limited-life vacuum tube, and then, when the transistors and all the important electronic components were miniaturized and converted into products that could be manufactured, mounted, and interconnected by photographic and chemical means without the detailed and clumsy intervention of human hands. Just as the replacement of handwritten manuscripts by printing largely eliminated copyists' errors in books, so the transition to the current method of printing circuits and components reduced circuit flaws of all kinds almost to the vanishing point. Today, although computers are much larger and more complicated than those of the 1950s, their flawless performance is almost taken for granted.

But even when hardware failures and glitches were common, no one ever asked how to go about putting a computer together correctly. It was clear that this was an electrical engineering problem like that of designing and building a radio set or a telephone network, or wiring a process control panel. The question of operating the resulting computer and coping with its flaws and faults was answered pragmatically and by demonstration.

What is different about software? Why is it always in crisis while the similar hardware crisis is over? First, there is lots more software being made than there are computers being designed, built, and used. This leads to lots of untrained and unskilled people being involved, and to lots of on-the-job training-by-making-major-mistakes. (Harry Ledgard addressed part of this question in "Programmers: The Amateur vs. the Professional" in ABACUS, Volume 3, Number 1, Summer 1985; this volume, page 35.)

Second, large, complex software systems are far more complicated than any hardware. As Brooks writes, "One can expect the human race to continue attempting systems just within or just beyond our reach: and software systems are perhaps the most intricate and complex of man's handiworks." Dijkstra says, "Programming will remain very difficult, because once we have freed ourselves from the circumstantial cumbersomeness, we will find ourselves free to tackle the problems that are now well beyond our programming capacity."

Third, while the electrical engineering of the hardware rests on a big stock of basic principles, some of them more than a century old, software engineering has only a few accepted, a few tentative, and many promised principles, but lots of art, craft, observed skill, and fumbling. That is, while software engineers are anxious to apply proven principles, there are not many at hand.

Finally, and most importantly, while we have good analogies between computers and other devices with which we have long experience, we have no good analogies for software. Paraphrasing what Brooks says in the first paragraph of his preface: Programming is like many other human endeavors—in more ways than most programmers believe. But in many other ways it is different—in more ways than most programmers expect. It is these similarities and differences that those who attack the software crisis try to identify and understand.

The Probable Future

Historically, we know that crises in our civilization that have seemed to be permanent in spite of vigorous attacks have had a variety of outcomes. A few have yielded completely and dramatically to some discovery; in this class we have the recent examples of infantile paralysis and smallpox. Some have vanished as technology and development have changed the surrounding environment; here we may look to the solutions of the streets-filled-with-horse-manure problem, of fire disasters from gas illumination, and of the dangers of evil witchcraft. Most crises have been ameliorated or had their character changed as curative attempts have been partially successful; for example, in spite of enormous efforts since antiquity, the problem of death has not been solved, but changing the objective from that of achieving immortality to extending life has yielded perceptible success.

But most continuing crises just continue, often unabated, supporting well-established industries devoted in part to coping with the crisis and in part to attempting to find solutions. Poverty, the common cold, old age, and taxes are in this class, and it is likely that the software crisis is too. As Brooks says, "The tar pit of software engineering will be sticky for some time to come." A less optimistic author might have said forever.

Books Discussed

Classics in Software Engineering, Edward N. Yourdon, editor; Yourdon Press, New York, 1979, 424 pages, paper, $33.50 (ISBN 0-917072-14-6).

Structured Programming, by O.-J. Dahl, E. W. Dijkstra, and C.A.R. Hoare; Academic Press, London, 1972, 220 pages, $27.00 (ISBN 0-12-200550-3).

A Discipline of Programming, by Edsger W. Dijkstra; Prentice-Hall, Englewood Cliffs, NJ, 1976, 217 pages, $32.50 (ISBN 0-13-215871-X).

Selected Writings on Computing: A Personal Perspective, by Edsger W. Dijkstra; Springer-Verlag, New York, 1982, 272 pages, $29.95 (ISBN 0-387-90652-5, or 3-540-90652-5 outside North America).

Systematic Programming: An Introduction, by Niklaus Wirth; Englewood Cliffs, NJ, Prentice-Hall, 1973, 169 pages, $28.95 (ISBN 0-13-880369-2).

Algorithms + Data Structures = Programs, by Niklaus Wirth; Englewood Cliffs, NJ, Prentice-Hall, 1975, 366 pages, $34.95 (ISBN 0-13-022418-9).

The Psychology of Computer Programming, by Gerald M. Weinberg; Von Nostrand Reinhold, New York, 1971, 288 pages, $16.95 (ISBN 0-442-29264-3).

The Mythical Man-Month: Essays on Software Engineering, by Frederick P. Brooks, Jr.; Addison-Wesley, Reading, MA, reprinted with corrections 1982, 195 pages, paper, $14.95 (ISBN 0-201-00650-2).

The Science of Programming, by David Gries; Springer-Verlag, New York, 1982, 366 pages, $19.95 (ISBN 0-387-90641-X, or 3-540-90641-X outside North America).

Structured Programming: Theory and Practice, by Richard C. Linger, Harlan D. Mills, and Bernard I. Witt; Addison-Wesley, Reading, MA, 1979, 402 pages, $32.95 (ISBN 0-201-14461-1).

The Art of Computer Programming, Volume I: Fundamental Algorithms, Second Edition, by Donald E. Knuth; Addison-Wesley, Reading, MA, 1974, 634 pages, $35.95 (ISBN 0-201-03809-9).

The Art of Computer Programming, Volume II: Semi-Numerical Algorithms, Second Edition, by Donald E. Knuth; Addison-Wesley, Reading, MA, 1981, 700 pages, $36.95 (ISBN 0-201-03822-6).

The Art of Computer Programming, Volume III: Sorting and Searching, by Donald E. Knuth; Addison-Wesley, Reading, MA, 1973, 722 pages, $35.95 (ISBN 0-201-03803-X).

The Elements of Programming Style, Second Edition, by Brian W. Kernighan and P.J. Plauger; Byte Books, McGraw-Hill, New York, 1978, 147 pages, paper, $15.95 (ISBN 0-07-034207-5).

Foundations of Program Verification, by Jacques Loeckx; John Wiley, New York, 1984, 230 pages, $29.95 (ISBN 0-471-90323-X).

The Program Development Process: Part 1, The Individual Programmer, by Joel D. Aron; Addison-Wesley, Reading, MA, 1974, 264 pages, $25.95 (ISBN 0-201-14451-4).

The Program Development Process: Part II, The Programming Team, by J.D. Aron; Addison-Wesley, Reading, MA, 1983, 690 pages, $31.95 (ISBN 0-201-14463-8).

IBM and Its Way

If you would know what the colossus is and how it works, you must go beyond the official account given by Buck Rodgers in The IBM Way.

Eric A. Weiss

To understand *computing* you must understand *IBM*, for not only does all the world consider the two synonymous, but, for better or worse, IBM bestrides the industry like the colossus it is. The company has been the subject of an almost uncountable infinity of popular articles as well as a few books (see the list on page 308), but never before has an IBM officer written a book about IBM. You might think that *The IBM Way* would be merely a shallow recitation of the company gospel as delivered by its finest preacher, thirty-four-year veteran F.G. "Buck" Rodgers, who retired in 1984 after ten years as corporate vice-president of marketing, then settled down to polish off the book (with some help from coauthor Robert L. Shook). To some extent what you expect is what you get, for at first glance the work appears to be a popular sermon that repeats ad nauseam the cliche-ridden message of its best-selling model, *In Pursuit of Excellence,* in the homely, friendly, and simplistic terms of a sales manager's speeches, while it romanticizes, justifies, and glorifies IBM and its ways. But out of this flood of superheated treacle, the informed and interested reader can fish more, much more, about the inner workings of Rodgers's beloved firm.

The book is important to computing professionals because in addition to its shallow recitation of the Golden Rule and the IBM Creed, it explicitly and implicitly gives a clear though highly polished, smoothed, shaped, and entirely wartless view, as the author says, of "the heart and soul of IBM: how it thinks and behaves behind closed doors; what goes into its decision making; what it deems important and how it stacks its priorities . . . "In other words, this is the approved IBM version of everything that makes IBM IBM, a view of the firm that tells much, although not nearly all and not entirely accurately, about the "most profitable business in the world."

Reprinted from ABACUS, Volume 3, Number 4, Summer 1986.

It is not a company history; it is not an autobiography; it is not an exposé; it provides no gossip; it says little that cannot be found elsewhere; but, like any book that is written from the heart, it tells a great deal both about its subject and its author. The book can be taken at face value as the official company explanation of why IBM is so great. It can be interpreted as a statement of how IBM wants to be perceived. Or it can be read in a more critical way. By keeping in mind what other sources have told us about IBM, the reader may get both a less glorified insight into why IBM is so great and some understanding of IBM's true nature, whether officially endorsed or not. I will try to help this critical analysis by mixing into my review of the book some of what I know of IBM, resulting in a review of both.

Disclaimer

First, to reveal and register my credentials, biases, and point of view, I must state that at various times in the past forty-five years I have been an observer, admirer, critic, friend, customer, and part owner of IBM, and am still all of the above, but I have never been an IBM employee, supplier, or competitor. All my textbooks have dealt with Big Blue products, although I wrote them without IBM's help or endorsement. I have long been fascinated by how IBM worked, how it crushed its opponents; how it bemused, hypnotized, hindered, and helped its customers; how it confused, manipulated, brainwashed, developed, rewarded, benefited, and motivated its employees; how it handled (and was handled by) the press, the government, and the computing community. Now, at last, in this book, I find many of my observations confirmed and coherently stated by an authoritative insider.

Sales, Sales, Sales

IBM is entirely devoted to sales. Anyone who has had even the slightest exposure to IBM knows this; but Rodgers, the quintessential salesman himself, makes the point even more strongly, repeating it again and again. "At IBM everybody sells" is more than a slogan or a gimmick; it is very close to a fact. Rodgers tells in detail, with examples and anecdotes, how IBM creates and maintains a "Totally Sales-Oriented Environment."

"The salesperson is the source from which everything in business starts." "The real heroes are the sales reps." "Every employee should feel a part of the selling effort." "All employees must realize how their jobs relate to the sales force." "Every employee is expected to contribute in some way to the overall marketing effort." "Everyone is working in harmony to make the sales rep's time more productive."

Those in sales and marketing are the IBM heroes and the best rewarded. "An extra effort is devoted to recognizing exceptional performance in the marketing arena." "A company must be generous in compensating its sales reps."

Sales reps get at least half of their income in commissions; they are not coddled; they are left pretty much on their own if their selling goes well, but find all their bosses on their backs when it does not. Successful salespeople get money, and plenty of it; but they also get recognition, compliments, titles, awards, certificates, and internal publicity. Rodgers is fond of the dramatic hoopla of the Hundred Percent Club and the Golden Circle, and of the drama of sales reps called to the sales-meeting podium to accept briefcases and wheelbarrows stuffed with cash; he obviously considers a blatant and innovative show-biz approach important to the motivation of salespeople.

Rodgers says little about unsuccessful sales reps, but it is clear that they are not long tolerated; after being encouraged, harassed, pushed, prodded, coached, advised, and punished, they are finally induced to leave. But the demand for IBM-trained salespeople is so great that even the rejects are usually avidly snapped up by others. R.W. McGrath's unofficial, unauthorized, and now out-of-print *IBM Alumni Directory* of the 1970s gave a strong indication that their success rate was high. (Some highly-placed alumni are listed in a box on page 312.) There is almost no inward flow of personnel. IBM grows its own, and almost never hires even a star salesman away from a competitor.

Until recently, all the major IBM executives—including both the Tom Watsons—started as salesmen calling on customers in the field. In their progression through the company hierarchy, they had management authority over research, development, engineering, manufacturing, or accounting, but they did not start in these sales-supporting departments, and these minor, cost-creating endeavors were not their primary fields of training or interest. They were salesmen first, super salesmen at their peak, and executives only in old age.

For a long time the only notable exception to this almost exclusive sales-path-to-the-top was the industry giant, John C. McPherson. Today, in the somewhat inflated upper reaches of the corporation, there are a few who followed the technical path or were brought in full-grown from outside: E.R. Piore, J.D. Kuehler, J.E. Bertram, R.E. Gomory, C.J. Conti, and L.M. Branscomb, to name those I can identify. But the sales route to the top is still the most common.

Products

Rodgers says almost nothing important about the nature of IBM's products or their technical content. He virtually ignores the fact that for thirty-five years IBM has been producing and selling hardware and software of increasingly great technological complexity. His attitude toward the details of computer technology is shown in one of his anecdotes, which tells how he beat out a competitor who had made an impressive presentation of his computer's "bits and bytes" by asking the confused but wavering customer, "Do you want to do business with a hardware vendor or do you want a partner?" In this story, in a few sentences, is the essential advice for IBM salespeople: Understand how to sell. Understand how to move your customer. Understand how to move your product. Leave the technical details to your sales support people.

Rodgers seems oblivious to IBM's technical accomplishments. He says almost nothing about how the decisions were made to undertake the IBM 701, Fortran, the 650, the 1401, or the 360 line—all important stories which are better told in recent issues of the *Annals of the History of Computing* and in *I.B.M.'s Early Computers* from MIT Press. Just as your friendly IBM salesperson has always done, Rodgers has learned not to deprecate IBM's competition, but rather to ignore it, thus ignoring the many occasions when other firms have taken technological leadership away from IBM in spite of its major R&D investments. You will learn nothing in this book about what IBM does, beyond amplifying the shouts of SELL! SELL! SELL! when its products are less than the best. This intense, almost closed-eyed salesperson's attitude toward the true nature of the product may explain, in part, why IBM has a reputation among many industry observers of being seldom first, seldom best, but always most. (Severe critics might substitute "never" for seldom.)

Technical People

IBM's technical people—engineers, mathematicians, and computer scientists—if not second-class employees, are at least not considered equal to the first-class employees, the salespeople. Of course there are technical heroes, like the eighty-eight IBM Fellows and the hundreds of recipients of Corporate Technical Awards (described in a box on page 312); although recognized with hurrahs and hoopla and well rewarded, even they are not considered to be as important as the sales heroes. Rodgers tells almost nothing about how IBM achieves the high technical quality of its products or the scientific and technical advances that are evident in its employees' patents and publications.

Customers

In keeping with IBM's overwhelming sales orientation, Rodgers says that the customer, not the product, is the center of every salesman's attention, and since at IBM, EVERYBODY SELLS, the customer is supposed to be the center of *everyone's* attention. The customer is contacted, called on,

Other Accounts of IBM

The *Annals of the History of Computing* has published several accounts of notable IBM technological achievements which give a better picture of the internal interaction among planning, development, design, manufacturing, and sales. While none of these accounts tells the "sales, sales, sales" story of this book, neither do any of them directly contradict it. IBM observers will find that taking the *Annals* articles with the Rodgers book and the books by Foy and by Bashe, Johnson, Palmer, and Pugh (mentioned below) gives a better rounded and more complete picture.

Annals articles that tell the IBM technical-development story include:

"The History of FORTRAN I, II, and III," by John Backus; Vol. 1, No. 1, July 1979, pp. 21–37.

"Early Electronic Computer Developments at IBM," by Byron E. Phelps; Vol. 2, No. 3, July 1980, pp. 253–67,

"Early IBM Computers: Edited Testimony," by Cuthbert C. Hurd; Vol. 3, No. 2, April 1981, pp. 163–82.

"The SSEC in Historical Perspective," by Charles J. Bashe; Vol. 4, No. 4, October 1982, pp. 296–312.

"Introduction to SPREAD Report," by Bob O. Evans; "Processor Products: Final Report of SPREAD Task Group, December 28, 1961," by John W. Haanstra et al.; "Discussion of the SPREAD Report, June 23, 1982," by Joel D. Aaron et al.; all in Vol. 5, No. 1, January 1983, pp. 4–44.

Special issue on the IBM 701, by Cuthbert C. Hurd et al.; Vol. 5, No. 2, April 1983, pp. 107–218.

Special issue on FORTRAN, by J. A. N. Lee and Henry S. Tropp et al.; Vol. 6, No. 1, January 1984, pp. 3–81.

Special issue on the IBM 650, by Cuthbert C. Hurd et al.; Vol. 8, No. 1, January 1986, pp. 3–88.

"System/360: A Retrospective View," by Bob O. Evans; Vol. 8, No. 2, April 1986, pp. 155–79.

Here is a small selection of other books about IBM:

The Lengthening Shadow: The Life of Thomas J. Watson, by Thomas and Marva Belden; Little, Brown and Co., Boston, 1962, 332 pages. This is the authorized life of the founder (1874–1956).

THINK: A Biography of the Watsons and IBM, by William Rodgers; Stein & Day, New York, 1969, 320 pages. An unauthorized biography by a very different Rodgers (no relation), with an excellent bibliography.

The Sun Never Sets on IBM: The Culture and Folklore of IBM World Trade, by Nancy Foy; William Morrow, New York, 1974, 218 pages. A somewhat antagonistic exploration of the overseas part of IBM, which nevertheless concludes: "I know of no other company that has the unique strength of IBM's Basic Beliefs, which are still reverently observed."

IBM's Early Computers: A Technical History, by C.J. Bashe, L.R. Johnson, J.H. Palmer, and E.W. Pugh; MIT Press, Cambridge, MA, 1986, $27.50, 650 pages. A detailed, definitive, authorized insiders' history of the company's development as an engineering organization. Starting with the days of the punched card and ending in the early 1960s, it focuses on technical alternatives rather than business or management considerations.

communicated with, consulted, flattered, pampered, educated, deferred to, used as an information source, sacrificed for, responded to, shown off to other customers. The customer's problems are the salesman's problems (at least until the sale is made), and a sales manager considers himself most successful when a customer treats IBM not as a vendor but as a partner and comes to the point of being unable to distinguish between IBM employees and his own. The object, of course, is to get customers, to keep customers, and to sell to customers. Salesmen are rewarded for doing these things well, particularly for selling, and punished for doing these things badly, particularly for not selling. The loss of a customer or the cancellation of a lease is treated as an unparalleled disaster, resulting in aggressive and persecutional full-dress investigations of how and why and who struck John, and in dramatic penalties. The most hard-felt penalty is that the current sales rep's future sales commissions on a lost account are reduced by the amount of all commissions previously paid on that account, including those that went to the rep's predecessors. When treated this way, sensible salespeople often resign.

Rodgers does not tell us how customers like this or how they respond, but my observation is that their reactions are varied. Some customers are flattered and delighted to be taken captive into the IBM camp. At the other extreme, some—particularly those whose organizational cultures are less sales-oriented than IBM, like writers and college professors—are repelled to the point of cutting off noses. Most customers are unevenly and alternately attracted and repelled. In *The Sun Never Sets on IBM,* Nancy Foy identifies the familiar "customer anxiety syndrome": every computer-selecting customer employee knows that if he or she chooses IBM and something goes wrong, no blame will be attached to the decision.

Individuals in customer firms soon realize that the IBM sales force is skilled at identifying its real and potential friends and enemies, and in applying all the techniques and pressures needed to handle both categories so as to sell, sell, sell. All customers notice that the IBM sales rep's deep interest in them and their problems seems to vanish or at least substantially diminish the instant the order is signed. (The interest is later restored when the sales rep has a new product and a new quota.)

On the whole, the process sells. Many customers like it. Some don't.

Service

For Rodgers, selling and servicing are inseparable parts of the IBM marketing function. This concept leads to the idea that IBM sells reliability, reputation, and service more than it sells its products; certainly many customers, especially the unsophisticated, commit themselves to IBM because of its reputation, especially its reputation for service. A standard IBM salesmen's promise quoted by Rodgers is, "If you incorporate my ideas and products into your operation, we will never let you down. Servicing your company will be our top priority.''

As with other promises in IBM's sales slogans, the service, on the whole, is a reality. The customer pays handsomely for service, in one way or another, but usually gets the kind of service that has been specifically promised—never less and seldom more. Although a marketing rep's attention to an account waxes and wanes as sales are promoted and completed, the level of service is more constant, although it often improves perceptibly when contract negotiations are in critical phases. Part of IBM's success must be ascribed to the fact that a majority of its customers want and like its service.

Training and Education

IBM is devoted to the training and education both of its employees and of its customers. This is an actual, practical, demonstrated devotion, in severe contrast to the hollow lip service often given to these areas by much of corporate America. IBM estimates that its training and education programs cost $600 million in 1984. Certainly the programs are unparalleled in the business world. In keeping with IBM's sales orientation, its sales people get the most and the best training. They are trained to sell, to understand the products and service that they sell, to sell, to understand their customers, to sell, to understand and sell IBM, and to sell. Each year, all the 40,000-odd IBM managers and executives, in and out of sales, get at least forty hours of off-the-job training, and their bosses must explain any lapses or delays in this schedule. Management education is conducted both in company schools and in selected colleges and universities.

Rodgers says little about customer education, but this too is done on a grand scale, giving education in IBM products, in their use, and in how other customers are using IBM products. Once it was free—that is, bundled; now some is free and some is charged for. Customers are also trained to love, honor, and respect IBM. It seems to work.

The internal training and education programs of many corporations go up and down with their business cycles. In good times everybody goes to school, but when things get tough the education program is the first to be cut back, and is often cut out. But IBM, as far as an outsider can tell, has maintained Tom Watson, Sr.'s commitment to training and education through good times and bad.

Rigidity

Rodgers tells much about IBM's cultural rigidity, sometimes without really meaning to. After denying that the dark suit, white button-down-collar shirt, and quiet tie is a corporate mandate, he says, ''But to be completely truthful, there is an unwritten dress code that's as effective as if it were engraved in steel—or as if it had a loaded gun behind it." He admits to a fierce personal intolerance of unreturned phone calls and tardiness. He expects managers to take "ownership" of orders and decisions, even if they dislike them, and to back them in public as their own. He wants no one to express disagreement in front of underlings, and he detests company gossip and rumors. In this book he demonstrates by example how to follow the well-known but unstated IBM rule forbidding public criticism of IBM, its motives, its actions, its leaders, or even the least of its employees. Any sensible subordinate—and IBM tries to hire and retain only sensible employees—would recognize these intolerances, expectations, opinions, preferences, and demonstrations as rigid rules backed with "a loaded gun."

How this rigid culture affects IBM and its people for good or ill cannot be known with any certainty, for the evidence is hidden by one of the rules, the implicit code of silence. We know that many free spirits have flown and been successful outside the IBM coop, but we also know that many brilliant and accomplished people, not all of them salespeople, have stayed and flourished under these rules, contributing greatly to IBM's achievements and to advances in computing.

Code of Behavior

IBM's corporate code of behavior rests on three tenets, originally stated by the senior Watson, reaffirmed by the junior, and now recited, repeated, returned to again and again, and enlarged on by Rodgers, who calls them *commitments:*

1. The individual must be respected.
2. The customer must be given the best possible service.
3. Excellence and superior performance must be pursued.

Rodgers says that every IBM action and policy is directly influenced by these principles, and that they have more to do with the company's success than its technological innovations, marketing skills, or financial resources.

IBM's formal "Business Conduct Guidelines," which derive from these commitments, make up a lengthy document of clear precepts which Rodgers excerpts in an appendix. (The whole ball of wax can be obtained from IBM on request.) The guidelines are complete and specific—chiefly concerned, as most such codes are, with telling employees how to act so as to keep the Board of Directors out of trouble and feeling good.

We have anecdotal evidence that the rules have been both followed and ignored in different cases. On the whole, however, IBM is respected by its customers, employees, observers, stockholders, and neighbors as being well-behaved and ethical, and certainly considered better than the average corporation. Competitors are not as sanguine, some charging anticompetitive practices and some winning settlements. The government's major

---

IBM Fellows and Technical Awards

While IBM's Corporate Technical Awards—cash prizes totalling two or three million dollars, given to several hundred technical professionals each year—are similar to those made on a much smaller scale by a few other companies, the IBM Fellow program is unique and especially noteworthy. Each year since 1963, a few employees are recognized for their accomplishments and contributions in engineering, programming, and science by being named IBM Fellows for life. The principal reward, beyond symbols, cash, and the title, is that for five years the fellows are free to pursue their own projects—anything they choose— within IBM and with the corporation's full support. John Backus, the father of Fortran, was one of the first to be so rewarded.

Well-Known IBM Alumni

Gene Amdahl, 63, left in 1970 after fourteen years, founded Amdahl Corp. and Trilogy Ltd.

H. Ross Perot, 55, left in 1962 after five years, founded Electronic Data Systems, now EDS chairman and a director of General Motors.

James D. Edwards, 45, left in 1980 after fifteen years, now president of AT&T's computer company.

David T. Kearns, 55, left in 1971 after seventeen years, now chairman and CEO of Xerox Corp.

Joe Henson, 52, left in 1981 after twenty-seven years, now president and CEO of Prime Computer Inc.

Robert S. Wiggins, 56, left in 1968 after thirteen years, now chairman, president, and CEO of Paradyne Corp.

Paul G. Stern, 47, left in 1976 after eight years, now president and CEO of Burroughs Corp.

---

charges of such behavior were dropped after twelve years of churning [see ABACUS, Winter 1984, 42–55]. The code says to be honest and ethical with competitors, but does not even hint that they should be thrashed gently!

There is a little-known multi-generation rule that describes how such codes gradually take effect. Originally a code may be promulgated for PR or sales reasons by a generation of managers who know that it is meaningless. Because of the restrictions on downward communication of embarrassing realities, the second generation of managers is not sure that the rules are merely window dressing. All they have to go on is their observation that their bosses give the code lip service and follow it part

IBM Jokes

An IBM Joke from Rodgers

One story tells how Tom Watson Jr. compassionately ordered the newly hired Rodgers to leave his final sales training class to be with his wife for the birth of their first child. It ends with these lines:

"Among the flowers that were delivered to the hospital room after the arrival of my daughter was a beautiful arrangement from Tom Watson. 'Do we know him?' Helen asked."

An Unapproved IBM Joke

The young wife of an IBM salesman complained that her marriage was still unconsummated: "For three years, he sat on the foot of the bed telling me how great it was going to be."

of the time, so they lip it and follow it half the time. But the third generation of managers has no secret message from the founding fathers. The only message they have is the written one, so they follow the code as if it had been intended to be real. The transition from fluff to fact took two hundred years in the case of the Declaration of Independence's "all men are created equal": in IBM's case the transition to complete acceptance and full implementation may come about sooner.

Women and Minorities

There has been less discrimination against women in computing than in most technical fields, and, in my view, IBM has been a leader in offering opportunities to women. As a top-level example: just this spring the number of female corporate vice presidents was doubled, so IBM now has two women officers in a total roster of 64. (This is a BIG company.) Yet, although three of those to whom the book is dedicated are women, the text hardly mentions women at all. The only paragraph on the subject, a short one, starts by saying that "women have created a series of problems and opportunities that most marketing departments are wrestling with today," and ends by stating, "Women must be reckoned with by marketing departments." Only one woman, the author's wife Helen, is named in the index, which names fourteen men. One might conclude that although people are important in Rodgers's IBM, women are not. Since in a great measure IBM is, in truth, Rodgers's IBM, this may be the general rule.

Blacks, Jews, and Asians are unmentioned by Rodgers. They, like women, were highly invisible in the IBM sales force before federal antidiscrimination legislation started to take effect. In the past, the percentage of these minorities throughout IBM was probably somewhat less than the corresponding minority enrollment and faculty limits then imposed by our leading universities. The effects of this traditional selectivity on the composition of IBM's work force, particularly its major management, are still apparent.

Unions

Rodgers says nothing about unions, giving the impression that since they do not exist at IBM, they are of no consequence. Why IBM has no unions, how this came about, and what the consequences are for both IBM and the computing industry remain unanswered questions. IBM management may know some of the answers but, as in so many other IBM personnel matters, it has never given a convincing account of the subject free of PR blather and circumlocution.

Stories and Jokes

Although the *Official IBM Song Book* is out of both print and favor, it has long been suspected that there is a parallel publication, a secret *Official IBM Joke Book* containing the funny stories that are approved for use by IBM sales reps and managers. If Rodgers's anecdotes and cautionary tales are not drawn from that legendary source, they certainly provide a supplement to it. All his stories are tasteful, dull, respectful company-pulpit parables. They are an accurate reflection of IBM's pompous and hearty official personality.

The unapproved inside IBM jokes, which Rodgers does not tell, are, as might be expected, often deprecatory stories about salesmen, chiefly concerning their childlike acceptance of IBM myths and hocum, their computer ignorance, and their unbridled promises to customers of the whole earth and pie in the sky. They reflect some internal antisales opinion that Rodgers is unaware of or chooses to ignore. (A sample of each kind of joke appears in the box on the previous page.)

The Future

Rodgers gives only a few hints about IBM's future. He cites IBM's trite and unrevealing goals for this decade as called out by John Opel: grow with the industry, exhibit leadership, be the most efficient and effective in everything, and sustain profitability. The advent of the personal computer has obviously caused changes. Rodgers mentions how IBM responded to this with a major overhaul of its marketing structure and the development of alternative methods of distribution and selling. Only by the phrase, "We're already late," does Rodgers admit that IBM was not the first to bring personal computing to a waiting world. He sees great promise in IBM's Independent Business Units, from one of which the IBM-PC belatedly sprang.

He does not seem to recognize the full magnitude or implications of these recent changes in the world of computing. It may be that no one does, but while a policy of "sell, sell, sell" may fit the new conditions as well as the old, IBM's unmentioned policies of forecasting, planning, organization, and product and customer development and selection will surely have to be greatly changed if IBM is to continue to dominate the industry.

Can IBM Be Copied?

Thomas J. Peters, coauthor of the enormously popular *In Search of Excellence* (3.4 million copies), claims in his introduction to *The IBM Way* that IBM can be a role model for other companies, while Rodgers explicitly states that others can learn from IBM and prosper by following its example. Of this there is grave doubt, for although IBM's philosophy, management techniques and practices, and corporate creed have never been kept secret, some computer firms that have tried to copy IBM have gone under. Indeed, the grand-scale failures of the computer ventures of both RCA and GE came about in spite of their direct imitation of IBM, and in spite of their armies of hired-away IBM-trained and -indoctrinated managers and sales reps. Perhaps these two failures, together with similar disasters, show that you cannot successfully graft the IBM culture onto very different and perhaps antagonistic cultures. Perhaps RCA, GE, and others failed because in each case the total sales orientation here preached by Rodgers did not pervade the entire company from the highest to the lowest levels. Perhaps success with the IBM model requires that the topmost leaders be salesmen and not lawyers, financiers, engineers, or spoiled children.

It is clear that IBM has been successful. It seems clear that it is not as easy as Peters and Rodgers imply to achieve equal success—at least in direct competition with IBM—by simply copying the company and following the precepts of this book. Perhaps there is more to success in computing than sell, sell, sell.

Book Reviewed

The IBM Way: Insights into the World's Most Successful Marketing Organization, by F.G. "Buck" Rodgers with Robert L. Shook; Harper & Row, New York, 1986, 235 pages, $17.95 (ISBN 0-06-015522-1).

Additional Publications Mentioned

In Search of Excellence: Lessons from America's Best-Run Companies, by Thomas J. Peters and Robert H. Waterman, Jr.; Harper & Row, New York, 1982, 360 pages, $19.95 (ISBN 0-06-015042-4).

IBM Alumni Directory, by R.W. McGrath; a quarterly started in 1973 by McGrath, but now apparently defunct.

INTERRUPT

A February 1984 article in the *Almanack* (published by the IEEE Philadelphia Section) commented on an earlier article in the newspaper *Video Print*, presenting "an analysis of the trends in consumer preferences in 1984":

" 'Long-range demographic trends are somewhat disturbing,' points out Debra Hurd of the *Video Print* research staff, 'because of the present trends towards home computers and away from children.' Hurd contends that 'children are essential if the home computer market is to have any future at all after about the year 2040;' otherwise, according to Hurd, 'there won't be anyone to buy the computers.'

"The *Video Print* article singles out Coleco Industries (Hartford, CT) as a 'major offender' because of its success in encouraging the acquisition of 'Cabbage Patch Kids and home computers, instead of real children.' Because this policy will, in the long run, turn out to be a self-defeating business strategy, *Video Print* suggests home computer manufacturers, while continuing to advertise home computers, donate 'equal time' for children."

If this analysis is correct, the problem is serious and urgent. We suggest that the President immediately appoint a National Commission on Increased Creation of Children Instead of Computers to make sure we put babies before bits.

Problems and Puzzles

Computer-Assisted Problem Solving

Demonstrating a systematic eight-step technique for solving difficult problems.

Richard V. Andree

How *do* you know how to solve a problem—with or without the help of a computer? How do you decide what program to write? These are frequently asked questions. During the past two decades, considerable study has gone into determining how successful problem-solvers do evolve their methods of solution. The subject of *artificial intelligence* has produced some partial answers.

Frequently, the solution method (the algorithm) used is the same method used earlier to solve a similar problem. This seems to be almost the only technique taught in many current mathematical textbooks, and may be why many students first examine the worked-out examples and then attempt to do the assigned problems, only reading the text material and considering the theory as a last resort.

A second and much rarer problem-solving technique is to rely upon the sudden presence of a new idea—an idea which a psychologist might call a "gestalt" or an "aha! reaction" [see M. Gardner's excellent book *Aha!*, W.H. Freeman, 1978], which a cartoonist might indicate by showing a lightbulb above the character's head. Such sudden insights are more apt to occur when one is doing something unrelated, perhaps sleeping, playing, or loafing, *after an intensive period of work on the problem.* This intensive

RICHARD V. ANDREE was the author or coauthor of 37 books on mathematics and computer science. He received his Ph.D. from the University of Wisconsin and published research papers in various branches of mathematics and computing and over 270 expository articles and papers. He taught at the University of Oklahoma where he was Computing Director and Mathematics Chairman and directed mathematics and computer workshops for 30 years. His death, while this book was in press, was a grievous loss to his family, friends, associates, and ABACUS.

Problems and Puzzles is a regular feature of ABACUS. The numbering of problems is consecutive from one issue to the next in order to avoid confusion when responses are received.

Reprinted from ABACUS, Volume 2, Number 3, Spring 1985.

Steps for Computer-Assisted Problem Solving

Successful problem solving usually involves several quite different stages. Here is a series of steps that is sincerely recommended to help you devise a program to solve mathematical problems that merit computer-assisted solution, but for which no feasible solution method, or algorithm, presents itself.

1. Be sure you understand the problem. Try to restate it in several ways. Be sure it is a finite problem, not one that requires you to examine infinitely many cases. Then try to find a general method, an algorithm, for solving the problem. If nothing satisfactory occurs to you, go to step 2.

2. Examine a simple special case first, *in detail.* Don't use a computer at this stage. Examine the easiest case (say "one-digit numbers," or "4-sided polygons," or "single persons who are not members of the union") first, using pencil and paper.

3. Then, if it seems appropriate, program a computer to examine another simple special case.

4. Modify your computer program to examine a third special case.

5. Modify and generalize your computer program so the program handles all of the special cases—and possibly others as well. Include tests to be sure the program is actually working as expected.

6. Run the new program, and examine the output or partial output.

7. Now reexamine the output. Use your common sense and mathematical acumen to see if you can devise a better (faster or safer) algorithm or prove a theorem that will help solve the problem, unless it is already solved.

8. Ask if the original problem has been solved to your satisfaction. If not, go back to step 5.

---

study period is vital. The change of pace from concentration to relaxation is apparently also helpful. Neither the use of an earlier solution nor the "wait for a novel insight" technique is sure-fire, but you should be aware of them because they often work.

Various think tanks have studied what successful problem solvers do when they get stuck. Their results fill several books (see, for example, the two-volume study *Results in a Theory of Problem Solving* by R. Banerji, published at Case Western Reserve, with support from N.S.F. and the Air Force, 1976; or the four-volume *Real-World Problem Solving* by H. Sackman and F. Blackwell, published by Rand Corp. with support from N.S.F.; or *The Art of Problem Solving* by M.S. Klamkin, published by Ford Motor Company's Scientific Research Staff, Dearborn, Michigan). Commercially available books in this area that merit perusal include G. Pólya's classic quintet: *How to Solve It* (Doubleday, 1957); *Mathematical Discovery I & II* (Princeton, 1954); *Mathematics and Plausible Reasoning*

I & II (Princeton, 1954). The latter volumes are perhaps the most mathematical, while the first are the most easily accessible. *How to Solve Problems* by W. Wickelgren (Freeman, 1974) also promises to become a classic.

From the myriad studies devoted to problem solving, a common thread may be abstracted into the sequence of steps listed in a box on page 318. Below we apply it to an actual problem, and then use the recommended refinement technique to produce a final solution using a reasonable amount of computer time.

Remember, this technique is designed to be used on *difficult* problems—problems that do not readily yield either to "prior experience" nor to "gestalt" methods. The technique seems laborious, and it is. However, it is less frustrating than not being able to solve the problem at all, so I urge you to give it a trial the next time you are stuck in tackling a computer-related problem.

The eight steps in the box may seem rather roundabout at first, but experienced computer problem-solvers have found it is a much better technique than the usual attack of the amateur, who tries to start by writing the final program, or at least jumps to steps 5 and 6 right away. This is fine on trivial problems, but on difficult problems it is better to start easy and work up gradually, testing each stage. Let us consider a problem for which we cannot seem to determine the answer by standard textbook methods.

—Sample Problem—

Find perfect square integers like 5776 which have the property that they end in their square roots: $\sqrt{5776} = 76$.

Admittedly, this problem is not earthshaking, but it is not easy to solve without a computer. Try it yourself before continuing—with or without a computer.

The problem, as given, is not a satisfactory computer problem since it has no bounds on where to seek solutions. Clearly 1 and 25 and 36 as well as 5776 are solutions, so such numbers exist. Let's limit our hunt to integers (S) having 16 or fewer digits to make the problem suitable for computer investigation. (You may wish to limit S to *fewer* than 16 digits at first, but many modern computers handle 16 digits without special programming.)

After you have made a serious attempt at solving this problem, let us use it as an example in examining the eight steps for computer-assisted problem solving.

1. Be sure you understand the problem. Try to restate it.

Original Problem: Find perfect square integers like 5776 which have the property that they end in their square roots: $\sqrt{5776} = 76$.

Computer Problem: Determine all positive integer squares S having 16 or fewer digits, such that $N = \sqrt{S}$ is an integer which constitutes the final digit(s) of S. Example: $S = 5776$, $N = \sqrt{5776} = 76$.

Restated Computer Problem (same problem, but from another viewpoint): Find non-negative integers N such that $S = N^2$ ends in N, with $S < 10^{16}$; *OR:* Find integers $N > 0$ such that their squares $N^2 = S < 10^{16}$ end in N.

The first technique that suggests itself may well be just to examine $S = N^2$ for each N and determine whether or not $S = N^2$ ends in N. That is, start with $N = 1$, square it, $S = N*N$, see if S ends in $N = 1$, then go to $N = 2$, and so on. . . . Later you may be able to devise a better algorithm.

2. Examine a simple special case first.

In attempting to solve any problem, it is well to examine special cases before plunging in. Let us examine the one-digit values of N.

N	N^2
0	0
1	1
2	4
3	9
4	16
5	25
6	36
7	49
8	64
9	81

So the one-digit numbers N whose squares end in N are $N = 0, 1, 5, 6$.

3. Write a computer program to examine another special case.

Let us write a program that will find the *three-digit* numbers N whose squares end in N. This idea displays two rather important problem-solving techniques:

1. It frequently pays to rephrase a question by turning it around a bit. We are looking for integers N such that $S = N*N$ ends in N, instead of seeking perfect squares S such that S ends in $\sqrt{S}$.

2. It is often helpful to examine a special case (here the three-digit case) of a more general problem.

Try writing such a program yourself before continuing.

To examine the last three digits of a number S, you need a technique for isolating the last three digits of a number. There is an easy way to do it using the INT( ) function of Basic, which produces the integer portion of a decimal value, INT(151.321) = 151. INT( ) produces the portion before the decimal point of the value inside of the parentheses. Thus,

$$\text{INT}(34.761) = 34$$
or
$$\text{INT}(953846.1) = 953846.$$

Similar functions are available in most computer languages.

The Basic instruction

$$T = S - 1000*\text{INT}(S/1000)$$

will produce the last three digits of S and store them as T. To see how it works, try it for a few integral values of S. For example:

$$S = 123456$$
$$S/1000 = 123.456$$
$$\text{INT}(S/000) = 123$$
$$1000*\text{INT}(S/1000) = 123000$$
$$S - 1000*\text{INT}(S/1000) = 123456 - 123000 = 456$$

—the last three digits of S, as required.

Using this instruction, see if you can devise the desired program to examine the squares of three-digit N values by yourself.

A Basic program to examine all the three-digit numbers N and print out those for which $S = N*N$ ends in N follows:

```
100    FOR N = 100 TO 999
110       S = N*N
120       T = S - 1000*INT(S/1000)
130       IF N <> T THEN 200
140       PRINT S;N
200    NEXT N
```

You may wish to run the above program before continuing. The results should be:

$$141376 \qquad 376$$
$$390625 \qquad 625$$

4. Modify your program to examine other special cases.

Can you change the program to obtain the one-digit values of N whose squares end in N—namely, 0, 1, 5, 6, as we saw when we worked the problem by hand?

Of course you can. Merely change instructions

```
100    FOR N = 100 TO 999
120    T = S - 1000*INT(S/1000)
```
to

```
100   FOR N = 0 to 9
120   T = S - 10*INT(S/10)
```

and run the program. Try it yourself.

What changes would you make in the program to obtain the two-digit values of N such that $S = N^2$ ends in the digits of N? Please try them before continuing. You should discover $N = 25$, $S = 625$ and $N = 76$, $S = 5776$.

Although our current attack is clumsy, even a clumsy approach is better than none at all. Let us now try to produce a program which will do the modifications. This is unnecessary in this particular problem, since the modifications are easily done by hand, but we may learn some useful tricks along the way.

5. Generalize your computer program to examine several cases using the same program.

Examine the following program and be sure you see how it works before running it. In this case we use P to detemine the number of digits we wish N to have, where P consists of a 1 followed by as many zeros as N has digits. To examine the three-digit N values, we set $P = 1000$.

Our new fundamental program:

```
10    INPUT P
100   FOR N = P/10 TO P - 1
110     S = N*N
120     T = S - P*INT(S/P)
130     IF N<>T THEN 200
140     PRINT S;N
200   NEXT N
```

If the program works well, see if there is a way to change P from 10 to 100 to 1000, etc., as the program goes along. If there is, you can use a slight modification of the above program. Modify the program yourself before continuing.

In any event, the modified program given below looks as if it would work:

```
10    P = 10
100   FOR N = P/10 TO P - 1
110     S = N*N
120     T = S - P*INT(S/P)
130     IF N <>T THEN 200
140     PRINT S;N
200   NEXT N
210   P = P*10
220   GOTO 100
```

Try it . . . it works! Well, it works for a while, anyway. Eventually, N becomes large enough that $S = N*N$ contains more digits than the computer will compute accurately. More on this problem later. The program really does need two more instructions.

> 90 PRINT "NOW WORKING ON N<";P
> (Also change 220 GOTO 90)

This will tell you how the program is doing by giving the general range of N-values on which the program is working. If it gets stuck, you at least know where it is stuck. It will also permit the user to see how much time the program spends on each set of k-digit N values, for $K = 1, 2, 3, \ldots$ Common sense suggests that three-digit numbers should take about ten times as long as two-digit numbers, since there are ten times as many of them.

The need for our second change is more involved. Computers are limited in the number of digits they can express precisely. They accept and calculate with numbers larger than this limit using floating-point arithmetic, but in doing so they usually lose track of the low-order (rightmost) digits of the number, and hence cannot tell if $S = N*N$ ends in N when S is too large. In fact, they cannot distinguish between a very large S and $S + 1$.

If a computer carries only six digits of accuracy, for example, and S is a 7-digit number, say (True S) = 7654321, the computer shows this as $7.65432E + 06$, which is read $7.65432 * 10^6$ or 7654320. Now consider (True $S + 1$) = 7654322; if your computer stores only six decimal digits, it will give $S + 1 = 7.65432 * 10^6$, which is precisely what you had for S. Thus, the computer does not distinguish between S and $S + 1$ if S is large enough.

In this case, the *final digit* of S is no longer known. The computer substitutes zero for it, and cannot tell if S ends in the same digits as N does. Surely you would wish your program to STOP automatically if such a crisis should arise (and it does, inevitably).

Make the STOP informative by inserting the instruction

> 115 IF S = S + 1 THEN PRINT "OVERFLOW ERROR
> ON S,N ="; S;N : STOP

If the computer cannot distinguish between S and $S + 1$, it will print the requested message and then STOP. Otherwise, the program will ignore instruction 115 and pass on to the next instruction.

The expanded program now reads:

```
 10    P = 10
 90    PRINT "NOW WORKING ON N<"; P
100       FOR N = P/10 TO P − 1
110       S = N*N
115       IF S = S + 1 THEN PRINT "OVERFLOW ERROR
          ON S,N = "; S;N : STOP
```

```
120    T = S − P*INT(S/P)
130    IF N <> T THEN 200
140  PRINT S,N
200  NEXT N
210  P = P*10
220  GOTO 90
```

Let's continue with our "steps for computer-assisted problem solving."

6. Run the general program and examine the output.

Give it a try on your own computer before continuing.

If the program is run on an old TRS-80 model I with level I Basic, the output will be:

```
NOW WORKING ON N < 10
        1      1
       25      5
       36      6
NOW WORKING ON N < 100
      625     25
     5776     76
NOW WORKING ON N < 1000
   141376    376
   390625    625
NOW WORKING ON N < 10000
OVERFLOW ERROR ON S,N = 3.35588E + 07, 5793
BREAK IN 115
```

Notice, on reaching P = 10000, our program "bombed off" with S,N = 3.35588E + 07, 5793 as a result of the test in instruction 115.

This seems to reach the limits of exploration using the old Basic, unless we are willing to construct our own special "multiple-precision" routines. However, level II Basic permits us to go further without having to create special subroutines, and I suspect your computer does also.

It is time to consider the concept of *double-precision arithmetic*. If you have extended precision or double precision (say TRS-80 model I, level 2 or higher), you can also investigate the problem for four- to eight-digit values of N (which produce eight- to sixteen-digit values of S) by including the instruction

$$5 \text{ DEFDBL S,P,}$$

which is read "define double." This produces "double-length" (sixteen-digit) values for any variable with a name beginning with S or P. Most other computers provide similar accommodation when greater precision is required.

However, troubles appear. Many computers do *not* produce a double-length product if single-length numbers are multiplied together. Thus,

$S = N*N$ will not produce a valid twelve-digit square if N is a single-precision six-digit number.

For $N = 9376$, (True S) = N^2 = 87909376. However, if the computer rounds this to six digits, it will produce $N*N$ = 8.79094E + 07, which is stored as S = 87909400, rather than the correct value, 87909376.

The obvious solution is to make all three, S, P, and N, double-precision by using

$$5 \text{ DEFDBL S,P,N.}$$

However, the instruction

$$\text{FOR } N = P/10 \text{ TO } P—1$$

Double-Precision Program
to Solve the Sample Problem

Comments

```
5 DEFDBL S, P, N
```
Defines variables beginning with S, P, and N as double-precision.

```
10 P = 10
```
The number of zeros in the current value of P is the number of digits in N.

```
90 PRINT "NOW WORKING ON N<";P
```
It is good practice in a program whose output may be sparse to include a statement displaying what the program is doing from time to time.

```
100 N = P/10
110 S = N*N
115 IF S = S+1 THEN PRINT
    "OVERFLOW ERROR ON
    S,N=";S;N : STOP
```
This is a necessary precaution; when the computer cannot tell the difference between S and $S+1$, the program will STOP and indicate this on the screen.

```
120 T = S - P*INT(S/P)
130 IF N<>T THEN 150
140 PRINT S;N
150 N = N + 1
200 IF N<P THEN 110
210 P = P*10
```
Changes P to the next higher power of 10.

```
215 PRINT
220 GOTO 90
```
Repeats program with new P value.

Figure 1

will not accept a double-precision variable for N on many computers.
This is easily fixed using

```
100   N = P/10
130   IF N <> T THEN 150
150   N = N + 1
200   IF N < P THEN 110
```

in place of

```
100   FOR N = P/10 TO P − 1
130   IF N <> T THEN 200
200   NEXT N
```

The Program now reads as shown in Figure 1, and yields the output shown
below as Figure 2.

Output from Figure 1

NOW WORKING ON N <10

1	1
25	5
36	6

NOW WORKING ON N <100

625	25
5776	76

NOW WORKING ON N <1000

141376	376
390625	625

NOW WORKING ON N <10000

87909376	9376

NOW WORKING ON N <100000

8212890625	90625

NOW WORKING ON N <1000000

11963109376	109376
793212890625	890625

—and so forth; this will continue for a long time.

Figure 2

You will notice that for each new *P* value, the program requires about *ten times as much* computer time as for the previous *P* value. Run the program again and time it. A rather slow microcomputer took almost a minute and a half to get from $P = 100$ to $P = 1000$. A faster micro took less than ten seconds to get from $P = 100$ to $P = 1000$, but the *increase* in time was still about ten-fold for each increase of the number of digits in *N*.

I hope your program did not "bomb out"; but it does require lots and lots of computing time. Let us consider our "slow micro." To get from $P = 100$ to $P = 1000$ takes about 1.5 minutes; from $P = 1000$ to $P = 10000$, 15 minutes; from $P = 10000$ to $P = 100000$, 2.5 hours. If the computer runs another twenty-four or forty-eight hours to go from $P = 100000$ to $P = 1000000$, you will also find

$$11963109376 \qquad 109376$$
$$793212890625 \qquad 890625$$

and who knows what else?

Now let's use our heads. This program really works the problem in a very crude brute-force way; we are just examining every number *N*. The number of numbers to be examined increases sharply as *P* increases; see Figure 3.

Clearly we can reasonably expect to examine $P < 10$, 100, 1000, 10000, and even 100000; but after that, the computer time involved becomes exorbitant. Of course, you may reason that the computer might just as well be working on your problem as sitting idle.

Back to our guidelines once more.

7. Reexamine the output. Use your common sense and mathematical knowledge to devise a better (faster) algorithm to help solve the problem.

We really should have recognized at the beginning that *N* must end in 0, 1, 5, or 6 if it is a satisfactory number (N^2 ending in *N*). This would have

Program Running Times

P	No. of Cases	Approximate Time
$1 < P < 10$	8	Less than 1 second
$10 < P < 100$	89	9 sec.
$100 < P < 1000$	899	90 sec. = 1.5 min
$1000 < P < 10000$	8999	15 min.
$10000 < P < 100000$	89999	150 min. = 2.5 hrs.
$100000 < P < 1000000$	899999	24 hr.
$1000000 < P < 10000000$	8999999	9 or 10 days
$10000000 < P < 100000000$	89999999	90^+ days = 3^+ months

Figure 3

saved almost 60% of our computing time. Actually, if $N>9$, N cannot end in 0, since then N^2 would tack on *another* 0 at the right. Similarly, if $N>9$, N cannot have the form $(10x + 1)$; that is, it cannot end in 1, since $N^2 = (10x+1)^2 = 100x^2 + 20x + 1$; the next-to-last digit is twice that in x, and therefore is not the same. Thus, mathematical arguments show that if $N>9$ and N^2 ends in N, then N ends in 5 or 6. So instead of increasing N by 1 each time, we can start with $N=5$ and jump by 10 each time, testing both N and $(N+1)$ to see if either has the desired property. The program shown as Figure 4 will cut out 80% of our running time, doing an hour's testing in twelve minutes. An 80% computer time savings on a problem pleases employers, and can lead to bonuses, salary increases, and eventual promotions. (But don't quit yet: our eight-step method has more to offer.)

Try the program. It works, and we really might have been smart enough to think of discarding 80% of the unsuccessful cases in the beginning.

However, now that there is some output to look at, it may be possible

A More Efficient Program

```
  5   DEFDBL S,P,N
 10   P=10
 90   PRINT "NOW WORKING ON N<";P

 98   REM
 99   REM THIS TESTS VALUES OF N ENDING IN 5.
100   N = 5 + INT(P/100)*10
110   S = N*N
115   IF S = S + 1 THEN PRINT "OVERFLOW ERROR ON
      S,N="S;N:STOP
120   T = S - P*INT(S/P)
130   IF N<>T THEN 150
135   PRINT S;N

148   REM
149   REM   THIS TESTS VALUES OF N ENDING IN 6.
150   N1 = N+1
152   S1 = N1*N1
154   T1 = S1 - P*INT(S1/P)
156   IF N1<>T1 THEN 160
158   PRINT S1;N1
160   N=N+10

198   REM
199   REM   THIS SENDS US BACK TO TRY NEXT N IF N<P.
200   IF N<P THEN 110

210   P = 10*P
215   PRINT
220   GOTO 90
```

Figure 4

to find an even more ingenious way to speed up our program. Look at the output. Do you notice anything special in the N column?

N^2	N
25	5
36	6
625	25
5776	76
141376	376
390625	625
87909376	9376
8212890625	90625
11963109376	109376
793212890625	890625

Two important points should be noticed:

Point 1. When we investigated the one-digit N's by hand and in the first program (modified to examine one-digit values of N), we found

N^2	N
0	0
1	1
25	5
36	6

—but our computer programs missed the first value $N=0$, and the latest program missed both $N=0$ and $N=1$. Why did that happen? Do you think that we missed any other values? Are you sure?

We did obtain all the values between $P=10$ and $P=1000000$, but missed $N=0$ and $N=1$ because the program did not test these values. If you didn't notice that earlier, you need more computing experience. Actually, 0, 1, and 2 are frequently special cases, and often need to be examined separately in number-theoretic problems.

Point 2. The only satisfactory values of $N>10$ ended in the exact digits of some satisfactory N we had already found.

Now that could be a real clue!
Consider the case starting at $P=1000$. We found

N^2	N
141376	376
390625	625

It seems reasonable to believe that any four-digit value of N whose square ends in N will itself end in either 376 or 625; for, according to the pattern we have noticed, remove the left-hand digit from any valid N, and you still have a valid N. Hmmm. Well, yes—that seems reasonable. Actually, it can be shown that there is only one possible extension X376 or Y625 for each value.

However, some ideas that "seem reasonable" turn out not to be true. For example, one of my students extended the above conjecture by asserting, "Since there is only one *four-digit value* of N such that N^2 ends in N, there can be only one such N having k digits for any $k>4$."

However, consider

$$N = 109376, \ N^2 = 11963109376;$$
$$N = 890625, \ N^2 = 793212890625;$$

—which blows that "reasonable conjecture."

What went wrong? The student realized that 9376 is the only suitable four-digit N, and assumed that any larger "suitable N" would have to use the same four digits—all other endings were out of the running. But glancing at the right-hand side of our output table (page 329), you can quickly see that the student overlooked 90625 as a suitable extension of the three-digit $N=625$, *with 0 as the fourth digit*—just as 109376 is a suitable extension of the four-digit 9376, with 0 as the fifth digit.

How about the original guess?

—Conjecture—

If a given N^2 ends in the digits $N>10$, then N itself must end in the same digits comprising some $M<N$, where M^2 ends in the digits of M.

Have we already proven this? If we *could* prove this, would it be helpful in our search? You bet it would be!

For example, in examining the five-digit N values, instead of examining 89,999 cases, we would only need to examine the 18 cases X9376, X0625 (and possibly the 9 more cases X0376, unless we can show that this is also impossible—which we can).

I'm not going to prove the conjecture, though it is true. High school students have produced acceptable proofs of the conjecture, and so could you; but that is not our purpose here.

To cut down from 89,999 cases to 18 cases for the five-digit N values is a savings of 99.98% of the values to be tested. The six-digit values produce even greater savings. What would formerly have taken months to RUN should now RUN in a few *minutes*, even if each number evaluated takes longer to test (since the program may be messier than before).

For now, let us assume the slightly stronger result:

—Assumption—

If N^2 ends in N, then N ends in the digits of some smaller K such that K^2 ends in K. Furthermore, the previous K will be a K with one fewer digit than N, granting the possibility of leading zeros on a smaller K (90625 being the N for $K = 0625$, $K^2 = 390625$). This means that if the number of digits in N is three or more, there are only two possible active values A and B whose extensions need be considered. These A and B will be the last two values N found such that N^2 ends in N.

Let's start our program investigating three-digit N values. This will enable us to test the program and see if it is running as we believe it should.

Store the "last two successful values of N" that we are trying to extend in locations A and B. To examine the three-digit values of N, the two-digit values to be extended will be $A = 25$, $B = 76$. We use

$$P = 1000$$
$$A = 25 \quad \text{(since when } N = 25,\ N^2 = 6\underline{25})$$
$$B = 76 \quad \text{(since when } N = 76,\ N^2 = 57\underline{76})$$

to "seed" our program with the successful two-digit values to be extended.

Continuing with "Steps for Computer-Assisted Problem Solving," we find:

8. Go back to step 5.

5. Modify and generalize your computer program. Include tests to be sure that the program is actually working as expected.

6. Run the new program and examine the output.

Figure 5 is a program that produces the desired results in a moderate time. Put it on your computer and see how it runs (Figure 6 shows the results).

8. Ask if the original problem has been solved to your satisfaction. If not, go back to step 5.

Now we need to ask whether the original problem has been solved. If it was to find all perfect squares N^2 such that N^2 ends in the digits of N, then it is only partially solved. The program has found all such $N < 412890625$, but there is no reason to suspect these are all that exist. There is also the possibility that our program is defective and may have overlooked some N values less than 10^9. (After all, we did overlook 0 and 1, remember?)

This is one way research is done. First, investigate a few special cases. Next, use a simple program to investigate a few more cases; if the results seem worthwhile, automate your program and let it run. Examine the

An Even Faster Program

```
  5   DEFDBL S,P,N,A,B
 10   P=1000
 20   A=25
 30   B=76

 90   PRINT " WORKING ON N < " ; P
 95   Q=P/10

 99   REM   THIS BLOCK EXTENDS A VALUE.
100   FOR K=1 TO 9
105   N = K*Q + A
110   S = N*N
115   IF S=S+1   THEN PRINT "OVERFLOW ERROR ON S,N = ";
      S;N:  STOP
120   T = S − P*INT(S/P)
130   IF N<>T THEN 200
140   PRINT S;N
150   A=N
160   GOTO 300
200   NEXT K
210   REM      END OF BLOCK THAT EXTENDS A VALUE.

250   REM

299   REM   THIS BLOCK EXTENDS B VALUE.
300   FOR K=1 TO 9
305   N = K*Q + B
310   S = N*N
320   T = S − P*INT(S/P)
330   IF N<>T THEN 400
340   PRINT S;N
350   B=N
360   GOTO 500
400   NEXT K
401   REM      END OF BLOCK THAT EXTENDS B VALUE.

450   REM

500   P = P*10
520   GOTO 90
```

Figure 5

output, make some conjectures and prove or disprove their validity. Then, devise a new technique (algorithm) for carrying out the investigation and implement it.

Now you are ready to try to prove the most general case. It may or may not yield to your effort—but, in any case, you have a pocketful of

Output from Figure 5

```
WORKING ON N < 1000
              390625              625
              141376              376
WORKING ON N < 10000
            87909376             9376
WORKING ON N < 100000
          8212890624            90625
WORKING ON N < 1000000
        793212890625           890625
         11963109376           109376
WORKING ON N < 10000000
       8355712890625          2890625
      50543227109376          7109376
WORKING ON N < 100000000
     166168212890625         12890625
    7588043387109376         87109376
WORKING ON N < 1000000000
OVERFLOW ERROR ON S,N = 1.704786682128906D+17    412890625
```

Figure 6

results that were previously unknown. We shall not attempt to go further here, but suspect some able reader will.

There is one additional check that should be made. Did our programs produce the same results, to the extent that they overlapped? If not, why not? This is important.

Take a look at Figure 7. The two rather different programs seem to agree as far as they go, but the longer program produces more results in one minute than the old program did in three months. *This* is what is meant by effective programming.

Actually, all satisfactory values of N where N has 100 or fewer digits are known, but their investigation uses more mathematical sophistication than we are willing to impose here.

Perhaps the two most important conclusions to remember from this article are:

1. You *do* have enough computer adroitness to undertake successfully the investigation (and at least partial solution) of problems so difficult that a year ago you wouldn't even have tried them.

2. You have discovered one of the fundamental truths of computer programming:

Comparison of Original and Final Programs

Original (slow-running) program	Faster program

```
  5 DEFDBL S,P,N
 10 P = 10




 90 PRINT "NOW WORKING ON
    N<";P
100 N = P/10







110 S = N*N
115 IF S = S+1 THEN PRINT
    "OVERFLOW ERROR ON
    S,N=";S;N:STOP
120 T = S - P*INT(S/P)
130 IF N<>T THEN 150
140 PRINT S;N
150 N = N + 1
200 IF N<P THEN 110
```

```
  5 DEFDBL S,P,N,A,B
 10 P = 1000
 20 A = 25
 30 B = 76

 90 PRINT "   WORKING ON
    N<";P
 95 Q=P/10

 99 REM   THIS BLOCK EXTENDS
    A VALUE
100 FOR K=1 TO 9
105 N = K*Q + A
110 S = N*N
115 IF S=S+1 THEN PRINT
    "OVERFLOW ERROR ON
    S,N=";S;N:STOP
120 T = S - P*INT(S/P)
130 IF N<>T THEN 200
140 PRINT S;N
150 A=N
160 GOTO 300
200 NEXT K
210 REM  END OF BLOCK THAT
    EXTENDS A VALUE

250 REM

299 REM   THIS BLOCK EXTENDS
    B VALUE
300 FOR K=1 TO 9
305 N = K*Q + B
310 S = N*N
320 T = S = P*INT(S/P)
330 IF N<>T THEN 400
340 PRINT S;N
350 B = N
360 GOTO 500
400 NEXT K
401 REM  END OF BLOCK THAT
    EXTENDS B VALUE

450 REM

500 P = P*10
520 GOTO 90
```

```
210 P = P*10
215 PRINT
220 GOTO 90
```

Figure 7

—Once you have a program written, debugged, and running properly, by reflecting on the problem you will often find a better way to attack it. If the problem is major, this is the time to think hard, then scrap your earlier effort and start over.—

Of course, if you are dealing with a "one-time-only" problem and your existing program produces the desired results while you are thinking, you can forget about any reprogramming—unless you want to show the program to someone else, or use it again later.

Problems

Here are some problems for your consideration.

Problem #20: Problem #1 (ABACUS, Fall 1983) asked you to determine all positive integer squares $S = N*N$ such that S contains each of the nine non-zero digits exactly once. This was solved neatly by a high school student (see Summer 1984) and by several others. The extension to cubes and 4th powers has also been solved (Summer 1984), but no reader has come forward with a program to solve the problem with "exactly once" changed to "exactly twice" or "exactly three times" in spite of the hint given in the Winter 1984 issue. Try it.

Problem #21: The current holder of the record for the longest palindromic square containing an *even number of digits* (Problem #3, Fall 1983) is still Rob Kolstad with the 26-digit
$(6360832925898)^2 =$
4046019551118811559106404.
Can you do better than this?

Problem #22: The determination of rational numbers (fractions) in lowest terms A, B, C, such that $A + B + C = 1 = A*B*C$—or a proof that they do not exist—(Problem #4, Winter 1984) is still open. Surely, some reader can produce at least partial results, such as: "If $A = X/D$, $B = Y/D$, $C = Z/D$ with $(X+Y+Z)^3 = X*Y*Z = D^3$, then there are no solutions for $D < \square$" (you choose the value of $\square$)—or, better yet, produce a solution.

Problem #23: Establish a new record for the number of ways in which an integer can be expressed as the sum of two abundant numbers (see Problem #12, Summer 1984). The current record is held by Mr. James Jones of Moore, Oklahoma, who has shown that 371280 can be expressed as a sum of two abundant numbers in more than 43000 different ways. James says record-breaking values are likely to be multiples of 60. Can you beat his record? Problems #13 and #14 are also open.

Problem #24: It is reasonably easy to find strings of consecutive integers *each* of which is divisible by some perfect square (greater than one). For example, in the string of seven consecutive integers beginning with 217070, each is divisible by the perfect square shown below it:

217070	217071	217072	217073	217074	217075	217076
7^2	3^2	2^2	113^2	11^2	5^2	2^2

Can you produce a longer string of consecutive integers each of which has a square factor greater than 1?

The reader submitting the best solution (along with program and explanation) for each one of the above problems will receive a gift book, regardless of whether or not he or she employs the "try this when you get stuck" method advocated in our column this month.

A Solution and Another Problem

Dr. Elvin J. Lee of Fargo, ND was the first reader to send in a mathematical proof that five is the maximum possible length of a string of consecutive deficient integers (Problem #15, Summer 1984), and he properly notes that the mathematical theorems needed for this proof are all given earlier in the article. A Springer-Verlag book goes to Dr. Lee.

Dr. Lee proved that there exist *infinitely many abundant pairs* (consecutive abundant numbers), and raised the still unanswered problem of the number of *deficient pairs*. Dr. Lee also introduced your author to a new concept—*weird numbers*. An abundant number, such as 12, has the property that the sum of its proper divisors is greater than the number itself ($12 \rightarrow 1 + 2 + 3 + 4 + 6 = 16 > 12$). However, for many abundant numbers *N*, some *subset* of the proper divisors of *N* will have *N* as its sum ($2 + 4 + 6 = 12$). (Is this true for most abundant numbers?) There do exist abundant numbers *W* for which *no* subset of the proper divisors of *W* will total W. The smallest such number $W = 70 \rightarrow 1, 2, 5, 7, 10, 14, 35$. These are not difficult to generate. 836 is a weird number. James Jones found 1,765 of them less than 1,000,000 with the help of a computer. Apparently, weird numbers were first discused by S.J. Benkowski in *American Mathematical Monthly* (1972, page 774) and by Benkowski and P. Erdös in *Mathematics of Computation* (Volume 28, April 1974, pages 617–23). If you know of an earlier reference, please let me know. Dr. Lee comments that all the *weird* numbers less than 100,000 are even, and he would like to know if there exist integers that are both *odd* and *weird*.

Problem #25: (a) Generate as many *weird* numbers as you can.
(b) Either find an *odd weird* number, or show that none exist.

Good solving!
—R.V.A.

Reproduction for Educational Use
Teachers have asked permission to reproduce this column for classroom distribution. Such permission is hereby granted providing both of the following conditions are met:

1. Copies are distributed for educational purposes, without charge.

2. The article is reproduced *in full,* including the page number and copyright line at the bottom of each page.

We encourage exploration of problems with the assistance of computers where appropriate.

Computers and the Law

Who's Liable When the Computer's Wrong?

Courts will not accept the defense, "It is the computer's fault."

Michael Gemignani

"Computer" mistakes may result from hardware, software, or human error. When users get inaccurate information from computer output, the source of the problem may be—among other possibilities—that

□ the original data was incorrect even before it was translated into a format the computer could manipulate;
□ the original data was translated incorrectly before being processed;
□ the software which processed the data contained either logical or semantic errors;
□ the output was incorrectly interpreted by the human user;
□ a hardware failure caused incorrect results to be produced;

—or some combination of these.

Incorrect information can cause damage both to individuals and to property. Billing errors are troublesome, and sometimes seem impossible to straighten out. Much more serious would be a faulty computer simulation of an airplane wing, which might cause the wing to fall off in midflight, with disastrous results to the aircraft and its occupants. Potentially still more disastrous would be an error like the one in 1979 in which a faulty NORAD computer called a false missile alert (shades of *War Games*). Such examples are not hypothetical. In March of 1979, the discovery of a mistake in computer software used in the design of nuclear plants caused a major reevaluation of the safety of several installations. With more and more of the world's commerce conducted by computer, and with gov-

MICHAEL C. GEMIGNANI holds a Ph.D. from Notre Dame and a J.D. from Indiana University. He is Dean of the College of Arts and Sciences and Professor of Computer Science at the University of Maine at Orono. A consultant on computer-related legal issues, he has written and spoken widely on this subject. His books include *Computer Law*, published by Lawyers Cooperative Publishing Co.

Reprinted from ABACUS, Volume 2, Number 1, Fall 1984.

ernments and private industry alike becoming increasingly dependent on computer systems, the potential for a major error (or breach of security) to cause massive damage is increasing daily. In this column, I want to consider a less dramatic but no less interesting aspect of computer error: What happens to the average citizen who is caught up in a computer error that causes him or her more than just minor inconvenience? What recourse does such a person have against the user of the machine that is creating the difficulty? Let's review one of the classic cases of this kind.

In February of 1963, a Mr. Swarens bought a 1962 Ford automobile, paid for in part with a loan from the dealer. This loan was secured by the automobile itself, meaning, of course, that if Swarens failed to make his payments on time, Ford Motor Credit Company, the party to whom the dealer assigned the loan, could repossess the car.

In June 1963, representatives of Ford informed Swarens in person that his payments were delinquent. He, however, produced cancelled checks proving that his payments were up-to-date. Two months later, Swarens was again visited by representatives of Ford who accused him of being behind in his payments; he, in turn, again produced cancelled checks to prove that all necessary payments had been made. Finally, in October, Swarens was visited by Ford's collection agents. Exasperated, Swarens displayed a shotgun, threw the agents out of his house, and stated that he would show them no more records. The agents, in turn, threatened that they could and would repossess the car.

On 2 December 1963, Swarens parked his car in the lot of the plant where he worked, but returned at the end of the day to find it missing. He reported the loss to the police, who advised him that the car had been repossessed. Swarens hitchhiked home.

The next morning Swarens went to Ford's collection office. The office manager admitted a mistake had been made and apologized, but he would not release the car until Swarens agreed to release Ford from any liability for the expenses and aggravation he had suffered because of Ford's mistake. Swarens refused to accept this condition and left without his car. Ford kept the car and later sold it, applying the proceeds to the outstanding balance on Swaren's debt. When Swarens failed to make the next payment due on the car he no longer had, Ford once again notified him that he was delinquent.

One marvels at Swaren's patience, for even after all of this, he waited several years before filing his suit against Ford. He asked for the market value of the car at the time it was repossessed as well as for punitive damages. (Punitive damages are an award a court can make in some civil cases to punish particularly offensive conduct and to try to prevent similar conduct in the future.) At the trial in 1968, more than five years after he had purchased the car and more than four years after it had been repossessed, Ford admitted that Swarens had been current in his payments at all times; he was awarded compensatory damages of $2000 and punitive damages of $5000. Ford appealed the ruling.

The appellate court upheld the award, including the punitive damages, rejecting each of Ford's arguments, most of which concerned procedural technicalities. Ford argued that the whole affair was caused by a computer error and that the damages awarded were therefore excessive. Nevertheless, in upholding the award of punitive damages, the appeals court concluded that the trial court had properly found that Ford had acted willfully and had not exercised good faith in its dealings with Swarens. The appeal court stated:

Men feed data to a computer and men interpret the answer the computer spews forth. In this computerized age, the law must require that men in the use of computerized data regard those with whom they are dealing as more important than a perforation on a card. Trust in the infallibility of a computer is hardly a defense, when the opportunity to avoid error is as apparent and repeated as was here presented.

One may conclude from this case that attributing the responsibility for harm to reliance on computer-generated data is not a defense if the means to avoid the mistake were readily available. What this means is that one ought not to be negligent in relying on computer-generated data; particularly, one ought not to be as grievously negligent as Ford had been with regard to Swarens when they persistently refused to correct their own mistakes or to make amends for the harm those mistakes had caused, even after they were presented with proof that they were wrong.

Other businesses besides Ford, of course, have incurred liability because of harm brought about by undue reliance on a computer. Consolidated Edison, for example, had to pay a builder for damages sustained by an unoccupied house when the utility company wrongfully turned off the electricity in the middle of January because of two unpaid bills totalling $25.11; the heating unit's power was cut off and some water pipes froze and burst, causing damage in the amount of $1030.

New York, like most states, has a statute which allows but does not require utilities to disconnect service to customers who do not pay their bills. The statute specifies that notice must be given prior to disconnection, and may be given by mail addressed to the customer at the place where service is provided. The court accepted that Consolidated Edison had complied with the notice requirement of the statute. Nevertheless, the court also stated that Consolidated Edison should have recognized from the letter which had requested the original connection that the customer was a builder who did not live in the house in question; in fact, the house was unoccupied.

The court reviewed one definition of negligence:

Negligence is the lack of ordinary care. It is a failure to exercise that degree of care which a reasonably prudent person would have exercised under such circumstances.

A "reasonably prudent person" would have recognized that the builder who had obtained the service wanted mail sent to the address on his letterhead, and that builders normally do not occupy the homes they build. A reasonably prudent person would also have consulted the customer's contact person at the utility office to determine the facts before disconnecting the electricity in the middle of winter. Where the possibility of damage can be clearly foreseen, there is a duty to exercise care.

Here is where the computer comes in. The disconnection was brought about by a "routine" action initiated by a computer. The court concluded:

> While the computer is a useful instrument, it cannot serve as a shield to relieve Consolidated Edison of its obligation to use reasonable care when terminating service. The statute gives it the discretionary power to do so, and this discretion must be exercised by a human brain. Computers can only issue mandatory instructions—they are not programmed to exercise discretion.

From this case we learn again that a human being who relies too heavily on the data that a computer provides runs the risk of having to pay damages for injuries caused by incorrect data. Moreover, these damages may have to be paid even if, as in the case just described, the data is actually correct but is used mindlessly.

Negligence is studied by every first-year law student. It is one of the central notions of the law, but it is not easily summarized. This does not mean that there is no short definition of negligence. It is understanding the implications of the definition that requires volumes. Basically, party A is negligent toward party B if A has a duty of care toward B and breaches that duty. If B suffers injury caused by A's negligence, then B may seek recovery in court.

But to whom does a programmer have a duty of care? And what is the standard of care required of programmers, that they may be certain of avoiding a breach of that duty? The classical test of the standard of care is what the reasonably prudent person would do under the circumstances. But what is expected of a reasonably prudent programmer? Certainly the answer will vary, depending on whether the programmer is coding software used in the design of nuclear power plants or coding some new arcade game.

If these questions are difficult, the issues of causation are even more troublesome. If a mistake is made in a program used in the design of nuclear power plants and a nuclear accident can be traced back to this mistake, to whom is the programmer liable? Only to his or her employer? To the contractors who built the plant? To the utility which runs the plant? To the persons injured in the accident? To those put out of work because of the power plant's failure?

The issue of negligent use of computers has only recently begun to be addressed by the courts, and the question of a programmer's duty of care has not yet come up. We will have more to say about both issues in future columns. In the meantime, computer professionals should recognize that they may be held legally responsible for injuries caused by errors in their work; and companies must realize that they may be held accountable for harm suffered, not only resulting from acting on incorrect computer output but also from the mindless use of correct data.

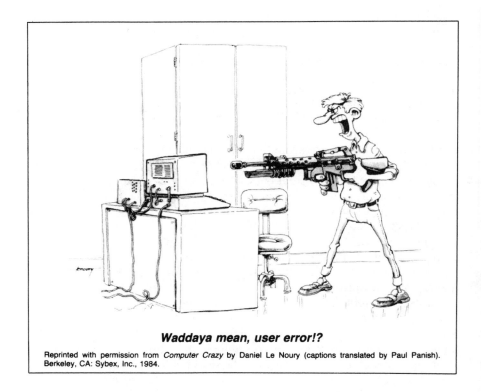

Waddaya mean, user error!?

Reprinted with permission from *Computer Crazy* by Daniel Le Noury (captions translated by Paul Panish). Berkeley, CA: Sybex, Inc., 1984.

Personal Computing

Is There Such a Thing as a Personal Computer?

What really distinguishes personal computers from larger machines? And how does this affect personal computing research?

LARRY PRESS

From 1977 through 1981, the National Computer Conference included a parallel Personal Computing Festival with its own sessions, proceedings, and exhibits. As cochairman of two of the festivals, I was often told that they should be abolished because there was nothing unique about personal computers, that they raised no new issues. The critics felt that personal computers were scaled-down versions of larger machines, and therefore that separate sessions on personal computer applications, hardware, operating systems, etc., were redundant.

Those people are nicely balanced by the folks who think there is nothing *but* personal computers; they dismiss "mainframes" and "minicomputers" as large file-servers for PCs.

I am convinced that there is such a thing as a personal computer although, like everyone else working with them, I've been too busy to figure out exactly why I hold that view. One possible reason is the existence of the personal computing "scene." People making and selling devices they call personal computers have created an industry bigger than the potato-chip industry, and no one questions the existence of the potato chip. The two thickest magazines ever published (*Byte* and *PC*) are devoted to what they perceive as personal computers. The term, however poorly defined, is working its way into our vocabulary.

If you don't consider potato chips and popular magazines sufficient authorities in matters of computer science, look at the March 1983 issue of *The Communications of the ACM*. There are two Apple computers on

In 1975 LARRY PRESS became aware of microcomputers, and now divides his time between consulting to personal computer manufacturers and users and writing about personal computers. He received a Ph.D. from UCLA in 1967, has taught in the United States and Europe, and is now a professor of Computer Information Systems at California State University, Dominguez Hills, CA.

Reprinted from ABACUS, Volume 1, Number 2, Winter 1984.

the cover and an article on two personal computer operating systems inside. More significant is a classified ad on page A-17 from MIT's Sloan School of Management, recruiting faculty with specialties in—among other areas—personal computers.

Some Differences

In addition to the existence of the scene, one can list some differences between what we've come to call personal computers and larger machines.

For a start, personal computers are closely coupled with their memory-mapped displays, whereas timesharing systems typically communicate with terminals at low (RS-232) speed and incur load-dependent delays. The high-band-width display of a personal computer facilitates graphic applications and those in which virtual metaphors such as unbounded spreadsheets or word-processing "scrolls" are easily implemented. Not only is this efficient, it narrows the gap between the abstract object inside the computer and its "real" manifestation when thought about or printed, making it relatively easy to learn to use a program. If you have a report to write or a budget forecast to prepare, you could use a Teletype-based line editor and a financial planning language on a timesharing system, but the job would surely go faster using a personal computer running a word-processing program such as Wordstar and a spreadsheet processor like VisiCalc. These programs would be easier to use and more efficient because they were designed to exploit the high-bandwidth displays found in personal computers.

Personal computer operating systems are also different. Some aspects are simpler, and others more complicated. With personal computers, we are interested in single-user, not multi-user systems. Issues of privacy and file protection are simplified, but rapid switching from one job to another is imperative. For instance, when the phone rings you may have to switch from editing a document to checking your calendar or updating a file, and then go back to the document. However, concurrent execution may not be necessary, since the system resources are not all that expensive. Personal computer operating systems must also be extended to support the high-bandwidth displays which are involved.

Ergonomic factors like styling, operator comfort, footprint (desk space required), and noise level take on increased importance with a personal computer. If we all are to have personal computers on our desks one day, the way we have personal telephones today, they will have to be small, attractive, and unobtrusive. In fact, they had better swallow up those telephones (and answering machines, rolodex files, and in-baskets) to free up some desk space.

Personal computers affect the surrounding culture in different ways than other computers have done. One way is that they have eroded the perceived status of our profession: "Oh, you're in computers, so is my cousin's little boy;" "Yes, I'm going to learn programming in junior college next semester;" or "What! the salesman at the computer store told me that most of the consultants in their files charge $5.00 per hour." Furthermore, it seems that the public sees personal computers as a symbol of our economic salvation through electronics—in contrast to earlier computers, which were a symbol of our alienation from the Earth and from each other.

Personal computers are marketed and supported in different ways from other machines. The record industry seems to be a better model than the traditional IBM branch office with its trained sales and systems people. Personal computer software companies attempt to build "star" authors, and industry periodicals publish "best-seller" lists. Packaging, art work, distribution channels, and retail shelf space are critical items. Software advertising budgets often exceed development costs by factors of ten and up.

Personal computers are designed with non-technical users in mind. Using application packages like word processors, file managers, and spreadsheet processors, these people are able to put their computers to good use. They often end up being used on an ad hoc basis, alongside of large machines that are used for ongoing systems and the maintenance of shared files. These people don't take their personal computers so seriously either. If it sits idle for a week, no one is concerned. There are no graveyard shifts.

Personal Computing Research

If there is such a thing as personal computers, we need to start thinking about the field of personal computing, and its research questions. In other words, if the Sloan School or a computer science department hires professors whose area of expertise is personal computers, what will they teach about, and what will their research deal with?

One area of research, particularly in a technically oriented business school, is the study of organizations using personal computers. How are personal computers used? Do they affect productivity? Are they status symbols? Are they feared? Have they affected organizational structures? Have commuting and communication patterns changed? And so forth. Margrethe Olson's article in the same March 1983 *Communications of the ACM* surveys these questions.

Other than the necessity for tightly-coupled displays, are there unique architectural requirements for personal computers? For example, what sort of intelligence do we need to build into peripherals to support the operational convenience and world view required by the casual user? We have the opportunity to design very intelligent peripherals (VIPs). Cygnet

Technology's programmable telephone controller and the Ungerman-Bass Ethernet controller (which handles low-level protocols and manages linked lists of I/O buffers in memory) are early steps in this direction. If every peripheral is to contain a 16-bit CPU with a megabyte address space and read/write memory, what should it look like?

That's a timid question on VIP architecture. The Japanese Fifth Generation Project [see BOOK REVIEWS in this volume] aims to produce a personal computer that will execute Prolog as its machine language, incorporating a backend database machine and a frontend for continuous voice and image input and output. In three years the Japanese hope to have an interim workstation running, executing one million logical inferences per second using a database of tens of thousands of 1K-byte objects (vectors of attribute values). When the prototype is debugged, they plan to implement the production models using ten-million-transistor chips. While the project may fall short of its goals, the Japanese are certainly interested in VIPs.

We need to develop operating systems that are unique to personal computers and suitable for casual users. The high-bandwidth displays require operating systems support for graphic I/O, callable text editors, interfaces for pointing devices, menu-generation and selection components, etc. Moving the operator interface to the operating system makes programming easier and also facilitates uniformity across programs.

Moving the user interface to the operating system will help, but it is not enough. We need to agree upon interface standards. Today, everyone in the U.S. knows that to use the telephone, you input a variable-length string of digits by pushing buttons or turning a dial and then speak into the receiver end nearest the cord. It wasn't always that way. My guess is that one day there will be a standard way to edit text or to connect to an electronic mail system, then compose and send a letter. We should be trying to shape those "application-level" standards. Intermediate format standards or intelligent filters are also needed for moving data between programs.

If personal computers do become pervasive, we had better take computer literacy more seriously. What should we be teaching? The answer probably won't be found in the catalog of a typical adult-education program because it is too difficult for the beginner to do anything useful with simple tools like Basic interpreters. Games, word-processing programs, spreadsheet processors, LOGO, Smalltalk, and expert systems are better starting places for thinking about the design of computer-literacy courses. We can now give the beginner three million transistors to learn with, and we should also provide a few hundred labor-years of software development.

How about investigating the human factors issues with interactive programs that are often used by people with little or no computer experience? Where do people make mistakes? Which operations are difficult to learn? Which features are frequently used, and which seldom? We have very little empirical data along these lines. For instance, when you use a word-processing editor, do you prefer that it overwrite old characters when you type something, or do you leave it in insert mode? Which is best for beginners? For experts? We should be instrumenting programs and studying users. Just as we gather statistics on I/O errors or as Nielsen gathers statistics on television viewing, we could distribute systems that record application and command usage. We could easily learn what was happening each time the "undo" key was pressed.

Should we be studying policy questions involving personal computers? Are they going to have a significant effect on the society? Some people rank the personal computer right up there with fire, agriculture, and moveable type. While I would not go that far, it will have some effect on our educational system and our communication and transportation infrastructure. As Senator Frank Lautenberg (D-NJ) pointed out in his maiden speech, there might be serious consequences of unequal access to personal computers by poor people and poor schools.

Even those who agree that personal computers are unique have to admit that they look an awful lot like the mainframe and minicomputers of the past. As I pointed out in my last column, most PC development to date has been a replay of the development of earlier computers; and a systematic perusal of mainframe applications and architectures should be made, with an eye toward technology transfer to personal computers. We should also be developing tools and standards to facilitate that transfer.

I've listed a few of the reasons why I think there is such a thing as personal computers, and have suggested a few questions to ask about them. I'd like to hear your comments on both subjects, particularly the second—what do you think the research issues are in the field of personal computing? You can write to me at 10726 Ester Avenue, Los Angeles, CA 90064.

Regardless of what the important questions turn out to be, I have a strong feeling that personal computers will democratize computer science research. I served my programming apprenticeship working on a multiprocessor operating system, a project requiring millions of dollars' worth of equipment. Today, any small university, or even a high school, could experiment with multiprocessor systems using only a personal computer and a wire-wrap tool. Take a look at the *Proceedings of the 1983 ACM Conference on Personal and Small Computers* for some examples of research being conducted at places like North Dakota State University, as well as at Bell Labs and IBM!

The Computer Press

Specialization in the Computer Press
Narrow specializations; do-it-yourself publishing; programs to the people.

ANNE A. ARMSTRONG

The 1980s are shaping up as the age of specialization in the computer press. The old adage about a specialist being a person who knows more and more about less and less is beginning to apply to many periodicals that cover some aspect of the computer industry.

Most early publications—such as *Byte, Computerworld, Datamation,* and *Electronic News*—cut horizontally across a broad topic area. As the industry grew and it became more difficult to cover everything, publishers tried to refine their focus and look for an application area that would set each publication apart from the competition. In this general category are such publications as *Business Software, Computer Graphics World, Family Computing,* and *MIS Week*. And finally the specialization increased until there was a whole shelf of magazines devoted to individual microcomputers—*A +, inCider, MacWorld, AmigaWorld,* and a host of PC pubs such as *PC Magazine, PC Week,* and *PC World*.

Unfortunately, publishers quickly found out that magazines devoted to a single computer could succeed only if the computer succeeded. The most visible proof of that theory was the fate of the three magazines devoted to IBM's PC*jr*. Announced even before the product was introduced, none outlasted the announcement that IBM was discontinuing its computer for the home.

ANNE ARMSTRONG, a graduate of Vanderbilt University and Johns Hopkins, has written about science and technology for more than fifteen years, focusing especially on computer and information technology for the trade press. She has edited *Information World*, the *Bulletin of the American Society for Information Science*, and *MicroSoftware Today*, and is currently managing editor of *CD Data Report*. Ms. Armstrong is also president of Langley Publications, Inc., a small publishing firm that specializes in optical storage technologies.

This is an editor-truncated version of a longer column that appeared in ABACUS, Volume 3, Number 4, Summer 1986.

Times have been hard in the world of computer magazines. *Communication Trends* reported that fifty computer magazines died in 1985 for lack of advertising revenues. Publishers have again been casting around, looking for another formula that will point the way to new successes.

One solution that several different publications are trying is a geographical limitation—a sort of city computer magazine. The Boston Computer Society publishes a bimonthly magazine for its members, the vast majority of whom live in the greater Boston area. The price of *Computer Update* is included in the society's $28 membership fee.

That magazine relies heavily on volunteer submissions by members—which in some cases might be the kiss of death for a publication, but BCS's membership roster reads like a who's who of the microcomputer world: Stewart Alsop, Dan Bricklin, Mitch Kapor, and Steve Wozniak. Although *Computer Update*'s columns and general features are not limited to Boston subject matter, the city and its computer society provide the common thread that runs throughout the publication.

San Francisco's *Computer Currents,* which may be the best bargain around, takes a similar approach by concentrating on a specific location. The concentration of high-technology companies and personalities in the Bay area saves the biweekly tabloid from seeming too parochial. Distributed free in that area, *Computer Currents* is also available by mail subscription at $40 per year for first-class mail delivery, or $18 for bulk rate. (Center Publications, 2550 9th Street, Berkeley, CA 94710.)

What that buys is a collection of contributions from some of the best columnists in the business, a couple of features, and ads. Although each issue seems to feature an interview with a big name in the computer industry, the part of the paper I like best is the columns. Regulars include John Dvorak, Stewart Alsop, Wendy Woods, Steve Rosenthal, and others on a rotating basis. George Morrow, president of Morrow Computers, was a recent contributor.

Each issue is loaded with opinion and some inside news. It's quirky and full of personality—almost like an on-line bulletin board that has found its way into print.

Another solution to publishers' search for a new success formula has been to get even more specific. The magazine would not be devoted to a broad software application, but would concentrate on the software offerings of a single company. This concept was pioneered with a magazine devoted entirely to Lotus products. There have been dozens of books devoted to a particular piece of software, and some users' group newsletters with a narrow focus; there are even magazines that focus on a single company like Digital Equipment or IBM, but a monthly magazine that concentrates solely on a couple of software packages from one company is a new twist.

My first reaction to the idea of *Lotus* magazine was that it was nothing but a sales gimmick; the notion that subscribers were expected to pay for this offering seemed even more ludicrous to me. But Lotus brought in big guns to handle the new publication. Chris Morgan, previously an editor of *Byte* and recently a corporate communications executive at Lotus, was the first editor, and Dan McMillan, previously at McGraw-Hill and International Thomson's *Management Technology,* was named publisher.

What changed my mind about trying the magazine, however, was that Lotus offered to send the magazine free for six months to anyone who used Lotus products and would agree to take it. I couldn't resist. Now, I have to admit, I'm impressed. The graphics and design are gorgeous. Although some of the articles are too hard-sell for Lotus ware, there are enough general-interest pieces in the features and in the "ideas and trends" section that I think the magazine is worth the $18 a year Lotus is asking.

But there is an underlying issue with the publication—the idea of advertising masquerading as news or objective reporting. Lotus is presenting its promotional material in this form because the format lends a legitimacy to the message. Presumably, most of the readers already own a Lotus product, and Lotus may defend the idea as a form of added support. However, everyone recognizes an ad for what it is. I wonder if the content of *Lotus* magazine is perceived in the same way.

The "pretend-it's-news" approach is a very popular one in the computer press. Some public relations firms will write complete stories about a product or company they represent and then offer the piece for free to papers and magazines. *Fortune* and *Business Week* regularly run special sections written by market research firms on some segment of the industry. The sections are used to sell advertising; they frequently mention in the copy companies that have purchased ads, and they are designed to look as much like the rest of the magazine as possible.

The most blatant example of an ad pretending to be news that I have encountered recently was in the March 10 issue of *Computerworld*. On page 33, the first page of a section on microcomputers, in the same position where news stories appear in all other sections was the headline, "Oracle Unveils Productivity Tools for SLQ/RT on the IBM RT PC." The type chosen was the same headline type used by *Computerworld* for its news stories; hence the confusion. Only on close examination could a reader see the small notation, "Advertisement." Oracle wanted the reader to think the announcement was news reported by *Computerworld*. I think less of CW Communications for allowing it to run this way.

Computing and the Citizen

SDI: A Violation of Professional Responsibility

Star Wars has lost a key scientist, who claims that many involved are accepting research funds under false pretenses.

DAVID LORGE PARNAS

In May of 1985 I was asked by the Strategic Defense Initiative Organization, the group within the Office of the U.S. Secretary of Defense that is responsible for the "Star Wars" program, to serve on a $1000/day advisory panel, the SDIO Panel on Computing in Support of Battle Management. The panel was to make recommendations about a research and development program to solve the computational problems inherent in space-based defense systems.

Like President Reagan, I consider the use of nuclear weapons as a deterrent to be dangerous and immoral. If there is a way to make nuclear weapons "impotent and obsolete" and end the fear of such weapons, there is nothing I would rather work on. However, two months later I had resigned from the panel. I have since become an active opponent of the SDI. This article explains why I am opposed to the program.

My View of Professional Responsibility

My decision to resign from the panel was consistent with long-held views about the individual responsibility of a professional. I believe this re-

---

DAVID LORGE PARNAS is a professor of computing and information science at Queen's University in Kingston, Ontario. Previously he was Lansdowne Professor of Computer Science at the University of Victoria in British Columbia. Professor Parnas has been Principal Investigator of the Software Cost Reduction Project at the Naval Research Laboratory in Washington, DC, and has also taught at Carnegie-Mellon University, the University of Maryland, the Technisch Hochschule Darmstadt, and the University of North Carolina at Chapel Hill. Dr. Parnas is interested in all aspects of software engineering. His special interests include program semantics, language design, program organization, process structure, process synchronization, and precise abstract specifications. An avid cyclist, Dave is best remembered by many students for lecturing with his pants tucked into his socks.

Reprinted from ABACUS, Volume 4, Number 2, Winter 1987.

sponsibility goes beyond an obligation to satisfy the short-term demands of the immediate employer.

As a professional:

☐ I am responsible for my own actions and cannot rely on any external authority to make my decisions for me.
☐ I cannot ignore ethical and moral issues. I must devote some of my energy to deciding whether the task that I have been given is of benefit to society.
☐ I must make sure that I am solving the real problem, not simply providing short-term satisfaction to my supervisor.

Some have held that a professional is a "team player" and should never "blow the whistle" on his colleagues and employer. I disagree. As the Challenger incident demonstrates, such action is sometimes necessary. One's obligations as a professional precede other obligations. One must not enter into contracts that conflict with one's professional obligations.

My Views on Defense Work

Many opponents of the SDI oppose all military development. I am not one of them. I have been a consultant to the Department of Defense and other components of the defense industry since 1971. I am considered an expert on the organization of large software systems, and I lead the U.S. Navy's Software Cost Reduction Project at the Naval Research Laboratory. Although I have friends who argue that "people of conscience" should not work on weapons, I consider it vital that people with a strong sense of social responsibility continue to work within the military/industrial complex. I do not want to see that power completely in the hands of people who are *not* conscious of social responsibility.

My own views on military work are close to those of Albert Einstein. Einstein, who called himself a militant pacifist, at one time held the view that scientists should refuse to contribute to arms development. Later in his life he concluded that to hold to a "no arms" policy would be to place the world at the mercy of its worst enemies. Each country has a right to be protected from those who use force, or the threat of force, to impose their will on others. Force can morally be used only against those persons who are themselves using force. Weapons development should be limited to weapons that are suitable for that use. Neither the present arms spiral nor nuclear weapons are consistent with Einstein's principles. One of our greatest scientists, he knew that international security requires progress in political education, not weapons technology.

SDI Background

The Strategic Defense Initiative, popularly known as "Star Wars," was initiated by a 1983 presidential speech calling on scientists to free us from

the fear of nuclear weapons. President Reagan directed the Pentagon to search for a way to make nuclear strategic missiles impotent and obsolete. In response, the SDIO has embarked upon a project to develop a network of satellites carrying sensors, weapons, and computers to detect intercontinental ballistic missiles (ICBMs) and intercept them before they can do much damage. In addition to sponsoring work on the basic technologies of sensors and weapons, SDI has funded a number of Phase I "architecture studies," each of which proposes a basic design for the system. The best of these have been selected, and the contractors are now proceeding to "Phase II," a more detailed design.

My Early Doubts

As a scientist, I wondered whether technology offered us a way to meet these goals. My own research has centered on computer software, and I have used military software in some of my research. My experience with computer-controlled weapon systems led me to wonder whether any such system could meet the requirements set forth by President Reagan.

I also had doubts about a possible conflict of interest. I have a project within the U.S. Navy that could benefit from SDI funding. I suggested to the panel organizer that this conflict might disqualify me. He assured me that if I did not have such a conflict, they would not want me on the panel. He pointed out that the other panelists—employees of defense contractors and university professors dependent on DoD funds for their research—had similar conflicts. Readers should think about such conflicts the next time they hear of a panel of "distinguished experts."

My Work for the Panel

The first meeting increased my doubts. In spite of the high rate of pay, the meeting was poorly prepared; presentations were at a disturbingly unprofessional level. Technical terms were used without definition; numbers were used without supporting evidence. The participants appeared predisposed to discuss many of the interesting but tractable technical problems in space-based missile defense, while ignoring the basic problems and "big picture." Everyone seemed to have a pet project of their own that they thought should be funded.

At the end of the meeting we were asked to prepare position papers describing research problems that must be solved in order to build an effective and trustworthy shield against nuclear missiles. I spent the weeks after the meeting writing up those problems and trying to convince myself that SDIO-supported research could solve them. I failed. I could not convince myself that it would be possible to build a system that we could trust, nor that it would be useful to build a system we did not trust.

Why Trustworthiness Is Essential

If the U.S. does not trust SDI, it will not abandon deterrence and nuclear missiles. Even so, the U.S.S.R. could not assume that SDI would be completely ineffective. Seeing both a "shield" and missiles, it would feel impelled to improve its offensive forces in an effort to compensate for SDI. The U.S., not trusting its defense, would feel a need to build still more nuclear missiles to compensate for the increased Soviet strength. The arms race would speed up. Further, because NATO would be wasting an immense amount of effort on a system it couldn't trust, we would see a weakening of our relative strength. Instead of the safer world that President Reagan envisions, we would have a far more dangerous situation. Thus, the issue of our trust in the system is critical. Unless the shield is trustworthy, it will not benefit any country.

The Role of Computers

SDI discussions often ignore computers, focusing on new developments in sensors and weapons. However, the sensors will produce vast amounts of raw data that computers must process and analyze. Computers must detect missile firings, determine the source of the attack, and compute the attacking trajectories. Computers must discriminate between threatening warheads and mere decoys designed to confuse our defensive system. Computers will aim and fire the weapons. All the weapons and sensors will be useless if the computers do not function properly. Software is the glue that holds such systems together. If the software is not trustworthy, the system is not trustworthy.

The Limits of Software Technology

Computer specialists know that software is always the most troublesome component in systems that depend on computer control. Traditional engineering products can be verified by a combination of mathematical analysis, case analysis, and prolonged testing of the complete product under realistic operating conditions. Without such validation, we cannot trust the product. None of these validation methods works well for software. Mathematical proofs verify only abstractions of small programs in restricted languages. Testing and case analysis sufficient to ensure trustworthiness take too much time. As E.W. Dijkstra has said, "Testing can show the presence of bugs, never their absence."

The lack of validation methods explains why we cannot expect a real program to work properly the first time it is really used. This is confirmed by practical experience. We can build adequately reliable software systems, but they become reliable only after extensive use in the field. Although responsible developers perform many tests, including simulations, before releasing their software, serious problems always remain when the first customers use the product. The test designers overlook the same problems the software designers overlook. No experienced person trusts a software system before it has seen extensive use under actual operating conditions.

Why Software for SDI Is Especially Difficult

SDI is far more difficult than any software system we have ever attempted. Some of the reasons are listed here; a more complete discussion can be found in an article published in *American Scientist* (see reference list).

SDI software must be based on assumptions about target and decoy characteristics, and those characteristics are controlled by the attacker. We cannot rely upon our information about them. The dependence of any program on local assumptions is a rich source of effective countermeasures. Espionage could render the whole multibillion-dollar system worthless without our knowledge. It could show an attacker how to exploit the inevitable differences between the computer model on which the program is based and the real world.

The techniques used to provide high reliability in other systems are hard to apply for SDI. In space, the redundancy required for high reliability is unusually expensive. The dependence of SDI on communicating computers in satellites makes it unusually vulnerable. High reliability can be achieved only if the failures of individual components are statistically independent; for a system subject to coordinated attacks, that is not the case.

Overloading the system will always be a potent countermeasure, because any computer system will have a limited capacity, and even crude decoys would consume computer capacity. An overloaded system must either ignore some of the objects it should track, or fail completely. For SDI, either option is catastrophic.

Satellites will be in fixed orbits that will not allow the same one to track a missile from its launch and to destroy it. The responsibility for tracking a missile will transfer from one satellite to another. Because of noise caused by the battle and enemy interference, a satellite will require data from other satellites to assist in tracking and discrimination. The result is a distributed real-time database. For the shield to be effective, the data will have to be kept up-to-date and consistent in real time. This means that satellite clocks will have to be accurately synchronized. None of this can be done when the network's components and communication links are unreliable, and unreliability must be expected during a real battle in which an enemy would attack the network. Damaged stations are likely to inject inaccurate or false data into the database.

Realistic testing of the integrated hardware and software is impossible. Thorough testing would require "practice" nuclear wars, including attacks that partially damage the satellites. Our experience tells us that many potential problems would not be revealed by lesser measures such as component testing, simulations, or small-scale field tests.

Unlike other weapon systems, this one will offer us no opportunity to modify the software during or after its first battle. It must work the first time.

These properties are inherent in the problem, not some particular system design. As we will see below, they cannot be evaded by proposing a new system structure.

My Decision to Act

After reaching the conclusions described above, I solicited comments from other scientists and found none that disagreed with my technical conclusions. Instead, they told me that the program should be continued, not because it would free us from the fear of nuclear weapons, but because the research money would advance the state of computer science! I disagree with that statement, but I also consider it irrelevant. Taking money allocated for developing a shield against nuclear missiles, while knowing that such a shield was impossible, seemed like fraud to me. I did not want to participate, and submitted my resignation. Feeling that it would be unprofessional to resign without explanation, I submitted position papers to support my letter. I sent copies to a number of government officials and friends, but did not send them to the press until after they had been sent to reporters by others. They have since been widely published.

SDIO's Reaction

The SDIO's response to my resignation transformed my stand on SDI from a passive refusal to participate to an active opposition. Neither the SDIO nor the other panelists reacted with a serious and scientific discussion of the technical problems that I raised.

The first reaction came from one of the panel organizers. He asked me to reconsider, but not because he disagreed with my technical conclusions. He accepted my view that an effective shield was unlikely, but argued that the money was going to be spent and I should help to see it well spent. There was no further reaction from the SDIO until a *New York Times* reporter made some inquiries. Then, the only reaction I received was a telephone call demanding to know who had sent the material to the *Times*.

After the story broke, the statements made to the press seemed, to me, designed to mislead rather than inform the public. Examples are given below. When I observed that the SDIO was engaged in "damage control," rather than a serious consideration of my arguments, I felt that I should inform the public and its representatives of my own view. I want the public to understand that no trustworthy shield will result from the SDIO-sponsored work. I want them to understand that technology offers no magic that will eliminate the fear of nuclear weapons. I consider this part of my personal professional responsibility as a scientist and an educator.

Critical Issues

Democracy can only work if the public is accurately informed. Again, most of the statements made by SDIO supporters seem designed to mislead the public. For example, one SDIO scientist told the public that there could be 100,000 errors in the software and it would still work properly. Strictly speaking, this statement is true. If one picks one's errors very carefully, they won't matter much. However, a single error caused the complete failure of a Venus probe many years ago. I find it hard to believe that the SDIO spokesman was not aware of that.

Another panelist repeatedly told the press that there was no fundamental law of computer science that said the problem could not be solved. Again, strictly speaking, the statement is true, but it does not counter my arguments. I did not say that a correct program was impossible; I said that it was impossible that we could trust the program. It is not impossible that such a program would work the first time it was used; it is also not impossible that 10,000 monkeys would reproduce the works of Shakespeare if allowed to type for five years. Both are highly unlikely. However, we could tell when the monkeys had succeeded; there is no way that we could verify that the SDI software was adequate.

Another form of disinformation was the statement that I—and other SDI critics—were demanding perfection. Nowhere have I demanded perfection. To trust the software we merely need to know that the software is free of catastrophic flaws, flaws that could cause massive failure or that could be exploited by a sophisticated enemy. That is certainly easier to achieve than perfection, but there is no way to know when we have achieved it.

A common characteristic of all these statements is that they argue with statements other than the ones I published in my papers. In fact, in some cases SDIO officials dispute statements made by earlier panels or by other SDIO officials, rather than debating the points I made.

The "90%" Distraction

One of the most prevalent arguments in support of SDI suggests that if there are three layers, each 90% effective, the overall "leakage" would be less than 1% because the effectiveness multiplies. This argument is accepted by many people who do not have scientific training. However,

□ There is no basis for the 90% figure; an SDI official told me it was picked for purpose of illustration.
□ The argument assumes that the performance of each layer is independent of the others, when it is clear that there are actually many links.
□ It is not valid to rate the effectiveness of such systems by a single "percentage." Such statistics are only useful for describing a random process. Any space battle would be a battle between two skilled opponents. A simple percentage figure is no more valid for such systems than it is as a way of rating chess players. The performance of defensive systems depends on the opponent's tactics. Many defensive systems have been completely defeated by a sophisticated opponent who found an effective countermeasure.

The "Loose Coordination" Distraction

The most sophisticated response was made by the remaining members of SDIO's Panel on Computing in Support of Battle Management, which named itself the Eastport group, in December 1985. This group of SDI proponents wrote that the system structures proposed by the best Phase I contractors, those being elaborated in Phase II, would not work because the software could not be built or tested. They said that these "architectures" called for excessively tight coordination between the "battle stations"—excessive communication—and they proposed that new Phase I studies be started. However, they disputed my conclusions, arguing that the software difficulties could be overcome using "loose coordination."

The Eastport Report neither defines its terms nor describes the structure that it had in mind. Parts of the report imply that "loose coordination" can be achieved by reducing the communication between the stations. Later sections of the report discuss the need for extensive communication in the battle-station network, contradicting some statements in the earlier section. However, the essence of their argument is that SDI could be trustworthy if each battle station functioned autonomously, without depending on help from others.

Three claims can be made for such a design:

☐ It decomposes an excessively large program to a set of smaller ones, each one of which can be built and tested.
☐ Because the battle stations would be autonomous, a failure of some would allow the others to continue to function.
☐ Because of the independence, one could infer the behavior of the whole system from tests on individual battle stations.

The Eastport group's argument is based on four unstated assumptions:

1. Battle stations do not need data from other satellites to perform their basic functions.
2. An individual battle station is a small software project that will not run into the software difficulties described above.
3. The only interaction between the stations is by explicit communication. This assumption is needed to conclude that test results about a single station allow one to infer the behavior of the complete system.
4. A collection of communicating systems differs in fundamental ways from a single system.

All of these assumptions are false!

1. The data from other satellites is essential for accurate tracking, and for discriminating between warheads and decoys in the presence of noise.
2. Each battle station has to perform all of the functions of the whole system. The original arguments apply to it. Each one is unlikely to work, impossible to test in actual operating conditions, and consequently impossible to trust. Far easier projects have failed.
3. Battle stations interact through weapons and sensors as well as through their shared targets. The weapons might affect the data produced by the sensors. For example, destruction of a single warhead or decoy might produce noise that makes tracking of other objects impossible. If we got a single station working perfectly in isolation, it might fail completely when operating near others. The failure of one station might cause others to fail because of overload. Only a real battle would give us confidence that such interactions would not occur.
4. A collection of communicating programs is mathematically equivalent to a single program. In practice, distribution makes the problem harder, not easier.

Restricting the communication between the satellites does not solve the problem. There is still no way to know the effectiveness of the system, and it would not be trusted. Further, the restrictions on communication are likely to reduce the effectiveness of the system. I assume that this is why none of the Phase I contractors chose such an approach.

The first claim in the list is appealing, and reminiscent of arguments made in the '60s and '70s about modular programming. Unfortunately, experience has shown that modular programming is an effective technique for making errors easier to correct, not for eliminating errors. Modular programming does not solve the problems described earlier in this paper. None of my arguments was based on an assumption of tight coupling; some of the arguments do assume that there will be data passed from one satellite to another. The Eastport Report, like earlier reports, supports that assumption.

The Eastport group is correct when it says that designs calling for extensive data communication between the battle stations are unlikely to work. However, the Phase I contractors were also right when they assumed that without such communication the system could not be effective.

Redefining the Problem

The issue of SDI software was debated in March 1986 at an IEEE computer conference. While two of us argued that SDI could not be trusted, the two SDI supporters argued that it did not matter. Rather than argue the computer-science issues, they tried to use strategic arguments to say that a shield need not be considered trustworthy. One of them argued, most eloquently, that the president's "impotent and obsolete" terminology was technical nonsense. He suggested that we ignore what "the President's speechwriters" had to say and look at what was actually feasible. Others argue that increased uncertainty is a good thing—quite a contrast to President Reagan's promise of increased security.

In fact, the ultimate response of the computer scientists working on SDI is to redefine the problem in such a way that there is a trivial solution and improvement is always possible. Such a problem is the ideal project for government sponsorship. The contractor can always show both progress and the need for further work. Contracts will be renewed indefinitely!

Those working on the project often disparage statements made by the president and his most vocal supporters, stating that SDIO scientists and officials are not responsible for such statements. However, the general public remains unaware of their position, and believes that the president's goals are the goals of those who are doing the scientific work.

Broader Questions

Is SDIO-Sponsored Work of Good Quality?

Although the Eastport panel were unequivocally supportive of continuing SDI, their criticisms of the Phase I studies were quite harsh. They assert that those studies, costing a million dollars each, overlooked elementary problems that were discussed in earlier studies. If the Eastport group is correct, the SDIO contractors and the SDIO evaluators must be considered incompetent. If the Eastport group's criticisms were unjustified, or if their alternative is unworkable, *their* competence must be questioned.

Although I do not have access to much of the SDIO-sponsored work in my field, I have had a chance to study some of it. What I have seen makes big promises, but is of low quality. Because it has bypassed the usual scientific review processes, it overstates its accomplishments and makes no real scientific contribution.

Do Those Who Take SDIO Funds Really Disagree with Me?

I have discussed my views with many who work on SDIO-funded projects. Few of them disagree with my technical conclusions. In fact, since the story became public, two SDIO contractors and two DoD agencies have sought my advice. My position on this subject has not made them doubt my competence.

Those who accept SDIO money give a variety of excuses. "The money is going to be spent anyway; shouldn't we use it well?" "We can use the money to solve other problems." "The money will be good for computer science."

I have also discussed the problem with scientists at the Los Alamos and Sandia National Laboratories. Here, too, I found no substantive disagreement with my analysis. Instead, I was told that the project offered lots of challenging problems for physicists.

In November 1985, I read in *Der Speigel* an interview with a leading German supporter of Star Wars. He made it clear that he thought of SDI as a way of injecting funds into high technology and not as a military project. He even said that he would probably be opposed to participation in any deployment should the project come to fruition.

The Blind Led by Those with Their Eyes Shut

My years as a consultant in the defense field have shown me that unprofessional behavior is common. When consulting, I often find people doing something foolish. Knowing that the person involved is quite competent, I may say something like, "You know that's not the right way to do that." "Of course," is the response, "but this is what the customer asked for." "Is your customer a computer scientist? Does he know what he is asking?" ask I. "No" is the simple reply. "Why don't you tell him?" elicits the response: "At XYZ Corporation, we don't tell our customers that what they want is wrong. We get contracts."

That may be a businesslike attitude, but it is not a professional one. It misleads the government into wasting taxpayers' money.

The Role of Academic Institutions

Traditionally, universities provide tenure and academic freedom so that faculty members can speak out on issues such as these. Many have done just that. Unfortunately, at U.S. universities there are institutional pressures in favor of accepting research funds from any source. A researcher's ability to attract funds is taken as a measure of his ability.

The president of a major university in the U.S. recently explained his acceptance of a DoD institute on campus by saying, "As a practical matter, it is important to realize that the Department of Defense is a major administrator of research funds. In fact, the department has more research funds at its disposal than any other organization in the country. . . . Increases in research funding in significant amounts can be received only on the basis of defense-related appropriations."

Should We Pursue SDI for Other Reasons?

I consider such rationalizations to be both unprofessional and dangerous. SDI endangers the safety of the world. By working on SDI, these scientists allow themselves to be counted among those who believe that the program can succeed. If they are truly professionals, they must make it very clear that an effective shield is unlikely, and a trustworthy one impossible. The issue of more money for high technology should be debated without the smoke screen of SDI. I can think of no research that is so important as to justify pretending that an ABM system can bring security to populations. Good research stands on its own merits; poor research must masquerade as something else.

I believe in research; I believe that technology can improve our world in many ways. I also agree with Professor Janusz Makowski of the Technion Institute, who wrote in the *Jerusalem Post,* "Overfunded research is like heroin, it leads to addiction, weakens the mind, and leads to prostitution." Many research fields in the U.S. are now clearly overfunded, largely because of DoD agencies. I believe we are witnessing the proof of Professor Makowski's statement.

My Advice on Participation in Defense Projects

I believe that it's quite appropriate for professionals to devote their energies to making the people of their land more secure. In contrast, it is not professional to accept employment doing "military" things that do not advance the legitimate defense interests of that country. If the project would not be effective, or if, in one's opinion, it goes beyond the legitimate defense needs of the country, a professional should not participate. Too many do not ask such questions. They ask only how they can get another contract.

It is a truism that if each of us lives as though what we do does matter, the world will be a far better place than it is now is. The cause of many serious problems in our world is that many of us act as if our actions do not matter. Our streets are littered, our environment polluted, and children neglected because we underestimate our individual responsibility.

The arguments given to me for continuation of the SDI program are examples of such thinking. "The government has decided; we cannot change it." "The money will be spent; all you can do is make good use of it." "The system will be built; you cannot change that." "Your resignation will not stop the program."

It is true, my decision not to toss trash on the ground will not eliminate litter. However, if we are to eliminate litter, I must decide not to toss trash on the ground. We all make a difference.

Similarly, my decision not to participate in SDI will not stop this misguided program. However, if everyone who knows that the program will not lead to a trustworthy shield against nuclear weapons refuses to participate, there will be no program. Every individual's decision is important.

It is not necessary for computer scientists to take a political position; they need only be true to their professional responsibilities. If the public were aware of the technical facts, if they knew how unlikely it is that such a shield would be effective, public support would evaporate. We do not need to tell the public not to build SDI. We only need to help them understand why it will never be an effective and trustworthy shield.

References

Einstein, Albert, and Freud, Sigmund. *Warum Krieg?* Zürich: Diogenes Verlag, 1972.

Parnas, D.L. "Software Aspects of Strategic Defense Systems." *American Scientist,* September-October 1985: 432–40. Also published in German in Kursbuch 83, *Krieg und Frieden—Streit um SDI,* by Kursbuch/Rotbuch Verlag, March 1986; and in Dutch in *Informatie,* Nr. 3, March 1986: 175–86.

Parnas, D.L. "On the Criteria to Be Used in Decomposing Systems into Modules." *Communications of the ACM* **15,** 12 (1972): 1053–8.

Eastport Group. "Summer Study 1985." A Report to the Director—Strategic Defense Initiative Organization, December 1985.

"Wer kuscht, hat keine Chance," *Der Speigel,* Nr. 47, 18 November 1985.

Reports from Correspondents

In keeping with the publisher's and editor's desire to have an international magazine, each ABACUS issue has reports from foreign correspondents concerned with computing outside the United States. In keeping with my desire to emulate *The New Yorker,* and as illustrated in two of the following samples, such reports are not always from overseas.

Report from Europe

France's Information Needs: Reality or Alibi?*

A Gallic approach to the information society; the success of French videotex.

REX MALIK

It is the annual gathering of some of the world's most sophisticated data shufflers—clever and demanding users. It is the ESOMAR (European Society for Opinion and Marketing Research) Congress, the nearest thing the intellectually respectable end of the industry has to a worldwide annual meeting. I go almost every year, but was particularly sure to attend the last one, as my wife was chairman of the program committee. (*Chairman*, will you note: she will have no truck with *chairperson*. Now that she is getting there, she says, they are not going to start changing the titles on her.)

It is 2 A.M. in the $6-a-Scotch bar of the conference headquarters hotel, the Nassauer Hof in Wiesbaden, and a conference keynote speaker is playing the piano. Jazz piano. Brilliantly. Almost sickeningly so.

The regular pianist is looking suitably impressed and wants to know if he is a professional. No, I say. I refrain from adding that he is another of those formidably intellectual French senior civil servants, brought up in the school of "if it is worth doing at all, it is worth doing well."

His name is Jean Salmona, best known internationally as the chairman of the Data for Development International Organization. He is also Director General of CESIA (Centre d'Etudes des Systems d'Information des

---

REX MALIK, probably the first European journalist to concentrate on computing, has been writing about that subject and related issues since 1956. Besides being the author of a well-known book, *And Tomorrow . . . The World? Inside IBM*, he is currently active as: Contributing Editor of *Intermedia,* the journal of the International Institute of Communications; London and Roving Correspondent for the French computing-industry paper *01 Informatique*; contributor/columnist for the leading Australian newspaper, The Australian, and columnist of the UK industry paper *Computer News*. He also works extensively for the British Broadcasting Corporation (BBC) and Independent Television.

*This is a truncated version of the original article that appeared in ABACUS, Volume 3, Number 3, Spring 1986.

Administrations), a unique and uniquely French consultancy, in that it has only one source of funds and one client—the French state.

CESIA, then, is well plugged into the power structure. Indeed the committee which sets its operational direction, determining what Salmona and his staff will look at and think about, is currently chaired by France's Prime Minister, Laurent Fabius. This alone would indicate that CESIA is not just another consultancy. Of course, it does the usual sorts of studies concerned with the near future, the experiments and trials dealing with what-do-we-do-next, but it also engages in much more theoretical work.

That you might expect; it is within the French tradition. A major project in France will typically start with a discussion of philosophy in relationship to whatever it may be. Then will follow structural analysis, and so on. Eventually someone will build something.

It is this approach that makes the French often seem so infuriating, particularly to American and British outsiders, brought up as they are in a different tradition. With them, it is more normal to build something first and then, when it is "out there," start worrying (or not) about what has been done and whether it should have been done in the first place.

Both systems have their virtues—and their drawbacks. Example: France is the only country to have created a nuclear power program of sufficient size that were there to be a sudden oil crisis or famine, France could still generate enough electricity to keep society going. America, by contrast, is almost disinvesting in nuclear power. The first situation is the result of intellectual theorizing and analysis prior to the event; the second results from the same processes occurring after.

The French approach, then, is to start by creating a master plan, during which process you set out to convince the actors who will take part that they should behave accordingly. It has been the same with computing, and this has led to the French failures and successes.

The French attitude, by which one means the attitude of those in power, is to recognize what copious experience and literature worldwide has shown: it would be foolish to say that the use of computer power changes the way organizations and companies act and behave—what they can do, how they operate—and then to deny that similar changes will occur in—and to—government. If the technology is as powerful as the literate end of the computing community believes, then obviously it will have structural effects across the board. But are the societal and governmental repercussions predictable?

Some obviously are. Jean Salmona is in heavy demand as a speaker, and naturally has standard bits in his speeches. One of them is that everywhere the costs of public administration are mounting, and everywhere they need to be reduced. So far, unexceptional.

The call on society's funds is heavy, and the state has better things to do with them than spend them on routine administration, particularly when there are more economical methods of achieving the same ends. But how is it to be done?

Currently going up in France is the world's largest videotex system, if you can call something which, by the end of the '80s, will probably have as many as ten million terminals accessing it a *system*. And why not? We talk of the "telephone system," and that is already far larger. Indeed, the French videotex system is a subset within it.*

Naturally, this will create a new infrastructure, new means for the citizen and administration to communicate and deal with each other. It follows that one must mount trials and experiments. This is now almost routine.

One of those trials, held in Marseilles so that it would deal with real, relatively unsophisticated nonmetropolitan users, involved 200 small and medium-sized companies, the sort without complex office structures, hierarchies, and routines. They were given access to an experimental interactive videotex module and terminals. The experimental system allowed them to enter those boring regular returns—taxes, salaries, insurance—which companies everywhere have to make on a routine and frequent basis.

Now under the traditional administrative paperwork system of the state, or even the system with batch-computer power grafted on, the error rate almost everywhere is high. In France, it is 30%. That error rate makes a substantial contribution to the employment levels of the modern state's administrative machine, again almost everywhere.

The Marseilles experimental trials used a system with system-led dialogues and inbuilt error-checking routines; it went so far as to check the sums and products. The result was that the error rate went down to *zero*. Salmona smiles as he says that. A substantial part of his career, after all, has been in the administration, and he can see some of the implications. For instance, almost all form-filling exercises could be handled on a similar basis, as long as the type of answer can be prior-specified and the answers are nonfuzzy.

But this is not the only step you can take. If you list out those routine reports that companies and businesses make every year to different ministries—central, local, and governmental agencies of all kinds—it turns out that most of them contain much of the same data. If anyone has done a full check, your reporter has not been able to discover it. However, the figures brandished about in Europe are that 80% of the data sought in any return either have already been submitted to some other agency, or will be. The suspicion is that it is much the same everywhere—France included.

The French solution, one being very slowly implemented, is first to organize a common feed to the agencies of the state so that they can share the data they are allowed to share (the French have quite tough regulations about data-sharing between ministries). Ministries can then take off the part of the return they need for their own approved purposes; the volume

---

*For a detailed discussion of videotex, see Jan Gecsei's article in Volume 3, Number 1 (Fall, 1985) issue.

French Videotex:

Other Conferences, Other Places, Later Times

Last September, Serge Chambaud, Director of *Direction des Bibliotheque des Musees et de L'information Scientifique et Technique,* spoke to the international information-handling professions conference Info '85 in Bournemouth, England. He produced data showing that by mid-summer there were twelve million transactions a month on the French national videotex system, that traffic was increasing at the rate of 17% a month, and that the number of new information-supplier businesses offering services was growing at the rate of two a day.

At the end of October, another key figure in French videotex circles, Georges Nahon, Director of Intelmatique, was reporting to the On-Line Videotex International Conference in Amsterdam in terms that were sometimes bullish, sometimes gleeful, sometimes arrogant, but always confident. There were now four Minitel terminals on offer, he said, and a fifth (ASCII-transparent, with 40/80-column options and local intelligence) would be available by next summer. The basic terminal was now available in quantity for third-party resale at around $250 each. By contrast, U.S. NALPS-standard terminals were not available in the shops at much below $900 each.

Nahon thought that the long four-year period needed to build up production had been worth it. The strategy chosen had worked so far, and gave every indication of continuing to do so. He pointed out that France had invested sums similar to those put in by West Germany for its service, yet had produced dramatically different results.

He reported that 140,000 Minitel terminals were out on lease and generating revenues of $1.5 million a month. The lease base alone was four times the number of terminals for the entire West German service. at that time.

He was speaking on the day on which it was claimed the millionth Minitel terminal had gone into service (a contrived coincidence, no doubt, if still accurate.)

He wished to point out that far from those terminals being free, paid for out of French state revenues, their funding in fact had been raised largely from commercial borrowings and telecommunications revenues. It had not come from government, and it was not free of interest charges.

In addition, the national videotex service was not, as it was generally thought abroad, a free service. True, there was a free minimum connection time to the telephone directory, but everything else was charged for at rates which varied from just under $3 an hour (for the most popular databases) to as much as $7 an hour. There were also some "closed user groups" (CUGs) charging up to $60 an hour. The average length of a videotex call was 7.7. minutes, and the traffic per Minitel terminal was at the level of 78 minutes a month.

Nahon could afford to be arrogant. The service was beginning to generate serious revenues, which was more than anyone else's had done so far. For years other suppliers had set out to rubbish the French approach. Now it looked as if the French had been right after all. When you read his remarks, you sense that his inward response to attacks is "Don't get mad, get even!" He was doing so, and with force. It did not exactly make him popular, but then that has never stopped a Frenchman yet.

of returns is decreased, and those who have to make them find their administrative load reduced. To do this, of course, you have to organize interagency tape transfer and interministry data transmission, as well as the electronic infrastructure, to enable society to communicate with the administration in machine-readable form.

Meanwhile, you have to reorganize the machinery of the state in other ways. This is where the French have been clever. You need equipment; you need training; but you also need to energize the system. The best way of doing this is to energize the major administrative actor, the department with the most power within and over the system, the one that will say, "If we have to change, all of you will change."

The most powerful arm of the French state is the Ministry of Finance and Economics, the equivalent of the Treasury elsewhere. The French joke has it that the country only has one ministry and this is it, and all the really powerful civil servants have served there at some time or are currently doing so.

That Ministry has been on the same historic site in the Louvre since prior to the Revolution. It is being moved to a totally new building, designed around electronic systems, computer power, local area networks, word processing, intelligent work stations, even a new archiving system in which all data will be held on videodiscs.

We turn to the subject of training. Shortly before Salmona spoke, it was announced that all of France's civil servants will eventually have some form of computing training. The top 1500 will be trained (or, as they prefer to put it at that level, "sensitized") within the next year; the next level down, middle-management-equivalent, within the next two; and the rest afterwards, though it is "the rest" who have had most of the training so far. Within ten years, the wider plan is to install over 600,000 intelligent workstations in the Civil Service, one for every two of France's 1,250,000 civil servants.

All this is short- to medium-term: an administrative restructuring of the state, and (as Salmona points out) the first such restructuring. But you have to think about the long term—what sort of society and administrative system is evolving out there—and for that you really have to do some very serious, very dry structural analysis.

If we are bound for the "Information Society," whatever that may be, does all information share the same characteristics, and is it used by all "actors" in a society in the same way?

Much of the Salmona speech was concerned with a first-stage analysis, in which he distinguished among three categories of information: Nonformalized, formalized active, and formalized passive (see the chart on the next page). The first category (*nonformalized* information) includes one's thoughts, which may have no rational basis at all—the input and output of conversations and meetings—all the material that does not get put down anywhere, at least not in a form useable by others.

Formalized active information is the data and information sent and received to influence action; it is the day-to-day stuff of organizations, the material of transaction processing. *Formalized passive* information includes the public record, the literature of particular fields, the output of the media which ends up in databases, the agreed laws, rules, and regulations of society. That material provides the bedrock on which the other categories of information rest.

It is of course much deeper and more complex than this. Nevertheless, the illustration gives a broad indication of the situation as Salmona sees it existing today in an average developed country.

But does the permeation of society by computing and communications bring about changes? His answer is yes, an answer that arises not from wishful thinking but analysis. Though there is a large potential market for the stuff of computing—formalized (passive and active) information—among individuals and small or medium enterprises, it is the enterprises that gain most from the introduction of widely disseminated, electronically based and carried information, for they are the ones more likely to come to decisions on its basis.

Conclusion: The power of the organized group, economic or otherwise, is going to be enhanced. What is more, he implies, as new generations, familiar with the tools, come increasingly to power within the sphere of local administration, traditionally a place of nonformalized political bargaining, central government is going to find its life made harder.

He asks tough questions, and gives equally tough if still tentative answers, picking the interesting examples. One has to remember, after all, that he is a skeptical (some might say cynical) senior French civil servant.

Do we really disclose the information that has led to a specific action? Do not be in a hurry to answer yes. Consider how often politicians—and others—will try to justify their actions on the basis of information which is not really the information that motivated those actions at all. Says Salmona:

The objective of a politician's actions is to maximize the probability of reelection; his action is therefore mainly based on data related to the opinion of his electorate, whereas he justifies his actions as being based on totally different information, this disclosure itself aimed at increasing his popularity.

Remember, he has met and dealt with a lot of politicians.

But what of the dynamic of the technology as it is introduced, and the consequent inability to forecast accurately all the major changes that will occur let alone the minor ones? He is willing to face that, too, and instances the way in which videotex is developing in France—not necessarily as might have been expected.

He says bluntly that the initial decision to provide all telephone users with videotex terminals and access to the system was technocratic, the view then taken being that in making this radical shift, supply and demand would follow—that is, if the initial decision was right.

It is turning out that way, creating surprises as it does so. By July, the French PTT, the telecommunications supplier, had given away more than 900,000 videotex terminals (actually they are subsumed in the telephone rental). There would be between two and three million installed within a few months.

Though he did not use the term, Salmona implied that a critical mass had now been achieved, and that some of the results were unexpected.

For a start, most of the database access expectations and forecasts were beginning to look on the low side. By July, usage was running at a million hours of database access a month. The initial and key database, the telephone directory, the excuse to set up the system in the first place, was pulling in 300,000 hours of access a month. So where was the other 700,000? Well, there were now well over a thousand service and information suppliers clustering around the system. (See the panel on French videotex.)

Surprises? The French newspaper *Le Liberation* set out earlier this year to offer a messaging service, though by almost everyone else's standards France still has a good postal system. They estimated and planned on a demand averaging 2500 hours a month for the short-term future, yet by summer the system was running at 2500 hours a day. It is still growing.

(All this is pleasing to your correspondent, who some years ago coauthored a book on the future of what was then known as *viewdata* but now is called *videotex*. In this book, it was argued that the messaging market

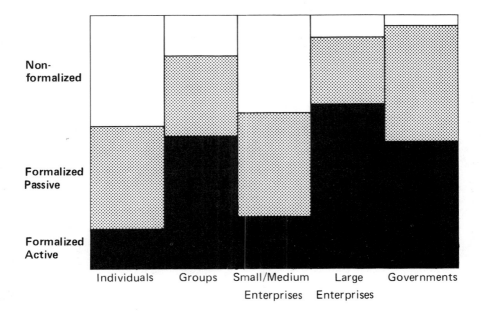

could well end up as large as the DB access market. The world rapidly became full of executives saying that we had it wrong.)

To be sure, the surprises have not all been of the pleasantly unexpected success type. There came a point during the summer—beautifully timed, as the country was all either at the beach or heading there—when Transpac (the packet-switched French national digital transmission network through which access to many such services is provided) almost had to be closed down and access restricted.

Transpac is the backbone of data transmission in France, and everybody uses it: videotex apart, more than 50,000 systems (and these are old figures) route their traffic through Transpac, including much of the French banking and financial system. They were beginning to complain that they just could not get through.

The problem was not channel capacity, it was ports. Transpac was initially devised with pre-videotex assumptions in mind, for more conventional network usage and system-to-system traffic. Transpac went down for a very simple reason. Those Minitels, the videotex terminals, have a "last-number redial" button. You cannot get through? Then redial by pressing one button. What clogged the system was not successful calls but unsuccessful calls, which led users to try again, sometimes hundreds of times. This was the classic business of port contention, but on a new and massive scale.

But surely, you will say, those callers did not hang on, listening into the phone handset for the *engaged* signal time after time. Of course not: Minitels are screenbased, and the screen is where the *engaged* message shows up. Which means that as a user, you will probably try many more times.

As Jean Salmona has said, we may not yet know by how much, but we do know that the information society *is* different.

Report from the Pacific

Tokyo: Fifth-Generation Reasoning*

This final installment of our Pacific Diary contains impressions of the computer scene in Japan.

REX MALIK

As a frequent visitor to Japan, observation leads me to believe that the country, its people, its organization, its habits are all much more complex than any book I have ever read or could write.

Consider the following proposition: The strengths and weaknesses of Japan do not come from innate character, but from historically derived social habit, custom, and organization (not to mention linguistic experience; see Neil Friedman's article on Japanese word processing, in this volume. Suppose, then, that one starts to change these. . . .

Senior hardware designers in the Japanese computer industry regard almost with awe Robb Wilmot, the chairman and former managing director of British computer manufacturer ICL, and not simply because he turned ICL around. He is a circuit designer of some repute, and in the very area where Japanese reputation and strengths are at their greatest.

The ICL/Fujitsu deal, in which the latter builds some ICL hardware to ICL design, has run surprisingly smoothly. What problems there are have often been at the level of marrying design to production, and these, when serious, are settled at joint meetings. The awe of Wilmot stems from his ability to sit, discuss the problem, and then redesign on the fly, on the spot. What is more, according to some who have sat in on these meetings, he is not simply right, he can usually arrive at an immediately practical—more often than not, optimum—solution.

Japanese engineers, using traditional Japanese methods of discussion, breaking a problem down and then seeking a consensus, find it difficult to improve his solutions more than marginally. The ability to shuffle elements and components around quickly to achieve a desired result is difficult to manage in Japan. What Wilmot does by redesigning in this way

*This is an editor-shortened version of the original article in ABACUS, Volume 3, Number 2, Winter 1986.

is to cut through a set of organizational processes built into the culture of the large Japanese corporation.

He does not seek opinions or search for consensus; he just does it. The problems this creates for Japanese are manifold. Managing directors at this level in Japan are not supposed to be technologically up to the speed to do what Wilmot does. They are expected to have left all that behind them, and now to be primarily concerned with leadership and the "higher strategy." To add to the Japanese confusion, he was managing director of ICL in his younger thirties, and does not look much older now. That, too, they are not prepared for. All the popular books on Japan are right in one respect: promotion in Japan comes with seniority and age. The Japanese solution, then, is to regard Wilmot as an eccentric, a genius, which promptly places him into a psychological containable framework.

Now contrast this with ICOT—Japan's Institute for New-Generation Computer Technology—where the joke has long been that if you look as if you can drive, you are probably too old. Apart from a central core of elderly team leaders and specialists, well into their thirties, the rest are mainly very young recent graduates, on two- or three-year secondments from the dozen or so corporations involved. Even so, the talent in Kazuhiro Fuchi's Fifth-Generation development team is the best talent those corporations and organizations could provide. Because some are the best, most are the best: corporate pride sees to that.

A substantial number of those skilled people, though not the key individuals, are now returning to their organizations. Many have already gone. This is a good way of ensuring that there is a rapid dissemination of results. And since, because of the nature of the project, there is fierce competition now to get into ICOT, onto a team which will be seventy-five strong by the year's end, the departing members can be replaced with other highly-qualified young candidates. Yet there are many hints that those who are leaving do not wish to go, for they will no longer have the free exchange of views, the wide-ranging discussion and arguments, the ability to offer input on anything when they have something to contribute, which are the norm at ICOT.

These are the norm by design. Japanese observation of American and European R&D organizational structures, looser and more generalized, had much to do with the way in which ICOT in turn was set up and organized—an attempt not so much to copy as to see whether differing structures played a role in invention. Of Japan's ability to innovate there is no doubt; but is invention different?

One of the results, I suspect, was not expected, and that is the loyalty transfer noted above. This will make many of the Japanese corporations even more suspicious of ICOT than they already are. For the ICOT "norm" contrasts with the much more tightly focused hard-project-bound, team-set-against-team system which is the corporate life norm.

Kazuhiro Fuchi (standing) is Director of Research at ICOT, Japan's Institute for New-Generation Computer Technology. Here he relaxes at home with his children, who are playing Othello on an MSX computer.

But ICOT does not simply cause problems for other Japanese; it causes just as many for outsiders, not least my Occidental journalist colleagues.

Much of the observation and comment about ICOT and its progress— or lack of it—from non-Japanese sources is suspect, for what ICOT is about cuts across both journalistic norms and the computing-based systems development approaches to which my colleagues are attuned. The problem is one of framework. Here, they say, is this supposedly massive effort; it is in its third year, yet all that is visible are a bunch of young men working on one office floor in downtown Tokyo. Where is the intelligent machine, or even a pilot model?

I have discussed this extensively with colleagues around the planet. I remind them, ever so gently, that ICOT is not supposed to produce that machine, however you care to define *intelligent,* until the nineties. The probable retort is that however this may be, surely they must have something they can demonstrate in which one can detect the germ of intelligence.

You will detect anthropomorphism here. If intelligent behavior is a simulacrum of human behavior, then surely it must follow that the machine's evolution will be on human-like terms or lines. Then one would begin by unveiling a system that demonstrates, however haltingly, that it might grow to become intelligent. This approach is buttressed by the history of systems development over the years, in which the initial system produced does one version of a given job, its successors building on it. The history of systems development in this industry sometimes does have strong anthropomorphic overtones.

I am tempted to reply, somewhat glibly, that an initial thought is not the same as physical conception, that pregnancy is a nine-month process. Well, reflect on this: from the time ICOT opened its doors to the time when it is expected to produce that hopefully mewing infant is nine months scaled up by twelve—nine years. Set within this framework, the approach of my colleagues is understandable; the time horizons of the news business are limited. But there is a further confusion. Projects funded by the Ministry of International Trade and Industry (MITI) are generally short-term, product-and-specific-application-bound. ICOT is neither; within the Japanese context, it is unique. It is about fundamental research (with the reservations discussed below), from which it is hoped that a basic technology can be created that will generate product.

Kazuhiro Fuchi must be weary of stating the following, so I will do it instead. What the Fifth-Generation Project is not about is computing as we understand it, or the derivatives and extensions from it we lump under the title of *AI*. Instead, it is about logic programming and a physically realized architecture derived from a logic-programming base. Which, in turn, means a machine architecture that is rule-based, not sequential-flow-based.

That thought is not original. Some of its implications are. When you set out to try to probe the mind of Fuchi—and I have tried a number of times—you get the impression that he decided early on that the only way to approach the Fifth Generation as a research effort was to go right back to starting premises and fundamentals, questioning just about everything that could be queried. It was almost as if digital electronics existed, and there was a software skills base, but no one had previously set out to build a system with any reasoning capability at all.

If they were to do that, they had to build their own sets of tools. The way to test, after all, is to set out to create tools which will replicate thought. So they had to target on specific isolatable functions—deduction, induction, abduction—and the result was relational database machines and inference machines, and their coupling.

But how did they go about this? Consider the Personal Sequential Inference Machine, a development tool. They built it fast—the technology is not very advanced—but then they did something we would probably find alien. They let a bunch of programmers loose on it, coding in Prolog, with little more than standard coding texts to guide them. If you take this approach, you get something done, you create hands-on experience, and you satisfy that seemingly basic Japanese need to build something, something that would enable them to operate on that Japanese incremental principle, and make improvements.

This approach, you can see already, is likely to cause problems for those accustomed to Occidental research methods. I urge caution on my colleagues. In the way we would recognize it, Fifth-Generation research is only beginning this year. Up till now, it has been tool-building and team-training. "From here on, it becomes difficult," says Fuchi.

We have not finished with the differences in approach. The key hardware designer, Dr. Uchida, points up the way ICOT is approaching the core problems by denying that ICOT is doing research in the traditional sense: it is doing research engineering. It is concerned with getting a grasp on the ambiguity of the observable external world, taking the fuzziness out, and producing an engineered result.

You may find this, too, a little baffling. But what he is clearly doing is making the classical distinction between pure and applied mathematics. What has been overlooked outside Japan is that for all the attempts to create something new, ICOT is still a Japanese organization, building itself on the basis of the strengths of Japanese organizational models, and seeking to insert into them what it conceives to be the strengths of others, so that

Dr. Shunichi Uchida, the key hardware designer at ICOT, poses next to the first Personal Sequential Inference Machine.

one model can be mapped onto the other without a reduction of effectiveness.

One of those Japanese strengths is the sensible habit of sweeping the field, the literature, the technology, building on what others have done. They do not simply sweep the rest of the world; good Japanese organizations also sweep Japan internally. Next, there usually follow attempts to build links with those whose work and approaches fit what they are trying to do, work they regard as promising. This allows gaps to be identified, and work can then be set in hand.

This has occurred with Fifth-Generation research. There are said to be around 300 Japanese projects that bear on ICOT's work, many of them set up before ICOT began, but many others since. This is what ICOT feeds on, and it is this which can lead Dr. Uchida almost to deny that ICOT is in fundamental research at all.

Every time I see them, I raise the same basic issues. When you cut through the disputes about machine replication of aspects of intelligence, starting with the assumption that such replication is inherently a worthwhile project to pursue (a large assumption in itself), you come to two central mechanistic problems.

One is the classic problem of what is it that you process (again, a minefield in itself), and how you go about processing it. This is what most research is concentrated on, and is the easiest topic—which does not mean that it is easy at all—for researchers to concentrate on and obtain support for, and for writers to report and discuss.

The other, I must admit, I find much more interesting, because of its inherent difficulty. It is the problem of externally anchoring and linking, more formally called the *knowledge acquisition process,* which naturally includes filtering processes such as forgetting, whatever processes those may be.

Progress in this field is slight almost everywhere, though there is reputedly interesting work going on in Japan and elsewhere on the modeling of analogy processes. In the second area, however, nowhere is there any serious work approaching engineered solutions. I am seeking a time scale, for I regard the second area as much more critical than the first. Dr. Uchida tells me that a discontinuity exists between my hopes and theirs: "We are not so ambitious."

The concentration so far remains on the first group of problems, for as Dr. Uchida remarks, toy problems in the field still require immense computing power, and even at this level, that power often does not exist. Some toys, after all, are more complex than others.

Videotex in Japan

It is an old rule of journalism that news is something that someone somewhere wishes you would not print; all the rest is public relations. But this does not satisfactorily cover all forms of journalism, some of which can fall through the cracks because of both aim and subject matter.

Like the following. There is a sense in which what follows is PR. It carries over from my REPORT FROM EUROPE in the previous issue; and to make it even more blatant, in the background is to be found the same company. It is, however, support—PR, if you wish—in favor of your correspondent's ideas and feel for the evolution of the technology. I hasten to write that I have no financial interest or connection with the company. For all I know, they could be going bust; I make it my business not to know. But I should be extremely upset if they were, for it would indicate that my judgment was seriously at fault, and my judgment is what I am paid for.

The company is called Aregon International. It is the result of my taking its founder, John Pearce, to visit British Telecom's equivalent to Bell Labs, its research center at Martlesham in eastern England, to see an invention now known as videotex and its inventor Sam Fedida. I was so enthusiastic that I went on to write a book on videotex with Fedida. Pearce went away and founded a videotex company, one concentrating on the business market. [For information on videotex around the world, see Jan Gecsei's article in the Fall 1985 issue.]

After more than seven years and a stream of installations worldwide, enter AT&T and Mitsubishi. Both sweep the offerings on the planet, and independently come to the conclusion that the Aregon solution is the one they should settle for, one for the North American market, the other for Japan and the Pacific. In both cases, of course, there is some redesign and some extensions—in the Japanese case, primarily to cope with language and character differences.

The redevelopment has occurred roughly concurrently this past year, much of it in London, with visits from both American and Japanese teams. This is giving Aregon's software people at various levels an opportunity to compare national styles as they show themselves in a third-party environment. We are talking here of two of the world's major corporations. The significance of AT&T will be obvious to ABACUS readers; what they may not know is that Mitsubishi, including its car-manufacturing operation, is a more-than-$70-billion-gross corporation.

American readers might find the Aregon equivalent of bar talk interesting, if perhaps a little worrying. For it is quite clear that they have a preference for dealing with the Japanese, even if there are occasionally some language problems.

"Americans? Friendly but aggressive."

"Patronizing. They will not admit that they might not know. Their attitude is, 'Whose basic technology is this anyway?' "

"You have to realize that their commitment is to themselves, not to the corporation in the long term. Anyway, they will probably not be there in five years' time."

As to the Japanese:

"Their cultural background makes them polite and pleasant to deal with. If they make an agreement, they honor it and stick to it."

"They are tough and astute, but they conduct themselves differently from Americans. They see others' problems, and they try to smooth the way. Where an American will say, 'Tough, but that's your problem, you solve it,' the Japanese is more likely to say, 'Yes, that is a problem; can we help solve it in any way?' There is a much more long-term commitment."

The next comment is really a summation of a number of remarks that bore on the same theme: "If he (the Japanese) is a manager of middle rank and any good, he may well have climbed further up the ladder by the time it is all up and running. He will still be with the corporation, but at a more senior level. If it goes wrong, it may still be partly his responsibility. It is then in his interest to ensure that it is done correctly the first time around, to try to limit a possible future headache."

The talk went further. Observation indicated the lack of a systems approach in Japanese thinking; they are good innovators at the micro level, but have blind spots at the macro. There is little lateral thinking; if it does not work, they find it difficult to turn a project proposal around or look at it from a different angle. (Remember the case of Robb Wilmot, discussed earlier).

Though one could generalize from these individual opinions, I would not do so except that they seem to fit with my own observation. Meanwhile, back in Tokyo, the two Mitsubishi managing directors who have to steer the company's entry into the videotex market—Kiyoshi Takahara (technical director) and Shinroku Morohashi (planning director)—tell you that they intend to take videotex in quite specific directions. They see it as a communications medium that allows the capture of data in the format of television-based text systems and the pulling down of data from news agency systems and more conventional computing databases.

The market they aim for is what is called in the jargon *closed user groups* (CUGs). Japan, they say, is full of experimental and often elementary videotex systems; indeed, the company is involved as an information provider in two localized public-access Tokyo systems.

They are of a size to enable them to go after very large CUGs, and few aims could be larger than the first contract they are seeking. They are the key system provider in a consortium that is bidding for the MITI network, or rather a network initially funded by MITI that has much larger ambitions.

It begins as a system to provide data for MITI, aiming initially at 500 terminals, going to 5000 in two years, and then hoping to be internationalized, with a terminal population that could go as high as 20,000 before the eighties are out. There is to be a two-part database of high-technology information, abstracts, diagrams, and text sourcing to enable users to search for ideas, technology, expertise. There will also be patent information, pricing, and product sourcing.

For Japan, of course, this has to be bilingual, hence everybody's problem. The talk is of allowing for different character sets, dictionary look-up techniques, split screens in which there is Kana input in the bottom part of the frame while the top part comes up with Kanji possibilities—and of the question of network response times if one puts Kana nodes in the network. [Neil Friedman discusses some of these complications in his article.] Clearly, it is a little bit much to expect even a PC-based terminal to have to cope with all this.

Whether or not they are successful, Mitsubishi is unlikely to be deterred. The MITI contract is not their starting point; that is the Japanese medical market, where they seek to create medical news services, under the name of Advanced Medical Information System or AMIS (for Japan is just as prone as the rest of us to stick titles on system proposals).

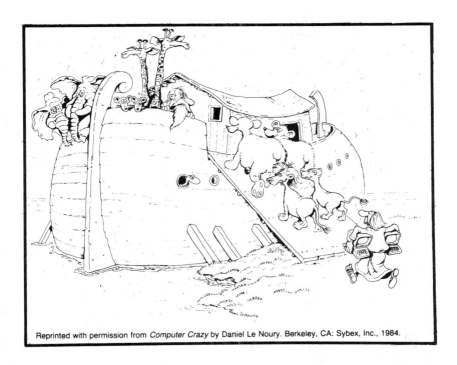

Reprinted with permission from *Computer Crazy* by Daniel Le Noury. Berkeley, CA: Sybex, Inc., 1984.

Report from Europe

Data Protection: Has the Tide Turned?

European nations, the first to enact laws protecting privacy in the computer age, may now be having second thoughts.

ANDREW LLOYD

There are signs of a backlash in Europe against one of the earliest forms of regulation affecting the data processing field. The Europeans, arguably, have been more inclined to press for computer regulation than their transatlantic friends. And regulate they did, with a series of data protection laws enacted in eight countries. These laws give citizens the right to know about and correct any name-linked computer data which concerns them— plus in most cases a variety of other rights. They apply to both public- and private-sector files; and many outlaw the interconnection of administrative files to catch out, for example, tax evaders.

But recent events on the old continent point to a swing away from the libertarian feelings which prompted the legislation. It was Sweden which first brought a data protection act onto its statute books in 1973 (though the German state of Hesse had implemented a local law as early as 1970). West Germany followed with a federal law in 1977, and France in 1978. A number of nations experienced "scandals" which prompted the legislators into action. One in France involved a government scheme to interconnect various files with a view to catching tax dodgers. The reputable daily paper *Le Monde* caught the mood of the anti-computer brigade with a headline using the proposed system's somewhat predatory acronym "SAFARI or Hunt the Frenchman."

As legislation in different countries has gone through, the debate over what should be contained in the laws has continued and evolved. All of these laws agree in giving the individuals the right of access to computer records which concern them (except for certain files said by governments

In addition to being ABACUS's first European correspondent, ANDREW LLOYD is European Editor of *New Scientist,* covering science and technology from Paris. After graduating in French from Oxford University, he spent five years as systems engineer with IBM, and later became European editor of *Datamation.*

Reprinted from ABACUS, Volume 1, Number 1, Fall 1983.

to concern state security), and the right to correct or delete incorrect data. Most laws also forbid the recording of information on religious or political opinions. Most impose on the operators of name-linked data files the obligation to register the nature and use of each system with an authority specially designated to look after data protection; this authority is usually separate from other administrative departments. Many levy heavy fines and even imprisonment on transgressors. Some of the heaviest sanctions may be taken against those who hand over name-linked information to third parties without authorization, or against those who use name-linked data for purposes other than those registered with the authority.

Predictably, the laws have led to outcries from private industry, and from those parts of the administration connected with the murkier areas of law and order, state security, and defense. Companies were particularly outraged by the attempts in some countries to include *legal* persons (meaning companies and institutions) in the law as well as private citizens. In some cases, this could theoretically have meant giving companies the right to inquire of a competitor what market research data the competitor had compiled on the inquirer.

Unsurprisingly to European eyes, it was the American multinationals who objected the most strongly to the proposed measures. Firstly, they tend to be the only companies which really know what is going on (and in this case the pending legislation was given precious little publicity). And secondly, their more sophisticated computer systems appeared more vulnerable to problems caused by such laws. Finally, the U.S. computer manufacturers made it their business to lobby hard—both as vendors whose business was at risk and as advanced computer users themselves. There is a good story about the French law, which had a particularly stormy passage through parliament. This originally included legal "persons" in the text; but the night before the bill was to go through the French parliament, the head of IBM France called the Justice Minister, Alain Peyrefitte, and persuaded him to drop the offending portion of the text. Careful reading of the parliamentary proceedings shows that this change in the bill was made with no debate at all—unlike the rowdy arguments which surrounded other changes.

Most laws are now well established; nations and their administrations have gotten used to living with them. At the time of this writing, 1983, the United Kingdom is still the odd man out, together with most of the Latin nations and Ireland. But even though nine Western European nations (plus Israel and Hungary) have already passed laws, while others including the United Kingdom, Spain, Portugal, Netherlands, and Belgium have legislation planned, a number of points remain unresolved.

The biggest area of uncertainty lies in just how far the data protection authority's power actually reaches. Though the DPA in various countries has (as required by many laws) given its opinion on government and private-sector name-linked file projects, and though it has apparently managed to influence the type of systems eventually installed, and though it has often commented unfavorably on administration plans and practices, there are indications that its power exists in theory but not in reality. Perhaps it is another symptom of a swing to the right in the face of recession, but the relationship between governments and the DPAs looks increasingly like the relationship in most countries between the government and the department of environmental control. The DPA is there because some deputies believe the electors like it. But it had better not step too far out of line; and to make sure, they refuse to allow it generous funding or adequate levels of staffing.

Several examples show where the limits of the potentially troublesome DPA's activities may lie. The proposed legislation in Great Britain places the power of regulation in the hands of the Home Office. As many right- and left-wing British commentators have pointed out, the interior department of any nation is probably the administration most likely to disregard individual rights when the occasion seems to make it opportune. The French government rode roughshod over the Commission Nationale de l'Informatique et des Libertés (CNIL) when it announced that it was setting up a file to fight terrorism (the German security services already have one) without seeking the approval of the CNIL. Following this announcement, the Socialist government made the gesture of consulting the nation's DPA, and not surprisingly got the go-ahead. The area is admittedly a gray one. But in the fight against crime, espionage, or terrorism, there is a grave danger that individual liberties can be encroached upon. The German system allows the security services to store data on suspects and even, for example, on people who have let accommodations to suspected terrorists. The French claim to have drawn the line more on the side of the presumably innocent individual.

Another and arguably related debate in the data protection field concerns the inclusion or exclusion of manual files along with computer files. Computer vendors and others have argued that there should be no unfair discrimination against their products, and by and large have managed to have at least some regulations imposed on manual files. Fervent defenders of civil rights have also argued that potentially dangerous files (such as lists of Jews) are still maintained in manual form by some security administrations. While investigating a proposed terrorist file, the French CNIL found that the nation's security services had some 22 million names on file, a good proportion of the adult population of France. (Civil rights campaigners, however, tell of reports that the Royal Canadian Mounted Police actually has data on more names than the entire Canadian population.)

But there are some who argue that leaving manual files out of data protection legislation altogether provides a golden opportunity for being extra strict on what governments can get away with on computers. If administrations are allowed to do pretty much what they like with manual files, subject to traditional checks and balances, the law can be tougher on making sure they do not go too far with the much more powerful tool, the computer. So far, it has not worked out that way—even though in the U.K., for example, the official reason why manual files are not included in the proposed legislation is that regulation is needed only for computers because they can handle data so much faster. Indeed, the British law looks particularly weak in the protection of civil rights vis-à-vis the government. Manual files are not affected, and the interior ministry will be in charge of monitoring its own abuses.

In Sweden, the government has begun to be tougher towards the first of the European data protection authorities. Earlier this year, a Swedish bank asked the Datainspektionen whether it could comply with a government tax authority request for data on the bank balances of suspected tax evaders. The Swedish DPA refused to give its assent, but the bank was finally pressured into handing over the data. The DPA then took the bank to court; at the time of this writing, the case is still pending. In yet another case, regional health authorities also asked a bank for account data on old-age pensioners suspected of being too wealthy to qualify for reduced-rate treatment in hospitals. Again, the Swedish DPA refused but was overruled, and the bank was forced to comply.

The chairman of the Datainspektionen, Jan Freese, something of a celebrity in data protection and other data regulation fields, is adamant that the latest cases are not the beginning of a trend. In the past, the government has taken ample notice of the DPA, he says.

But there are two other important ways in which the data protection tide may be turning. The public is still generally apathetic about its privacy. Data protection authorities are reduced to making declarations that the public should be more interested. But the question is: *will* it start to get worried about computer data use? If the DPAs have to resort to publicity campaigns to make the public aware of the dangers, then perhaps they are not really needed.

The other awakening of consciousness in Europe at the moment is also militating against overly strict data regulation. In most countries, official, financial, and industrial opinion is aware of the technological gap between the old continent and the United States and Japan. Culturally, the Europeans are far behind the Americans, not only in their use of computers but also in the receptivity to information technology (even in the willingness of middle management to sit down at a keyboard). One of the big complaints from British small and medium business lobbies in the run-up to the new data protection bill was that the regulations could slow down progress towards the efficient use of computers. Similar feelings are present elsewhere in Europe, and most governments are doing their best to accelerate computer literacy as fast as possible. This is one more reason why, in today's economic climate, data protection may be coming upon hard days.

Report from Anaheim

ABACUS Goes to the 1983 National Computer Conference

The National Computer Conference ain't what it used to be; but is that good or bad?

Eric A. Weiss

I have been faithfully attending NCCs since the first of its predecessors, the Old Joint in Philadelphia in 1951. As they grew from friendly gatherings of cronies into noisy, swirling monsters of hoopla and promotion, I learned to apply a metaphorical framework to them so that I could get my mind around each one and extract its essence without being overwhelmed by the glitter, the detail, the sound, and the fury. So now I think of each NCC as a great art gallery through which I stroll, getting a general feeling of the ambience, now and then meeting a friend, pausing here and there to examine some particularly interesting painting, and forming an opinion of the state of the art world.

So my metaphor for the 1983 NCC is Modest Mussorgsky's *Pictures at an Exhibition,* taken up theme by theme.

Promenade

There is hardly room in Anaheim to stroll. Almost all the strawberry fields have been paved for parking lots. Sixty motel-hotels are "Sorry, no vacancy." The officially secret attendance is known by every bellboy to be 105,000, the biggest NCC yet. Exhibits have grown from none in 1951, to being able to fit in the LA Ambassador Hotel ballroom in 1961, to filling the Anaheim exhibit hall with the Big Stuff while relegating the minis, hobbyists and their personal computers to the Disneyland Hotel ballroom and basement in 1980, to this sprawl of more than 600 exhibitors today. It is too big for any convention space in the U.S. except here, Las Vegas, Chicago, and New York, and it even stretches their acreages.

The Exhibit Hall is so vast that there is a perceptible temperature difference due to latitude between its two ends, hot in the south and cool in the north. The Japanese are here in force, exhibiting, looking, picking

Reprinted from ABACUS, Volume 1, Number 1, Fall 1983.

up literature, asking, taking notes. There are not as many exhibit gimmicks as last year, but plays—theatrical performances about the products—are fashionable with the Biggies. Giveaways, funny hats, and clever buttons are fewer. *Datamation* magazine wins the most-used-loot-bag sweepstakes and, as always, the prize for the best and most sought-after reception. The prize is an overstuffed room.

The Gnome

No one who was there (maybe 2% of the registrants) will forget the keynote speaker's show. Folksy John P. Imlay, head packager of the software house, Management Science America, set a new standard of showmanship for NCC keynote speakers. He swung a golf club to illustrate a corny golf joke; showed slides and movies; engaged in a real-time conversation with a giant moving, talking, satellite-transmitted image of software's only U.S. senator, Frank Lautenberg of New Jersey, and ended with a recitation of his own original poem while a live violinist played "The Impossible Dream." What was his message? The good news is: computers are fine but people are more important. The bad news is: the industry needs government help to set a consistent strategy to combat the Japanese invasion.

Wild applause. A two-minute standing ovation.

Promenade

I see a friend. He has changed. Now he has no beard, all his long hair has fallen out, he wears shoes and a show badge of some company with a computer-created name combining the okay words of 1983, microproductivity-personalcomputer-network, into unpronounceability.

"What's new?"

"Four of the Dwarfs have standardized on Unix V. Perpetual computing may make it this time. Try to find a punched card anywhere. My feet hurt up to the knees."

"What's best in the show?"

"Look in on Votan and their speech recognizer and the tiny portable Grid computer. They were unadvertised sleepers hidden in the hotel ballroom and basement."

I lose him—the gawking, shuffling crowd pushes us apart.

The Old Castle

Pioneer Day honors Howard Aiken, the Harvard Computation Laboratory, and the Marks I thru IV, inclusive. Captain Grace Murray Hopper, who was there when she was just a lieutenant jg, keynotes. (In a curious inversion, Grace gets the Ada Lovelace award. Since Grace has done far more for computing than Ada ever did, it should be the other way around: the women should give Ada an award named for Grace.) A panel of Aiken's students tell of his efforts, accomplishments, and tangible contributions. They praise his vision and perspective, recall the research and educational environment of the good old days and the atmosphere that Aiken generated. Reference is made to his blind spots in regard to programming but, except for a few brief asides, no one recalls his aggressive, abrasive, self-aggrandizing personality, his stubbornness and rigidity which kept things moving when a lesser man would have faltered but which also caused him to cling too long to bad ideas. Already history is being trimmed, smoothed, straightened and prettified into myth.

Promenade

Where are the Aikens, the Hoppers, the Turings, the Goodes, the Ahmdahls, the Watsons, the Backuses, the Kemenys, the Mauchlys, the Eckerts, the Norrisses, the Hammings, the Grosches for tomorrow? Some may be pressing around me now. Others are too young to go to the NCC; under-fourteens are barred from the show. Where are the apprentices? Not with the big names, for surely the big companies, the big universities, the big government agencies can't stand the single-minded drive and scornful iconoclasm of creative youth or the aggressive self-assurance of an Aiken. Probably the young geniuses are alone or with small firms that are at daily risk of bankruptcy, stubbornly and joyfully doing what everyone knows is hopelessly naive, optimistic, and doomed to failure. But it is on them that the future depends. What do they need? They don't need capture by the rich and powerful. They don't need specific direction and guidance, for that is what kills good new ideas. Certainly they don't need a consistent national strategy set by a government-industry Temporary National Information Committee. Certainly they don't need protection from the Japanese. (We gave them that protection in 1941–5.) They need a little unrestricted help, a lot of free rein, and generalized cheering and encouragement. "Go it, world! Go it, kids!"

Tuileries

There stands Micropro, in a booth as big as the biggest and oldest of the hardware houses, selling its software as if it were hard. Wordstar, the writer's friend, built the booth. Can it go on? Will it go on? Is the small software house the wave of the future? Can the act be repeated? Improved? Will getting big make it bad? Will success spoil sales? Will the big hard boys allow the small and soft to live?

Bydlo

The publishers are all swollen up like the immense wheels of a Polish ox-cart. Their booths are big, open, inviting, stuffed with books. The college and professional texts are there, but being pushed aside by the books for the public and for children and by books specific to certain hardware and software. Publishers are getting into selling software itself, first to the markets they know, the schools, but gingerly trying out the general public by way of the computer stores. As always, they are investing in the future because books feed the minds of the young and set the agenda, the tone, and the style of tomorrow.

Promenade

Where is computing going? Terminals, keyboards, graphics, color displays are everywhere. Everything is networked to everything else. Storage in every form and shape is bigger, cheaper, faster: more bits, more bits to the buck, more bits to the cubic centimeter, more bits to the microsecond, more bytes. All hardware is smaller, cheaper, more powerful. All software is friendlier, smarter, faster. Everything helps productivity. Lots of things are fun to do or to see, but nobody comes right out and says so. Where is the imagination? What will fill the floor of the 1993 NCC? More of the same? Will it be AI? Games? Graphics? Robotory? National consistency?

Ballet of the Unhatched Chicks

This fits the NCC theme, "The Emerging Information Age: Computers, Communication, and People." Some chicks' heads pop through shells. Some chickens come home to roost.

But I see a better link with the little chicken ballet in the sky-is-falling panel session on Japan's Fifth Generation Computer project. Here experts from Stanford, both the university and the research institute, and the DOD terrified their audience by predicting that the Japanese government's long-term plans for the development of computer technology will make Japan the world leader by the 1990s. But then the panel offered hope. The U.S. government must quickly organize and direct a nationwide computer research program, forcing all the "sleepy, sluggish U.S. companies" that are overconcerned with their profits and independence into participation in the technological developments that the government and industry leaders select. These are developments that won't make money but that will be good for the nation and for national defense. Specifically mentioned were those specialities of the panelists that now suffer from industrial neglect, supercomputer number crunchers, artificial intelligence, and the software that goes with them. To some it sounded as if once more those who mistrust the chaos and confusion of pragmatic, profit-driven, independent competing enterprises and who prefer the efficiencies of central planning and precise command and control were telling us that to save our independence we must destroy it.

Fat chance. Fortunately a chaotic and profit-driven Congress would sooner let the sky fall than let pointy-headed, non-Congressional experts plan and direct the nation's destiny.

Catacombae

Six huge, white, plastic, air-conditioned circus tents at the far end of the grounds handle the overflow of new exhibitors in Tent City. Here are those who are low on the complex NCC exhibitor rating scale, a scale which is calculated to keep everybody coming but puts the most faithful, long-time, big-spending exhibitors near the front door. This location algorithm often puts the newest and most interesting things in the worst locations, like the hotel ballroom and basement, but it also puts the curiosities in the tents. Australia is here without kangaroos or koalas. In the tents too are China—the anti-red one, not the real one; France, in a curiously detached but Gallic stance; DuPont, only selling Teflon-insulated wire; and Springer-Verlag with the first ABACUS flyers.

The most exciting event at the NCC, although noticed by only a few, was the Big Wind on Tuesday. This spot cyclone swirled in at 10 A.M., raised a cloud of dust higher than the Hyatt, flattened the outside canopies and ripped off the roof-mounted air-conditioners of Tent City, leaving this part of the swamp to steam and swelter. (But I must admit that the ambient light in these tents was a lot better than the California saloon gloom of the permanent halls.)

The Market Place at Limoges

The Apple booth, under its great white arches, is jammed. Those on the outer rim of the crowd press forward trying to see and hear. Apple brags "biggest, biggest, biggest." Everybody knows Apple. Everybody wants to see Lisa. Everybody wants his or her very own. How will Apple come through the PC shakeout that the common wisdom knows must come? Surely Apple exemplifies the wave of the recent past. Is it the wave of the future?

Promenade

I meet a friend, older, experienced, wise, philosophical. We stand together, blocking the aisle, looking over each other's shoulders as we talk, looking for other friends.

"Tell me," I say, "have personal computers caught on in business? Will they become common in corporate use? Will they make any difference?"

"They've almost caught on," he says. "You will be sure that they have been found useful and important to business and have really caught on when you see all the consultants telling managers how to limit the use of personal computers and control their proliferation. This is always the signal that something useful and important has appeared in the business scene. Whenever this happens, consultants and auditors go to work to show managers how to stop it. Remember when the use of copying machines was being limited and controlled? Before that there was the 'limit air travel' drive, before that the 'hold down the use of the telephone' period, and there is evidence of an early Egyptian drive to save papyrus by writing smaller. The signal is infallible. The limit-and-control action is the clear indication that even the most blind and obtuse managers, those who pile up their savings by doing nothing, have recognized the inevitability of something new and different. When personal computers in business get this kind of attention, they will have arrived. In the next step, as with the copying machines and the telephone, personal computers will become accepted and indispensable."

With our eyes still fixed in the convention stare, we part.

Con mortuis in lingua mortua

GE is down to printers only. Xerox, in its grey tower, seems not sure what to do next. Honeywell, NCR, Sperry-Univac, RCA, and American Bell, once belles of the ball, the biggest and the brightest, are fading back. They all have brave fronts, brave plans, and brave announcements, but in a few years some of them will be as well known for computers as Philco and Bendix. The small, the excited, and the newly named companies, many now ripe for acquisition, purchase, merger, and death, press forward.

The Hut on Fowls' Legs

The eighty technical sessions, the twenty-two Professional Development Seminars, and the countless society meetings and receptions go on day and night in the Big Hall and the surrounding hotels. These, not the exhibits, were the original reason for the NCC; but the exhibits draw the crowds and the admissions, besides which the booth rentals at $15 per square foot make the funds that pay the bills for everyone except the vendors. The technical sessions are seldom outstanding, and often thinly attended. The Proceedings, once widely referenced, now age and die quickly, but the PD seminars teach and the society meetings keep the juices flowing for those so inclined. The success and growth of several commercial imitators of the NCC prove the viability and need for what must appear to strangers and foreigners a strange computing folk rite. If you don't like to think of the NCC as a house walking on chicken legs, you may prefer to think of it as a great primordial jellyfish of many symbiotic parts, which eats, swims, and grows in the warm beneficent nutrient-laden computing sea—a sea that is untroubled by the obvious lack of any consistent national computing policy.

The Great Gate at Kiev

This, naturally, is IBM. Its current misleading slogan is "Leadership in products and technology." Humbug! IBM is a leader, but it always seems embarrassed to name its greatest strength, to take credit for how it has always led. It knows its markets, it knows its customers, it knows how to sell. It is in these areas that it is the leader. With products and technology it is almost never firstest but is always mostest. Peters and Waterman in the current business best-seller, *In Search of Excellence,* tell the story of IBM's strength and leadership better than any IBM brochure or slogan ever has.

What's in the dark IBM booth? (It's not blue this year. Has Big Blue left us?) It has PC's (not afraid to show a video game this year), flat plasma displays at $7500, a light-duty robot plugging chips into boards, thin film disks, a new system—system/36—as the way to get rid of the system/34 problems, and keyboards and screens like everybody else. At the hotel, IBM demonstrates the difference between the thinking of computer engineers and writer/editors. The example provided is a lash-up for in-house publishing, going from typing through composing (in all kinds of typefaces, graphs, charts, and simple line diagrams) to camera-ready metallized-paper page masters. It will not live in this form long, for it reflects an engineer's view of how authors, copy editors, makeup editors, and designers ought to work and ought to want to use this sensational technology. The customers will straighten it all out.

Promenade (Encore)

What is the wave of the future? Will IBM set it with its great moving mass? Is it the dinosaur death of the old giants? Is it the lower-case personal computers? (Personal-business computers, Fujitsu says. Personal-business-professional computers, some PR clown will soon say. Then it will go back to what we all say, personal computers.) Is it user-friendly software, networks, AI, artificial respiration, portable computing, voice recognition, enthusiastic children, university technology, books, magazines, video games, or the power-operated, sneeze-actuated Kleenex dispenser? Is it all of these, and, as they say on TV, more, much more, probably coming from the hearts and minds of people who never heard of the NCC.

And will this bubbling ferment be helped or hurt by government-industry cooperative direction, by a Temporary National Information Committee, by protection against the Japanese? Or are all these proposals to save a healthy business like the Great Wind that swoops past, unheard and unnoticed by most of the players?

The industry is frantically healthy, still growing by doubling and splitting and finding new directions long before it has fully explored the old ones.

So what is the state of the art? The art is okay. It's the critics who are in a state.

INTERRUPT

An editorial in the *Detroit Free Press* (May 18, 1985) comments on the development of a robotic automobile at Carnegie-Mellon University. This "wheeled robot" is expected to do everything from laying undersea pipe to delivering weapons to soldiers.

Development of wheeled robots has become somewhat old-hat by now, although CMU's car uses the latest in high tech—lasers, acoustic devices, and stereo television—to sense its environment and respond accordingly. So why the editorial? It seems the car embarrassed its creators in a recent test drive. "The car navigated well for a while until the curves became sharper. It then veered off the track, climbed a tree and began clawing at the bark."

As the editorial notes, humans can certainly empathize with this very human reaction, but it "is hardly what one would expect of a sophisticated vehicle." Maybe CMU should try developing a robotic spouse passenger to cool down the hot-tempered robot driver.

Report from Washington

MCC: One U.S. Answer to the Japanese

EDITH HOLMES

Strange bedfellows are made not only by politics, but also, it seems, by competition. Ten U.S. computer manufacturers who ordinarily compete fiercely among themselves for business have joined together in a new effort to share information, research, and resources as they try to catch up with the Japanese, who have a head start in developing a "fifth generation" computer. The new enterprise, which has been named Microelectronics and Computer Technology Corp. (and is known, somewhat selectively, by the initials MCC), joins together the resources of Advanced Micro Systems, Digital Equipment Corp., Harris Corp., Honeywell, Motorola, NCR, National Semiconductor, RCA, and Sperry Univac.

First mentioned by Robert Price of Control Data Corp. to a Computer & Business Equipment Manufacturers Association meeting in 1980, the idea of some type of cooperative research venture was sparked by the success which Japanese government-supported efforts seemed to be producing. When the U.S. government showed no interest in getting involved, William Norris, chairman of Control Data, invited fifty executives from sixteen companies to a hush-hush meeting in Orlando, Florida, in February 1982. There the companies discussed ways to work together. Task forces were formed to determine the amount of funding needed, where to locate the company, and what work to begin with.

By August 1982, the organization had progressed well enough for the company to be incorporated in Delaware. In late February of this year, a chief executive was selected and announced for the fledgling venture— former deputy director of the Central Intelligence Agency, retired admiral

EDITH HOLMES is a free-lance journalist who covers Washington and the computer and communications industries for a number of clients. Her undergraduate degree was from Dickinson College, and she has a master's degree in science journalism from Boston University.

Reprinted from ABACUS, Volume 1, Number 1, Fall 1983.

and intelligence specialist Bobby R. Inman. He has set about the task of hiring staff and attacking four areas which the participants agreed on: 1) advanced computer architecture, 2) software technology, 3) integrated circuit packaging, and 4) computer-aided design and manufacturing.

Under the terms of the cooperative agreement, each of the member companies will supply funds and technical experts. To many firms, one of the attractive features of the project is that it relieves them of the burden of trying to maintain staff experts in the more than two dozen subspecialities that contribute to modern computer design. Several companies poured millions of dollars into bubble memories, for example, in an effort to determine whether these memories held more promise for some applications than semiconductor memories. MCC will give companies a chance to evaluate a technique or technology before committing large sums of money to it.

MCC will not produce any products, according to Inman. That will be up to the individual companies. It will hold patents and license their production as commercial products. Companies subscribing to a particular project expect to get a head start to the marketplace for any products developed.

MCC expects to begin business with somewhere between $50 million and $100 million in working capital, made up primarily from the contributions required of the participating companies. They must all take part in and help finance at least one project for a period of three years.

Although antitrust implications have been raised, the Justice Department has followed carefully the development of the venture, and assistant attorney general William F. Baxter has indicated that the department does not intend to challenge the company at this point.

Missing from the ranks of the new company are some big names—IBM, Xerox, and Burroughs, for instance—but there are reportedly several dozen firms still considering either full or some form of associate membership.

How well the new research firm will do in competing with foreign technology may depend in large part on how many firms agree to participate and how trusting they become of each other. Some analysts wonder whether market rivalries—which have existed for a very long time—can disappear quickly.

Author's Update

MCC has continued to evolve and now appears to be entering a new and difficult phase. Admiral Inman left the consortium at the beginning of 1987 and several of the charter members departed, as well, forcing MCC to consider opening its ranks to foreign companies—including the Japanese—and to slash its $1 million entry fee to $250,000 in an effort to attract new shareholders.

Features

Miscellaneous Features, items that cannot be included in any other category and that are intended to be entertaining, are sprinkled throughout ABACUS. Interrupts—short whimsical or humorous paragraphs and cartoons—are used in this volume as they are in ABACUS, to fill what would otherwise be blank spaces at the ends of pages. An ABACUS Competition, modeled on that in the *New York Magazine,* appears in every recent issue. The Competition Results, appended to the following sample, come out two issues later. The Editors' Forecast, here spread between the Competition and Results, is ABACUS's only intentional parody.

ABACUS COMPETITION #1:
Old and New Computing Aphorisms

In the late 1950s Richard W. Hamming originated the famous aphorism, "The purpose of computing is insight, not numbers." George E. Forsythe later suggested the modification. "The purpose of computing numbers is not yet in sight."

Competitors are invited to suggest similar aphorisms about computing, in matched pairs or singly. If not original, give the author and the documentary source. Only one entry per reader and no more than 200 words, please.

Competition rules: TYPEWRITTEN POSTCARDS, PLEASE. *ONE ENTRY ONLY* should be sent to Competition Number 1, ABACUS, Box 232, Springfield, PA 19064. It must be received by 1 July 1986; foreign postmarks will be given one month's grace. The editors' decisions are final, and all entries become the property of ABACUS, and runners-up will receive one-year subscriptions. Results and winners' names will appear in the Fall issue.

Reprinted from ABACUS, Volume 3, Number 3, Spring 1986.

The Editors of ABACUS Present Their Forecast

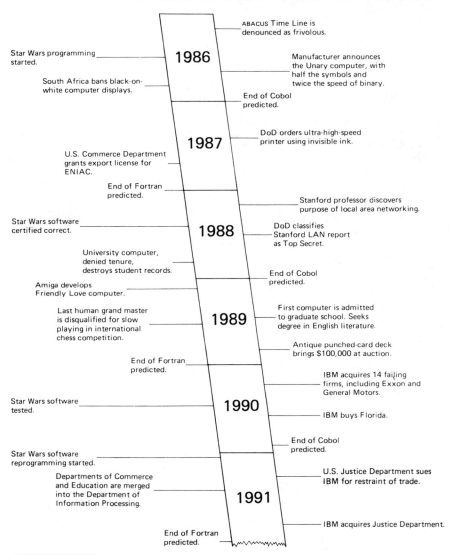

ABACUS Time Line is denounced as frivolous.

Star Wars programming started.

1986

Manufacturer announces the Unary computer, with half the symbols and twice the speed of binary.

South Africa bans black-on-white computer displays.

End of Cobol predicted.

1987

DoD orders ultra-high-speed printer using invisible ink.

U.S. Commerce Department grants export license for ENIAC.

End of Fortran predicted.

Stanford professor discovers purpose of local area networking.

Star Wars software certified correct.

1988

DoD classifies Stanford LAN report as Top Secret.

University computer, denied tenure, destroys student records.

End of Cobol predicted.

Amiga develops Friendly Love computer.

Last human grand master is disqualified for slow playing in international chess competition.

1989

First computer is admitted to graduate school. Seeks degree in English literature.

Antique punched-card deck brings $100,000 at auction.

End of Fortran predicted.

IBM acquires 14 failing firms, including Exxon and General Motors.

Star Wars software tested.

1990

IBM buys Florida.

End of Cobol predicted.

Star Wars software reprogramming started.

U.S. Justice Department sues IBM for restraint of trade.

Departments of Commerce and Education are merged into the Department of Information Processing.

1991

IBM acquires Justice Department.

End of Fortran predicted.

Reprinted from ABACUS, Volume 3, Number 3, Spring 1986.

for The Coming Decade in Computing

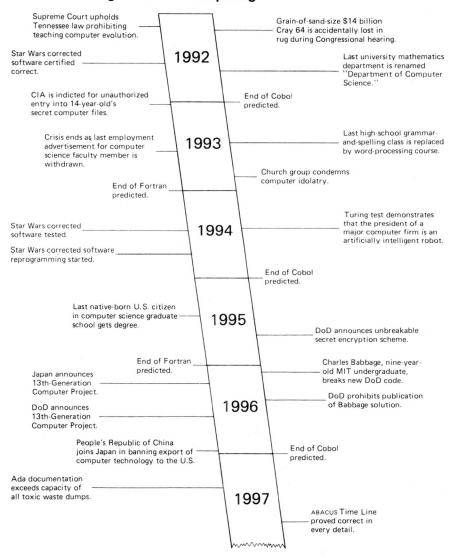

Supreme Court upholds Tennessee law prohibiting teaching computer evolution.

Star Wars corrected software certified correct.

CIA is indicted for unauthorized entry into 14-year-old's secret computer files.

Crisis ends as last employment advertisement for computer science faculty member is withdrawn.

End of Fortran predicted.

Star Wars corrected software tested.

Star Wars corrected software reprogramming started.

Last native-born U.S. citizen in computer science graduate school gets degree.

End of Fortran predicted.

Japan announces 13th-Generation Computer Project.

DoD announces 13th-Generation Computer Project.

People's Republic of China joins Japan in banning export of computer technology to the U.S.

Ada documentation exceeds capacity of all toxic waste dumps.

1992

1993

1994

1995

1996

1997

Grain-of-sand-size $14 billion Cray 64 is accidentally lost in rug during Congressional hearing.

Last university mathematics department is renamed "Department of Computer Science."

End of Cobol predicted.

Last high-school grammar-and-spelling class is replaced by word-processing course.

Church group condemns computer idolatry.

Turing test demonstrates that the president of a major computer firm is an artificially intelligent robot.

End of Cobol predicted.

DoD announces unbreakable secret encryption scheme.

Charles Babbage, nine-year-old MIT undergraduate, breaks new DoD code.

DoD prohibits publication of Babbage solution.

End of Cobol predicted.

ABACUS Time Line proved correct in every detail.

RESULTS OF ABACUS COMPETITION #1:
Old and New Computing Aphorisms

In the Spring issue, readers were invited to suggest computing aphorisms like the famous line originated by Richard W. Hamming, "The purpose of computing is insight, not numbers," later twisted by the late George E. Forsythe into "The purpose of computing numbers is not yet in sight."

WINNER: "Bit by bit computers are learning to program their users."

Originated and submitted by Alfred R. Fregly of Fort Washington, MD, who has been given a two-year subscription to ABACUS.

RUNNER-UP: "Old programs do not learn, they simply fade away."

Originated by Herbert A. Simon and submitted by Arnulfo P. Azcarraga of Bangkok, Thailand, who has been given a one-year subscription to ABACUS.

More Computing Aphorisms

Typical sayings are listed below. Although any of these would have won, none were submitted. Most of them have been copied, with permission, from Jim Haynes's column "The Open Channel" in *Computer,* March 1986.

The Analytical Engine weaves Algebraical patterns just as the Jacquard loom weaves flowers and leaves.
—*Ada, Countess of Lovelace*

Don't worry about people stealing your ideas. If your ideas are any good, you'll have to ram them down people's throats.
—*Howard Aiken*

On a clear disk you can seek forever.
—*Jeff Mischkinsky*

To iterate is human, to recurse, divine.
—*L. Peter Deutsch*

Upward compatible means we get to keep all our old mistakes.
—*Dennie van Tassel*

Computer Science is the only discipline in which we consider adding a new wing to a building to be maintenance.
—*Jim Horning*

The [XYZ-11]/785 is bug-for-bug compatible with the 780.
—*Anonymous*

To the systems programmer, the customers and users serve only to provide a test load.
—*P. Des Jardins*

APL is a write-only language. (I can write programs in APL but I can't read any of them.)
—*Roy Keir*

Base 8 is just like base 10 if you don't have any thumbs.
—*Tom Lehrer*

Counting in binary is just like counting in decimal if you are all thumbs.
—*Glaser & Way*

Systems programmers are the high priests of a low cult.
—*R.S. Barton*

Maybe Computer Science should be in the College of Theology.
—*R.S. Barton*

You cannot fix a bug you do not know about.
—*E.W. Dijkstra*

Reprinted from ABACUS, Volume 4, Number 1, Fall 1986.

The First Fourteen Issues:
Fall 1983–Winter 1987

Contents

Reprinted selections appear in boldface type.

VOL. 1   No. 3   SPRING 1984

Due to a lack of space, Larry Press's PERSONAL COMPUTING column
does not appear, but will return in our next issue.

VOL. 3   No. 2   WINTER 1986

VOL. 3 No. 4 SUMMER 1986

VOL. 4   No. 1   FALL 1986

The First Fourteen Issues:
Fall 1983–Winter 1987
Index

Reprinted selections appear in bold face type.

EDITORIALS
By Anthony Ralston (unless otherwise noted)

Volume Index

c. = cartoon, f. = figure, n. = footnote, p. = photo, t. = table

Xenakis, Yannis, 143, 166
Xerox, 186–187, 393, 397

Yedinaya Sistema. *See* ES
Yourdon, Edward N., 295–296, 300,
    302

Zave, Pamela, 294
Zemanek, Heinz, xviii
Zilog, 226, 228, 230*t.*, 232–233
Zipf, G. K., 155
Zipf's Law, 155